Praise for *Road Work*
by Mark Bowden

"[Bowden] delivers fascinating, and sometimes outsized, slices of life."   —*Publishers Weekly*

"Astute character reading and solid research combine with ingenious and stylish prose: a superior portfolio from a journalist who stays at the top of his game with remarkable consistency."
                     —*Kirkus Reviews* (starred review)

"A great sample of a politically mainstream but adventurous writer."   —*Library Journal*

"[Bowden] excels at sharply drawn, painstakingly reported stories about oddballs, losers and con men. . . . [He] is that rare reporter whose writing works as well on a small canvas as it does on the big screen."   —*The New York Times Book Review*

"Whether the topic is preserving the black rhino in Africa or a traditional high school football rivalry, Bowden is at the top of his form at drawing the reader into the narrative."
                     —*Rocky Mountain News*

ABOUT THE AUTHOR

Mark Bowden is the author of *Guests of the Ayatollah*, *Finders Keepers*, *Killing Pablo*, *Black Hawk Down*, *Bringing the Heat*, and *Doctor Dealer*. He is a national correspondent for *The Atlantic*.

ROAD WORK

AMONG TYRANTS, HEROES, ROGUES, AND BEASTS

MARK BOWDEN

PENGUIN BOOKS

PENGUIN BOOKS

Published by the Penguin Group
Penguin Group (USA) Inc., 375 Hudson Street, New York, New York 10014, U.S.A.
Penguin Group (Canada), 90 Eglinton Avenue East, Suite 700, Toronto,
Ontario, Canada M4P 2Y3 (a division of Pearson Penguin Canada Inc.)
Penguin Books Ltd, 80 Strand, London WC2R 0RL, England
Penguin Ireland, 25 St Stephen's Green, Dublin 2, Ireland (a division of Penguin Books Ltd)
Penguin Group (Australia), 250 Camberwell Road, Camberwell,
Victoria 3124, Australia (a division of Pearson Australia Group Pty Ltd)
Penguin Books India Pvt Ltd, 11 Community Centre, Panchsheel Park, New Delhi – 110 017, India
Penguin Group (NZ), cnr Airborne and Rosedale Roads, Albany,
Auckland 1310, New Zealand (a division of Pearson New Zealand Ltd)
Penguin Books (South Africa) (Pty) Ltd, 24 Sturdee Avenue,
Rosebank, Johannesburg 2196, South Africa

Penguin Books Ltd, Registered Offices:
80 Strand, London WC2R 0RL, England

First published in the United States of America by Grove / Atlantic, Inc. 2004
Published in Penguin Books 2006

10 9 8 7 6 5 4 3 2 1

"Tales of the Tyrant," "The Kabul-Ki Dance," "The Dark Art of Interrogation," "Pompadour
with a Monkey Wrench," and "A Beautiful Mind" originally appeared in *The Atlantic Monthly*.

"Gore's Stiff Competition" originally appeared on Salon.com.

"The Game of a Lifetime" and "The Unkindest Cut" originally appeared in *Sports Illustrated*.

"The Great Potato Pick-Off Play," "Schmidt's Misfortune," "Rhino," "The Urban Gorilla," "Breeding
the Better Cow," "Battling 'the Baddies' in Fantasyland," "Fight to the Finish," "Fight with Fame,"
"The Fight Rocky Lost," and "Cops on the Take" originally appeared in *The Philadelphia Inquirer*.

"Mayberry Vice" originally appeared in *Rolling Stone*.

THE LIBRARY OF CONGRESS HAS CATALOGED THE HARDCOVER EDITION AS FOLLOWS:
Bowden, Mark, 1951–
Road work : among tyrants, heroes, rogues, and beasts / Mark Bowden.
p. cm.
ISBN 0-87113-876-X (hc.)
ISBN 0 14 30.3673 4 (pbk.)
I. Title.
PN4874.B6297A25 2004
070'.92—dc22   1004052841

Printed in the United States of America

To Jim Naughton and Gene Roberts,
for enlarging my ambition

C O N T E N T S

INTRODUCTION

Ben Bradlee, the iconic editor of *The Washington Post*, was not impressed when he interviewed me for a job in 1979. I had worn a suit and a new pair of shoes for the occasion, and had stepped off the Metro on my way to the newspaper building into the heart of Hurricane David. It was only a two-block walk, but I was soaked to the skin.

He appeared before me in all his craggy magnificence, straight white hair falling across his forehead, the immaculate starched white collar of his blue shirt worn unbuttoned, silk tie askew. Bradlee was tan and athletic, prosperous and in charge. I confess to being in awe. Just six years from Watergate and only three years after being portrayed by Jason Robards in *All the President's Men*, he was the most famous and esteemed newspaper editor in the world.

My damp entrance immediately triggered an anecdote.

"When I was just starting out," he began in his gravelly voice with a grin, "I had two job interviews scheduled, one with *The Baltimore Sun* and the other with *The Post.* ..." It was a story he would retell years later in his memoirs. When he got to Baltimore, riding down on a train from Boston, there was a downpour, so he decided to forgo *The Sun* interview and just to proceed on down to D.C. The rest was history.

He probably didn't mean anything by it, but his telling me that story as I sat dripping across from him made it seem like the most famous and esteemed newspaper editor in the world was telling me that a cleverer fellow might have avoided the rain.

Clearly, coming down on the train from Harvard, Bradlee had had reason to be more complacent about landing a job with a good newspaper than I did. For six years I had been writing for the declining and little-read *Baltimore News-American,* a backwater in the unimpressive Hearst newspaper chain. I craved the respectability of a good newspaper and, with two small children at home, needed a better paycheck if I was going to stick with journalism. *The Sun*, the newspaper Bradlee had so cavalierly written off, had been the object of my fervent desires for years, and had for all that time been spurning my applications.

But I had gotten lucky. All at once opportunity had knocked. By the time I met with Bradlee, I already had a job offer from *The Philadelphia Inquirer.*

"Before you take the job in Philly, you ought to at least see what *The Post* has to offer," said Jon Katz, my editor in Baltimore, a former reporter at both *The Post* and *The Inquirer* who was kindly trying to further my career. He had arranged for a day of interviews in Washington.

I had already met that rainy day with Bob Woodward, of Woodward and Bernstein, one of the two most celebrated newspaper reporters in America. He was then metro editor of *The Post.* It had been a peculiar session. Woodward has a broad, friendly face and the flat hard accent of his hometown of Wheaton, Illinois. I had grown up in the town next door, Glen Ellyn, so we had some common ground. Early in our conversation he noted that I had been covering Maryland politics, and asked me, "Who do you think is the most corrupt official in high office in Maryland?"

It took me a moment to figure out what to say.

"I don't know," I said at last. "I don't assume people are corrupt unless I know something that suggests they are, and if I had information like that I would have written about it."

He seemed satisfied with that answer, and we talked for a while more about other things. Then he leaned abruptly across the desk, thrusting that wide face at me, and asked, conspiratorially, "No, just between you and me, who do you think is the most corrupt official in high office in Maryland?"

I was taken aback. I wondered if this was some high-powered interrogation technique I had never heard about. I couldn't think of what to say.

"I already answered that question," I said.

Woodward moved on to other things, and didn't seem put out, but I felt like I had disappointed him. The exchange had left me feeling that there was something basically different between his approach to reporting and mine. So I was already feeling a little off balance when I went in to see Bradlee. Other than that first anecdote—and I'm sure he didn't mean anything by it—Bradlee was charming. He is an accomplished raconteur, and he told me a number of good stories. Then, perhaps remembering that I was the one who was supposed to be answering questions, he asked, "Tell me, what is your biggest weakness as a journalist?"

I was not accustomed to evaluating myself in such terms, but I felt I owed him an honest answer.

"I think I am a better writer than I am a reporter," I said. "I know I enjoy writing more than I enjoy reporting."

That was all I told Bradlee, and it was the truth. Whenever I set out to report a story I felt like I was inventing the process. Every story was different, and I always felt there was something else I ought to be doing but didn't know what. Whenever I sat down to write, it was with the feeling that I didn't know enough yet to do so. There was always something else to find out, someone else to talk to, some other fact to run down. The truth is that I'd never had a particularly strong ambition to be a newspaper reporter. I had met ones for whom the job was a life goal, people who had grown up devouring newspapers, memorizing bylines, imagining themselves in far-flung places covering the big breaking story. I was a newspaper reporter because I wanted to write, and it was a place where you got paid to do it. I had taken the Baltimore job because I figured it would be better to get paid for writing than for running a cash register at a supermarket, which was how I had put myself through school. I had what real newspapermen would have called, somewhat disparagingly, a "features mentality." I was perfectly happy working on stories that had nothing to do with breaking news, that interested no one else, and that ran deep inside the paper. I had actually conspired on occasion to keep my stories off the front page, where most would be hacked and reedited over the course of the day's various editions. My stories were safer inside. What I really wanted was to write books and articles like those of the "New Journalists" of that era—Tom Wolfe, Gay Talese, Norman Mailer, Truman Capote and others—but that goal seemed as distant as Mars. I did love the newsroom: the characters, the hustle, and the deadlines. I loved working all day, driving out to meet people and interview them, gathering enough information to write a story, and then picking up the newspaper the next day and seeing it in print. Even ideas that didn't appeal to me grabbed me once I got started. There was something about the drama of real life that always kicked in. But my favorite part of the process always came when I had a chance to sit down and write.

I left Bradlee feeling uncertain about my prospects at *The Post*. Most reporters in 1979 would have given a lot for a job at that newspaper, myself included. It still shone with the afterglow of Watergate, one of the great investigative efforts in the history of journalism. When I returned to my desk in Baltimore the next day there was a message asking me to call Woodward.

"Bowden, you idiot, why did you tell Bradlee that you are a lousy reporter?" he asked.

I had not told Bradlee that. Woodward told me not to worry about it, that he was sure a job offer was still forthcoming, but I decided not to wait for it. I made up my mind then and there to take the job at *The Inquirer*.

It was the best decision I ever made. In retrospect I am grateful that Bradlee and Woodward made it easier for me. Interviewing in Philadelphia, I had liked immediately Jim Naughton, then *The Inquirer's* eccentric metro editor (one could not help but notice the giant chicken head hanging outside his cubicle), and Gene Roberts, its shrewd, slow-talking, no-nonsense editor. Roberts was genuinely odd. Throughout his interview with me, between long silences after each of my replies, he would pour amber liquid from a decanter into a small glass and chug it. I only found out later that it was tea. They had played no games with me, and seemed to share an interest in the things that most excited me about journalism. I had been picking up the *Sunday Inquirer* for several years because it was startlingly good, the talk of the business. All through the 1970s it had been winning prizes for remarkably ambitious and original work. It didn't have the same high profile as *The Post* or *The New York Times*—where both Naughton and Roberts had worked before Philadelphia—but it had a hip luster that the bigger papers didn't. It was the hot place to work, a newspaper where you could do great things the day you walked in the door, as opposed to climbing a long-established employment ladder. What appealed to me most was the emphasis Naughton and Roberts placed on creative writing. My friend Richard Ben Cramer had recently won a Pulitzer for his amazing and original writing from the Middle East. Donald Drake, the paper's medical reporter, was turning out four- and five-part series that read like plays. This was precisely the kind of work I had always wanted to do.

The Inquirer was my home for more than twenty years, and it was, as Roberts once put it, the greatest care and feeding system for writers in the world. A little more than a year after I started, he dispatched me to Africa for several months to research and write a series of stories about the threatened extinction of the black rhinoceros—a series that became a notorious symbol of Roberts's excesses, but one that nearly every reporter I knew would have thrilled to get (one piece of that series is reprinted here). Before leaving on that assignment, I traveled to New York City to meet with the late Harold Hayes, the legendary editor who had coached Tom Wolfe's breakthrough articles in *Esquire*. Hayes had a lifelong interest in African wildlife, and had written a good book on the subject, entitled *The Last Place on Earth*.

"Let me get this straight," he said. "Your newspaper is going to send you flying all over Africa to research and write about what's happening to the rhino?"

He shook his head with amazement.

"That's just extraordinary," he said, "and wonderful. It restores my faith in daily newspapers. Don't blow it."

Don't blow it—those words stayed with me through all my years at *The Inquirer*. It was an extraordinary place to work. The paper hired some of the best and most ambitious young journalists in America, and *enlarged* their ambition. It let reporters grow in whatever direction their talent and interests led. Some specialized in "investigative" work, others became foreign correspondents, still others became specialists in certain areas of reporting. For me, the goal was always to become a better writer. My instincts drove me to work on ever-bigger, longer, more complex stories. I was evolving from a newspaper reporter into a magazine writer and author, and *The Inquirer* let me do it. Many of the articles reprinted in this collection were originally published in *The Inquirer*'s Sunday magazine. The process wasn't always easy. For instance, when I was writing "Cops on the Take," the last article in this collection, I realized early on that the dimensions of the story wouldn't fit into a single issue of the magazine. I warned my editor, the ever-practical David Boldt, what was coming.

"Then stop," he said. "Don't write the whole story. Just write a piece of it."

"But why leave out so much good material if I have it?" I asked.

"Because it won't fit in the magazine," he said.

"Why not run it as a series over several weeks," I suggested, never one to be timid about granting myself more space.

"Because we don't do that at the magazine," David said.

"Why don't we do it?"

"Because people would lose track of the story from week to week. Because it's our policy. It has come up before. Roberts says we can't do it."

Invoking Roberts was the final word in all arguments at *The Inquirer*. I ignored David. I figured that even if the whole story didn't get published, I wanted to write it. I wanted to write it fully, to push myself, to see if I could sustain such an extended narrative. When I gave it to David, he was horrified.

"What am I supposed to do with this?" he said.

"If we have to, I'll cut it, but I at least wanted you to see the whole thing."

David read it, and liked it.

"But I can't use it as is," he said.

"If Roberts is the one who made the rule, can't he also break it?" I asked.

So David showed the piece to Roberts, who suggested in his soft Southern drawl, "Why don't you run it as a series."

It ran over four successive weekends.

The Inquirer was like that. Whenever I pushed at the paper's limits, it bent to accommodate me. It was famous for pulling out all the stops for a big story, and breaking any rule in order to encourage its reporters to come up with something new. Three of my books—*Finders Keepers, Black Hawk Down,* and *Killing Pablo*—were originally printed in the newspaper, the latter two in twenty-nine and thirty-one parts, respectively. *The Inquirer* was the only newspaper in America that would do that.

In a way, a strong body of magazine articles is proof that a writer really loves what he is doing. Because here is the sad truth about writing for magazines: You will never make a living at it when you need the living, and if you ever are in a position to make enough writing for them, you will no longer need it. It is very much like a piece of wisdom I heard from a friend in college about sex. He said, "The more you want it, the less you get it; the less you get it, the more you want it." I have found this to be true about life. Nobody except those famous and established enough not to need it can make a living wage writing for magazines. Most newspapers don't pay extra for the longer works. So writing long was always a struggle, driven by ego and ambition, never encouraged. For reasons I cannot fully fathom, I was born stubborn enough to persist. Here is the proof. My goal was always to be working on the most ambitious thing that I had ever done, and most of these stories, particularly the older ones, represent the best work I had done to date. Today, *The Atlantic Monthly* affords me the same kind of opportunity, and all of the recent work in this collection originally appeared there.

My answer to Bradlee's question twenty-five years ago might have bollixed my chances at *The Post,* but I stand by it. I am more confident today than I was then about my reporting skills, but I still enjoy the writing more than the reporting, and I still think I am a better writer than I am a reporter.

Mark Bowden
April 2004

TALES OF
THE TYRANT

MAY 2002

This story was the late Michael Kelly's idea. I had been working on it for a few weeks, just gathering some reading material, when the September 11th attacks happened. Kelly, editor of The Atlantic Monthly, *tracked me down to* The Philadelphia Inquirer *newsroom, where I had gone to help cover the extraordinary events of that day. He told me to drop the Saddam story. "I want you to start working on something—I don't know yet what it will be—about the events of today. I'm thinking of devoting an entire issue to a story a year from today. We can talk about ideas later, but I just want you to start thinking along those lines." I did think about it a lot over the next few days, and ultimately decided that I wanted to stick with the Saddam story. I figured the subject of September 11th was going to be studied and written about by everyone, and my instinct—something* Inquirer *editor Gene Roberts had always encouraged—was to "zig when everyone else zags." Besides, I had read enough about Saddam to be intrigued. I wanted to try to understand what it would be like to be a tyrant, how someone like Saddam Hussein really saw himself. The "big" September 11th story that Michael had in mind became my colleague William Langewiesche's brilliant three-part "American Ground." This story was* The Atlantic's *cover story in May 2002, and less than a year later Michael was killed in Iraq, riding toward Baghdad with the troops that brought Saddam down.*

SHAKHSUH (HIS PERSON)

Today is a day in the Grand Battle, the immortal Mother of All Battles. It is a glorious and a splendid day on the part of the self-respecting people of Iraq and their history, and it is the beginning of the great shame for those who ignited its fire on the other part. It is the first day on which the vast military phase of that battle started. Or rather, it is the first day of that battle, since Allah decreed that the Mother of All Battles continue till this day.
—Saddam Hussein, in a televised address to the Iraqi people,
January 17, 2002

The tyrant must steal sleep. He must vary the locations and times. He never sleeps in his palaces. He moves from secret bed to secret bed. Sleep and a fixed routine are among the few luxuries denied him. It is too dangerous to be predictable, and whenever he shuts his eyes, the nation drifts. His iron grip slackens. Plots congeal in the shadows. For those hours he must trust someone, and nothing is more dangerous to the tyrant than trust.

Saddam Hussein, the Anointed One, Glorious Leader, Direct Descendant of the Prophet, President of Iraq, chairman of its Revolutionary Command Council, field marshal of its armies, doctor of its laws, and Great Uncle to all its peoples, rises at about three in the morning. He sleeps only four or five hours a night. When he rises, he swims. All his palaces and homes have pools. Water is a symbol of wealth and power in a desert country like Iraq, and Saddam splashes it everywhere—fountains and pools, indoor streams and waterfalls. It is a theme in all his buildings. His pools are tended scrupulously and tested hourly, more to keep the temperature and the chlorine and pH levels comfortable than to detect some poison that might attack him through his pores, eyes, mouth, nose, ears, penis, or anus—although that worry is always there too.

He has a bad back, a slipped disk, and swimming helps. It also keeps him trim and fit. This satisfies his vanity, which is epic, but fitness is critical for other reasons. He is now sixty-five, an old man, but because his power is grounded in fear, not affection, he cannot be seen to age. The tyrant cannot afford to become stooped, frail, and gray. Weakness invites challenge, coup d'état. One can imagine Saddam urging himself through a fixed number of laps each morning, pushing to exceed the number he swam the previous year, as if time could be undone by effort and will. Death is an enemy he cannot defeat—only, perhaps, delay. So he works. He also dissembles. He dyes his gray hair black and avoids using his reading glasses in public. When he is to give a speech, his aides print it out in huge letters, just a few lines per page. Because his back problem forces him to walk with a slight limp, he avoids being seen or filmed walking more than a few steps.

He is long-limbed, with big, strong hands. In Iraq the size of a man still matters, and Saddam is impressive. At six feet two he towers over his shorter, plumper aides. He lacks natural grace but has acquired a certain elegance of manner, the way a country boy learns to match the right tie with the right suit. His weight fluctuates between about 210 and 220 pounds, but in his custom-tailored suits the girth isn't always easy to see. His paunch shows when he takes off his suit coat. Those who watch him carefully know he has a tendency to lose weight in times of crisis and to gain it rapidly when things are going well.

Fresh food is flown in for him twice a week—lobster, shrimp, and fish, lots of lean meat, plenty of dairy products. The shipments are sent first to his nuclear scientists, who x-ray them and test them for radiation and poison. The food is then prepared for him by European-trained chefs, who work under the supervision of al Himaya, Saddam's personal body-guards. Each of his more than twenty palaces is fully staffed, and three meals a day are cooked for him at every one; security demands that palaces from which he is absent perform an elaborate pantomime each day, as if he were in residence. Saddam tries to regulate his diet, allotting servings and por-tions the way he counts out the laps in his pools. For a big man he usually eats little, picking at his meals, often leaving half the food on his plate. Sometimes he eats dinner at restaurants in Baghdad, and when he does, his security staff invades the kitchen, demanding that the pots and pans, dishware, and utensils be well scrubbed, but otherwise interfering little. Saddam appreciates the culinary arts. He prefers fish to meat, and eats a lot of fresh fruits and vegetables. He likes wine with his meals, though he is hardly an oenophile; his wine of choice is Mateus rosé. But even though he indulges only in moderation, he is careful not to let anyone outside his most trusted circle of family and aides see him drinking. Alcohol is for-bidden by Islam, and in public Saddam is a dutiful son of the faith.

He has a tattoo on his right hand, three dark-blue dots in a line near the wrist. These are given to village children when they are only five or six years old, a sign of their rural, tribal roots. Girls are often marked on their chins, forehead, or cheeks (as was Saddam's mother). For those who, like Saddam, move to the cities and come up in life, the tattoos are a sign of humble origin, and some later have them removed, or fade them with bleach until they almost disappear. Saddam's have faded, but apparently just from age; although he claims descent from the prophet Muhammad, he has never disguised his humble birth.

The president-for-life spends long hours every day in his office—whichever office he and his security minders select. He meets with his ministers and generals, solicits their opinions, and keeps his own counsel. He steals short naps during the day. He will abruptly leave a meeting, shut himself off in a side room, and return refreshed a half hour later. Those who meet with the president have no such luxury. They must stay awake and alert at all times. In 1986, during the Iran-Iraq war, Saddam caught Lieutenant General Aladin al-Janabi dozing during a meeting. He stripped the general of his rank and threw him out of the army. It was years before al-Janabi was able to win back his position and favor.

Saddam's desk is always immaculate. Reports from his various department heads are stacked neatly, each a detailed accounting of recent accomplishments and spending topped by an executive summary. Usually he reads only the summaries, but he selects some reports for closer examination. No one knows which will be chosen for scrutiny. If the details of the full report tell a story different from the summary, or if Saddam is confused, he will summon the department head. At these meetings Saddam is always polite and calm. He rarely raises his voice. He enjoys showing off a mastery of every aspect of his realm, from crop rotation to nuclear fission. But these meetings can be terrifying when he uses them to cajole, upbraid, or interrogate his subordinates. Often he arranges a surprise visit to some lower-level office or laboratory or factory—although, given the security preparations necessary, word of his visits outraces his arrival. Much of what he sees from his offices and on his "surprise" inspections is doctored and full of lies. Saddam has been fed unrealistic information for so long that his expectations are now also uniformly unrealistic. His bureaucrats scheme mightily to maintain the illusions. So Saddam usually sees only what those around him want him to see, which is, by definition, what he wants to see. A stupid man in this position would believe he had created a perfect world. But Saddam is not stupid. He knows he is being deceived, and he complains about it.

He reads voraciously—on subjects from physics to romance—and has broad interests. He has a particular passion for Arabic history and military history. He likes books about great men, and he admires Winston Churchill, whose famous political career is matched by his prodigious literary output. Saddam has literary aspirations himself. He employs ghostwriters to keep up a ceaseless flow of speeches, articles, and books of history and philosophy; his oeuvre includes fiction as well. In recent years he appears to have written and published two romantic fables, *Zabibah and the King* and *The Fortified Castle;* a third, as-yet-untitled work of fiction is due out soon. Before publishing the books Saddam distributes them quietly to professional writers in Iraq for comments and suggestions. No one dares to be candid—the writing is said to be woefully amateurish, marred by a stern pedantic strain—but everyone tries to be helpful, sending him gentle suggestions for minor improvements. The first two novels were published under a rough Arabic equivalent of "Anonymous" that translates as "Written by He Who Wrote It," but the new book may bear Saddam's name.

Saddam likes to watch TV, monitoring the Iraqi stations he controls and also CNN, Sky, al Jazeera, and the BBC. He enjoys movies, particularly those involving intrigue, assassination, and conspiracy—*The Day of the Jackal, The Conversation, Enemy of the State.* Because he has not traveled extensively, such movies inform his ideas about the world and feed his inclination to believe broad conspiracy theories. To him the world is a puzzle that only fools accept at face value. He also appreciates movies with more literary themes. Two of his favorites are *The Godfather* series and *The Old Man and the Sea.*

Saddam can be charming, and has a sense of humor about himself. "He told a hilarious story on television," says Khidhir Hamza, a scientist who worked on Iraq's nuclear-weapons project before escaping to the West. "He is an excellent storyteller, the kind who acts out the story with gestures and facial expressions. He described how he had once found himself behind enemy lines in the war with Iran. He had been traveling along the front lines, paying surprise visits, when the Iranian line launched an offensive and effectively cut off his position. The Iranians, of course, had no idea that Saddam was there. The way he told the story, it wasn't boastful or self-congratulatory. He didn't claim to have fought his way out. He said he was scared. Of the troops at his position, he said, 'They just left me!' He repeated 'Just left me!' in a way that was humorous. Then he described how he hid with his pistol, watching the action until his own forces retook the position and he was again on safe ground. 'What can a pistol do in the middle of battle?' he asked. It was charming, extremely charming."

General Wafic Samarai, who served as Saddam's chief of intelligence during the eight-year Iran-Iraq war (and who, after falling out of favor in the wake of the Persian Gulf War, walked for thirty hours through the rugged north of Iraq to escape the country), concurs: "It is pleasant to sit and talk to him. He is serious, and meetings with him can get tense, but you don't get intimidated unless he wants to intimidate you. When he asks for your opinion, he listens very carefully and doesn't interrupt. Likewise, he gets irritated if you interrupt him. 'Let me finish!' he will say sharply."

Saddam has been advised by his doctors to walk at least two hours a day. He rarely manages that much time, but he breaks up his days with strolls. He used to take these walks in public, swooping down with his entourage on neighborhoods in Baghdad, his bodyguards clearing sidewalks and streets as the tyrant passed. Anyone who approached him unsolicited was beaten nearly to death. But now it is too dangerous to walk in public—and the limp must not be seen. So Saddam makes no more unscripted public appearances. He limps freely behind the high walls and patrolled fences of his vast estates. Often he walks with a gun, hunting deer or rabbit in his private preserves. He is an excellent shot.

Saddam has been married for nearly forty years. His wife, Sajida, is his first cousin on his mother's side and the daughter of Khairallah Tulfah, Saddam's uncle and first political mentor. Sajida has borne him two sons and three daughters, and remains loyal to him, but he has long had relationships with other women. Stories circulate about his nightly selecting young virgins for his bed, like the Sultan Shahryar in *The Thousand and One Nights,* about his having fathered a child with a longtime mistress, and even about his having killed one young woman after a kinky tryst. It is hard to sort the truth from the lies. So many people, in and out of Iraq, hate Saddam that any disgraceful or embarrassing rumor is likely to be embraced, believed, repeated, and written down in the Western press as truth. Those who know him best scoff at the wildest of these tales.

"Saddam has personal relationships with women, but these stories of rape and murder are lies," Samarai says. "He is not that kind of person. He is very careful about himself in everything he does. He is fastidious and very proper, and never wants to give the wrong impression. But he is occasionally attracted to other women, and he has formed relationships with them. They are not the kind of women who would ever talk about him."

Saddam is a loner by nature, and power increases isolation. A young man without power or money is completely free. He has nothing, but he also has everything. He can travel, he can drift. He can make new acquaintances every day, and try to soak up the infinite variety of life. He can seduce and be seduced, start an enterprise and abandon it, join an army or flee a nation, fight to preserve an existing system or plot a revolution. He can reinvent himself daily, according to the discoveries he makes about the world and himself. But if he prospers through the choices he makes, if he acquires a wife, children, wealth, land, and power, his options gradually and inevitably diminish. Responsibility and commitment limit his moves. One might think that the most powerful man has the most choices, but in reality he has the fewest. Too much depends on his every move. The tyrant's choices are the narrowest of all. His life—the nation!—hangs in the balance. He can no longer drift or explore, join or flee. He cannot reinvent himself, because so many others depend on him—and he, in turn, must depend on so many others. He stops learning, because he is walled in by fortresses and palaces, by generals and ministers who rarely dare to tell him what he doesn't wish to hear. Power gradually shuts the tyrant off from the world. Everything comes to him second or third hand. He is deceived daily. He becomes ignorant of his land, his people, even his own family. He exists, finally, only to preserve his wealth and power, to build his legacy. Survival becomes his one overriding passion. So he regulates his diet, tests his food for poison, exercises behind well-patrolled walls, trusts no one, and tries to control everything.

Major Sabah Khalifa Khodada, a career officer in the Iraqi army, was summoned from his duties as assistant to the commander of a terrorist training camp on January 1, 1996, for an important meeting. It was nighttime. He drove to his command center at Alswayra, southwest of Baghdad, where he and some other military officers were told to strip to their underwear. They removed their clothing, watches, and rings, and handed over their wallets. The clothing was then laundered, sterilized, and x-rayed. Each of the officers, in his underwear, was searched and passed through a metal detector. Each was instructed to wash his hands in a disinfecting permanganate solution.

They then dressed, and were transported in buses with blackened windows, so that they could not see where they were going. They were driven for a half hour or more, and then were searched again as they filed off. They had arrived at an official-looking building, Khodada did not know where. After a time they were taken into a meeting room and seated at a large round table. Then they were told that they were to be given a great honor: the president himself would be meeting with them. They were instructed not to talk, just to listen. When Saddam entered, they were to rise and show him respect. They were not to approach or touch him. For all but his closest aides, the protocol for meeting with the dictator is simple. He dictates.

"Don't interrupt," they were told. "Don't ask questions or make any requests."

Each man was given a pad of paper and a pencil, and instructed to take notes. Tea in a small glass cup was placed before each man and at the empty seat at the head of the table.

When Saddam appeared, they all rose. He stood before his chair and smiled at them. Wearing his military uniform, decorated with medals and gold epaulets, he looked fit, impressive, and self-assured. When he sat, everyone sat. Saddam did not reach for his tea, so the others in the room didn't touch theirs. He told Khodada and the others that they were the best men in the nation, the most trusted and able. That was why they had been selected to meet with him, and to work at the terrorist camps where warriors were being trained to strike back at America. The United States, he said, because of its reckless treatment of Arab nations and the Arab people, was a necessary target for revenge and destruction. American aggression must be stopped in order for Iraq to rebuild and to resume leadership of the Arab world. Saddam talked for almost two hours. Khodada could sense the great hatred in him, the anger over what America had done to his ambitions and to Iraq. Saddam blamed the United States for all the poverty, backwardness, and suffering in his country.

Khodada took notes. He glanced around the room. Few of the others, he concluded, were buying what Saddam told them. These were battle-hardened men of experience from all over the nation. Most had fought in the war with Iran and the Persian Gulf War. They had few illusions about

Saddam, his regime, or the troubles of their country. They coped daily with real problems in cities and military camps all over Iraq. They could have told Saddam a lot. But nothing would pass from them to the tyrant. Not one word, not one microorganism.

The meeting had been designed to allow communication in only one direction, and even in this it failed. Saddam's speech was meaningless to his listeners. Khodada despised him, and suspected that others in the room did too. The major knew he was no coward, but, like many of the other military men there, he was filled with fear. He was afraid to make a wrong move, afraid he might accidentally draw attention to himself, do something unscripted. He was grateful that he felt no urge to sneeze, sniffle, or cough.

When the meeting was over, Saddam simply left the room. The tea-cups had not been touched. The men were then returned to the buses and driven back to Alswayra, from which they drove back to their camps or homes. The meeting with Saddam had meant nothing. The notes they had been ordered to take were worthless. It was as if they had briefly visited a fantasy zone with no connection to their own world.

They had stepped into the world of the tyrant.

TUMOOH (AMBITION)

The Iraqis knew that they had the potential, but they did not know how to muster up that potential. Their rulers did not take the responsibility on the basis of that potential. The leader and the guide who was able to put that potential on its right course had not yet emerged from amongst them. Even when some had discovered that potential, they did not know how to deal with it. Nor did they direct it where it should be directed so as to enable it to evolve into an effective act that could make life pulsate and fill hearts with happiness.
—Saddam Hussein, in a speech to the Iraqi people,
July 17, 2000

In Saddam's village, al-Awja, just east of Tikrit, in north-central Iraq, his clan lived in houses made of mud bricks and flat, mud-covered wooden roofs. The land is dry, and families eke out a living growing wheat and vegetables. Saddam's clan was called al-Khatab, and they were known to be violent and clever. Some viewed them as con men and thieves, recalls Salah Omar al-Ali, who grew up in Tikrit and came to know Saddam well in later life. Those who still support Saddam may see him as Saladinesque, as a great pan-Arab leader; his enemies may see him as Stalinesque, a cruel dictator; but to al-Ali, Saddam will always be just an al-Khatab, acting out a family pattern on a much, much larger stage.

Al-Ali fixed tea for me in his home in suburban London last January. He is elegant, frail, gray, and pale, a man of quiet dignity and impeccable manners who gestures delicately with long-fingered hands as he speaks. He was the information minister of Iraq when, in 1969, Saddam (the real power in the ruling party), in part to demonstrate his displeasure over Arab defeats in the Six-Day War, announced that a Zionist plot had been discovered, and publicly hanged fourteen alleged plotters, among them nine Iraqi Jews; their bodies were left hanging in Baghdad's Liberation Square for more than a day. Al-Ali defended this atrocity in his own country and to the rest of the world. Today he is just one of many exiled or expatriated former Iraqi government officials, an old socialist who served the revolutionary pan-Arab Baath Party and Saddam until running afoul of the Great Uncle. Al-Ali would have one believe that his conscience drove him into exile, but one suspects he has fretted little in his life about human rights. He showed me the faded dot tattoos on his hand, which might have been put there by the same Tikriti who gave Saddam his.

Although al-Ali was familiar with the al-Khatab family, he did not meet Saddam himself until the mid-sixties, when they were both socialist revolutionaries plotting to overthrow the tottering government of General Abd al-Rahman Arif. Saddam was a tall, thin young man with a thick mop of curly black hair. He had recently escaped from prison, after being caught in a failed attempt to assassinate Arif's predecessor. The attempt, the arrest, the imprisonment, had all added to Saddam's revolutionary luster. He was an impressive combination: not just a tough capable of commanding respect from the thugs who did the Baath Party's dirty work, but also well-read, articulate, and seemingly open-minded; a man of action who also understood policy; a natural leader who could steer Iraq into a new era. Al-Ali met the young fugitive at a café near Baghdad University. Saddam arrived in a Volkswagen Beetle and stepped out in a well-cut gray suit. These were exciting times for both men. The intoxicating aroma of change was in the air, and prospects for their party were good. Saddam was pleased to meet a fellow Tikriti. "He listened to me for a long time," al-Ali recalled. "We discussed the party's plans, how to organize nationally.

The issues were complicated, but it was clear that he understood them very well. He was serious, and took a number of my suggestions. I was impressed with him."

The party seized control in 1968, and Saddam immediately became the real power behind his cousin Ahmad Hassan al-Bakr, the president and chairman of the new Revolutionary Command Council. Al-Ali was a member of that council. He was responsible for the north-central part of Iraq, including his home village. It was in Tikrit that he started to see Saddam's larger plan unfold. Saddam's relatives in al-Awja were throwing their newly ascendant kinsman's name around, seizing farms, ordering people off their land. That was how things worked in the villages. If a family was lucky, it produced a strongman, a patriarch, who by guile, strength, or violence accumulated riches for his clan. Saddam was now a strongman, and his family was moving to claim the spoils. This was all ancient stuff. The Baath philosophy was far more egalitarian. It emphasized working with Arabs in other countries to rebuild the entire region, sharing property and wealth, seeking a better life for all. In this political climate Saddam's family was a throwback. The local party chiefs complained bitterly, and al-Ali took their complaints to his powerful young friend. "It's a small problem," Saddam said. "These are simple people. They don't understand our larger aims. I'll take care of it." Two, three, four times al-Ali went to Saddam, because the problem didn't go away. Every time it was the same: "I'll take care of it."

It finally occurred to al-Ali that the al-Khatab family was doing exactly what Saddam wanted them to do. This seemingly modern, educated young villager was not primarily interested in helping the party achieve its idealistic aims; rather, he was using the party to help him achieve his. Suddenly al-Ali saw that the polish, the fine suits, the urbane tastes, the civilized manner, and the socialist rhetoric were a pose. The real story of Saddam was right there in the tattoo on his right hand. He was a true son of Tikrit, a clever al-Khatab, and he was now much more than the patriarch of his clan.

Saddam's rise through the ranks may have been slow and deceitful, but when he moved to seize power, he did so very openly. He had been serving as vice-chairman of the Revolutionary Command Council, and as vice president of Iraq, and he planned to step formally into the top positions. Some of the party leadership, including men who had been close to Saddam for years, had other ideas. Rather than just hand him the reins, they had begun advocating a party election. So Saddam took action. He staged his ascendancy like theater.

On July 18, 1979, he invited all the members of the Revolutionary Command Council and hundreds of other party leaders to a conference hall in Baghdad. He had a video camera running in the back of the hall to record the event for posterity. Wearing his military uniform, he walked slowly to the lectern and stood behind two microphones, gesturing with a big cigar. His body and broad face seemed weighted down with sadness. There had been a betrayal, he said. A Syrian plot. There were traitors among them. Then Saddam took a seat, and Muhyi Abd al-Hussein Mashhadi, the secretary-general of the Command Council, appeared from behind a curtain to confess his own involvement in the putsch. He had been secretly arrested and tortured days before; now he spilled out dates, times, and places where the plotters had met. Then he started naming names. As he fingered members of the audience one by one, armed guards grabbed the accused and escorted them from the hall. When one man shouted that he was innocent, Saddam shouted back, "*Itla! Itla!*"—"Get out! Get out!" (Weeks later, after secret trials, Saddam had the mouths of the accused taped shut so that they could utter no troublesome last words before their firing squads.) When all of the sixty "traitors" had been removed, Saddam again took the podium and wiped tears from his eyes as he repeated the names of those who had betrayed him. Some in the audience, too, were crying—perhaps out of fear. This chilling performance had the desired effect. Everyone in the hall now understood exactly how things would work in Iraq from that day forward. The audience rose and began clapping, first in small groups and finally as one. The session ended with cheers and laughter. The remaining "leaders"—about 300 in all—left the hall shaken, grateful to have avoided the fate of their colleagues, and certain that one man now controlled the destiny of their entire nation. Videotapes of the purge were circulated throughout the country.

It was what the world would come to see as classic Saddam. He tends to commit his crimes in public, cloaking them in patriotism and in effect turning his witnesses into accomplices. The purge that day reportedly resulted in the executions of a third of the Command Council. (Mashhadi's performance didn't spare him; he, too, was executed.) During the next few weeks scores of other "traitors" were shot, including government officials, military officers, and people turned in by ordinary citizens who responded to a hotline phone number broadcast on Iraqi TV. Some Council members say that Saddam ordered members of the party's inner circle to participate in this bloodbath.

While he served as vice-chairman, from 1968 to 1979, the party's goals had seemed to be Saddam's own. That was a relatively good period for Iraq, thanks to Saddam's blunt effectiveness as an administrator. He orchestrated a draconian nationwide literacy project. Reading programs were set up in every city and village, and failure to attend was punishable by three years in jail. Men, women, and children attended these compulsory classes, and hundreds of thousands of illiterate Iraqis learned to read. UNESCO gave Saddam an award. There were also ambitious drives to build schools, roads, public housing, and hospitals. Iraq created one of the best public-health systems in the Middle East. There was admiration in the West during those years, for Saddam's accomplishments if not for his methods. After the Islamic fundamentalist revolution in Iran, and the seizure of the U.S. embassy in Tehran in 1979, Saddam seemed to be the best hope for secular modernization in the region.

Today all these programs are a distant memory. Within two years of his seizing full power, Saddam's ambitions turned to conquest, and his defeats have ruined the nation. His old party allies in exile now see his support for the social-welfare programs as an elaborate deception. The broad ambitions for the Iraqi people were the party's, they say. As long as he needed the party, Saddam made its programs his own. But his single, overriding goal throughout was to establish his own rule.

"In the beginning the Baath Party was made up of the intellectual elite of our generation," says Hamed al-Jubouri, a former Command Council member who now lives in London. "There were many professors, physicians, economists, and historians—really the nation's elite. Saddam was charming and impressive. He appeared to be totally different from what we learned he was afterward. He took all of us in. We supported him because he seemed uniquely capable of controlling a difficult country like Iraq, a difficult people like our people. We wondered about him. How could such a young man, born in the countryside north of Baghdad, become such a capable leader? He seemed both intellectual and practical. But he was hiding his real self. For years he did this, building his power quietly, charming everyone, hiding his true instincts. He has a great ability to hide his intentions; it may be his greatest skill. I remember his son Uday said one time, 'My father's right shirt pocket doesn't know what is in his left shirt pocket.'"

What does Saddam want? By all accounts, he is not interested in money. This is not the case with other members of his family. His wife, Sajida, is known to have gone on million-dollar shopping sprees in New York and London, back in the days of Saddam's good relations with the West. Uday drives expensive cars and wears custom-tailored suits of his own design. Saddam himself isn't a hedonist; he lives a well-regulated, somewhat abstemious existence. He seems far more interested in fame than in money, desiring above all to be admired, remembered, and revered. A nineteen-volume official biography is mandatory reading for Iraqi government officials, and Saddam has also commissioned a six-hour film about his life, called *The Long Days,* which was edited by Terence Young, best known for directing three James Bond films. Saddam told his official biographer that he isn't interested in what people think of him today, only in what they will think of him in five hundred years. The root of Saddam's bloody, single-minded pursuit of power appears to be simple vanity.

But what extremes of vanity compel a man to jail or execute all who criticize or oppose him? To erect giant statues of himself to adorn the public spaces of his country? To commission romantic portraits, some of them twenty feet high, portraying the nation's Great Uncle as a desert horseman, a wheat-cutting peasant, or a construction worker carrying bags of cement? To have the nation's television, radio, film, and print devoted to celebrating his every word and deed? Can ego alone explain such displays? Might it be the opposite? What colossal insecurity and self-loathing would demand such compensation?

The sheer scale of the tyrant's deeds mocks psychoanalysis. What begins with ego and ambition becomes a political movement. Saddam embodies first the party and then the nation. Others conspire in this process in order to further their own ambitions, selfless as well as selfish. Then the tyrant turns on them. His cult of self becomes more than a political strategy. Repetition of his image in heroic or paternal poses, repetition of his name, his slogans, his virtues, and his accomplishments, seeks to make his power seem inevitable, unchallengeable. Finally he is praised not out of affection or admiration but out of obligation. One *must* praise him.

Saad al-Bazzaz was summoned to meet with Saddam in 1989. He was then the editor of Baghdad's largest daily newspaper and the head of the ministry that oversees all of Iraq's TV and radio programming. Al-Bazzaz took the phone call in his office. "The president wants to ask you something," Saddam's secretary said.

Al-Bazzaz thought nothing of it. He is a short, round, garrulous man with thinning hair and big glasses. He had known Saddam for years, and had always been in good odor. The first time Saddam had asked to meet him had been more than fifteen years earlier, when Saddam was vice-chairman of the Revolutionary Command Council. The Baath Party was generating a lot of excitement, and Saddam was its rising star. At the time, al-Bazzaz was a twenty-five-year-old writer who had just published his first collection of short stories and had also written articles for Baghdad newspapers. That first summons from Saddam had been a surprise. Why would the vice-chairman want to meet with him? Al-Bazzaz had a low opinion of political officials, but as soon as they met, this one struck him as different. Saddam told al-Bazzaz that he had read some of his articles and was impressed by them. He said he knew of his book of short stories, and had heard they were very good. The young writer was flattered. Saddam asked him what writers he admired, and after listening to al-Bazzaz, told him, "When I was in prison, I read all of Ernest Hemingway's novels. I particularly like *The Old Man and the Sea.*" Al-Bazzaz thought, *This is something new for Iraq—a politician who reads real literature.* Saddam peppered him with questions at that meeting, and listened with rapt attention. This, too, al-Bazzaz thought was extraordinary.

By 1989 much had changed. Saddam's regime had long since abandoned the party's early, idealistic aims, and al-Bazzaz no longer saw the dictator as an open-minded man of learning and refinement. But he had prospered personally under Saddam's reign. His growing government responsibilities left him no time to write, but he had become an important man in Iraq. He saw himself as someone who advanced the cause of artists and journalists, as a force for liberalization in the country. Since the end of the war with Iran, the previous year, there had been talk of loosening controls on the media and the arts in Iraq, and al-Bazzaz had lobbied quietly in favor of this. But he wasn't one to press too hard, so he had no worries as he drove the several miles from his office to the Tashreeya area of Baghdad, near the old Cabinet Building, where an emissary from the president met him and instructed him to leave his car. The emissary drove al-Bazzaz in silence to a large villa nearby. Inside, guards searched him and showed him to a sofa, where he waited for half an hour as people came and went from the president's office. When it was his turn, he was handed a pad and a pencil, reminded to speak only if Saddam asked a direct question, and then ushered in. It was noon. Saddam was wearing a military uniform. Staying seated behind his desk, Saddam did not approach al-Bazzaz or even offer to shake his hand.

"How are you?" the president asked.

"Fine," al-Bazzaz replied. "I am here to listen to your instructions."

Saddam complained about an Egyptian comedy show that had been airing on one of the TV channels: "It is silly, and we shouldn't show it to our people." Al-Bazzaz made a note. Then Saddam brought up something else. It was the practice for poems and songs written in praise of him to be aired daily on TV. In recent weeks al-Bazzaz had urged his producers to be more selective. Most of the work was amateurish—ridiculous doggerel written by unskilled poets. His staff was happy to oblige. Paeans to the president were still aired every day, but not as many since al-Bazzaz had changed the policy.

"I understand," Saddam said, "that you are not allowing some of the songs that carry my name to be broadcast."

Al-Bazzaz was stunned, and suddenly frightened. "Mr. President," he said, "we still broadcast the songs, but I have stopped some of them because they are so poorly written. They are rubbish."

"Look," Saddam said, abruptly stern, "you are not a judge, Saad."

"Yes. I am not a judge."

"How can you prevent people from expressing their feelings toward me?"

Al-Bazzaz feared that he was going to be taken away and shot. He felt the blood drain from his face, and his heart pounded heavily. The editor said nothing. The pencil shook in his hand. Saddam had not even raised his voice.

"No, no, no. You are not the judge of these things," Saddam reiterated.

Al-Bazzaz kept repeating, "Yes, sir," and frantically wrote down every word the president said. Saddam then talked about the movement for more freedoms in the press and the arts. "There will be no loosening of controls," he said.

"Yes, sir."

"Okay, fine. Now it is all clear to you?"

"Yes, sir."

With that Saddam dismissed al-Bazzaz. The editor had sweated through his shirt and sport coat. He was driven back to the Cabinet Building, and then drove himself back to the office, where he immediately rescinded his earlier policy. That evening a full broadcast of the poems and songs dedicated to Saddam resumed.

Hadafuh (His Goal)

You are the fountain of willpower and the wellspring of life, the essence of earth, the sabers of demise, the pupil of the eye, and the twitch of the eyelid. A people like you cannot but be, with God's help. So be as you are, and as we are determined to be. Let all cowards, piggish people, traitors, and betrayers be debased.
—Saddam Hussein, addressing the Iraqi people, July 17, 2001

Iraq is a land of antiquity. It is called the Land of Two Rivers (the Tigris and the Euphrates); the land of Sumerian kings, Mesopotamia, and Babylon; one of the cradles of civilization. Walking the streets of Baghdad gives one a sense of continuity with things long past, of unity with the great sweep of history. Renovating and maintaining the old palaces is an ongoing project in the city. By decree, one of every ten bricks laid in the renovation of an ancient palace is now stamped either with the name Saddam Hussein or with an eight-pointed star (a point for each letter of his name spelled in Arabic).

In 1987 Entifadh Qanbar was assigned to work on the restoration of the Baghdad Palace, which had once been called al-Zuhoor, or the Flowers Palace. Built in the 1930s for King Ghazi, it is relatively small and very pretty; English in style, it once featured an elaborate evergreen maze. Qanbar is an engineer by training, a short, fit, dark-haired man with olive skin. After earning his degree he served a compulsory term in the army, which turned out to be a five-year stint, and survived the mandatory one-month tour on the front lines in the war with Iran.

Work on the palace had stalled some years earlier, when the British consultant for the project refused to come to Baghdad because of the war. One of Qanbar's first jobs was to supervise construction of a high and ornate brick wall around the palace grounds. Qanbar is a perfectionist, and because the wall was to be decorative as well as functional, he took care with the placement of each brick. An elaborate gate had already been built facing the main road, but Qanbar had not yet built the portions of the wall on either side of it, because the renovation of the palace itself was unfinished, and that way large construction equipment could roll on and off the property without danger of damaging the gate.

One afternoon at about five, as he was preparing to close down work for the day, Qanbar saw a black Mercedes with curtained windows and custom-built running boards pull up to the site. He knew immediately who was in it. Ordinary Iraqis were not allowed to drive such fancy cars. Cars like this one were driven exclusively by al Himaya, Saddam's bodyguards.

The doors opened and several guards stepped out. All of them wore dark-green uniforms, black berets, and zippered boots of reddish-brown leather. They had big moustaches like Saddam's, and carried Kalashnikovs. To the frightened Qanbar, they seemed robotic, without human feelings.

The bodyguards often visited the work site to watch and make trouble. Once, after new concrete had been poured and smoothed, some of them jumped into it, stomping through the patch in their red boots to make sure that no bomb or listening device was hidden there. Another time a workman opened a pack of cigarettes and a bit of foil wrapping fluttered down into the newly poured concrete. One of the guards caught a glimpse of something metallic and reacted as if someone had thrown a hand grenade. Several of them leaped into the concrete and retrieved the scrap. Angered to discover what it was, and to have been made to look foolish, they dragged the offending worker aside and beat him with their weapons. "I have worked all my life!" he cried. They took him away, and he did not return. So the sudden arrival of a black Mercedes was a frightening thing.

"Who is the engineer here?" the chief guard asked. He spoke with the gruff Tikriti accent of his boss. Qanbar stepped up and identified himself. One of the guards wrote down his name. It is a terrible thing to have al Himaya write down your name. In a country ruled by fear, the best way to survive is to draw as little attention to yourself as possible. To be invisible. Even success can be dangerous, because it makes you stand out. It makes other people jealous and suspicious. It makes you enemies who might, if the opportunity presents itself, bring your name to the attention of the police. For the state to have your name for any reason other than the most conventional ones—school, driver's license, military service—is always dangerous. The actions of the state are entirely unpredictable, and they can take away your career, your freedom, your life. Qanbar's heart sank and his mouth went dry.

"Our Great Uncle just passed by," the chief guard began. "And he said, 'Why is this gate installed when the two walls around it are not built?'"

Qanbar nervously explained that the walls were special, ornamental, and that his crew was saving them for last because of the heavy equipment coming and going. "We want to keep it a clean construction," he said.

"Our Great Uncle is going to pass by again tonight," said the guard. "When he does, it must be finished."

Qanbar was dumbfounded. "How can I do it?" he protested.

"I don't know," said the guard. "But if you don't do it, you will be in trouble." Then he said something that revealed exactly how serious the danger was: "And if you don't do it, we will be in trouble. How can we help?"

There was nothing to do but try. Qanbar dispatched Saddam's men to help round up every member of his crew as fast as they could—those who were not scheduled to work as well as those who had already gone home. Two hundred workers were quickly assembled. They set up floodlights. Some of the guards came back with trucks that had machine guns mounted on top. They parked alongside the work site and set up chairs, watching and urging more speed as the workers mixed mortar and threw down line after line of bricks.

The crew finished at nine-thirty. They had completed in four hours a job that would ordinarily have taken a week. Terror had driven them to work faster and harder than they believed possible. Qanbar and his men were exhausted. An hour later they were still cleaning up the site when the black Mercedes drove up again. The chief guard stepped out. "Our Uncle just passed by, and he thanks you," he said.

Walls define the tyrant's world. They keep his enemies out, but they also block him off from the people he rules. In time he can no longer see out. He loses touch with what is real and what is unreal, what is possible and what is not—or, as in the case of Qanbar and the wall, what is just barely possible. His ideas of what his power can accomplish, and of his own importance, bleed into fantasy.

Each time Saddam has escaped death—when he survived, with a minor wound to his leg, a failed attempt in 1959 to assassinate Iraqi President Abd al-Karim Qasim; when he avoided the ultimate punishment in 1964 for his part in a failed Baath Party uprising; when he survived being trapped behind Iranian lines in the Iran-Iraq war; when he survived attempted coups d'état; when he survived America's smart-bombing campaign against Baghdad, in 1991; when he survived the nationwide revolt after the Gulf War—it has strengthened his conviction that his path is divinely inspired and that greatness is his destiny. Because his worldview is essentially tribal and patriarchal, destiny means blood. So he has ordered genealogists to construct a plausible family tree linking him to Fatima, the daughter of the prophet Muhammad. Saddam sees the prophet less as the bearer of divine revelation than as a political precursor—a great leader who unified the Arab peoples and inspired a flowering of Arab power and culture. The concocted link of bloodlines to Muhammad is symbolized by a 600-page, hand-lettered copy of the Koran that was written with Saddam's own blood, which he donated a pint at a time over three years. It is now on display in a Baghdad museum.

If Saddam has a religion, it is a belief in the superiority of Arab history and culture, a tradition that he is convinced will rise up again and rattle the world. His imperial view of the grandeur that was Arabia is romantic, replete with fanciful visions of great palaces and wise and powerful sultans and caliphs. His notion of history has nothing to do with progress, with the advance of knowledge, with the evolution of individual rights and liberties, with any of the things that matter most to Western civilization. It has to do simply with power. To Saddam, the present global domination by the West, particularly the United States, is just a phase. America is infidel and inferior. It lacks the rich ancient heritage of Iraq and other Arab states. Its place at the summit of the world powers is just a historical quirk, an aberration, a consequence of its having acquired technological advantages. It cannot endure.

In a speech this past January 17, the eleventh anniversary of the start of the Gulf War, Saddam explained, "The Americans have not yet established a civilization, in the deep and comprehensive sense we give to civilization. What they have established is a metropolis of force. . . . Some people, perhaps including Arabs and plenty of Muslims and more than these in the wide world . . . considered the ascent of the U.S. to the summit as the last scene in the world picture, after which there will be no more summits and no one will try to ascend and sit comfortably there. They considered it the end of the world as they hoped for, or as their scared souls suggested it to them."

Arabia, which Saddam sees as the wellspring of civilization, will one day own that summit again. When that day comes, whether in his lifetime or a century or even five centuries hence, his name will rank with those of the great men in history. Saddam sees himself as an established member of the pantheon of great men—conquerors, prophets, kings and presidents, scholars, poets, scientists. It doesn't matter if he understands their contributions and ideas. It matters only that they are the ones history has remembered and honored for their accomplishments.

In a book titled *Saddam's Bombmaker* (2000), Khidhir Hamza, the nuclear scientist, remembers his first encounter with Saddam, when the future dictator was still nominally the vice-chairman. A large new computer had just been installed in Hamza's lab, and Saddam came sweeping through for a look. He showed little interest in the computer; his attention was drawn instead to a lineup of pictures that Hamza had tacked to the wall, each of a famous scientist, from Copernicus to Einstein. The pictures had been torn from magazines.

"What are those?" Saddam asked.

"Sir, those are the greatest scientists in history," Hamza told him.

Then, as Hamza remembers it, Saddam became angry. "What an insult this is! All these great men, these great scientists! You don't have enough respect for these great men to frame their pictures? You can't honor them better than this?"

To Hamza, the outburst was irrational; the anger was out of all proportion. Hamza interpreted it as Saddam's way of testing him, of putting him in his place. But Saddam seemed somehow *personally* offended. To understand his tantrum one must understand the kinship he feels with the great men of history, with history itself. Lack of reverence for an image of Copernicus might suggest a lack of reverence for Saddam.

In what sense does Saddam see himself as a great man? Saad al-Bazzaz, who defected in 1992, has thought a lot about this question, during his time as a newspaper editor and TV producer in Baghdad, and in the years since, as the publisher of an Arabic newspaper in London.

"I need a piece of paper and a pen," he told me recently in the lobby of Claridge's Hotel. He flattened the paper out on a coffee table and tested the pen. Then he drew a line down the center. "You must understand, the daily behavior is just the result of the mentality," he explained. "Most people would say that the main conflict in Iraqi society is sectarian, between the Sunni and the Shia Muslims. But the big gap has nothing to do with religion. It is between the mentality of the villages and the mentality of the cities."

"Okay. Here is a village." On the right half of the page al-Bazzaz wrote a *V* and beneath it he drew a collection of separate small squares. "These are houses or tents," he said. "Notice there are spaces between them. This is because in the villages each family has its own house, and each house is sometimes several miles from the next one. They are self-contained. They grow their own food and make their own clothes. Those who grow up in the villages are frightened of everything. There is no real law enforcement or civil society. Each family is frightened of each other, and all of them are frightened of outsiders. This is the tribal mind. The only loyalty they know is to their own family, or to their own village. Each of the families is ruled by a patriarch, and the village is ruled by the strongest of them. This loyalty to tribe comes before everything. There are no values beyond power. You can lie, cheat, steal, even kill, and it is okay so long as you are a loyal son of the village or the tribe. Politics for these people is a bloody game, and it is all about getting or holding power."

Al-Bazzaz wrote the word "city" atop the left half of the page. Beneath it he drew a line of adjacent squares. Below that he drew another line, and another. "In the city the old tribal ties are left behind. Everyone lives close together. The state is a big part of everyone's life. They work at jobs and buy their food and clothing at markets and in stores. There are laws, police, courts, and schools. People in the city lose their fear of out-siders, and take an interest in foreign things. Life in the city depends on cooperation, on sophisticated social networks. Mutual self-interest defines public policy. You can't get anything done without cooperating with oth-ers, so politics in the city becomes the art of compromise and partnership. The highest goal of politics becomes cooperation, community, and keep-ing the peace. By definition, politics in the city becomes nonviolent. The backbone of urban politics isn't blood, it's law."

In al-Bazzaz's view, Saddam embodies the tribal mentality. "He is the ultimate Iraqi patriarch, the village leader who has seized a nation," he explained. "Because he has come so far, he feels anointed by destiny. Every-thing he does is, by definition, the right thing to do. He has been chosen by Heaven to lead. Often in his life he has been saved by God, and each escape makes him more certain of his destiny. In recent years, in his speeches, he has begun using passages and phrases from the Koran, speak-ing the words as if they are his own. In the Koran, Allah says, 'If you thank me, I will give you more.' In the early nineties Saddam was on TV, pre-senting awards to military officers, and he said, 'If you thank me, I will give you more.' He no longer believes he is a normal person. Dialogue with him is impossible because of this. He can't understand why journalists should be allowed to criticize him. How can they criticize the father of the tribe? This is something unacceptable in his mind. To him, strength is every-thing. To allow criticism or differences of opinion, to negotiate or com-promise, to accede to the rule of law or to due process—these are signs of weakness."

Saddam is, of course, not alone in admiring *The Godfather* series. They are obvious movies for him to like (they were also a favorite of the Colom-bian cocaine tycoon Pablo Escobar). On the surface it is a classic patriar-chal tale. Don Vito Corleone builds his criminal empire from nothing, motivated in the main by love for his family. He sees that the world around him is vicious and corrupt, so he outdoes the world at its own cruelty and preys upon its vices, creating an apparent refuge of wealth and safety for himself and his own. We are drawn to his single-mindedness, subtle intel-ligence, and steadfast loyalty to an ancient code of honor in a changing world—no matter how unforgiving that code seems by modern standards.

The Godfather suffers greatly but dies playing happily in the garden with his grandson, arguably a successful man. The deeper meaning of the films, however, apparently eludes Saddam. *The Godfather* saga is more the story of Michael Corleone than of his father, and the film's message is not a happy one. Michael's obsessive loyalty to his father and to his family, to the ancient code of honor, leads him to destroy the very things it is designed to protect. In the end Michael's family is torn by tragedy and hatred. He orders his own brother killed, choosing loyalty to code over loyalty to family. Michael becomes a tragic figure, isolated and unloved, ensnared by his own power. He is a lot like Saddam.

In Saddam's other favorite movie, *The Old Man and the Sea,* the old man, played by Spencer Tracy, hooks a great fish and fights alone in his skiff to haul it in. It is easy to see why Saddam would be stirred by the image of a lone fisherman, surrounded by a great ocean, struggling to land this impossible fish. "I will show him what a man can do and what a man endures," the old man says. In the end he succeeds, but the fish is too large for the dinghy, and is devoured by sharks before the trophy can be displayed. The old man returns to his hut with cut and bleeding hands, exhausted but happy in the knowledge that he has prevailed. It would be easy for Saddam to see himself in that old man.

Or is he the fish? In the movie it leaps like a fantasy from the water—a splendid, wild, dangerous thing, magnificent in its size and strength. It is hooked, but it refuses to accept its fate. "Never have I had such a strong fish, or one that acted so strangely," the old man proclaims. Later he says, "There is no panic in his fight." Saddam believes that he is a great natural leader, the likes of which his world has not seen in thirteen centuries. Perhaps he will fail in the struggle during his lifetime, but he is convinced that his courage and vision will fire a legend that will burn brightly in a future Arab-centered world.

Even as Saddam rhapsodizes over the rich history of Arabia, he concedes the Western world's clear superiority in two things. The first is weapons technology—hence his tireless efforts to import advanced military hardware and to develop weapons of mass destruction. The second is the art of acquiring and holding power. He has become a student of one of the most tyrannical leaders in history: Joseph Stalin.

Saïd Aburish's biography, *Saddam Hussein: The Politics of Revenge* (2000), tells of a meeting in 1979 between Saddam and the Kurdish politician

Mahmoud Othman. It was an early-morning meeting, and Saddam received
Othman in a small office in one of his palaces. It looked to Othman as if
Saddam had slept in the office the night before. There was a small cot in the
corner, and the president received him wearing a bathrobe.

Next to the bed, Othman recalled, were "over twelve pairs of expensive shoes. And the rest of the office was nothing but a small library of books
about one man, Stalin. One could say he went to bed with the Russian
dictator."

In the villages of Iraq the patriarch has only one goal: to expand and
defend his family's power. It is the only thing of value in the wide, treach-
erous world. When Saddam assumed full power, there were still Iraqi intellectuals who had hopes for him. They initially accepted his tyranny as
inevitable, perhaps even as a necessary bridge to a more inclusive government, and believed, as did many in the West, that his outlook was essentially modern. In this they were gradually disappointed.

In September of 1979 Saddam attended a conference of unaligned
nations in Cuba, where he formed a friendship with Fidel Castro, who still
keeps him supplied with cigars. Saddam came to the gathering with Salah
Omar al-Ali, who was then the Iraqi ambassador to the United Nations, a
post he had accepted after a long period of living abroad as an ambassador. Together Saddam and al-Ali had a meeting with the new foreign
minister of Iran. Four years earlier Saddam had made a surprise conces-
sion to the soon-to-be-deposed Shah, reaching an agreement on navigation in the Shatt-al-Arab, a sixty-mile strait formed by the confluence of
the Tigris and Euphrates Rivers as they flow into the Persian Gulf. Both
countries had long claimed the strait. In 1979, with the Shah roaming the
world in search of cancer treatment, and power in the hands of the Ayatollah Khomeini (whom Saddam had unceremoniously booted out of Iraq
the year before), relations between the two countries were again strained,
and the waters of the Shatt-al-Arab were a potential flash point. Both countries still claimed ownership of two small islands in the strait, which were
then controlled by Iran.

But al-Ali was surprised by the tone of the discussions in Cuba. The
Iranian representatives were especially agreeable, and Saddam seemed to
be in an excellent mood. After the meeting al-Ali strolled with Saddam in
a garden outside the meeting hall. They sat on a bench as Saddam lit a big
cigar.

"Well, Salah, I see you are thinking of something," Saddam said. "What are you thinking about?"

"I am thinking about the meeting we just had, Mr. President. I am very happy. I'm very happy that these small problems will be solved. I'm so happy that they took advantage of this chance to meet with you and not one of your ministers, because with you being here we can avoid another problem with them. We are neighbors. We are poor people. We don't need another war. We need to rebuild our countries, not tear them down."

Saddam was silent for a moment, drawing thoughtfully on his cigar. "Salah, how long have you been a diplomat now?" he asked.

"About ten years."

"Do you realize, Salah, how much you have changed?"

"How, Mr. President?"

"How should we solve our problems with Iran? Iran took our lands. They are controlling the Shatt-al-Arab, our big river. How can meetings and discussions solve a problem like this? Do you know why they decided to meet with us here, Salah? They are weak is why they are talking with us. If they were strong there would be no need to talk. So this gives us an opportunity, an opportunity that only comes along once in a century. We have an opportunity here to recapture our territories and regain control of our river."

That was when al-Ali realized that Saddam had just been playing with the Iranians, and that Iraq was going to go to war. Saddam had no interest in diplomacy. To him, statecraft was just a game whose object was to outmaneuver one's enemies. Someone like al-Ali was there to maintain a pretense, to help size up the situation, to look for openings, and to lull foes into a false sense of security. Within a year the Iran-Iraq war began.

It ended horrifically, eight years later, with hundreds of thousands of Iranians and Iraqis dead. To a visitor in Baghdad the year after the war ended, it seemed that every other man on the street was missing a limb. The country had been devastated. The war had cost Iraq billions. Saddam claimed to have regained control of the Shatt-al-Arab. Despite the huge losses, he was giddy with victory. By 1987 his army, swelled by compulsory service and modern Western armaments, was the fourth largest in the world. He had an arsenal of Scud missiles, a sophisticated nuclear-weapons program under way, and deadly chemical and biological weapons in development. He immediately began planning more conquest.

* * *

Saddam's invasion of Kuwait, in August of 1990, was one of the great military miscalculations of modern history. It was a product of grandiosity. Emboldened by his "victory" over Iran, Saddam had begun to plan other improbable undertakings. He announced that he was going to build a world-class subway system for Baghdad, a multibillion-dollar project, and then proclaimed that he would construct a state-of-the-art nationwide rail system along with it. Ground was never broken for either venture. Saddam didn't have the money. One thing he did have, however, was an army of more than a million idle soldiers—easily enough men to overrun the neighboring state of Kuwait, with its rich oil deposits. He gambled that the world would not care, and he was wrong. Three days after Saddam's takeover of the tiny kingdom President George Bush announced, "This will not stand," and immediately began assembling one of the largest military forces ever in the region.

Through the end of 1990 and into 1991 Ismail Hussain waited in the Kuwaiti desert for the American counterattack. He is a short, stocky man, a singer, musician, and songwriter. The whole time he was forced to wear a uniform, he knew that he did not belong in one. Although some of the men in his unit were good soldiers, none of them thought they belonged in Kuwait. They hoped that they would not have to fight. Everyone knew that the United States had more soldiers, more supplies, and better weapons. Surely Saddam would reach an agreement to save face, and his troops would be able to withdraw peacefully. They waited and waited for this to happen, and when word came that they were actually going to fight, Hussain decided that he was already dead. There was no hope: he foresaw death everywhere. If you went toward the American lines, they would shoot you. If you stayed in the open, they would blow you up. If you dug a hole and buried yourself, American bunker-buster bombs would stir your remains with the sand. If you ran, your own commanders would kill you—because they would be killed if their men fled. If a man was killed running away, his coffin would be marked with the word "*jaban*," or "coward." His memory would be disgraced, his family shunned. There would be no pension for them from the state, no secondary school for his children. "*Jaban*" was a mark that would stain the family for generations. There was no escaping it. Some things are worse than staying with your friends and waiting to die. Hussain's unit manned an antiaircraft gun. He never even saw the American fighter jet that took off his leg.

It was apparent to everyone in the Iraqi military, from conscripts like Hussain to Saddam's top generals, that they could not stand up against such force. Saddam, however, didn't see it that way. Al-Bazzaz remembers being shocked by this. "We had the most horrible meeting on January 14, 1991, just two days before the allied offensive," he told me. "Saddam had just met with the UN secretary-general, who had come at the final hour to try to negotiate a peaceful resolution. They had been in a meeting for more than two and a half hours, so hopes were running high that some resolution had been reached. Instead Saddam stepped out to address us, and it was clear he was going to miss this last opportunity. He told us, 'Don't be afraid. I see the gates of Jerusalem open before me.' I thought, *What is this shit?* Baghdad was about to be hit with this terrible firestorm, and he's talking to us about visions of liberating Palestine?"

Wafic Samarai was in a particularly difficult position. How does one function as chief of intelligence for a tyrant who does not wish to hear the truth? On the one hand, if you tell him the truth and it contradicts his sense of infallibility, you are in trouble. On the other, if you tell him only what he wants to hear, time will inevitably expose your lies and you will be in trouble.

Samarai was a lifelong military officer. He had advised Saddam throughout the long war with Iran, and he had seen him develop a fairly sophisticated understanding of military terminology, weaponry, strategy, and tactics. But Saddam's vision was clouded by a strong propensity for wishful thinking—the downfall of many an amateur general. If Saddam wanted something to happen, he believed he could will it to happen. Samarai kept up a steady stream of intelligence reports as the United States and its allies assembled an army of nearly a million soldiers in Kuwait, with air power far beyond anything the Iraqis could muster, with artillery, missiles, tanks, and other armored vehicles decades more advanced than Iraq's arsenal. The Americans didn't hide these weapons. They wanted Saddam to understand exactly what he was up against.

Yet Saddam refused to be intimidated. He had a plan, which he outlined to Samarai and his other generals in a meeting in Basra weeks before the American offensive started. He proposed capturing U.S. soldiers and tying them up around Iraqi tanks, using them as human shields. "The Americans will never fire on their own soldiers," he said triumphantly, as if such squeamishness was a fatal flaw. It was understood that he would have no such compunction. In the fighting, he vowed, thousands of enemy prisoners would be taken for this purpose. Then his troops would roll unopposed into eastern Saudi Arabia, forcing the allies to back down. This was his plan, anyway.

Samarai knew that this was nothing more than a hallucination. How were the Iraqis supposed to capture thousands of American soldiers? No one could approach the American positions, especially in force, without being discovered and killed. Even if it could be done, the very idea of using soldiers as human shields was repulsive, against all laws and international agreements. Who knew how the Americans would respond to such an act? Might they bomb Baghdad with a nuclear weapon? Saddam's plan was preposterous. But none of the generals, including Samarai, said a word. They all nodded dutifully and took notes. To question the Great Uncle's grand strategy would have meant to admit doubt, timidity, and coward- ice. It might also have meant demotion or death.

Still, as chief of intelligence, Samarai felt compelled to tell Saddam the truth. Late in the afternoon of January 14 the general reported for a meeting in Saddam's office in the Republican Palace. Dressed in a well-cut black suit, the president was behind his desk. Samarai swallowed hard and delivered his grim assessment. It would be very difficult to stand fast against the as- sault that was coming. No enemy soldiers had been captured, and it was unlikely that any would be. There was no defense against the number and variety of weapons arrayed against Iraq's troops. Saddam had refused all previous military advice to withdraw the bulk of his forces from Kuwait and move them back across the Iraqi border, where they might be more effec- tive. Now they were so thinly strung out across the desert that there was little to stop the Americans from advancing straight to Baghdad itself. Samarai had detailed evidence to back up his views—photographs, news reports, num- bers. The Iraqis could expect nothing more than swift defeat, and the threat that Iran would take advantage of their weakness by invading from the north.

Saddam listened patiently to this litany of pending disaster. "Are these your personal opinions or are they facts?" he asked. Samarai had presented many facts in his report, but he conceded that some of what he was offer- ing was educated conjecture.

"I will now tell you my opinion," Saddam said calmly, confidently. "Iran will never interfere. Our forces will put up more of a fight than you think. They can dig bunkers and withstand America's aerial attacks. They will fight for a long time, and there will be many casualties on both sides. Only we are willing to accept casualties; the Americans are not. The American people are weak. They would not accept the losses of large numbers of their soldiers."

Samarai was flabbergasted. But he felt he had done his duty. Saddam would not be able to complain later that his chief intelligence officer had misled him. The two men sat in silence for a few moments. Samarai could feel the looming American threat like a great weight pressing on his shoulders. There was nothing to be done. To Samarai's surprise, Saddam did not seem angry with him for delivering this bad news. In fact, he acted appreciative that Samarai had given it to him straight. "I trust you, and that's your opinion," he said. "You are a trustworthy person, an honorable person."

Heavy aerial attacks began three days later. Five weeks after that, on February 24, the ground offensive began, and Saddam's troops promptly surrendered or fled. Thousands were pinned at a place called Mutla Ridge as they tried to cross back into Iraq; most were incinerated in their vehicles. Iran did not invade, but otherwise the war unfolded precisely as Samarai had predicted.

In the days after this rout Samarai was again summoned to meet with Saddam. The president was working out of a secret office. He had been moving from house to house in the Baghdad suburbs, commandeering homes at random in order to avoid sleeping where American smart bombs might hit. Still, Samarai found him looking not just unfazed but oddly buoyed by all the excitement.

"What is your evaluation, general?" Saddam asked.

"I think this is the biggest defeat in military history," Samarai said.

"How can you say that?"

"This is bigger than the defeat at Khorramshahr [one of the worst Iraqi losses in the war with Iran, with Iraqi casualties in the tens of thousands]."

Saddam didn't say anything at first. Samarai knew the president wasn't stupid. He surely had seen what everyone else had seen—his troops surrendering en masse, the slaughter at Mutla Ridge, the grinding devastation of the U.S. bombing campaign. But even if Saddam agreed with the general's assessment, he could not bring himself to say so. In the past, as at Khorramshahr, the generals could always be blamed for defeat. Military people would be accused of sabotage, betrayal, incompetence, or cowardice. There would be arrests and executions, after which Saddam could comfortably harbor the illusion that he had rooted out the cause of failure. But this time the reasons for defeat rested squarely with him, and this, of course, was something he could never admit. "That's your opinion," he said curtly, and left it at that.

Defeated militarily, Saddam has in the years since responded with even wilder schemes and dreams, articulated in his typically confused, jargon-laden, quasi-messianic rhetoric. "On this basis, and along the same central concepts and their genuine constants, together with the required revolutionary compatibility and continuous renewal in styles, means, concepts, potentials, and methods of treatment and behavior, the proud and loyal people of Iraq and their valiant armed forces will win victory in the final results of the immortal Mother of All Battles," he declared in a televised address to the Iraqi people in August of last year. "With them and through them, good Arabs will win victory. Their victory will be splendid, immortal, immaculate, with brilliance that no interference can overshadow. In our hearts and souls as in the hearts and souls of the high-minded, glorious Iraqi women and high-spirited Iraqi men, victory is absolute conviction, Allah willing. The picking of its final fruit, in accordance with its description which all the world will point to, is a matter of time whose manner and last and final hour will be determined by the Merciful Allah. And Allah is the greatest!"

To help Allah along, Saddam had already started secret programs to develop nuclear, chemical, and biological weapons.

QASWAH (CRUELTY)

The flood has reached its climax and after the destruction, terror, murder, and sacrilege practiced by the aggressive, terrorist, and criminal Zionist entity, together with its tyrannical ally, the U.S., has come to a head against our brothers and our faithful struggling people in plundered Palestine. If evil achieves its objectives there, Allah forbid, its gluttony for more will increase and it will afflict our people and other parts of our wide homeland too.
—Saddam Hussein, in a televised address to the Iraqi people,
December 15, 2001

In the early 1980s a mid-level Iraqi bureaucrat who worked in the Housing Ministry in Baghdad saw several of his colleagues accused by Saddam's regime of accepting bribes. The accusations, he believes, were probably true. "There was petty corruption in our department," he says. The accused were all sentenced to die.

"All of us in the office were ordered to attend the hanging," says the former bureaucrat, who now lives in London. "I decided I wasn't going to go, but when my friends found out my plans, they called me and urged me to reconsider, warning that my refusal could turn suspicion on me." So he went. He and the others from his office were led into a prison courtyard, where they watched as their colleagues and friends, with whom they had worked for years, with whose children their children played, with whom they had attended parties and picnics, were marched out with sacks tied over their heads. They watched and listened as the accused begged, wept, and protested their innocence from beneath the sacks. One by one they were hanged. The bureaucrat decided then and there to leave Iraq.

"I could not live in a country where such a thing takes place," he says. "It is wrong to accept bribes, and those who do it should be punished by being sent to jail. But to hang them? And to order their friends and colleagues to come watch? No one who has witnessed such cruelty would willingly stay and continue to work under such conditions."

Cruelty is the tyrant's art. He studies and embraces it. His rule is based on fear, but fear is not enough to stop everyone. Some men and women have great courage. They are willing to brave death to oppose him. But the tyrant has ways of countering even this. Among those who do not fear death, some fear torture, disgrace, or humiliation. And even those who do not fear these things for themselves may fear them for their fathers, mothers, brothers, sisters, wives, and children. The tyrant uses all these tools. He commands not just acts of cruelty but cruel spectacle. So we have Saddam hanging the fourteen alleged Zionist plotters in 1969 in a public square, and leaving their dangling bodies on display. So we have Saddam videotaping the purge in the Baghdad conference hall, and sending the tape to members of his organization throughout the nation. So we have top party leaders forced to witness and even to participate in the executions of their colleagues. When Saddam cracks down on Shia clerics, he executes not just the mullahs but also their families. Pain and humiliation and death become public theater. Ultimately, guilt or innocence doesn't matter, because there is no law or value beyond the tyrant's will; if he wants someone arrested, tortured, tried, and executed, that is sufficient. The exercise not only serves as warning, punishment, or purge but also advertises to his subjects, his enemies, and his potential rivals that he is strong. Compassion, fairness, and concern for due process or the law are all signs of indecision. Indecision means weakness. Cruelty asserts strength.

Among the Zulu, tyrants are said to be "full of blood." According to one estimate, in the third and fourth years of Saddam's formal rule (1981 and 1982) more than 3,000 Iraqis were executed. Saddam's horrors over the more than thirty years of his informal and formal rule will someday warrant a museum and archives. But lost among the most outrageous atrocities are smaller acts that shed light on his personality. Tahir Yahya was the prime minister of Iraq when the Baath Party took power, in 1968. It is said that in 1964, when Saddam was in prison, Yahya had arranged for a personal meeting and tried to coerce him into turning against the Baathists and cooperating with the regime. Yahya had served Iraq as a military officer his whole adult life, and had at one time even been a prominent member of the Baath Party, one of Saddam's superiors. But he had earned Saddam's enduring scorn. After seizing power, Saddam had Yahya, a well-educated man whose sophistication he resented, confined to prison. On his orders Yahya was assigned to push a wheelbarrow from cell to cell, collecting the prisoners' slop buckets. He would call out "Rubbish! Rubbish!" The former prime minister's humiliation was a source of delight to Saddam for years. He would tell the story, chuckling over the words, "Rubbish! Rubbish!"

In another case Lieutenant General Omar al-Hazzaa was overheard speaking ill of the Great Uncle in 1990. He was not just sentenced to death. Saddam ordered that prior to his execution his tongue be cut out; for good measure, he also executed al-Hazzaa's son, Farouq. Al-Hazzaa's homes were bulldozed, and his wife and other children left on the street.

Saddam is realistic about the brutal reprisals that would be unleashed should he ever lose his grip on power. In their book *Out of the Ashes* (1999), Andrew and Patrick Cockburn tell of a family that complained to Saddam that one of their members had been unjustly executed. He was unapologetic, and told them, "Do not think you will get revenge. If you ever have the chance, by the time you get to us there will not be a sliver of flesh left on our bodies." In other words, if he ever becomes vulnerable, his enemies will quickly devour him.

Even if Saddam is right that greatness is his destiny, his legend will be colored by cruelty. It is something he sees as regrettable, perhaps, but necessary—a trait that defines his stature. A lesser man would lack the stomach for it. His son Uday once boasted to a childhood playmate that he and his brother, Qusay, had been taken to prisons by their father to witness torture and executions—to toughen them up for "the difficult tasks ahead," he said.

Yet no man is without contradictions. Even Saddam has been known to grieve over his excesses. Some who saw him cry at the lectern during the 1979 purge dismiss it as a performance, but Saddam has a history of bursting into tears. In the wave of executions following his formal assumption of power, according to Saïd Aburish's biography, he locked himself in his bedroom for two days and emerged with eyes red and swollen from weeping. Aburish reports that Saddam then paid a brazen though apparently sincere condolence call on the family of Adnan Hamdani, the executed official who had been closest to him during the previous decade. He expressed not remorse—the execution was *necessary*—but sadness. He told Hamdani's widow apologetically that "national considerations" must outweigh personal ones. So on occasion, at least, Saddam the person laments what Saddam the tyrant must do. During the Civil War, Abraham Lincoln drew a sharp distinction between what he personally would do—abolish slavery—and what his office required him to do: uphold the Constitution and the Union. Saddam ought to feel no such conflict; by definition, the interests of the state are his own. But he does.

The conflict between his personal priorities and his presidential ones has been particularly painful in his own family. Two of his sons-in-law, the brothers Saddam and Hussein Kamel, fled to Jordan and spilled state secrets—about biological, chemical, and nuclear-weapons programs—before inexplicably returning to Iraq and their deaths. Uday Hussein, Saddam's eldest son, is by all reports a sadistic criminal, if not completely mad. He is a tall, dark-skinned, well-built man of thirty-seven, who in his narcissism and willfulness is almost a caricature of his father. Uday has all his father's brutal instincts and, apparently, none of his discipline. He is a flamboyant drunk, and famous for designing his own wild apparel. Photographs show him wearing enormous bow ties and suits in colors to match his luxury cars, including a bright-red one with white stripes, and one that is half red, half white. Some of his suit jackets have a lapel on one side but not the other.

Ismail Hussain, the hapless Iraqi soldier who lost his leg in the Kuwaiti desert, attracted Uday's attention as a singer after the war. He became the First Son's favorite performer, and was invited to sing at the huge parties Uday threw every Monday and Thursday night. The parties were often held at a palace, which Saddam built, on an island in the Tigris near Baghdad. The opulence was eye-popping. All the door handles and fixtures in the palace were made of gold.

"At the parties," says Ismail, who now lives in Toronto, "I would be performing, and Uday would climb up on the stage with a machine gun and start shooting it at the ceiling. Everyone would drop down, terrified. I was used to being around weapons, bigger weapons than Uday's Kalashnikov, so I would just keep on singing. Sometimes at these parties there would be dozens of women and only five or six men. Uday insists that everyone get drunk with him. He would interrupt my performance, get up onstage with a big glass of cognac for himself and one for me. He would insist that I drink all of it with him. When he gets really drunk, out come the guns. His friends are all terrified of him, because he can have them imprisoned or killed. I saw him once get angry with one of his friends. He kicked the man in the ass so hard that his boot flew off. The man ran over and retrieved the boot and then tried to put it back on Uday's foot, with Uday cursing him all the while."

Uday's blessing paves the way for a singer like Ismail to perform regularly on Iraqi television. For this service Uday demands a kickback, and he can unmake a star as quickly as he can make one. The same is true in sports. Raed Ahmed was an Olympic weight lifter who carried the Iraqi flag during the opening ceremonies of the Atlanta games, in 1996. "Uday was head of the Olympic Committee, and all sports in Iraq," Ahmed told me early this year, in his home in a suburb of Detroit. "During training camp he would closely monitor all the athletes, keeping in touch with the trainers and pushing them to push the athletes harder. If he's unhappy with the results, he will throw the trainers and even the athletes into a prison he keeps inside the Olympic Committee building. If you make a promise of a certain result and fail to achieve it in competition, then the punishment is a special prison where they torture people. Some of the athletes started to quit when Uday took over, including many who were the best in their sports. They just decided it was not worth it. Others, like me, loved their sports, and success can be a stepping-stone in Iraq to better things, like a nice car, a nice home, a career. I always managed to avoid being punished. I was careful never to promise anything that I couldn't deliver. I would always say that there was a strong possibility that I would be beaten. Then, when I won, Uday was so happy."

Ahmed sat like a giant in his small living room, his shoulders nearly as wide as the back of the couch. The world of Saddam and Uday now strikes him as a bizarre wonderland, an entire nation hostage to the whims of a tyrant and his crazy son. "When I defected, Uday was very angry," he said. "He visited my family and questioned them. 'Why would Ahmed do such a thing?' he asked. 'He was always rewarded by me.' But Uday is despised."

Saddam tolerated Uday's excesses—his drunken parties, his private jail in the Olympic Committee headquarters—until Uday murdered one of the Great Uncle's top aides at a party in 1988. Uday immediately tried to commit suicide with sleeping pills. According to the Cockburns, "As his stomach was being pumped out, Saddam arrived in the emergency room, pushed the doctors aside, and hit Uday in the face, shouting: 'Your blood will flow like my friend's!'" His father softened, and the murder was ruled an accident. Uday spent four months in custody and then four months with an uncle in Geneva before he was picked up by the Swiss police for carrying a concealed weapon and asked to leave the country. Back in Baghdad, in 1996, he became the target of an assassination attempt. He was hit by eight bullets, and is now paralyzed from the waist down. His behavior has presumably disqualified him from succeeding his father. Saddam has made a show in recent years of grooming Qusay, a quieter, more disciplined and dutiful heir.

But the shooting of Uday was a warning to Saddam. Reportedly, a small group of well-educated Iraqi dissidents—none of whom has ever been apprehended, despite thousands of arrests and interrogations—carried it out. The would-be assassins are rumored to be associated with the family of General Omar al-Hazzaa, the officer whose tongue was cut out before he and his son were executed. This may be true; but there is no shortage of aggrieved parties in Iraq.

* * *

As Saddam approaches his sixty-sixth birthday, his enemies are numerous, strong, and determined. He celebrated the 1992 electoral defeat of George Bush by firing a gun from a palace balcony. Ten years later a new President Bush is in the White House, with a new national mission to remove Saddam. So the walls that protect the tyrant grow higher and higher. His dreams of pan-Arabia and his historical role in it grow ever more fanciful. In his clearer moments Saddam must know that even if he manages to hang on to power for the remainder of his life, the chances of his fathering a dynasty are slim. As he retreats to his secret bed each night, sitting up to watch a favorite movie on TV or to read one of his history books, he must know it will end badly for him. Any man who reads as much as he does, and who studies the dictators of modern history, knows that in the end they are all toppled and disdained.

"His aim is to be leader of Iraq forever, for as long as he lives," Samarai says. "This is a difficult task, even without the United States targeting you. The Iraqis are a divided and ruthless people. It is one of the most difficult nations in the world to govern. To accomplish his own rule, Saddam has shed so much blood. If his aim is for his power to be transferred to his family after his death, I think this is far into the realm of wishful thinking. But I think he lost touch with reality in that sense long ago."

This, ultimately, is why Saddam will fail. His cruelty has created great waves of hatred and fear, and it has also isolated him. He is out of step. His speeches today play like a broken record. They no longer resonate even in the Arab world, where he is despised by secular liberals and Muslim conservatives alike. In Iraq itself he is universally hated. He blames the crippling of the state on UN sanctions and U.S. hostility, but Iraqis understand that he is the cause of it. "Whenever he would start in blaming the Americans for this and that, for everything, we would look at each other and roll our eyes," says Sabah Khalifa Khodada, the former Iraqi major who was stripped and decontaminated for a meeting with the Great Uncle. The forces that protect him know this too—they do not live full-time behind the walls. Their loyalty is governed by fear and self-interest, and will tilt decisively if and when an alternative appears. The key to ending Saddam's tyranny is to present such an alternative. It will not be easy. Saddam will never give up. Overthrowing him will almost certainly mean killing him.

He guards his hold on the state as he guards his own life. There is no panic in his fight.

But for all the surrounding threats, Saddam sees himself as an immortal figure. Nothing could be more illustrative of this than the plot of his first novel, *Zabibah and the King*. Set in a mythical Arabian past, it is a simple fable about a lonely king, trapped behind the high walls of his palace. He feels cut off from his subjects, so he sets out on occasion to mingle. On one such outing, to a rural village, the king is struck by the beauty of the young Zabibah. She is married to a brutish husband, but the king summons her to his palace, where her rustic ways are at first scorned by the sophisticated courtiers. In time Zabibah's sweet simplicity and virtue charm the court and win the king's heart—although their relationship remains chaste. Questioning his own stern methods, the king is reassured by Zabibah, who tells him, "The people need strict measures so that they can feel protected by this strictness." But dark forces invade the kingdom. Infidel outsiders pillage and destroy the village, aided by Zabibah's jealous and humiliated husband, who rapes her. (The outrage occurs on January 17, the day in 1991 when the United States and allied powers began aerial attacks on Iraq.) Zabibah is later killed; the king defeats his enemy and slays Zabibah's husband. He then experiments with giving his people more freedoms, but they fall to fighting among themselves. Their squabbles are interrupted by the good king's death and their realization of his greatness and importance. The martyred Zabibah's sage advice reminds them: the people need strict measures.

And so Saddam champions the simple virtues of a glorious Arab past, and dreams that his kingdom, though universally scorned and defiled, will rise again and triumph. Like the good king, he is vital in a way that will not be fully understood until he is gone. Only then will we all study the words and deeds of this magnificent, defiant soul. He awaits his moment of triumph in a distant, glorious future that mirrors a distant, glorious past.

THE KABUL-KI DANCE

NOVEMBER 2002

I had been trying to get on the Air Force base outside Kuwait City long before the Afghanistan War to write a story about American pilots who were engaged in a shooting war over Iraq that nobody cared about anymore. They were flying daily patrols over Saddam's territory, enforcing UN-mandated no-flight zones, dodging SAMs and bombing the Iraqi launching and targeting sites. I was exchanging e-mail with some of the fliers, but the Air Force wouldn't let me on the base. Then September 11th happened and things really shut down. But my contacts with the pilots paid off. The Bold Tigers were pulled into the Afghan war, and they contacted me when they came home. I met with them in two trips to their home base of Mountain Home, Idaho. They had video and audio of all their missions. As I interviewed them, they would tell me about a particular bombing run and then ask, "You want to see it?" Air power is the most remarkable asset in the U.S. military, the one thing more than any other that gives the United States unassailable war-fighting superiority. This was a chance to see how it worked, to dissect a big part of the technology and methods that so quickly routed the Taliban.

One of the unadvertised downsides of being a god of the night sky, of delivering America's smartest bombs, of owning the twenty-first-century battlefield and then getting home in time to dine on surf 'n' turf and Häagen-Dazs and catch the latest episode of *Friends*, is the capability of the U.S. Air Force to record every word and image from the cockpit of your F-15 for digital playback. It's fine for showing off marksmanship and relishing derring-do; but some moments are not meant to be relived every time some wise-ass desk jock in the Mission Planning Cell, the MPC, cues up a certain audio file and punches a button on his keyboard.

"Holy shit! Missile launch!"

Heart in the throat, sphincter puckered, a trace of panic in the voice. It's a little embarrassing. It's the exact opposite of the purely utilitarian pilotese they teach in training.

"Holy shit! Missile launch!"

At war over Afghanistan, an Air Force captain called Snitch learned to live with the fact that his moment of genuine alarm had been preserved on audio. Snitch is one of the thirty-six crew members of the 391st Fighter Squadron, the Bold Tigers, a force of twelve F-15 Strike Eagles out of Mountain Home, Idaho. He is a slender, cheerful man in his early thirties, with brown eyes, short brown hair that looks as if it just came out from under a helmet, and freckles that still show under a dark tan. He grew up in Wisconsin, graduated from the Air Force Academy in 1992, and spent two years in Alaska as an Air Force criminal investigator. Hence his nickname. (The fliers in this story asked to be identified only by their call signs, to protect themselves and their families.) Snitch is a backseater, a weapons-systems officer, or "wizzo"—and something of a laser-guidance artist, so he's plenty secure with his skills. He also has a good sense of humor. But Snitch was annoyed to have his moment of panic become a squadron joke—especially the hundredth time he heard it. The fear was certainly defensible. Snitch knows pilotese and speaks it with the best of them, but the first time you see one of those surface-to-air motherfuckers corkscrewing up right at *you* . . . well, something primitive takes over.

For Snitch the joke was also a point of pride. Not many of the other guys had to dodge SAMs in this war. Besides, the joke was useful. It reminded the entire squadron, whose members saw this engagement as the greatest turkey shoot of all time, that there were real hazards up there, and that the long stretches of cramped, tense routine in the bubble cockpits of their jets, where even traveling at the speed of sound could get tedious, demanded an unflagging vigilance.

"Holy shit! Missile launch!"

It happened like this:

Snitch and his pilot, Slokes, had been airborne for hours, doing what the fliers of the 391st call the Kabul-ki Dance, circling Kabul with the full force of the U.S. air armada. They had completed the long night flight to Afghanistan after traveling down the Persian Gulf southeast from al Jaber (none of the Air Force personnel would disclose the location of their desert base outside Kuwait City, but it was widely reported during the conflict), avoiding Iran's airspace, rendezvousing with tankers over the Gulf of Oman to refuel, making a sharp left turn at Gwadar to cross over Pakistan and the great jagged peaks of the Siahan Range, and finally making their way northeast to Kabul. On daytime missions this same flight would reveal hours of dusty red-brown mountain ranges, miles and miles of hostile nothing, a seemingly endless expanse of saw-toothed ridges, a country harsher and emptier than any they had ever seen. On nighttime missions like this one they flew enveloped in darkness, under stars and a moon that seemed close enough to dodge. When they reached Kabul, in east-central Afghanistan, they joined the scores of American warplanes operating at various altitudes. At 20,000 feet the F-15s waited for "fragged" targets from Boss Man, the Airborne Warning and Control System (AWACS) aircraft that choreographs the terribly complicated and dangerous dance of the modern air assault. A target is fragged when it is assigned to be hit. Depending on its importance and the potential for "collateral damage," or civilian deaths (and thus political fallout), getting a target fragged may mean running all the way up the permission chain to the White House. On that mission Snitch and Slokes had already hit several targets and were given another, time-critical one: a SAM site just outside the city that had unwisely lobbed a missile into the dark sky full of American warplanes, revealing its position and thereby sealing its fate.

Their Strike Eagle, a sleek two-engine jet, the premier precision air-to-ground attack instrument in the U.S. arsenal, was still carrying five 500-pound laser-guided bombs, called GBU-12s (GBU stands for "guided bomb unit"), and Slokes and Snitch were still eager for a chance to lay into something. To be sent home carrying bombs was the worst. With comic futility Slokes would plead with Boss Man, "Please, sir, can I ask somebody else?" Nobody wanted to face the three-hour flight back to Kuwait with packages undelivered—it made the flight longer and burned fuel like crazy; and to face the crew that had worked like dogs to ready the aircraft, load the bombs, and paint love notes to Osama bin Laden and Mullah Mohammed Omar on the ordnance was a full-bore bummer.

Working with the AWACS coordinates, Snitch quickly located the SAM site in his target pod, and Slokes maneuvered the jet into the approach. They felt the familiar push of their backs into their seats, and the lurch of their guts against their spines, but both were much too busy to think about the discomfort. Snitch couldn't have said if the jet was upside down or right side up. His nose was glued to the green of his eight-inch target monitor. Manipulating the laser with his hand control, he cleared Slokes to "pickle"—release the bomb. The pilot pressed the button that gives the jet final permission to drop a bomb once it has calculated the perfect trajectory, and fractions of a second later the thing was off. Slokes banked the jet to the left as Snitch, gently nudging his hand controller, kept the laser zeroed; his pod stays fixed on the target no matter how the jet moves. The bomb hit "shack on," or dead center, and the SAM launcher vanished in a satisfactory black splash on the monitor. Job well done . . . but then up out of the burning mess spiraled a missile that the GBU had evidently cooked right off the pad.

It was then that Snitch famously exclaimed, *"Holy shit! Missile launch!"*

Slokes immediately threw the jet off its course, and Snitch punched out some chaff and flares (the chaff distracts radar guidance, and the flares confuse a heat-seeker), after which ensued thirty weighty seconds—or, as Snitch puts it, "half the known age of the universe"—of listening to each other's nervous breathing in the headphones, waiting to be torn into oblivion, until the pilot of a trailing jet commented, in perfect pilotese, "It burned out co-altitude."

"Holy sheepshit!" Slokes said, breaking the silence.

"I got that in the pod, brother," Snitch said, meaning that the event was digitally preserved and they could show it off later.

"Fuckin' party!" Slokes said, deep into the euphoria of being shot at and missed.

"Fun" is a word not often applied to warfare. It's unseemly; you aren't supposed to enjoy yourself while killing people. But the high-intensity enthusiasm of the Bold Tigers was unmistakable. They are young (most of them in their twenties), slender, fit, smart, patriotic, highly motivated, exhaustively trained, and crisply able. They are all in love with flight, with riding their silver bullets to the edges of the sky, peering down at the broad curvature of the earth, feeling the great surge of supersonic engines beneath them. Given the chance to show what they could do, taking on a cause that both inspired and excited them, added a tincture of danger to the heady mix. It's no wonder the pilots and wizzos of the 391st came to feel that this was the time of their lives.

What is most telling about Slokes and Snitch's brush with danger is that it was memorable at all. The Bold Tigers trace their history back to the days of flying P-47s in combat over Europe in World War II. The unit has known times when being shot at was all too common, as was being shot at and hit. But the days of jousting with the enemy in the sky, of flirting daily with death in the clouds, are all but over—and have been for some time. At the dawn of World War II the French pilot and author Antoine de Saint-Exupéry was already mourning the flying duelists of the Great War and anticipating the tremendous bombing raids that would define the coming conflict. The fighter plane was being replaced by the flying truck, and war seemed to call less for aerial artistry than for the capacity to deliver or endure wave after wave of bombs. Saint-Exupéry could not have foreseen today's conflicts, in which bombing has become an exercise in precision and fighter pilots (or, in the case of the Strike Eagles, fighter crews) are essentially technicians who—the close call of Snitch and Slokes notwithstanding—fight wars that are nearly stripped of passion and danger. Combat has become a procedure, deliberate and calculated, more cerebral than visceral—even if it does still have its moments. The modern American air war is almost never about air-to-air combat. Squadrons like the 391st now go to war virtually unopposed. Few nations have the capability to contest American fighters in the sky, and those that do would probably fare badly. Air warfare as practiced today by the U.S. military is about delivering weapons accurately and with impunity. The goal is to destroy an enemy's ability to make war, with minimal risk above and minimal carnage and destruction below.

Given the ineffectiveness of surface-to-air missiles in recent conflicts, those on the receiving end of this juggernaut are left with few weapons. Perhaps the most powerful one, apart from suicidal acts of terror, is the world's indignation. Victimhood affords the enemy a claim to higher moral ground. The shedding of enough innocent blood can eclipse the meaning of even the noblest cause. So civilian deaths are trumpeted by the enemy with each new air assault. Whether in Iraq, Bosnia, or Afghanistan, the number of casualties is often exaggerated. Western journalists are given tours of shattered neighborhoods and villages, where images of real death, dismemberment, and grief counter the Pentagon's antiseptic videos of guided bombs striking toy houses and cars. These images stir outrage in the United States and Europe and fuel the now familiar rearguard American movements to stop such bombings and end such wars.

The astonishing precision of modern American weaponry deflates this outrage. Compared with other "bomb-delivery systems," such as the old B-52s and the F-16 Falcons, the Bold Tigers in their Strike Eagles are artists of aerial bombardment. They worry less about being shot at than about missing their "dimpie," or designated mean point of impact. Slokes subscribes to an adage he read in a history book about pilots in World War II, which goes, "God, please don't let me fuck up . . . but if I do, please don't let me fuck up and live."

B-52s—or "Buffs," for "Big Ugly Fat Fuckers"—drop the less accurate, less smart joint direct attack munitions, or JDAMs. In the Afghanistan campaign they took off from Diego Garcia, an island in the Indian Ocean; cruised way up to somewhere in the "Bozosphere" (meaning "way the fuck up there"); and, visible from below only as bright white contrails, opened their bomb bays and let fly. They are the wholesale-delivery teams of the modern air-war industry. F-16s, direct heirs of the single-seat combat-fighter tradition, are sleek and cool, excellent for providing air cover for bombers—but there was no call for that over Afghanistan. The Bold Tigers affectionately call F-16s "Lawn Darts," because that's what they look like, because they carry relatively light loads, and because if their single engine fails, they perform a graceful nosedive straight into the ground.

In contrast, the Bold Tigers are hunters. They prowl around in shoulder-held-missile territory, skimming the terrain, looking, as they say, to paint their bull's-eyes right on terrorist assholes. These crews are the sharp end of the most effective death-and-destruction delivery system ever devised.

The air campaign that was waged over Afghanistan is of a significantly higher order than the one conducted over Vietnam, where flying a fighter-bomber was still essentially a solo act. Today's air assault is a feat of aerial coordination. From early October of 2001 until the following January the sky over Afghanistan caterwauled with warplanes and support aircraft from the British and American Army, Navy, Marines, and Air Force—so many that the greatest danger faced by crews like those of the Bold Tigers was colliding with one another or being clipped by JDAMs from above.

At the highest level, in orbit hundreds of miles up, were scores of satellites. Below them, at 40,000 feet or so, were the Buffs and B-1s, which dropped more than half the bombs used on Afghanistan. There were EA-6 Prowlers to jam enemy communications. There were A-10 Thunderbolts and AC-130s for close air support, and air-rescue teams in helicopters— Pave Lows (MH-53Js), Black Hawks (UH-60s), and Jolly Green Giants (HH-53s). Finally, there were the strikers—the F-15s, the F-16s, and the Navy and Marine Corps F-18 Hornets and F-14 Tomcats, which delivered laser-guided precision bombs. There were also the unmanned aerial vehicles (UAVs), armed with cameras and missiles—drones like the Predator (RQ-1), which made a name for itself for the first time in this conflict. Add to these dozens of Extenders (KC-10s) and Stratotankers (KC-135s)— flying gas stations that enabled the armada to stay aloft for hours and hours. And last there were Boss Man and its British equivalent, Spartan, whose job it was to coordinate the whole Kabul-ki Dance.

Over Afghanistan the twelve Strike Eagles of the 391st usually carried nine GBU-style bombs, including, on five occasions, the GBU-28, a 5,000-pound bunker buster. The Bold Tigers were the busiest of three Air Force fighter squadrons in the war; they flew 230 sorties from October 17 to January 6. The squadron's eighteen crews (thirty-five men and one woman, a twenty-six-year-old wizzo nicknamed Baldie, who had a full head of medium-brown hair), backed up by about 230 maintenance workers and munitions experts, delivered a goodly portion of the precision bombs dropped in the war. This small group of fliers played a major role in dismantling a totalitarian theocracy and chasing al Qaeda back into the hills.

The F-15 is an old aircraft, older than many of the crew members who fly it. Originally designed as a single-seat air-to-air fighter, it made its debut flight in 1972. It was the first operational jet with enough thrust to actually accelerate in a vertical climb. Sixty-four feet long and forty-three feet wide from wingtip to wingtip, it is slightly larger than a deluxe tour bus and considerably less accommodating for its crew. Adding a seat behind the pilot's became useful for bombing missions, because the additional systems required for finding and hitting targets were too much for a single flier to handle. Apart from all of its electronic wizardry, the twin-tailed jet consists of little more than fuel tanks and two huge Pratt & Whitney jet engines. The cockpit is tight. Instruments fill the displays in front of both pilot and wizzo and line panels to the left and the right. There is enough room for the fliers to stretch their legs forward, but not enough to raise their arms far over their heads, and little room to shift from side to side. Fearing deep-vein thrombosis on such long flights, doctors teach the crews isometric exercises to perform in the cramped space. The seats, which are attached to ejection rockets in case of emergency, have no cushioning, because any space for it would allow the hard shell of the chair to hit a flier's backside on ejection with enough impact to crush a pelvis or snap a spine. With an average sortie length for the squadron of about ten hours, the crews put up with sore rumps.

And insistent bladders. That issue did present itself, especially on the longer flights (the record was fifteen and a half hours). Urination was a struggle even for the men, who are provided with "piddle packs"—tube-like plastic bags with a powder inside that turns urine into a gel. In theory, piddle packs are easy to use, fitting right over the tip of the penis; but the crews are wearing flight suits, heavy jackets (the air temperature is sub-freezing at altitude), G-suits, and survival vests (with loaded 9-mm pistols), and are strapped down in spaces no larger than the backseat of a Honda Civic. More than one crew member had to strip down mid-flight and bring his skivvies home in a plastic bag.

It is even worse for women. The Air Force has been working on the concept of a woman's urinating in a cockpit for several years now, and if Baldie is a fair judge, it has not yet solved the problem. Poor Baldie. (Her nickname comes from the fact that she is married to an F-16 pilot and thus "Bangs a Lawn Dart Driver": BALD-D.) Sitting just a few feet in front of or behind a male flier, a woman is forced to disrobe in an immodest series of contortions, exposing her hands and hindquarters to the stinging cold, and then has to negotiate a funnel attached to a bag. It's little wonder that Baldie became known as the "super camel," for her holding ability. ("I did sprint to the bathroom a few times the second we landed," she says.) Bowel movements? Too horrible to contemplate, and no accommodations what-soever. The bowels are easier to regulate, of course, and during the Af-ghanistan campaign Imodium became a staple of the Bold Tiger diet; but dining on not always familiar food in a foreign land has been known to create digestive emergencies that can confound even the strongest over-the-counter medications. One flier earned the nickname "B-NOK," for "buck naked over Kuwait," when seized by a call that had to be answered. He relieved himself into a small cardboard fast-food container with the jet on autopilot. Most of these fliers can strip, crap, and fly all at once—a proud accomplishment. These are not the kinds of skills they package in the "Go Air Force" pitch.

The crews gladly accept their discomfort. Baldie announced her career intentions at age four. They were reinforced two years later, when her father was doing some contract work for NASA in Providence, Rhode Island, and one day brought home a collection of colorful prints of jet aircraft. He gave them to his daughter, who, thrilled, declared that in the future she was going to fly one. (She has recently started pilot training.) Slokes, a big, boisterous, confident man with short-clipped blond hair, is the son of a World War II fighter pilot, but he swears that this had nothing to do with his desire to be a flier. He attended the Air Force Academy because he got in, and because it was free. He aimed to be one of the twenty grads each year whom the academy sends on to medical school, and he had a GPA to qualify, but along the way he got a chance to fly. The stethoscope could not compete with the throttle. Snitch wanted to go to flight school when he graduated from the academy, but imperfect eyesight initially eliminated him from both the front and backseat. Undaunted, he applied for a waiver and started his job in Alaska as a criminal investigator for the Air Force. When the waiver was approved, he was torn. He liked his work, but in the Air Force the most prestigious job is in a bubble cockpit. His commanding officer, noticing how avidly Snitch watched the fighters take off and land every day, asked, "So, Lieutenant, what was it that brought you here in the first place?"

"I was waiting for my waiver to come through," he said.

"And . . . ?"

Super Dave, a balding, fair-haired wizzo of thirty-four, was raised on a dairy farm in Virginia. His goal had been to design airplanes, until a friend took him up in a Cessna: he was hooked. Push, a tall, lean Army brat with dark hair and blue eyes, accepted an Air Force ROTC scholarship as a means of paying his way through Duke University. It was not long before flying in an F-15 eclipsed his enthusiasm for civil engineering. Two Fish, who flew with Baldie, wants to be an astronaut. An Air Force Academy grad with a master's degree in astrodynamics, he is aiming to keep alive a family tradition—his grandfather worked for NASA. Tank is on the same path. Growing up in Minnesota, he used to cut the lawn of a pilot who took him up in a plane a couple of times. He earned his pilot's license as a teenager, attended the academy, and is working on getting a graduate degree in aerospace engineering from the University of Washington.

Their commander, AJ, a trim man with a pink complexion who seems uncomfortable when not in motion, is an older version of them all. In his forties, AJ is the kind of man who could long ago have moved on to more lucrative employment as a commercial pilot but who has never been able to shake the thrill of flying fighters. An Air Force brat whose father was a wizzo on missions over Korea and Vietnam, he has moved around so much in his life that he's not sure where he comes from. ("I think I'm from Idaho," he says.) AJ has an unabashed sense of commitment to his country.

Despite the high level of talent and motivation, flight crews are, by virtue of being flesh and blood, one of the weak links in the war machine. The Air Force tries to regulate them like delicate instruments, with pills to clog their bowels and pills to clean their bowels, "go" pills to speed crews up and "no go" pills to slow them down. The crews are pampered, not out of kindness but out of necessity. The job demands a great deal of mental and emotional clarity. So the base at al Jaber is by no means a hardship post. Crew members share air-conditioned mobile homes with a bathroom and a shower, cable TV, a DVD player, and PlayStation 2. They have hearty food, workout facilities, and an officers' club with a paperback library, twenty La-Z-Boy recliners, a big screen for movie viewing, a popcorn machine, and snacks (but no alcohol). The cable TV carries all the major networks and European MTV, and—perhaps owing to the generosity of the installer—receives unsolicited X-rated fare late at night. AJ got to see more of his beloved Green Bay Packers' games that fall than he ever gets to see at home in Idaho.

The crew members were entitled to one fifteen-minute satellite phone call home each week, and unlimited Internet access, resulting in constant e-mail traffic with spouses, family, and friends. Some of the fliers got in trouble for revealing too much in their excited stories. They quickly learned that the recipients were forwarding their private electronic messages to other friends, who forwarded them again, until the crews were getting return mail from perfect strangers all over the world. Each crew usually had a sortie to Afghanistan only every three or four days, and although they also flew missions over the no-fly zone in Iraq, there was still plenty of downtime. When she wasn't dropping bombs, Baldie, ever the multitasker, spent much of her time completing course work for a master's

degree in engineering from Oklahoma State University. (Her professors
FedExed her videotapes of their classes.) Some of the fliers drove into
Kuwait City on occasion to dine out at restaurants or shop at the Western-
style malls. AJ and some others even attended an air show in Dubai, the
third largest in the world. War was never like this before.

Chaz, a lieutenant colonel who served as the Bold Tigers' ops officer,
had the job of keeping the squadron flying, which involved artfully managing rest and maintenance. A longtime wizzo from Mississippi, blond and
stocky at age forty-three, he would review charts, ask questions, listen
intently, and, above all, peer deeply into the eyes of the young crew members while trying to decide if they were rested and alert enough to fly. They
all wanted to fly as often as they were allowed, but Chaz made up his own
mind about it. He was less interested in what they said than in the look in
their eyes. If he didn't like what he saw there, if he saw jumpiness or flat-
ness, they were grounded.

With all the direct hits recorded by the Bold Tigers in the campaign,
Chaz is proudest of a shot that missed. "One of my young wizzos got dis-
oriented while his bomb was in flight," he says, smiling beatifically. "He
directed it into a dirt field. That's good judgment, good training."

For the Bold Tigers flying over Afghanistan, the most excitement came at
the beginning of the campaign. The squadron flew its first sortie of the war
on October 17. After leaving Kuwait, two F-15s felt their way into unfamiliar space out over the Persian Gulf on a perfectly black night, their
initial objective to find an Extender, because they couldn't make the long
flight without repeated refueling.

AJ flew alongside an F-15 piloted by Slokes. Each jet carried nine
500-pound bombs. It was just over a month after the attacks on the United
States, and both crews felt a strong sense of purpose heading off to war.
There was a powerful urge to act. Wearing night optical goggles, known
as NOGs, they occasionally saw the green outlines of a carrier force in the
smooth black waters below. But for Air Force planes carriers were not an
option for refueling; they needed to find an airborne tanker. Fuel management was critical, and on that first flight AJ was nervous. "Whenever a
pilot tells me he gets bored on a long flight," he says, "I tell him he should
learn to worry more." They had to maintain enough fuel to fly to a friendly

base in an emergency, which meant they had to keep topping off their fuel tanks in the air. AJ, working with an AWACS, was finally able to spot an Extender before the sortie would have needed to be aborted. They took no chances after finding the big tanker. They just slowed down and flew alongside it over Pakistan and into southern Afghanistan.

In the early days of the war the Bold Tigers tended to rendezvous over Kandahar, near the Pakistani border in the southeastern corner of the country, where they would wait for a fragged target. At that point they faced plenty of antiaircraft artillery, or "triple A." The shots would come in bursts of three to five. The Zeus (ZSU-23) snaked up, a twisting line of orange light. KS-19s, which fire 100-mm shells, were more worrisome; sometimes when the jets were under 20,000 feet, a shell would burst in a sudden white flash above them. That got the attention of the crew, like someone flipping on a floodlight in the darkness. The 57-mm guns sent up red tracers that usually fizzled well below the jets. But the smaller rounds came up faster. The shells rose as brightening balls of light. The crews worried when they saw out their canopy a ball centered on their plane rather than sliding away; that meant it was bearing straight at them. At 20,000 to 30,000 feet they were pretty much out of range, but in a country with 12,000-foot mountain peaks even that altitude wasn't completely safe. It was always a comfort to be flying at night. Flying that high, they could be spotted only as a faint moving shadow on the stars.

On that first sortie they were given a target in Jalalabad, a two-building radio relay station inside a walled compound. Snitch had already typed the ground coordinates from Boss Man into his computer, and once over the area he pointed his target pod in the general direction. He then began to search his video screen for the radio relay station, trying to pick up visual clues from the surrounding neighborhood based on the description he had been given. Some descriptions were better than others. When he had the ground coordinates before beginning the mission, he would draw himself a map that made it easier to locate the target. This time he hadn't made a sketch, because from his preflight target study it looked like what Slokes had called "a dog-balls target," meaning it stood out conspicuously.

When they flew into the air over Jalalabad, their jet noise alerted ground defenses, and the sky erupted around them with triple A. They heard no sound, just saw lines of light and sudden flashes of white, yellow, and red around and above them. AJ and his wizzo hit their target on the first pass, but Slokes and Snitch had trouble pinpointing theirs. In daylight the target may have stood out like dog balls, but they had arrived at a time of night known as "thermal crossover"—that is, the point when ground temperatures had dropped enough to match the temperature of the buildings. Because the imaging equipment in the target pod was thermal, Snitch had a hell of a time making the target out. Three times Slokes swung the jet around and flew back into the light show, as Snitch tried to zero in on the building.

"Come on, dude, we need to get these bombs off," Slokes urged.

Snitch knew from the first two passes that the building would become more visible the closer they got. The GBU was equipped with a laser sensor in its tip, and with small steering mechanisms in its fins, called servo motors, to redirect its flight. So he could release the bombs before the building was completely visible and then steer them in as the picture came into better focus. He approximated the target and told Slokes, "Captured, cleared to pickle."

Slokes pushed the button, and the first bomb dropped. Snitch then placed the cursor on his screen at the precise spot he wanted it to hit— "painting the target," the fliers called it—and fired his laser. The wizzo guided the bomb directly into the second building.

Both crews, first elated, grew sober. They had spent years practicing, so bombing was routine, even sport. Now they were dropping real 500-pound bombs on real people. Packed with high explosives, encased in hard metal designed to fracture into hot shrapnel, a GBU-12 would vaporize anyone or anything within a few yards of its detonation, which would be seen as a black splash on Snitch's screen. No one inside a radius of about 200 meters would be likely to survive the shock wave and shrapnel. A safe distance (behind cover) was considered to be 500 meters—a meter for every pound of explosives. No matter how accurate the crews were, they could only hope that they were hitting appropriate targets; they were only as good as their intel. They all tried to imagine what it would be like to be on the receiving end of their delivery. An American pilot captive in Baghdad during the Persian Gulf War, who survived a GBU-12 hit on the prison where he was being held, said the approaching bomb made a sound like tearing canvas. (Older bombs, less aerodynamic, whistled.) Then came the *click! click! click!* of the servo motors as the bomb was steered home, followed by the loud static noise of the laser ionizing the air around it. Then *WHAM!*

The adrenaline rush faded on the long flight home. The pilots and wizzos talked, popped go pills as necessary, and checked and rechecked their navigation. Sometimes they broke out peanut butter and jelly sandwiches or croissants they'd provisioned from the mess hall. Mach One can feel like a crawl in the final hours of a nine-hour sortie.

It was hard in the beginning to tell if they were making a difference. One of the first sorties that seemed to strike a blow came about a week into the campaign, when two Bold Tiger Strike Eagles took out the Ministry for the Prevention of Vice and Propagation of Virtue in Kandahar, which intel later assured them was a big deal. "We want you to hit a building," Boss Man said. When Super Dave plotted out the coordinates, he saw that it was in the center of Kandahar.

"Oh, boy, this is going to be good," he told his pilot, Curly. The targeting directions were somewhat vague. Super Dave was told to look at his screen for a big intersection, and to aim for the large building on the northeast corner. He was trying to memorize Kandahar (that's how he spent the long hours on the flight over), and one thing he knew for sure was that the city had lots of intersections. He told the controller that he needed better information.

"The building has columns," the controller said.

There was no way, looking straight down, that they were going to see columns. So Super Dave and Fang, the wizzo in the other F-15, went to work on the problem. Comparing the global-positioning coordinates with the infrared image on his screen, they asked for clarification from Boss Man, and finally zeroed in on a building that was several city blocks long. Super Dave's first bomb hit the domed front corner of the structure. The two jets took their time, making runs just as they did in target practice. On the video of the sortie the targeted end of the building collapses neatly, folding in on itself, more like the object of a professional demolition than the victim of an improvised bombing run.

In those early days of the campaign there were more targets than time to hit them, and sometimes the crews found themselves being pushed to do more than they thought wise. The crews classified missions by priority: low (could be put off until another day), medium (time-sensitive), or high (urgent because U.S. forces were under fire on the ground). In high-priority circumstances the crews were willing to take bigger risks, including flying off to remote areas without knowing whether they would be able to find a tanker to refuel, and flying low over lofty mountain ranges where they knew they would be vulnerable to shoulder-fired SAMs.

For low- and medium-priority missions they learned to dicker with the AWACS. Push was the wizzo on an early sortie when Spartan, the British AWACS, assigned his and another F-15, flying wing, a target in Tarin Kowt, a city north of Kandahar. It was described as a Taliban headquarters building, housing government leaders. The jets had been in the air for hours, earlier in northern Afghanistan, and were low on fuel. They knew that the target area was fairly distant and that tankers were unlikely to be in the vicinity. They didn't relish the prospect of having to make an emergency landing somewhere in northern Pakistan, which is what Spartan recommended. So they bargained. If Spartan would assign them two tankers, they'd do the job. Push remembers wondering whether this was the right thing to do. The crews discussed it among themselves and concluded that if the target was of high enough priority to put them in this situation, it was worth a couple of tankers. They sweated it out for a few minutes until Spartan coughed up the tankers, and then they flew north.

In the end they destroyed their target, but it was a stressful ride home. When they landed at al Jaber, concluding a thirteen-hour sortie, their group commander was waiting for them on the tarmac. That had not happened before. It signified something either very good or very bad. Maybe the brass were displeased with their dickering.

But when the men climbed down from their cockpits, it was to handshakes and praise.

The war gave the crews opportunities to stretch their skills, to try things they had never attempted during practice. Two Fish and Baldie were midway through a sortie when an AWACS assigned them an important target, a convoy of trucks. Baldie estimated the speed of the vehicles to be 100 miles an hour. ("How fast would you be driving down the road if you knew that an F-15 was trying to kill you?" she asks.) She made a rough calculation of where the trucks would be when the bomb reached the road, and cleared Two Fish to pickle. Guiding the GBU with her laser, teasing it along with her hand controller, like a kite at the end of a string, she put it right through the lead truck's front grille.

"You have just been killed by a girl," Two Fish said.

Few things are more satisfying in war than watching the enemy employ outmoded tactics. Snitch and Slokes, flying over Kabul one night, stared in wonder as all the city's lights went out in a matter of seconds. An alarm had obviously sounded, and someone was throwing main switches at a power plant. The lights went out in four sectors—one, two, three, four. Just like that the entire city went black, which would have made perfect sense, say, twenty years ago, when technologically primitive Soviet MiGs were overhead. But turning off all the artificial light had the effect of reducing the "noise" in the fliers' NOG reception. It gave them a clearer view below.

What was the human cost of all this state-of-the-art expertise? The Pentagon does not attempt to tally casualties among enemy combatants, but given how many bombs were dropped and targets destroyed, the numbers in Afghanistan had to be well into the thousands. As for innocent victims, there are likewise no good estimates. Casualty counts are effectively propaganda, so they are all suspect. Human-rights groups, many of which oppose war categorically, say thousands of innocents died. Marc W. Herold, a professor of economics at the University of New Hampshire, who has a decided antiwar bent, used primarily media accounts but also interviews with refugees to calculate that the two-month campaign produced at least 3,767 civilian casualties. But that number appears to be grandly inflated. A study by the Project on Defense Alternatives, a nonprofit academic defense-policy group, using fewer data but more stringent categories than Herold did, estimated 1,000 to 1,300 civilian deaths, and a *New York Times* investigation last summer put the total closer to 400.

No bombing campaign—no matter how sophisticated or scrupulous—can completely avoid mistakes, whether from errant bombs or faulty intelligence. Given one target in a crowded urban neighborhood, Slokes warned Boss Man, "Make sure you got this one on tape." He did not want to be held responsible for the consequences. They all knew that mistakes could take the lives of kids sleeping in the wrong houses, people crossing the wrong streets. Some of the Bold Tigers wrestled with this grim knowledge. Baldie, who flew five bombing missions and describes herself as "a Catholic who goes to church every Sunday," sometimes found the consequences of her work "hard to think about." After viewing sortie videos she would brood over the fact that the job she had done that day had killed some people and ruined others' lives. The first bomb she dropped in

Afghanistan missed. She had aimed at a tank but made a big crater in the side of a nearby mountain instead. She knew that a miss like that over a city or a town could have terrible consequences.

By any account (including Herold's), the bombing campaign in Afghanistan hit fewer unintended targets than any other in history. Pentagon analysts say that more than 75 percent of the bombs dropped in Afghanistan exploded where targeted, compared with fewer than half in the Persian Gulf War, in 1991, and in the much-touted bombings over Serbia in 1999.

For the Bold Tigers the deaths of innocents were part of the price of war. As long as they believed that the war was necessary and was improving the lives of millions oppressed by the Taliban, that cost was acceptable. Baldie recalls an interview with a Taliban official that aired on CNN. He was asked by a reporter how his regime could use an Olympic soccer stadium to hold public executions, in which men were hanged from goalposts and women were shot at the goal lines for offenses such as adultery. The mullah mistook the moral question for a practical one. He protested that if only international money were available to build a separate stadium for executions, then soccer matches might be able to resume in the current one. Baldie was so appalled that she later found those remarks comforting when she steered home her bombs.

Among the squadron's recorded collection of audio-video "greatest hits" was the artful destruction of a purported Taliban building in Kandahar. Last summer I reviewed the event with a group of crew members at their base in Idaho. On the monitor we watched a negative black-and-white thermal image of a building at the center of the city. Vehicles and people were moving on the street out front. Abruptly four black darts flashed into the picture from the upper left-hand side, quick as an eye blink, and the screen was filled with a black splash.

On the recording the gleeful voice of a wizzo named Buzzer shouted, *"Shack, baby! Die like the dogs that you are!"*

We all sat in silence for a moment as the outburst hung awkwardly in the air. Buzzer is known for raw commentary like this, and months removed from the heat of battle, with a writer there and all, the six crew members in the room were clearly having second thoughts about having played this particular clip. On the screen, in the form of tiny black dots, people could be seen emerging from the flaming building, fleeing down the street.

Finally, Slokes spoke. His face creased with disapproval, he said sternly, "That's just wrong." He held his expression for a few seconds, and no one in the room was sure about whether to take him seriously. Then he grinned. Everyone laughed.

In the early weeks of the campaign the American effort to topple the Taliban and rout al Qaeda was not showing big results. By late October there were signs that the campaign was getting bogged down. With winter approaching, skeptics predicted that experienced Taliban and al Qaeda fighters might hang tough for years, as they had two decades earlier against the Soviet Union. According to *The New York Times,* Ahmed Rashid, one of the foremost authorities on the Taliban, was predicting that the Taliban leaders and their fighters could survive for "at least six months." R. W. Apple, the veteran *Times* news analyst, invoked the historically loaded term "quagmire."

On November 13 Kabul fell. Three weeks after that the Taliban fled Kandahar, their final stronghold, and jubilant citizens danced in the streets, tearing down Taliban flags and raising the traditional black, red, and green Afghan banner. The heart of the American military campaign had taken exactly two months.

The turning point, as experienced from the cockpit of an F-15, was the introduction on the ground of small numbers of U.S. soldiers—Rangers, Delta Force, and the Air Force's own combat controllers—known as forward air controllers, or FACs, whose voices started crackling into the fliers' headsets in late October. These extraordinarily brave stealth operators found themselves alone or in small groups deep in enemy territory, calling down air strikes and orchestrating what quickly became victory. They had parachuted or been helicoptered into Afghanistan at night, and had been left on the ground to fend for themselves. Some Special Forces teams, Green Berets, went to work helping to mobilize friendly Afghan forces against the Taliban and al Qaeda. Others usually hunkered down in dangerous places—the vicinity of airports, forts, and enemy troop concentrations, for example—to become the forwardmost eyes and ears of the air assault.

Tank was flying wing on October 25 on a four-plane mission from Kandahar up to Mazar-i-Sharif. He listened in on the communications as a team of F-16s dove into their bombing runs. To Tank's delight, the jets were talking to a ground FAC. When the Lawn Darts had shot their load, the F-15s moved in and started working with the operative. The landscape below was all enemy-controlled territory, but somewhere in the stark hills was this American voice and a keen pair of eyes. The ground FAC was trying to coordinate an attack on a collection of enemy tanks and trucks. This flight was code-named Zesty (like many F-15 sorties).

"Can you ID a vehicle, Zesty?" the ground FAC asked.

"We're at twenty-five thousand feet," answered Stab, one of the pilots, meaning, "Not likely."

"Do you see the main road?" the ground FAC asked.

"Roger."

"Any vehicle north of that road is bad. The good guys are all on horses and camels."

Slokes and Snitch were in awe of the guys on the ground, who were so far from anything friendly, huddled down between rocks on cold mountainsides, eating their packaged meals (or bugs and snakes), and sleeping in bags on hard terrain, while the Bold Tigers dined on steak and lobster, watched European MTV, and slept in air-conditioned comfort. It made the pilots doubly disappointed when they were unable to hit what the ground FACs wanted them to.

One night Slokes and Snitch were assigned to a Special Forces team perched temporarily on a hillside just south of Kandahar, not far from the city's airport. Four miles above, at 20,000 feet, the fliers watched as the ground FAC waved an infrared laser pointer to draw them a map on the hillside. He traced a waving line, and gradually narrowed its swing down to a point. "We're here," one Special Forces operative told them.

He was part of a team of eight men, code-named Texas One Seven, with whom the Bold Tigers would work for weeks. Using the steep hillside to provide protective cover from the north, the eight had set up camp in a valley, complete with a big plastic bag of fuel, called a bladder, to serve as a filling station for their four-wheeled vehicles.

There was one ground controller working near Kabul whom the crews dubbed the Crack FAC, because his ground-to-air instructions were so vague and at times so misleading that he seemed to be on crack. Not that they didn't respect the guy. He must have been, as they put it, "crazy brave" to be down where he was. But whenever Boss Man ordered a crew to work with the guy, there were groans in the cockpit. The Crack FAC didn't sound any older than nineteen. (The squadron never found out who he was.)

"Okay, you see the first ridgeline?" he said on one run. "Go one ridge over." From the cockpit at 20,000 feet, the world was made up of ridgelines. "You're going to have to be more specific than that," the pilot told him.

On one occasion he pleaded with a crew to drop on a village. "Just go ahead and drop a bomb," he said.

"We can't do that, dude," a pilot nicknamed Bait replied, meaning they couldn't just wipe out an entire village.

"There haven't been any good guys in that village for years," the Crack FAC argued.

"I might hit you," Bait said.

"You're not going to hit me, man, I'm standing in snow."

Still, the crews declined to drop their bombs.

But even the Crack FAC got better at communicating, and the crews grew fonder of him. After directing a strike on a Taliban tank that had begun firing on his position, a relieved Crack FAC called back, "Zesty, that was *excellent!*"

On the last day of October, just before the course of the air war started to turn dramatically, a Strike Eagle flown by Zuni with a wizzo named Gunner, veterans both, got a call from Spartan, directing it north to help some U.S. forces under fire. With a full load of GBU-12s and fuel, the jet was what the crews call a "pig in space," and flew at what seemed to them a snail's pace. Once in the vicinity, they started calling for Tiger Three, the ground FAC. When his voice came up into the headphones, it was clear they were dealing with a cool customer.

"Hey, Zesty, I'm ready to give a nine-line brief," he said—jargon for a quick assessment of the situation. He wanted them to get right to work. What he needed wasn't going to be easy. This was a daylight sortie, but cloud cover had been building. Now the crew could see nothing below but an ocean of cotton. Here and there mountain peaks poked through. Zuni wanted to know exactly how urgent the situation was.

"Tiger Three, this is Zesty. Are you under fire?"

"Roger, Zesty. We are under fire by tank."

That was about as urgent as things could get. The two fliers were going to have to try something. Zuni asked if the ground FAC had the capability of changing his laser code to steer the F-15's bombs. He did, so it was theoretically possible to drop the bombs into the clouds and let him take over.

At first the fliers struggled to relay the numbers of their laser code through the static. Then Zuni asked the ground FAC to read him the latitude and longitude coordinates for the tanks. The ground FAC proceeded to read out a list of numbers, which Gunner quickly realized were calculated somewhat differently from what he was used to. For some inexplicable reason the Army uses a system different from the Air Force's—one of those interservice snafus that have cropped up throughout the history of American warfare. The Air Force uses degrees, minutes, and thousandths of a minute, whereas the Army uses degrees, minutes, and seconds. All the numbers would have to be converted, and Gunner didn't have a chart.

"I don't have a nine-line card," he complained. "I've got a fucking piece of paper."

So at 20,000 feet, with friendly forces taking fire beneath an opaque canopy of clouds, flying a multimillion-dollar aircraft equipped with the U.S. military's state-of-the-art targeting software, Gunner went to work with a pencil, a piece of paper, and the calculator on his Casio watch. He has a degree in aerospace engineering with a minor in physics, but this was going to call for long-dormant computational skills.

Gunner worked frantically. Under the pressure of the moment, hurtling forward at hundreds of miles per hour, he felt as if his brain were functioning at half speed as he pounded away on the tiny keys of his calculator. He was muttering to himself, "Ah, he gave me two-nine-point-six-nine. I made that four-five—shit! Four-five, three-seven, oh-six, five. And he gave me six-nine-two-two-point-four-one. I made that a point-seven . . ."

The jet moved into heavy clouds and kept descending, hoping for clearer skies.

"Zesty, when do I turn on the laser?" the ground FAC asked.

"Wilco, stand by," Zuni told the ground FAC. Then he said to his wizzo, "As soon as you get it in, Gunner, I'm going."

"You're good," Gunner said with a sigh. He had just punched in the last conversion.

They now asked Tiger Three for an elevation reading, and once more the numbers had to be converted. Gunner started pounding away again on his watch.

"That'll make it—ah, goddammit! That'll make it sixteen hundred and six-nine feet for elevation."

The jet was still socked in by clouds. In a land of high peaks it wasn't safe to fly low with zero visibility for long.

"I don't think I want to go underneath this, Gunner," Zuni said.

"Nope," the wizzo agreed. They would have to release the bomb blind.

"Turn your laser on," Zuni instructed the ground FAC.

"Roger. Laser on."

"I want you to keep it on. Keep it on for at least about a minute and a half."

"Our laser will only allow sixty seconds," the ground FAC said.

"Okay, turn your laser *off*," Zuni instructed immediately, realizing that the battery would be dead by the time the ground FAC could pick up the bombs.

"Okay," Gunner said. "Five seconds."

"Turn your laser on *now*," Zuni told the ground FAC.

"Roger," came the voice from the ground. "Laser on."

"Weapon away," Zuni said. "Weapon away."

Zuni turned the jet and headed steeply up out of the clouds. Things got quiet. There was just the sound of the F-15 and the inhaling and exhaling of its anxious pilot and wizzo, waiting. Thirty seconds. Half the known age of the universe. At thirty seconds Zuni said hopefully, "You should have impact."

Nothing. More quiet breathing. Then, crackling in their headphones, "Zesty one-one. Laser off. Shack on target."

The pilot and the wizzo cheered in the cockpit.

"Prepare for immediate reattack," Tiger Three said.

Making one run after another for the next twenty minutes, Zuni and Gunner repeated this procedure, doing the conversions, dropping the bombs blind, and waiting for the report back from the ground. Between runs the ground FAC changed the batteries in his laser.

Down under the clouds, unbeknownst to Zuni and Gunner, a miracle had taken place. When the squadron met with the ground FAC months later, he explained how things had looked from his end. He had been with a Northern Alliance unit equal in number to the Taliban forces but outgunned. With the Taliban fighters stretched in front of them in tanks, the Northern Alliance fighters were about to withdraw when the ground FAC persuaded them to wait for air support. This was early in the ground war, and the local fighters were still dubious of their new allies' technological claims. The Northern Alliance fighters eyed the opaque cloud cover skeptically. Who could hit anything through that? What could these scruffy American soldiers who showed up at their camps in teams of two or three accomplish in a real battle on unfamiliar terrain? What did they know about fighting? Many of the Northern Alliance soldiers were veterans of numerous campaigns. They didn't need Americans to tell them what they could or could not do on familiar battlefields. They knew when they were overmatched. Some of them were already falling back.

Then, like a thunderbolt, the first bomb blew up the lead Taliban tank. Minutes later another bomb shot through the clouds and destroyed a second tank. This happened again and again, until the imposing armored force arrayed before them was in smoking ruins. Mystified but jubilant, the Northern Alliance forces descended from the hills, routing the Taliban troops. It was a preview of what would happen in the coming weeks all over the country. How could one fight a foe that could rain pinpoint destruction through the clouds, day or night, 24/7?

When it was over, an exhausted Gunner complained to Zuni, "The recruiter said there would be no math in the cockpit."

After the ground FACs arrived, in late October, things moved fast. Mazar-i-Sharif fell, and then Kabul, and then Kandahar, marking the formal collapse of the Taliban. In the end the entire armada of fighters, AWACS, jammers, tankers, and rescue planes was dancing in the skies over Kandahar, every crew eager for a chance to do its thing, trying to stay out of the other crews' paths. The relentless pounding broke the spirits of the Taliban, whose forces began to defect in ever-larger numbers.

By mid-November most concentrations of enemy fighters would disperse at the sound of a jet overhead. Some of the more stubborn ones, however, continued to hang tough. The F-15 crews would spot them at camps in the hills, but neither the jet noise nor even bombing runs seemed to faze them. But when they started hearing the *click! click! click!* of the servo motors steering a GBU-12 in for the kill, they would begin fleeing in all directions. By then, of course, it was too late. In truth, the only safe place to be was underground, and with bunker busters, and Special Forces guys prowling the hills, even the caves became unsafe. Some thought they could escape in a speeding car or truck, and a few years ago they would have been right—but Baldie's grille shot demonstrated the folly of that tactic. Afghanistan was the greatest pickle run in history.

The science of war will keep advancing. A half century from now the exploits of the Bold Tigers over Afghanistan will be as anachronistic as Saint-Exupéry's battling biplanes. Snitch's grandfather, a retired military pilot, clips and sends him articles about the coming of an age of UAVs and teases him about fliers' being "the limiting factor in aviation." Pilots and wizzos of the future will "fly" their machines from comfy chairs at a safe distance, with both feet on solid ground and bathroom facilities close at hand. Today's fighter jocks will reminisce to their grandchildren about what it was actually like to ride bullets high over the clouds, and to reign supreme in the night sky.

It will sound more glamorous then. For the fliers of the 391st it was sometimes hard to keep their eyes open on the ride home. Fatigue and relief from the stress of bombing runs would overtake them. Up there in their bubble canopy among the stars, to help stay awake, Baldie would chat nonstop with Two Fish, about their families, their futures, their friends, her plans to attend pilot school. ("Baldie, you took another one of those go pills, didn't you?" Two Fish would ask.) Slokes and Snitch ate their Thanksgiving meal high over the peaks of Pakistan. Before the sortie they had stocked Styrofoam carryout meal boxes with drumsticks, stuffing, cranberry sauce, and pumpkin pie—there had been quite a spread in the mess hall. Neither had wanted to eat a big meal before setting out on a nine-to-ten-hour flight. But with their bomb racks empty, Slokes put the F-15 on autopilot, muttering his thanks into the thin air of dawn, and the two feasted, finding the food by the finger lights on their gloves. By that time the meal had grown very cold, but Slokes says, "It was definitely the most memorable Thanksgiving dinner of my life. Sorry, Mom."

On those long rides home, in the hours before the sun cracked the planet's purple rim, they would survey the jagged peaks of the Siahan Range and peer out past the Gulf of Oman to the great fires that leap up

from the oil fields of the United Arab Emirates. The seaport of Dubai glim-
mered like a jewel on the Persian Gulf coast, lit up so improbably at the
edge of the desert that it looked as if someone had misplaced Las Vegas.
Sometimes thunderstorms in the distance would flash waves of light across
the clouds for hundreds of miles and throw sudden shadows across their
cockpit. The constellation Orion was always over their heads on those fall
and winter nights, as familiar and as distant as it was at home. Sometimes
the radar stations along the Iranian coast would paint the jets ominously,
and alarms would go off in the cockpits—a reminder of hazards still lurk-
ing in the dark.

   And some nights the sky would explode with shooting stars. Showers of light. They moved in blue streaks across the heavens, one or two
every couple of seconds. There were so many that the squadron's intel
officer would warn the crews not to mistake them for enemy fire. Using
their NOGs, the crews saw them as lines of bright white against a glowing
field of green.

THE DARK ART OF
INTERROGATION

OCTOBER 2003

This story grew out of my curiosity about what was happening to top al Qaeda leaders after their arrest. Published accounts kept reporting that this captive or that was "cooperating" with interrogators and providing useful information. At the same time, the Bush administration was reiterating U.S. support for international agreements banning torture. So, I wondered, How were they getting from point A to point B? Cullen Murphy, the Atlantic's *managing editor, had been asking himself a lot of the same questions. As I wrote this, I kept imagining the scene from Ang Lee's film* The Hulk, *in which the monster's alter ego, Bruce Banner, is suspended inside a sensory deprivation tank, tethered by wires to monitoring devices from head to toe. Scientists arrayed around the tank literally peer inside him. Hollywood excels at building fantasies on the margin between what people think technology can do and what it actually can do. The truth is that there is no such thing as a truth serum, or a machine that enables scientists to peer into another person's thoughts. Extracting information in real life, it turns out, is a lot more interesting. This was a story that gave me nightmares.*

Rawalpindi, Pakistan

On what may or may not have been a Saturday, on what may have been March 1, in a house in this city that may have been this squat two-story white one belonging to Ahmad Abdul Qadoos, with big gray-headed crows barking in the front yard, the notorious terrorist Khalid Sheikh Mohammed was roughly awakened by a raiding party of Pakistani and American commandos. Anticipating a gunfight, they entered loud and fast. Instead they found him asleep. He was pulled from his bed, hooded, bound, hustled from the house, placed in a vehicle, and driven quickly away.

Here was the biggest catch yet in the war on terror. Sheikh Mohammed is considered the architect of two attempts on the World Trade Center:

the one that failed, in 1993, and the one that succeeded so catastrophically, eight years later. He is also believed to have been behind the attacks on the U.S. embassies in Kenya and Tanzania in 1998, and on the USS *Cole* two years later, and behind the slaughter last year of the *Wall Street Journal* reporter Daniel Pearl, among other things. An intimate of Osama bin Laden's, Sheikh Mohammed has been called the operations chief of al Qaeda, if such a formal role can be said to exist in such an informal organization. Others have suggested that an apter designation might be al Qaeda's "chief franchisee." Whatever the analogy, he is one of the terror organization's most important figures, a burly, distinctly modern, cosmopolitan thirty-seven-year-old man fanatically devoted to a medieval form of Islam. He was born to Pakistani parents, raised in Kuwait, and educated in North Carolina to be an engineer before he returned to the Middle East to build a career of bloody mayhem.

Some say that Sheikh Mohammed was captured months before the March 1 date announced by Pakistan's Inter-Services Intelligence (ISI). Abdul Qadoos, a pale, white-bearded alderman in this well-heeled neighborhood, told me that Sheikh Mohammed was not there "then or ever." The official video of the takedown appears to have been faked. But the details are of minor importance. Whenever, wherever, and however it happened, nearly everyone now agrees that Sheikh Mohammed is in U.S. custody, and has been for some time. In the first hours of his captivity the hood came off and a picture was taken. It shows a bleary-eyed, heavy, hairy, swarthy man with a full black moustache, thick eyebrows, a dark outline of beard on a rounded, shaved face, three chins, long sideburns, and a full head of dense, long, wildly mussed black hair. He stands before a pale tan wall whose paint is chipped, leaning slightly forward, like a man with his hands bound behind him, the low cut of his loose-fitting white T-shirt exposing matted curls of hair on his chest, shoulders, and back. He is looking down and to the right of the camera. He appears dazed and glum.

Sheikh Mohammed is a smart man. There is an anxious, searching quality to his expression in that first postarrest photo. It is the look of a man awakened into nightmare. Everything that has given his life meaning, his role as husband and father, his leadership, his stature, plans, and ambitions, is finished. His future is months, maybe years, of imprisonment and interrogation; a military tribunal; and almost certain execution. You can practically see the wheels turning in his head, processing his terminal predicament. How will he spend his last months and years? Will he maintain a dignified, defiant silence? Or will he succumb to his enemy and betray his friends, his cause, and his faith?

If Sheikh Mohammed felt despair in those first hours, it didn't show. According to a Pakistani officer who sat in on an initial ISI questioning, the al Qaeda sub-boss seemed calm and stoic. For his first two days in custody he said nothing beyond confirming his name. A CIA official says that Sheikh Mohammed spent those days "sitting in a trancelike state and reciting verses from the Koran." On the third day he is said to have loosened up. Fluent in the local languages of Urdu, Pashto, and Baluchi, he tried to shame his Pakistani interrogators, lecturing them on their responsibilities as Muslims and upbraiding them for cooperating with infidels.

"Playing an American surrogate won't help you or your country," he said. "There are dozens of people like me who will give their lives but won't let the Americans live in peace anywhere in the world." Asked if Osama bin Laden was alive, he said, "Of course he is alive." He spoke of meeting with bin Laden in "a mountainous border region" in December. He seemed smug about U.S. and British preparations for war against Saddam Hussein. "Let the Iraq War begin," he said. "The U.S. forces will be targeted inside their bases in the Gulf. I don't have any specific information, but my sixth sense is telling me that you will get the news from Saudi Arabia, Qatar, and Kuwait." Indeed, in the following months al Qaeda carried out a murderous attack in Saudi Arabia.

On that third day, once more hooded, Sheikh Mohammed was driven to Chaklala Air Force base, in Rawalpindi, and turned over to U.S. forces. From there he was flown to the CIA interrogation center in Bagram, Afghanistan, and from there, some days later, to an "undisclosed location" (a place the CIA calls "Hotel California")—presumably a facility in another cooperative nation, or perhaps a specially designed prison aboard an aircraft carrier. It doesn't much matter where, because the place would not have been familiar or identifiable to him. Place and time, the anchors of sanity, were about to come unmoored. He might as well have been entering a new dimension, a strange new world where his every word, move, and sensation would be monitored and measured; where things might be as they seemed but might not; where there would be no such thing as day or night, or normal patterns of eating and drinking, wakefulness and sleep;

where hot and cold, wet and dry, clean and dirty, truth and lies, would all be tangled and distorted.

Intelligence and military officials would talk about Sheikh Mohammed's state only indirectly, and conditionally. But by the time he arrived at a more permanent facility, he would already have been bone-tired, hungry, sore, uncomfortable, and afraid—if not for himself, then for his wife and children, who had been arrested either with him or some months before, depending on which story you believe. He would have been warned that lack of cooperation might mean being turned over to the more direct and brutal interrogators of some third nation. He would most likely have been locked naked in a cell with no trace of daylight. The space would be filled night and day with harsh light and noise, and would be so small that he would be unable to stand upright, to sit comfortably, or to recline fully. He would be kept awake, cold, and probably wet. If he managed to doze, he would be roughly awakened. He would be fed infrequently and irregularly, and then only with thin, tasteless meals. Sometimes days would go by between periods of questioning, sometimes only hours or minutes. The human mind craves routine, and can adjust to almost anything in the presence of it, so his jailers would take care that no semblance of routine developed.

Questioning would be intense—sometimes loud and rough, sometimes quiet and friendly, with no apparent reason for either. He would be questioned sometimes by one person, sometimes by two or three. The session might last for days, with interrogators taking turns, or it might last only a few minutes. He would be asked the same questions again and again, and then suddenly be presented with something completely unexpected— a detail or a secret that he would be shocked to find they knew. He would be offered the opportunity to earn freedom or better treatment for his wife and children. Whenever he was helpful and the information he gave proved true, his harsh conditions would ease. If the information proved false, his treatment would worsen. On occasion he might be given a drug to elevate his mood prior to interrogation; marijuana, heroin, and sodium pentothal have been shown to overcome a reluctance to speak, and methamphetamine can unleash a torrent of talk in the stubbornest subjects, the very urgency of the chatter making a complex lie impossible to sustain. These drugs could be administered surreptitiously with food or drink, and given the bleakness of his existence, they might even offer a brief period of relief and pleasure, thereby creating a whole new category of longing—and new leverage for his interrogators.

Deprived of any outside information, Sheikh Mohammed would grow more and more vulnerable to manipulation. For instance, intelligence gleaned after successful al Qaeda attacks in Kuwait and Saudi Arabia might be fed to him, in bits and pieces, so as to suggest foiled operations. During questioning he would be startled regularly by details about his secret organization—details drawn from ongoing intelligence operations, new arrests, or the interrogation of other captive al Qaeda members. Some of the information fed to him would be true, some of it false. Key associates might be said to be cooperating, or to have completely recanted their allegiance to *jihad*. As time went by, his knowledge would decay while that of his questioners improved. He might come to see once-vital plans as insignificant, or already known. The importance of certain secrets would gradually erode.

Isolated, confused, weary, hungry, frightened, and tormented, Sheikh Mohammed would gradually be reduced to a seething collection of simple needs, all of them controlled by his interrogators.

The key to filling all those needs would be the same: *to talk*.

SMACKY-FACE

We hear a lot these days about America's overpowering military technology; about the professionalism of its warriors; about the sophistication of its weaponry, eavesdropping, and telemetry. But right now the most vital weapon in its arsenal may well be the art of interrogation. To counter an enemy who relies on stealth and surprise, the most valuable tool is information, and often the only source of that information is the enemy himself. Men like Sheikh Mohammed who have been taken alive in this war are classic candidates for the most cunning practices of this dark art. Intellectual, sophisticated, deeply religious, and well trained, they present a perfect challenge for the interrogator. Getting at the information they possess could allow us to thwart major attacks, unravel their organization, and save thousands of lives. They and their situation pose one of the strongest arguments in modern times for the use of torture.

Torture is repulsive. It is deliberate cruelty, a crude and ancient tool of political oppression. It is commonly used to terrorize people, or to wring confessions out of suspected criminals who may or may not be guilty. It is the classic shortcut for a lazy or incompetent investigator. Horrifying examples of torturers' handiwork are catalogued and publicized annually by Amnesty International, Human Rights Watch, and other organizations that battle such abuses worldwide. One cannot help sympathizing with the innocent, powerless victims showcased in their literature. But professional terrorists pose a harder question. They are lockboxes containing potentially life-saving information. Sheikh Mohammed has his own political and religious reasons for plotting mass murder, and there are those who would applaud his principled defiance in captivity. But we pay for his silence in blood.

The word "torture" comes from the Latin verb *torquere,* "to twist." *Webster's New World Dictionary* offers the following primary definition: "The inflicting of severe pain to force information and confession, get revenge, etc." Note the adjective "severe," which summons up images of the rack, thumbscrews, gouges, branding irons, burning pits, impaling devices, electric shock, and all the other devilish tools devised by human beings to mutilate and inflict pain on others. All manner of innovative cruelty is still commonplace, particularly in Central and South America, Africa, and the Middle East. Saddam Hussein's police force burned various marks into the foreheads of thieves and deserters, and routinely sliced tongues out of those whose words offended the state. In Sri Lanka prisoners are hung upside down and burned with hot irons. In China they are beaten with clubs and shocked with cattle prods. In India the police stick pins through the fingernails and fingers of prisoners. Maiming and physical abuse are legal in Somalia, Iran, Saudi Arabia, Nigeria, Sudan, and other countries that practice *sharia;* the hands of thieves are lopped off, and women convicted of adultery may be stoned to death. Governments around the world continue to employ rape and mutilation, and to harm family members, including children, in order to extort confessions or information from those in captivity. Civilized people everywhere readily condemn these things.

Then there are methods that, some people argue, fall short of torture. Called "torture lite," these include sleep deprivation, exposure to heat or cold, the use of drugs to cause confusion, rough treatment (slapping, shoving, or shaking), forcing a prisoner to stand for days at a time or to sit in uncomfortable positions, and playing on his fears for himself and his family. Although excruciating for the victim, these tactics generally leave no permanent marks and do no lasting physical harm.

The Geneva Convention makes no distinction: it bans any mistreatment of prisoners. But some nations that are otherwise committed to ending brutality have employed torture lite under what they feel are justifiable circumstances. In 1987 Israel attempted to codify a distinction between torture, which was banned, and "moderate physical pressure," which was permitted in special cases. Indeed, some police officers, soldiers, and intelligence agents who abhor "severe" methods believe that banning all forms of physical pressure would be dangerously naive. Few support the use of physical pressure to extract confessions, especially because victims will often say anything (to the point of falsely incriminating themselves) to put an end to pain. But many veteran interrogators believe that the use of such methods to extract information is justified if it could save lives—whether by forcing an enemy soldier to reveal his army's battlefield positions or forcing terrorists to betray the details of ongoing plots. As these interrogators see it, the well-being of the captive must be weighed against the lives that might be saved by forcing him to talk. A method that produces life-saving information without doing lasting harm to anyone is not just preferable; it appears to be morally sound. Hereafter I will use "torture" to mean the more severe traditional outrages, and "coercion" to refer to torture lite, or moderate physical pressure.

There is no clear count of suspected terrorists now in U.S. custody. About 680 were detained at Camp X-Ray, the specially constructed prison at Guantánamo, on the southeastern tip of Cuba. Most of these are now considered mere foot soldiers in the Islamist movement, swept up in Afghanistan during the swift rout of the Taliban. They come from forty-two different nations. Scores of other detainees, considered leaders, have been or are being held at various locations around the world: in Pakistan, Saudi Arabia, Egypt, Sudan, Syria, Jordan, Morocco, Yemen, Singapore, the Philippines, Thailand, and Iraq, where U.S. forces now hold the top echelon of Saddam Hussein's dismembered regime. Some detainees are in disclosed prisons, such as the facility at Bagram and a camp on the island of Diego Garcia. Others—upper-tier figures such as Sheikh Mohammed, Abu

Zubaydah, Abd al-Rashim al-Nashiri, Ramzi bin al-Shibh, and Tawfiq bin Attash—are being held at undisclosed locations.

It is likely that some captured terrorists' names and arrests have not yet been revealed; people may be held for months before their "arrests" are staged. Once a top-level suspect is publicly known to be in custody, his intelligence value falls. His organization scatters, altering its plans, disguises, cover stories, codes, tactics, and communication methods. The maximum opportunity for intelligence gathering comes in the first hours after an arrest, before others in a group can possibly know that their walls have been breached. Keeping an arrest quiet for days or weeks prolongs this opportunity. If March 1 was in fact the day of Sheikh Mohammed's capture, then the cameras and the headlines were an important intelligence failure. The arrest of the senior al Qaeda figure Abu Anas Liby, in Sudan in February of 2002, was not made public until a month later, when U.S. efforts to have him transferred to custody in Egypt were leaked to the *Sunday Times* of London. So, again, there is no exact count of suspected terrorists in custody. In September of last year, testifying before the House and Senate Intelligence Committees, Cofer Black, the State Department's coordinator for counterterrorism, said that the number who have been detained was about 3,000.

All these suspects are questioned rigorously, but those in the top ranks get the full coercive treatment. And if official and unofficial government reports are to be believed, the methods work. In report after report hardcore terrorist leaders are said to be either cooperating or, at the very least, providing some information—not just vague statements but detailed, verifiable, useful intelligence. In late March, *Time* reported that Sheikh Mohammed had "given U.S. interrogators the names and descriptions of about a dozen key al Qaeda operatives believed to be plotting terrorist attacks on America and other western countries" and had "added crucial details to the descriptions of other suspects and filled in important gaps in what U.S. intelligence knows about al Qaeda's practices." In June, news reports suggested that Sheikh Mohammed was discussing operational planning with his captors and had told interrogators that al Qaeda did not work with Saddam Hussein. And according to a report in June of last year, Abu Zubaydah, who is said to be held in solitary confinement somewhere in Pakistan, provided information that helped foil a plot to detonate a radioactive bomb in the United States.

Secretary of Defense Donald Rumsfeld said in September of last year that interrogation of captured terrorist leaders had yielded "an awful lot of information" and had "made life an awful lot more difficult for an awful lot of folks." Indeed, if press accounts can be believed, these captured Islamist fanatics are all but dismantling their own secret organization. According to published reports, Sheikh Mohammed was found in part because of information from bin al-Shibh, whose arrest had been facilitated by information from Abu Zubaydah. Weeks after the sheikh's capture, Bush administration officials and intelligence experts told *The Washington Post* that the al Qaeda deputy's "cooperation under interrogation" had given them hopes of arresting or killing the rest of the organization's top leadership.

How much of this can be believed? Are such reports wishful thinking, or deliberate misinformation? There is no doubt that intelligence agencies have scored big victories over al Qaeda in the past two years, but there is no way to corroborate these stories. President Bush himself warned, soon after 9/11, that in war mode his administration would closely guard intelligence sources and methods. It would make sense to claim that top al Qaeda leaders had caved under questioning even if they had not. Hard men like Abu Zubaydah, bin al-Shibh, and Sheikh Mohammed are widely admired in parts of the world. Word that they had been broken would demoralize their followers, and would encourage lower-ranking members of their organization to talk; if their leaders had given in, why should they hold out?

To some, all this jailhouse cooperation smells concocted. "I doubt we're getting very much out of them, despite what you read in the press," says a former CIA agent with experience in South America. "Everybody in the world knows that if you are arrested by the United States, nothing bad will happen to you."

Bill Cowan, a retired Marine lieutenant colonel who conducted interrogations in Vietnam, says, "I don't see the proof in the pudding. If you had a top leader like Mohammed talking, someone who could presumably lay out the whole organization for you, I think we'd be seeing sweeping arrests in several different countries at the same time. Instead what we see is an arrest here, then a few months later an arrest there."

These complaints are all from people who have no qualms about using torture to get information from men like Sheikh Mohammed. Their concern is that merely using coercion amounts to handling terrorists with

kid gloves. But the busts of al Qaeda cells worldwide, and the continuing
roundup of al Qaeda leaders, suggest that some of those in custody are
being made to talk. This worries people who campaign against all forms
of torture. They believe that the rules are being ignored. Responding to
rumors of mistreatment at Bagram and Guantánamo, Amnesty International and Human Rights Watch have written letters and met with Bush
administration officials. They haven't been able to learn much.

Is the United States torturing prisoners? Three inmates have died in
U.S. custody in Afghanistan, and reportedly eighteen prisoners at Guantánamo have attempted suicide; one prisoner there survived after hanging
himself but remains unconscious and is not expected to revive. Shah
Muhammad, a twenty-year-old Pakistani who was held at Camp X-Ray for
eighteen months, told me that he repeatedly tried to kill himself in despair.
"They were driving me crazy," he said. Public comments by administration officials have fueled further suspicion. An unnamed intelligence official told *The Wall Street Journal,* "What's needed is a little bit of smacky-face.
Some al Qaeda just need some extra encouragement." Then there was the
bravado of Cofer Black, the counterterrorism coordinator, in his congressional testimony last year. A pudgy, balding, round-faced man with glasses,
who had served with the CIA before taking the State Department position,
Black refused to testify behind a screen, as others had done. "The American
people need to see my face," he said. "I want to look the American people in
the eye." By way of presenting his credentials he said that in 1995 a group of
"Osama bin Laden's thugs" were caught planning "to kill me."

Describing the clandestine war, Black said, "This is a highly classified
area. All I want to say is that there was 'before 9/11' and 'after 9/11.' After
9/11 the gloves came off." He was referring to the overall counterterrorism
effort, but in the context of detained captives the line was suggestive. A story
in December of 2002 by the *Washington Post* reporters Dana Priest and Barton
Gellman described the use of "stress and duress" techniques at Bagram, and
an article in *The New York Times* in March described the mistreatment of
prisoners there. That month Irene Kahn, the secretary-general of Amnesty
International, wrote a letter of protest to President Bush.

> The treatment alleged falls clearly within the category of torture and
> other cruel, inhuman or degrading treatment or punishment which is
> absolutely prohibited under international law ... [We] urge the US
> government to instigate a full, impartial inquiry into the treatment of

detainees at the Bagram base and to make the findings public. We further urge the government to make a clear public statement that torture and other cruel, inhuman or degrading treatment of suspects in its custody will not be tolerated under any circumstances, and that anyone found to have engaged in abuses will be brought to justice.

In June, at the urging of Amnesty and other groups, President Bush reaffirmed America's opposition to torture, saying, "I call on all governments to join with the United States and the community of law-abiding nations in prohibiting, investigating, and prosecuting all acts of torture . . . and we are leading this fight by example." A slightly more detailed response had been prepared two months earlier by the Pentagon's top lawyer, William J. Haynes II, in a letter to Kenneth Roth, the executive director of Human Rights Watch. (My requests for interviews on this subject with the Pentagon, the White House, and the State Department were declined.) Haynes wrote,

> The United States questions enemy combatants to elicit information they may possess that could help the coalition win the war and forestall further terrorist attacks upon the citizens of the United States and other countries. As the President reaffirmed recently to the United Nations High Commissioner for Human Rights, United States policy condemns and prohibits torture. When questioning enemy combatants, US personnel are required to follow this policy and applicable laws prohibiting torture.

As we will see, Haynes's choice of words was careful—and telling. The human-rights groups and the administration are defining terms differently. Yet few would argue that getting Sheikh Mohammed to talk doesn't serve the larger interests of mankind. So before tackling the moral and legal questions raised by interrogation, perhaps the first question should be, What works?

ACID TESTS AND MONKEY ORGASMS

The quest for surefire methods in the art of interrogation has been long, ugly, and generally fruitless. Nazi scientists experimented on concentration-camp inmates, subjecting them to extremes of hot and cold, to drugs, and to raw pain in an effort to see what combination of horrors would induce cooperation. The effort produced a long list of dead and maimed, but no reliable ways of getting people to talk.

In 1953 John Lilly, of the National Institute of Mental Health, discovered that by placing electrodes inside the brain of a monkey, he could stimulate pain, anger, fear—and pleasure. He placed one inside the brain of a male monkey and gave the monkey a switch that would trigger an immediate erection and orgasm. (The monkey hit the switch roughly every three minutes, thus confirming the male stereotype.) The idea of manipulating a brain from the inside promptly attracted the interest of the CIA, which foresaw, among other things, the possibility of sidestepping a reluctant informant's self-defenses. But Lilly dropped the line of research, pointing out that merely inserting the electrodes caused brain damage.

These experiments and others are recorded in detail in John Marks's somewhat overheated book *The Search for the "Manchurian Candidate": The CIA and Mind Control* (1979) and in George Andrews's book *MKULTRA: The CIA's Top Secret Program in Human Experimentation and Behavior Modification* (2001). Andrews summarized information revealed in congressional probes of CIA excesses. Marks was more sensational. In the spirit of the times, he tended to interpret the Agency's interest in behavioral science, hypnosis, and mind-altering drugs as a scheme to create zombielike secret agents, although it appears that the real goal was to make people talk.

There was a lot of hope for LSD. Discovered by accident in a Swiss pharmaceutical lab in 1943, it produced powerful mind-altering effects in very small doses. It was more powerful than mescaline, which had its own adherents, and could easily be administered without the victim's knowledge, slipped into food or drink. The hope was that an informant in such an artificially open-minded state would lose sight of his goals and sense of loyalty and become putty in the hands of a skilled interrogator. Studies on LSD began at a number of big universities, and as word of the drug's properties spread, it started to attract a broad range of interest. Theologians, scholars, and mental-health workers visited the Maryland Psychiatric Research Institute, just outside Baltimore, to turn on and tune in, and similar programs began in Boston, New York, Chicago, and other cities. Almost twenty years ago I interviewed a number of those who took part in these experiments; all of them were apparently motivated only by professional curiosity. The CIA's role was kept quiet. But the most notorious of its efforts at LSD experimentation involved Frank Olson, an Army scientist who was dosed without his knowledge and subsequently committed suicide. The U.S. Army conducted field tests of LSD as an interrogation tool in 1961 (Operation Third Chance), dosing nine foreigners and an American soldier named James Thornwell, who had been accused of stealing classified documents. Thornwell subsequently sued the government and was awarded $650,000. Most of these efforts led to little more than scandal and embarrassment. The effects of the drug were too wildly unpredictable to make it useful in interrogation. It tended to amplify the sorts of feelings that inhibit cooperation. Fear and anxiety turned into terrifying hallucinations and fantasies, which made it more difficult to elicit secrets, and added a tinge of unreality to whatever information was divulged. LSD may have unlocked the mind in some esoteric sense, but secrets tended to ride out the trip intact.

Experiments were also conducted with heroin and psychedelic mushrooms, neither of which reliably delivered up the secrets of men's souls. Indeed, drugs seemed to enhance some people's ability to be deceptive. Scopolamine held out some early hope, but it often induced hallucinations. Barbiturates were promising, and were already used effectively by psychiatrists to help with therapy. Some researchers advocated electroshock treatments, to, as it were, blast information from a subject's brain. Drugs such as marijuana, alcohol, and sodium pentothal can lower inhibitions, but they do not erase deep-seated convictions. And the more powerful the drug, the less reliable the testimony. According to my intelligence sources, drugs are today sometimes used to assist in critical interrogations, and the preferred ones are methamphetamines tempered with barbiturates and cannabis. These tools can help, but they are only as effective as the interrogator.

Better results seemed to come from sensory deprivation and solitary confinement. For most people severe sensory deprivation quickly becomes misery; the effects were documented in the notorious 1963 CIA manual on interrogation, called the *Kubark Manual*. It remains the most comprehensive and detailed explanation in print of coercive methods of questioning—given the official reluctance to discuss these matters or put them in writing, because such things tend to be both politically embarrassing and secret. Treatises on interrogation in the public domain are written primarily for police departments and address the handling of criminal defendants—with all the necessary concern for protecting a defendant's rights. Unearthed in 1997, through the Freedom of Information Act, by the *Baltimore Sun* reporters Gary Cohn, Ginger Thompson, and Mark Matthews, the *Kubark Manual* reveals the CIA's insights into the tougher methods employed by the military and intelligence agencies. Much of the practice and theory it details is also found unchanged in the 1983 *Human Resource Exploitation Training Manual*, usually known as the *Honduras Manual*—which the CIA had tried to soften with a hasty edit prior to releasing it. The manual was shaken loose at the same time by Cohn and Thompson. And the more summary discussions of technique in later U.S. Army manuals on interrogation, including the most recent, also clearly echo *Kubark*. If there is a bible of interrogation, it is the *Kubark Manual*.

The manual cites a 1954 study at the National Institute of Mental Health (again led by John Lilly) in which two volunteers attempted to see how long they could stay suspended in water wearing blackout masks and hearing only the sound of their own breathing and "some faint sounds of water from the piping." Neither lasted more than three hours. According to the study, "Both passed quickly from normally directed thinking through a tension resulting from unsatisfied hunger for sensory stimuli and concentration upon the few available sensations to provide reveries and fantasies and eventually to visual imagery somewhat resembling hallucinations." John Marks reported in his book that in a similar experiment a volunteer kicked his way out of a sensory-deprivation box after an hour of tearful pleas for release had been ignored.

The summary of another experiment concluded,

> The results confirmed earlier findings. 1) The deprivation of sensory stimuli induces stress; 2) the stress becomes unbearable for most subjects; 3) the subject has a growing need for physical and social stimuli; and 4) some subjects progressively lose touch with reality, focus inwardly, and produce delusions, hallucinations, and other pathological effects.

But these effects didn't trouble everyone. One man's misery is another man's mind-altering experience. Some people found they liked sensory-deprivation tanks; indeed, in later years people would pay for a session in one. Lilly was fond of injecting himself with LSD and then closing himself off in his tank—a series of experiments made famous in the 1980 film *Altered States*. In Canada a scientist put a fifty-two-year-old woman identified only as Mary C. in a sensory-deprivation chamber for thirty-five days. She never asked to be let out.

One thing all these experiments made clear was that no matter what drugs or methods were applied, the results varied from person to person. So another major area of inquiry involved trying to define certain broad personality types and discover what methods would work best for each. The groups were ridiculously general—the *Kubark Manual* lists "The Orderly-Obstinate Character," "The Greedy-Demanding Character," "The Anxious, Self-Centered Character"—and the prescriptions for questioning them tended to vary little and were sometimes silly (the advice for questioning an Orderly-Obstinate Character recommends doing so in a room that is especially neat). The categories were useless. Everyone, and every situation, is different; some people begin a day greedy and demanding and end it orderly and obstinate.

The one constant in effective interrogation, it seems, is the interrogator. And some interrogators are just better at it than others.

"You want a good interrogator?" Jerry Giorgio, the New York Police Department's legendary third-degree man, asks. "Give me somebody who people like, and who likes people. Give me somebody who knows how to put people at ease. Because the more comfortable they are, the more they talk, and the more they talk, the more trouble they're in—the harder it is to sustain a lie."

Though science has made contributions, interrogation remains more art than science. Like any other subject, Sheikh Mohammed presented his interrogators with a unique problem. The critical hub of a worldwide secret network, he had a potential road map in his head to the whole shadow world of *jihad*. If he could be made to talk, to reveal even a few secrets, what an intelligence bonanza that would be! Here was a man who lived to further his cause by whatever means, who saw himself as morally, spiritually, and intellectually superior to the entire infidel Western world, a man for whom capitulation meant betraying not just his friends and his cherished cause but his very soul.

What makes a man like that decide to talk?

ALLIGATOR CLIPS

Bill Cowan spent three and a half years fighting the war in Vietnam. He was a young Marine captain assigned to the Rung Sat Special Zone, a putrid swamp that begins just south of Saigon. Miles and miles of thick, slurping mud that swallowed soldiers to their waists, it is populated by galaxies of mosquitoes and other biting insects, snakes, crocodiles, and stands of rotting mangrove. It is intersected by the saltwater rivers of the Mekong Delta, and features occasional stretches of flat, open farmland. The Marines knew that several battalions of Vietcong were in the Rung Sat. The enemy would lie low, building strength, and then launch surprise attacks on South Vietnamese or U.S. troops. The soldiers in Cowan's unit played cat-and-mouse with an enemy that melted away at their approach.

So when he captured a Vietcong soldier who could warn of ambushes and lead them to hidden troops but who refused to speak, wires were attached to the man's scrotum with alligator clips and electricity was cranked out of a 110-volt generator.

"It worked like a charm," Cowan told me. "The minute the crank started to turn, he was ready to talk. We never had to do more than make it clear we could deliver a jolt. It was the fear more than the pain that made them talk."

Fear works. It is more effective than any drug, tactic, or torture device. According to unnamed scientific studies cited by the *Kubark Manual* (it is frightening to think what these experiments might have been), most people cope with pain better than they think they will. As people become more familiar with pain, they become conditioned to it. Those who have suffered more physical pain than others—from being beaten frequently as a child, for example, or suffering a painful illness—may adapt to it and come to fear it less. So once interrogators resort to actual torture, they are apt to lose ground.

"The threat of coercion usually weakens or destroys resistance more effectively than coercion itself," the manual says.

> The threat to inflict pain, for example, can trigger fears more damaging than the immediate sensation of pain . . . Sustained long enough, a strong fear of anything vague or unknown induces regression, whereas the materialization of the fear, the infliction of some form of punishment, is likely to come as a relief. The subject finds that he can hold out, and his resistances are strengthened.

Furthermore, if a prisoner is subjected to pain after other methods have failed, it is a signal that the interrogation process may be nearing an end. "He may then decide that if he can just hold out against this final assault, he will win the struggle and his freedom," the manual concludes. Even if severe pain does elicit information, it can be false, which is particularly troublesome to interrogators seeking intelligence rather than a confession. Much useful information is time-sensitive, and running down false leads or arresting innocents wastes time.

By similar logic, the manual discourages threatening a prisoner with death. As a tactic "it is often found to be worse than useless," the manual says, because the sense of despair it induces can make the prisoner withdraw into depression—or, in some cases, see an honorable way out of his predicament.

Others disagree.

"I'll tell you how to make a man talk," a retired Special Forces officer says. "You shoot the man to his left and the man to his right. Then you can't shut him up."

John Dunn found the truth to be a little more complicated. In his case the threat of execution forced him to bend but not break. He was a U.S. Army intelligence officer in the Lam Dong Province of Vietnam, in March of 1968, when he was captured by the Vietcong. He and other captives were marched for weeks to a prison camp in the jungle, where initially he was treated quite well. The gentle treatment lulled him, Dunn says, and contributed to his shock when, in his first interrogation session, he was calmly told, "We don't need you. We did not sign the Geneva Convention, and you are not considered a prisoner of war anyway. You are a war criminal. If you don't cooperate with us, you will be executed."

He was sent back to his hammock to think things over. Dunn had never considered himself a superaggressive soldier, a "warrior type," and had never imagined himself in such a situation. His training for captivity had been basic. He had been instructed to tell his captors only his name, rank, and serial number. Anything beyond that was considered a breach of duty—a betrayal of his country, his role as a soldier, and his personal honor. Faced with death, Dunn weighed his devotion to this simple code. He felt it was unrealistic. He wrestled to come up with a solution that would keep him alive without completely compromising his dignity. He figured there were certain details about his life and service that were not worth dying to protect. Some things needed to be kept secret, and others did not. Struggling with shame, he decided to answer any questions that did not intrude on that closed center of secrecy. He would not tell them he was an intelligence officer. ("Not out of patriotism," he says. "Out of fear, strictly self-preservation.") He would not reveal accurate details about fortifications around his company's headquarters, in Di Linh. He would not tell them about upcoming plans, such as the Phoenix Program (an assassination program targeting Vietcong village leaders), and above all, he would not make any public statements. But he would talk. The threat of execution in his case was not "worse than useless." It shook Dunn to his core.

In a subsequent session he talked, but not enough to satisfy his captors. Again and again he refused to make a public statement. Starved, sore, and still frightened, Dunn was told, "You will be executed. After dark."

When the sun set, the interrogator, his aide, and the camp commander came for Dunn with a group of soldiers. They unlocked his chain, and he carried it as they led him away from the encampment into the jungle. They stopped in front of a pit they had dug for his grave and put a gun to his head. The interrogator gave him one more chance to agree to make a statement.

"No," Dunn said. He had gone as far as he was willing to go.

"Why do you want to die?" he was asked.

"If I must, I must," Dunn said. He felt resigned. He waited to be killed.

"You will not be executed," the camp commander said abruptly, and that was that.

Judging by Dunn's experience, the threat of death may be valuable to an interrogator as a way of loosening up a determined subject. But, as with pain, the most important factor is fear. An unfrightened prisoner makes an unlikely informer.

If there is an archetype of the modern interrogator, it is Michael Koubi. The former chief interrogator for Israel's General Security Services, or Shabak, Koubi probably has more experience than anyone else in the world in the interrogation of hostile Arab prisoners, some of them confirmed terrorists and religious fanatics—men, he says, "whose hatred of the Jews is unbridgeable." He has blue eyes in a crooked face: time, the greatest caricaturist of all, has been at work on it for more than sixty years, and has produced one that is lean, browned, deeply lined, and naturally concave. His considerable nose has been broken twice, and now ends well to the right of where it begins, giving him a look that is literally off-center. His wisdom, too, is slightly off-center, because Koubi has been given a uniquely twisted perspective on human nature. For decades he has been experimenting with captive human beings, cajoling, tricking, hurting, threatening, and spying on them, steadily upping the pressure, looking for cracks at the seams.

I met Koubi at his home on the beach in Ashkelon, just a short drive north of the border with the Gaza Strip, in whose prisons he worked for much of his career. He is comfortably retired from his Shabak job now, a grandfather three times over, and works for the municipal Inspection and Sanitation Department. There are still many things he is not free to discuss, but he is happy to talk about his methods. He is very proud of his skills, among them an ability to speak Arabic so fluently that he can adopt a multitude of colloquial flavors. Koubi came to his career as an interrogator through his love of language. He grew up speaking Hebrew, Yiddish, and Arabic, and he studied Arabic in high school, working to master its idiom and slang. He also had a knack for reading the body language and facial expressions of his subjects, and for sensing a lie. He is a skilled actor who could alternately befriend or intimidate a subject, sometimes turning on a dime. Blending these skills with the tricks he had learned over the years for manipulating people, Koubi didn't just question his subjects, he orchestrated their emotional surrender.

To many, including many in Israel, Koubi and the unit he headed are an outrage. The games they played and the tactics they employed are seen as inhuman, illegal, and downright evil. It is hard to picture this pleasant grandfather as the leader of a unit that critics accuse of being brutal; but then, charm has always been as important to interrogation work as toughness or cruelty—perhaps more important. Koubi says that only in rare instances did he use force to extract information from his subjects; in most cases it wasn't necessary.

"People change when they get to prison," Koubi says. "They may be heroes outside, but inside they change. The conditions are different. People are afraid of the unknown. They are afraid of being tortured, of being held for a long time. Try to see what it is like to sit with a hood over your head for four hours, when you are hungry and tired and afraid, when you are isolated from everything and have no clue what is going on." When the captive believes that *anything* could happen—torture, execution, indefinite imprisonment, even the persecution of his loved ones—the interrogator can go to work.

Under pressure, he says, nearly everyone looks out first and foremost for No. 1. What's more, a very large part of who a man is depends on his circumstances. No matter who he is before his arrest, his sense of self will blur in custody. Isolation, fear, and deprivation force a man to retreat, to reorient himself, and to reorder his priorities. For most men, Koubi says, the hierarchy of loyalty under stress is 1) self, 2) group, 3) family, 4) friends. In other words, even the most dedicated terrorist (with very rare exceptions), when pushed hard enough, will act to preserve and protect himself at the expense of anyone or anything else. "There's an old Arab saying," Koubi says. "'Let one hundred mothers cry, but not my mother—but better my mother than me.'"

With older men the priorities shift slightly. In middle age the family often overtakes the group (the cause) to become the second most important loyalty. Young men tend to be fiercely committed and ambitious, but older men—even men with deeply held convictions, men admired and emulated by their followers—tend to have loves and obligations that count for more. Age frays idealism, slackens zeal, and cools ferocity. Abstractions lose ground to wife, children, and grandchildren. "Notice that the leaders of Hamas do not send their own sons and daughters, and their own grandchildren, to blow themselves up," Koubi says.

So it is often the top-level men, like Sheikh Mohammed, who are easier to crack. Koubi believes that having the al Qaeda leader's wife and children in custody gives his interrogators powerful leverage. The key is to find a man's weak point and exploit it.

For Koubi the three critical ingredients of that process are preparation, investigation, and theater.

Preparing a subject for interrogation means softening him up. Ideally, he has been pulled from his sleep—like Sheikh Mohammed—early in the morning, roughly handled, bound, hooded (a coarse, dirty, smelly sack serves the purpose perfectly), and kept waiting in discomfort, perhaps naked in a cold, wet room, forced to stand or to sit in an uncomfortable position. He may be kept awake for days prior to questioning, isolated and ill-fed. He may be unsure where he is, what time of day it is, how long he has been or will be held. If he is wounded, as Abu Zubaydah was, pain medication may be withheld; it is one thing to cause pain, another to refuse to relieve it.

Mousa Khoury, a Palestinian businessman, knows the drill all too well. A slender thirty-four-year-old man with a black goatee and thinning hair, he is bitter about the Israeli occupation and his experiences in custody. He has been arrested and interrogated six times by Israeli forces. He was once held for seventy-one days.

"My hands were cuffed behind my back, and a potato sack was over my head," he says. "My legs were cuffed to a tiny chair. The chair's base is ten centimeters by twenty centimeters. The back is ten centimeters by ten centimeters. It is hard wood. The front legs are shorter than the back ones, so you are forced to slide forward in it, only your hands are bound in the back. If you sit back, the back of the chair digs into the small of your back. If you slump forward, you are forced to hang by your hands. It is painful. They will take you to the toilet only after screaming a request one hundred times." He could think about only one thing: how to make the treatment stop. "Your thoughts go back and forth and back and forth, and you can no longer have a normal stream of consciousness," he says.

Preparing an interrogator means arming him beforehand with every scrap of information about his subject. U.S. Army interrogation manuals suggest preparing a thick "dummy file" when little is known, to make it appear that the interrogator knows more than he does. Nothing rattles a captive more than to be confronted with a fact he thought was secret or obscure. It makes the interrogator seem powerful, all-knowing. A man's sense of importance is wounded, and he is slower to lie, because he thinks he might be caught at it. There are many ways that scraps of information—gathered by old-fashioned legwork or the interrogation of a subject's associates—can be leveraged by a clever interrogator into something new. Those scraps might be as simple as knowing the names of a man's siblings or key associates, the name of his girlfriend, or a word or phrase that has special meaning to his group. Uncovering privileged details diminishes the aura of a secret society, whether it is a social club, a terrorist cell, or a military unit. Joining such a group makes an individual feel distinct, important, and superior, and invests even the most mundane of his activities with meaning. An interrogator who penetrates that secret society, unraveling its shared language, culture, history, customs, plans, and pecking order, can diminish its hold on even the staunchest believer. Suspicion that a trusted comrade has betrayed the group—or the subject himself—undermines the sense of a secretly shared purpose and destiny. Armed with a few critical details, a skilled interrogator can make a subject doubt the value of information he has been determined to withhold. It is one thing to suffer in order to protect a secret, quite another to cling to a secret that is already out. This is how a well-briefed interrogator breaches a group's defenses.

Koubi believes that the most important skill for an interrogator is to know the prisoner's language. Working through interpreters is at best a necessary evil. Language is at the root of all social connections, and plays a critical role in secret societies like Hamas and al Qaeda. A shared vocabulary or verbal shorthand helps to cement the group.

"I try to create the impression that I use his mother tongue even better than he does," Koubi says. "No accent, no mistaken syntax. I speak to him like his best friend speaks to him. I might ask him a question about a certain word or sentence or expression, how it is used in his culture, and then demonstrate that I know more about it than he does. This embarrasses him very much."

Once a prisoner starts to talk, rapid follow-up is needed to sort fact from fiction, so that the interrogator knows whether his subject is being cooperative or evasive, and can respond accordingly. Interrogation sessions should be closely observed (many rooms designed for this purpose have one-way mirrors), and in a well-run unit a subject's words can sometimes be checked out before the session is over. Being caught so quickly in a lie demonstrates the futility of playing games with the interrogator, and strengthens his hand. It shames and rattles the subject. When information checks out, the interrogator can home in for more details and open up new avenues of exploration.

Religious extremists are the hardest cases. They ponder in their own private space, performing a kind of self-hypnosis. They are usually well educated. Their lives are financially and emotionally tidy. They tend to live in an ascetic manner, and to look down on nonbelievers. They tend to be physically and mentally strong, and not to be influenced by material things—by either the incentives or the disincentives available in prison.

Often the rightness of their cause trumps all else, so they can commit any outrage—lie, cheat, steal, betray, kill—without remorse. Yet under sufficient duress, Koubi says, most men of even this kind will eventually break—most, but not all. Some cannot be broken.

"They are very rare," he says, "but in some cases the more aggressive you get, and the worse things get, the more these men will withdraw into their own world, until you cannot reach them."

Mousa Khoury, the Palestinian businessman who has been interrogated six times, claims that he never once gave in to his jailers. Koubi has no particular knowledge of Khoury's case, but he smiles his crooked, knowing smile and says, "If someone you meet says he was held by our forces and did not cooperate at all, you can bet he is lying. In some cases men who are quite famous for their toughness were the most helpful to us in captivity."

Interrogation is also highly theatrical. The *Kubark Manual* is very particular about setting the stage.

> The room in which the interrogation is to be conducted should be free of distractions. The colors of the walls, ceiling, rugs, and furniture should not be startling. Pictures should be missing or dull. Whether the furniture should include a desk depends not upon the interrogator's convenience but rather upon the subject's anticipated reaction to the connotations of superiority and officialdom. A plain table may be preferable. An overstuffed chair for the use of the interrogatee is sometimes preferable to a straight-backed, wooden chair because if he is made to stand for a lengthy period or is otherwise deprived of physical comfort, the contrast is intensified and increased disorientation results.

The manual goes on to recommend lighting that shines brightly in the face of the subject and leaves the interrogator in shadow. There should be no phone or any other means of contact with those outside the room, to enhance concentration and the subject's feeling of confinement. In Koubi's experience it was sometimes helpful to have associates loudly stage a torture or beating session in the next room. In old CIA interrogation training, according to Bill Wagner, a retired agent, it was recommended that mock executions take place outside the interrogation room.

A good interrogator is a deceiver. One of Koubi's tricks was to walk into a hallway lined with twenty recently arrested, hooded, uncomfortable,

hungry, and fearful men, all primed for interrogation, and shout commandingly, "Okay, who wants to cooperate with me?" Even if no hands, or only
one hand, went up, he would say to the hooded men, "Okay, good. Eight
of you. I'll start with you, and the others will have to wait." Believing that
others have capitulated makes doing so oneself much easier. Often, after
this trick, many of the men in the hall would cooperate. Men are herd
animals, and prefer to go with the flow, especially when moving in the other
direction is harsh.

In one case Koubi had information suggesting that two men he was
questioning were secretly members of a terrorist cell, and knew of an impending attack. They were tough men, rural farmers, very difficult to intimidate or pressure, and so far neither man had admitted anything under
questioning. Koubi worked them over individually for hours. With each
man he would start off by asking friendly questions and then grow angrier
and angrier, accusing the subject of withholding something. He would slap
him, knock him off his chair, set guards on him, and then intervene to pull
them off. Then he would put the subject back in the chair and offer him a
cigarette, lightening the mood. "Let him see the difference between the
two atmospheres, the hostile one and the friendly one," Koubi says. Neither man budged.

Finally Koubi set his trap. He announced to one of the men that his
interrogation was over. The man's associate, hooded, was seated in the
hallway outside the room. "We are going to release you," Koubi said. "We
are pleased with your cooperation. But first you must do something for
me. I am going to ask you a series of questions, just a formality, and I need
you to answer 'Yes' in a loud, clear voice for the recorder." Then, in a voice
loud enough for the hooded man outside in the hall to hear, but soft enough
so that he couldn't make out exactly what was being said, Koubi read off a
long list of questions, reviewing the prisoner's name, age, marital status,
date of capture, length of detainment, and so forth. These were regularly
punctuated by the prisoner's loud and cooperative "Yes." The act was
enough to convince the man in the hall that his friend had capitulated.

Koubi dismissed the first man and brought in the second. "There's
no more need for me to question you," Koubi said. "Your friend has confessed the whole thing." He offered the second prisoner a cigarette and gave
him a good meal. He told him that the information provided by his friend
virtually ensured that they would both be in prison for the rest of their

lives ... unless, he said, the second prisoner could offer him something, anything, that would dispose the court to leniency in his case. Convinced that his friend had already betrayed them both, the second prisoner acted promptly to save himself. "If you want to save Israeli lives, go immediately," he told Koubi. "My friends went with a car to Yeshiva Nehalim [a religious school]. They are going to kidnap a group of students ..." The men were found in Erez, and the operation was foiled.

There are other methods of keeping a prisoner confused and off balance, such as rapidly firing questions at him, cutting off his responses in mid-sentence, asking the same questions over and over in different order, and what the manual calls the "Silent" technique, in which the interrogator "says nothing to the source, but looks him squarely in the eye, preferably with a slight smile on his face." The manual advises forcing the subject to break eye contact first. "The source will become nervous, begin to shift around in his chair, cross and recross his legs, and look away," the manual says. "When the interrogator is ready to break silence, he may do so with some quite nonchalant questions such as 'You planned this operation a long time, didn't you? Was it your idea?'"

Then there is "Alice in Wonderland."

> The aim of the Alice in Wonderland or confusion technique is to confound the expectations and conditioned reactions of the interrogatee ... The confusion technique is designed not only to obliterate the familiar but to replace it with the weird ... Sometimes two or more questions are asked simultaneously. Pitch, tone, and volume of the interrogators' voices are unrelated to the import of the questions. No pattern of questions and answers is permitted to develop, nor do the questions themselves relate logically to each other.

If this technique is pursued patiently, the manual says, the subject will start to talk "just to stop the flow of babble which assails him."

Easily the most famous routine is "Good Cop/Bad Cop," in which one interrogator becomes the captive's persecutor and the other his friend. A lesser-known but equally effective technique is "Pride and Ego," "Ego Up/Ego Down," or (as the more pretentious *Kubark Manual* puts it) "Spinoza and Mortimer Snerd," in which the "Ego Down" part involves repeatedly asking questions that the interrogator knows the subject cannot answer. The subject is continually berated or threatened ("How could you not know the answer to that?") and accused of withholding, until, at long last, he is asked a simple question that he can answer. An American POW subjected to this technique has said, "I know it seems strange now, but I was positively grateful to them when they switched to a topic I knew something about."

CIA psychologists have tried to develop an underlying theory for interrogation—namely, that the coercive methods induce a gradual "regression" of personality. But the theory is not convincing. Interrogation simply backs a man into a corner. It forces difficult choices, and dangles illusory avenues of escape.

A skillful interrogator knows which approach will best suit his subject; and just as he expertly applies stress, he continually opens up these avenues of escape or release. This means understanding what, at heart, is stopping a subject from cooperating. If it is ego, that calls for one method. If it is fear of reprisal or of getting into deeper trouble, another method might work best. For most captives a major incentive to keep quiet is simply pride. Their manhood is being tested, not just their loyalty and conviction. Allowing the subject to save face lowers the cost of capitulation, so an artful interrogator will offer persuasive rationales for giving in: others already have, or the information is already known. Drugs, if administered with the subject's knowledge, are helpful in this regard. If a subject believes that a particular drug or "truth serum" renders him helpless, he is off the hook. He cannot be held accountable for giving in. A study cited in George Andrews's book *MKULTRA* found that a placebo—a simple sugar pill—was as effective as an actual drug up to half of the time.

Koubi layered his deception so thick that his subjects never knew exactly when their interrogation ended. After questioning, captives usually spent time in a regular prison. The Israelis had bugged the prison with a system that was disguised well enough to *appear* hidden but not well enough to avoid discovery. In this way prisoners were led to believe that only certain parts of the prison were bugged. In fact, all of the prison was bugged. Conversations between prisoners could be overheard anywhere, and were closely monitored. They were an invaluable source of intelligence. Prisoners who could hold out through the most intense interrogation often let their guard down later when talking to comrades in jail.

To help such inadvertent confessions along, Koubi had yet another card to play. Whenever an interrogated subject was released to the general prison, after weeks of often grueling questioning, he was received with open arms by fellow Palestinians who befriended him and congratulated him for having endured interrogation. He was treated like a hero. He was fed, nursed, even celebrated. What he didn't know was that his happy new comrades were working for Koubi.

Koubi calls them "birdies." They were Palestinians who, offered an incentive such as an opportunity to settle with their families in another country, had agreed to cooperate with Shabak. Some days or weeks after welcoming the new prisoner into their ranks, easing his transition into the prison, they would begin to ask questions. They would debrief the prisoner on his interrogation sessions. They would say, "It is very important for those on the outside to know what you told the Israelis and what you *didn't* tell them. Tell us, and we will get the information to those on the outside who need to know." Even prisoners who had managed to keep important secrets from Koubi spilled them to their birdies.

"The amazing thing is that by now the existence of the birdies is well-known," Koubi says, "and yet the system still works. People come out of interrogation, go into the regular prison, and then tell their darkest secrets. I don't know why it still works, but it does."

BIG DADDY UPTOWN

Most professional interrogators work without the latitude given the CIA, the FBI, or the military in the war on terror. A policeman's subjects all have to be read their Miranda rights, and cops who physically threaten or abuse suspects—at least nowadays—may find themselves in jail. Jerry Giorgio, the legendary NYPD interrogator, has operated within these rules for nearly forty years. He may not know all the names of the CIA and military techniques, but he has probably seen most of them at work. Known as "Big Daddy Uptown," Giorgio now works for the New York County district attorney in a cramped office in Lower Manhattan that he shares with two others. He is a big man with a big voice, thinning gray hair, a broad belly, and wide, searching greenish-brown eyes. He is considered a wizard by his former colleagues in the NYPD. "All of us of a certain generation came out of the Jerry Giorgio school of interrogation," says John Bourges, a recently retired Manhattan homicide detective.

"Everybody knows the Good Cop/Bad Cop routine, right?" Giorgio says. "Well, I'm always the Good Cop. I don't work with a Bad Cop, either. Don't need it. You want to know the truth? The truth is—and this is important—everybody down deep *wants* to tell his or her story. It's true. No matter how damaging it is to them, no matter how important it is for them to keep quiet, they want to tell their story. If they feel guilty, they want to get it off their chests. If they feel justified in what they did, they want to explain themselves. I tell them, 'Hey, I know what you did and I can prove it. Now what are you going to do about it? If you show remorse, if you help me out, I'll go to bat for you.' I tell them that. And if you give them half a reason to do it, they'll tell you everything."

The most important thing is to get them talking. The toughest suspects are those who clam up and demand a lawyer right at the start. Giorgio believes that once he gets a suspect talking, the stream of words will eventually flow right to the truth. One murderer gave him three voluntary statements in a single day, each one signed, each one different, each one slightly closer to the truth.

The murderer was Carlos Martinez, a hulking former football player who in May of 1992 killed his girlfriend, Cheryl Maria Wright, and dumped her body in New York, right at the Coliseum overlook off the Henry Hudson Parkway. Since many young female murder victims are killed by their boyfriends, Giorgio started looking for Wright's. Martinez phoned Giorgio when he heard that the detective wanted to ask him some questions. Giorgio had pictures of Wright with Martinez, and in all the pictures the young beau had a giant head of Jheri curls. But he showed up in Giorgio's office bald. The detective was immediately more suspicious; a man who worries that somebody might have seen him commit a crime generally tries to alter his appearance.

Here is how Giorgio summarizes what turned out to be a very long and fruitful conversation:

"I was at home last night," Martinez said. "She did call me."

"Really, why?"

"She wanted me to pick her up. I told her, 'I'm watching the Mets game; I can't pick you up.'"

That was it. Giorgio acted very pleased with this statement, thanked Martinez, wrote it up, and asked the young man to sign it. Martinez did.

Then Giorgio stared at the statement and gave Martinez a quizzical look.

"You know, Carlos, something about this statement doesn't look right to me. You two had been going out for, what? Seven years? She calls you and asks you to pick her up at night where she's just gotten off work. It's not a safe neighborhood, and you tell her no? You mean a ball game on TV was more important to you?"

The question was cunning. The detective knew that Martinez was trying to make a good impression; he definitely didn't want to leave Giorgio with any unresolved issues to play in his mind. So it concerned him that his first statement didn't sound right. Giorgio's question also touched Martinez's sense of chivalry, an important quality for many Hispanic men. It wouldn't do to be seen as ungentlemanly. Here was a young woman who had just been brutally killed. How would it look to her family and friends if he admitted that she had called and asked him for a ride and he had left her to her fate—for a ball game on TV? The question also subtly suggested an out: The neighborhood wasn't safe. People got hurt or killed in that neighborhood all the time. Maybe Martinez could admit that he had seen Cheryl on the night of the murder without directly implicating himself. No one ever accused the former footballer of being especially bright. He rose to Giorgio's bait immediately.

He said, "Jerry, let me tell you what really happened." ("Note," Giorgio says proudly, "already I'm *Jerry!*") Martinez now said that he had left his place to pick Wright up after work, but they had gotten into an argument. "She got mad at me and told me she didn't need a ride, so I waited until she got on the bus, and then I left." ("Look, now he's the picture of chivalry!" Giorgio says happily.)

"Let me take that down," Giorgio said, again acting pleased with the statement. He wrote it out neatly and asked Martinez to look it over and sign it. Martinez did.

Again Giorgio squinted at the paper. "You know, Carlos, something is still not right here. Cheryl was a strikingly beautiful girl. People who saw her remembered her. She's taken that bus home from work many nights, and people on that bus know who she is. And you know what? Nobody who rode that bus saw her on it last night."

(This was, in Giorgio's words, "pure bullshit." He hadn't talked to anybody who rode that bus. "Sometimes you have to just take a chance," he says.)

Again Martinez looked troubled. He had not allayed the detective's suspicions. So he tried again. "Okay, okay," he said. "This is really it. Let me tell you what really happened. Cheryl called, and I left to pick her up, but I ran into a friend of mine—I can't tell you his name—and we picked her up together. Then Cheryl and I got in this argument, a big fight. My friend got fed up. So we drove away, up Broadway to 181st Street, and stopped at the McDonald's there. He pulled out a gun, my friend, and he told me to get out of the car. 'Wait here,' he told me. 'I'm going to get rid of your problem.' Then he left. I waited. Then he came back. He said he had gotten rid of my problem."

Giorgio nodded happily and started to write up statement No. 3. He acted troubled over the fact that Martinez refused to name the friend, and the young man quickly coughed up a name. Giorgio's lieutenant, who had been watching the session through a one-way mirror, immediately got to work tracking down Martinez's friend. By the time the third statement had been written up, signed, and nestled neatly on top of the other two, Giorgio had a new problem to pose to Martinez: it seemed that his friend was in South Carolina, and had been for some time.

"We never did get to finish the fourth statement," Giorgio says. "Martinez's family had hired a lawyer, and he called the station forbidding us to further question his client." It was, of course, too late.

CAPTAIN CRUNCH VERSUS THE TREE HUGGERS

On a spring morning in the offices of Amnesty International, in Washington, D.C., Alistair Hodgett and Alexandra Arriaga were briefing me on their organization's noble efforts to combat torture wherever in the world it is found. They are bright, pleasant, smart, committed, attractive young people, filled with righteous purpose. Decent people everywhere agree on this: torture is evil and indefensible.

But is it always?

I showed the two an article I had torn from that day's *New York Times*, which described the controversy over a tragic kidnapping case in Frankfurt, Germany. On September 27 of last year a Frankfurt law student kidnapped an eleven-year-old boy named Jakob von Metzler, whose smiling face appeared in a box alongside the story. The kidnapper had covered Jakob's mouth and nose with duct tape, wrapped the boy in plastic, and hidden him in a wooded area near a lake. The police captured the suspect when he tried to pick up ransom money, but the suspect wouldn't reveal where he had left the boy, who the police thought might still be alive. So the deputy police chief of Frankfurt, Wolfgang Daschner, told his subordinates to threaten the suspect with torture. According to the suspect, he was told that a "specialist" was being flown in who would "inflict pain on me of the sort I had never experienced." The suspect promptly told the police where he'd hidden Jakob, who, sadly, was found dead. The newspaper said that Daschner was under fire from Amnesty International, among other groups, for threatening torture.

"Under these circumstances," I asked, "do you honestly think it was wrong to even *threaten* torture?"

Hodgett and Arriaga squirmed in their chairs. "We recognize that there are difficult situations," said Arriaga, who is the group's director of government relations. "But we are opposed to torture under any and all circumstances, and threatening torture is inflicting mental pain. So we would be against it."

Few moral imperatives make such sense on a large scale but break down so dramatically in the particular. A way of sorting this one out is to consider two clashing sensibilities: the warrior and the civilian.

The civilian sensibility prizes above all else the rule of law. Whatever the difficulties posed by a particular situation, such as trying to find poor Jakob von Metzler before he suffocated, it sees abusive government power as a greater danger to society. Allowing an exception in one case (saving Jakob) would open the door to a greater evil.

The warrior sensibility requires doing what must be done to complete a mission. By definition, war exists because civil means have failed. What counts is winning, and preserving one's own troops. To a field commander in a combat zone, the life of an uncooperative enemy captive weighs very lightly against the lives of his own men. There are very few who, faced with a reluctant captive, would not in certain circumstances reach for the alligator clips, or something else.

"It isn't about getting mad, or payback," says Bill Cowan, the Vietnam interrogator. "It's strictly business. Torturing people doesn't fit my moral compass at all. But I don't think there's much of a gray area. Either the guy has information you need or not. Either it's vital or it's not. You know which guys you need to twist."

The official statements by President Bush and William Haynes reaffirming the U.S. government's opposition to torture have been applauded by human-rights groups—but again, the language in them is carefully chosen. What does the Bush administration mean by "torture"? Does it really share the activists' all-inclusive definition of the word? In his letter to the director of Human Rights Watch, Haynes used the term "enemy combatants" to describe those in custody. Calling detainees "prisoners of war" would entitle them to the protections of the Geneva Convention, which prohibits the "physical or mental torture" of POWs, and "any other form of coercion," even to the extent of "unpleasant or disadvantageous treatment of any kind." (In the contemptuous words of one military man, they "prohibit everything except three square meals, a warm bed, and access to a Harvard education.") Detainees who are American citizens have the advantage of constitutional protections against being held without charges, and have the right to legal counsel. They would also be protected from the worst abuses by the Eighth Amendment, which prohibits "cruel and unusual punishment." The one detainee at Guantánamo who was discovered to have been born in the United States has been transferred to a different facility, and legal battles rage over his status. But if the rest of the thousands of detainees are neither POWs (even though the bulk of them were captured during the fighting in Afghanistan) nor American citizens, they are fair game. They are protected only by this country's international promises—which are, in effect, unenforceable.

What are those promises? The most venerable are those in the Geneva Convention, but the United States has sidestepped this agreement in the case of those captured in the war on terror. The next most important would be those in the Universal Declaration of Human Rights, which asserts, in Article 5, "No one shall be subjected to torture or to cruel, inhuman or degrading treatment or punishment." There is also the Convention Against Torture, the agreement cited by Bush in June, which would seem to rule out any of the more aggressive methods of interrogation. It states, in Article 1, "For the purposes of this Convention, torture means any act by which severe pain or suffering, whether physical or mental, is intentionally inflicted on a person." Again, note the word "severe." The United States is avoiding the brand "torturer" only by sleight of word.

The history of interrogation by U.S. armed forces and spy agencies is one of giving lip service to international agreements while vigorously using coercion whenever circumstances seem to warrant it. However, both the Army and the CIA have been frank in their publications about the use of coercive methods. The *Kubark Manual* offers only a few nods in its 128 pages to qualms over what are referred to, in a rare euphemism, as "external techniques": "Moral considerations aside, the imposition of external techniques of manipulating people carries with it the grave risk of later lawsuits, adverse publicity, or other attempts to strike back." The use of the term "strike back" here is significant; it implies that criticism of such unseemly methods, whether legal, moral, or journalistic, would have no inherent validity but would be viewed as an enemy counterattack.

Bill Wagner, the former CIA agent, remembers going to the Agency's three-week interrogation course at "The Farm," in Williamsburg, Virginia, in 1970. Until it was shut down, a few years later, it was considered the Agency's "premier course," Wagner says, and only the best recruits were invited to take it. "To say you had been through it was a real feather in your cap."

Volunteers played the role of captives in return for guaranteed space in a future session of the coveted course. They were deprived of sleep, kept doused with water in cold rooms, forced to sit or stand in uncomfortable positions for long periods, isolated from sunlight and social contacts, given food deliberately made unappetizing (oversalted, for instance, or tainted with a green dye), and subjected to mock executions. At least 10 percent of the volunteers dropped out, even though they knew it was just a training exercise. Wagner says that many of those who had served as victims later refused to take the course and victimize others. "They lost their stomach for it," he says.

Several years after Wagner took the course, he says, the Agency dropped it entirely. The scandals of the Nixon years put the CIA under unprecedented scrutiny. Over the next three decades spying schools and most human-intelligence networks were gradually dismantled. The United States itself was losing its stomach for hands-on intelligence gathering— and with it, interrogation.

Nobody experienced the effects of this shift more dramatically than Keith Hall, who earned the nickname Captain Crunch before he lost his job as a CIA agent. Now he describes himself as "a poster child for political correctness." He is a pugnacious brick of a man, who at age fifty-two is just a thicker (especially in the middle) version of the young man who joined the Marines thirty years ago. After his discharge he earned a master's degree in history and international relations; he took a job as a police officer, because he craved a more physical brand of excitement than academia had to offer. His nickname comes from this craving.

The CIA hired Hall immediately after he applied, in 1979, because of his relatively rare combination of academic and real-world credentials. He was routed into the Investigation and Analysis Directorate, where he became one of the Agency's covert operators, a relatively small group ("about forty-eight guys, total," Hall says) known as the "knuckle-draggers." Most CIA agents, especially by the 1980s, were just deskmen.

Hall preferred traveling, training, and blowing things up, even though he felt that the rest of the Agency looked down its patrician nose at guys like him. When the U.S. embassy in Beirut was bombed, on April 18, 1983, eight of the seventeen Americans killed were CIA employees. There were going to be plenty of official investigations, but the Agency wanted one of its own. Hall was selected to carry it out.

"They flew me to Langley on one of their private planes, and delivered me to the seventh floor," he says. "They told me, 'We want you to go to Beirut and find out who blew up the embassy and how they did it. The president himself is going to be reading your cables. There is going to be some retribution here.'"

Hall was honored, and excited. This was a mission of singular purpose, of the highest priority, and he knew he was expected to get results. Having been a police officer and a Marine, he knew that the official investigations had to build a case that might someday stand up in court. His goal was not to build a case but just to find out who did it.

He slept on rooftops in Beirut, changing the location every two nights. It was a dangerous time to be an American—especially a CIA officer—there, and Hall kept moving. He worked with the Lebanese Special Security Force, and set up a computer in the police building.

Hall says he took part without hesitation in brutal questioning by the Lebanese, during which suspects were beaten with clubs and rubber hoses or wired up to electrical generators and doused with water. Such methods eventually led him to the suspected "paymaster" of the embassy bombing, a man named Elias Nimr. "He was our biggest catch," Hall says—a man with powerful connections. "When I told the Lebanese minister of defense, I watched the blood drain out of his face."

Nimr was a fat, pampered-looking twenty-eight-year-old, used to living the good life, a young man of wealth, leisure, and power. He came to the police building wearing slacks, a shiny sport shirt, and Gucci shoes. He had a small, well-trimmed moustache at the center of his soft, round face, and wore gold on his neck, wrists, and fingers. When he was marched into the building, Hall says, some of the officers "tried to melt into the shadows" for fear of eventual retribution. Nimr was nonchalant and smirking in his initial interview, convinced that when word got back to his family and connections, he would promptly be released.

When Hall got a chance to talk to him, he set out to disabuse Nimr. "I'm an American intelligence officer," he said. "You really didn't think that you were going to blow up our embassy and we wouldn't do anything about it, did you? You really should be looking inside yourself and telling yourself that it's a good idea to talk to me. The best way to go is to be civilized. . . . I know you think you are going to walk right out of here in a few minutes. That's not going to happen. You're mine. I'm the one who will make the decisions about what happens to you. The only thing that will save your ass is to cooperate." Nimr smiled at him dismissively.

The next time they met, Nimr wasn't in such good shape. In this case his connections were failing him. No one had roughed him up, but he had been kept standing for two days. Hall placed him in a straight-backed metal chair, with hot floodlights in his face. The agent sat behind the light, so that Nimr couldn't see him. Nimr wasn't as cocky, but he was still silent.

At the third interrogation session, Hall says, he kicked Nimr out of his chair. It was the first time anyone had physically abused him, and he seemed stunned. He just stared at Hall. He hadn't eaten since his arrest, four days earlier. But he still had nothing to say.

"I sent him back to his cell, had water poured over him again and again while he sat under a big fan, kept him freezing for about twenty-four hours. He comes back after this, and you can see his mood is changing. He hasn't walked out of jail, and it's beginning to dawn on him that no one is going to spring him."

Over the next ten days Hall kept up the pressure. During the questioning sessions he again kicked Nimr out of his chair, and both he and the Lebanese captain involved cracked him occasionally across the shins with a wooden bat. Finally Nimr broke. According to Hall, he explained his role in the bombing, and in the assassination of Lebanon's president.

He explained that Syrian intelligence agents had been behind the plan. (Not everyone in the CIA agrees with Hall's interpretation.)

Soon afterward, Nimr died in his cell. Hall was back in Washington when he heard the news. He assumed that Nimr had been killed to prevent him from testifying and naming others involved in the plot. Armed with tapes of Nimr's confession, Hall felt he had accomplished his mission; but several months after finishing his report he was fired. As he understood it, word had leaked out about torture sessions conducted by a CIA agent, and the U.S. government was embarrassed.

None of the men charged was ever prosecuted for the bombing. Hall believes that the United States may have paid dearly for backing away from his investigation and letting the matter drop. William Buckley, who was Hall's station chief, was subsequently kidnapped, tortured, and killed. He was among fourteen Western civilians kidnapped in Beirut in 1984. In October of the previous year, 241 American servicemen were killed in the bombing of their barracks at the Beirut airport. Some analysts believe that all these atrocities were committed by the same group, the one Hall believes he unearthed in his investigation. Still bitter about it nineteen years later, Hall says, "No one was punished for it, except me!"

Hall sees the loss of his career as dramatic proof that the CIA sold out to the "tree huggers" two decades ago, and points with scorn to a directive from President Bill Clinton that effectively barred intelligence agents from doing business with unsavory characters. The full-scale U.S. retreat from the uglier side of espionage is well documented—but has, by all accounts, been sharply reversed in the aftermath of 9/11.

"People are being very careful, very legal, and very sensible," one former top intelligence official says. "We are not inflicting intense pain, or doing anything damaging or life-threatening. We are once again asking, 'How do you take people down a series of steps in such a way that it has an impact?' That's the only game in town."

Despite the hue and cry over mistreatment of prisoners at Guantánamo, two former Pakistani inmates there—Shah Muhammad and Sahibzada Osman Ali—told me that except for some roughing up immediately after they were captured, they were not badly treated at Camp X-Ray. They both felt bored, lonely, frustrated, angry, and helpless (enough for Shah Muhammad to attempt suicide), but neither believed that he would be harmed by his American captors, and both regarded the extreme precautions (shackles, handcuffs, hoods) that so outraged the rest of the world as comical. "What did the American soldiers think I could do to them?" asked Sahibzada, who stands about five feet eight and weighs little more than 150 pounds. Indeed, the lack of fear at Camp X-Ray no doubt made it more difficult to sort out foot soldiers from dedicated terrorists.

The perfect model of an interrogation center would be a place where prisoners lived in fear and uncertainty, a place where they could be isolated or allowed to mingle freely, as the jailer wished, and where conversations anywhere could be overheard. Interrogators would be able to control the experience of their subjects completely, shutting down access to other people, or even to normal sensation and experience, or opening that access up. Subjects' lives could be made a misery of discomfort and confusion, or restored to an almost normal level of comfort and social interaction within the limitations of confinement. Hope could be dangled or removed. Cooperation would be rewarded, stubbornness punished. Interrogators would have ever-growing files on their subjects, with each new fact or revelation yielding new leads and more information—drawn from field investigations (agents in the real world verifying and exploring facts gathered on the inside), the testimony of other subjects, collaborators spying inside the prison, and surreptitious recordings. The interrogators in this center would have the experience and the intuition of a Jerry Giorgio or a Michael Koubi.

Serious interrogation is clearly being reserved for only the most dangerous men, like Sheikh Mohammed. So why not lift the fig leaf covering the use of coercion? Why not eschew hypocrisy, clearly define what is meant by the word "severe," and amend bans on torture to allow interrogators to coerce information from would-be terrorists?

This is the crux of the problem. It may be clear that coercion is sometimes the right choice, but how does one allow it yet still control it? Sadism is deeply rooted in the human psyche. Every army has its share of soldiers who delight in kicking and beating bound captives. Men in authority tend to abuse it—not all men, but many. As a mass, they should be assumed to lean toward abuse. How does a country best regulate behavior in its dark and distant corners, in prisons, on battlefields, and in interrogation rooms, particularly when its forces number in the millions and are spread all over the globe? In considering a change in national policy, one is obliged to anticipate the practical consequences. So if we formally lift the ban on torture, even if only partially and in rare, specific cases (the attorney and author Alan Dershowitz has proposed issuing "torture warrants"), the question will be, How can we ensure that the practice does not become commonplace—not just a tool for extracting vital, life-saving information in rare cases but a routine tool of oppression?

As it happens, a pertinent case study exists. Israel has been a target of terror attacks for many years, and has wrestled openly with the dilemmas they pose for a democracy. In 1987 a commission led by the retired Israeli Supreme Court justice Moshe Landau wrote a series of recommendations for Michael Koubi and his agents, allowing them to use "moderate physical pressure" and "nonviolent psychological pressure" in interrogating prisoners who had information that could prevent impending terror attacks. The commission sought to allow such coercion only in "ticking-bomb scenarios"—that is, in cases like the kidnapping of Jakob von Metzler, when the information withheld by the suspect could save lives.

Twelve years later the Israeli Supreme Court effectively revoked this permission, banning the use of any and all forms of torture. In the years following the Landau Commission recommendations, the use of coercive methods had become widespread in the Occupied Territories. It was estimated that more than two thirds of the Palestinians taken into custody were subjected to them. Koubi says that only in rare instances, and with court permission, did he slap, pinch, or shake a prisoner—but he happens to be an especially gifted interrogator. What about the hundreds of men who worked for him? Koubi could not be present for all those interrogations. Every effort to regulate coercion failed. In the abstract it was easy to imagine a ticking-bomb situation, and a suspect who clearly warranted rough treatment. But in real life where was the line to be drawn? Should coercive methods be applied only to someone who knows of an immediately pending attack? What about one who might know of attacks planned for months or years in the future?

"Assuming you get useful information from torture, then why not always use torture?" asks Jessica Montell, the executive director of B'Tselem, a human-rights advocacy group in Jerusalem. "Why stop at the bomb that's already been planted and at people who know where the explosives are? Why not people who are building the explosives, or people who are donating money, or transferring the funds for the explosives? Why stop at the victim himself? Why not torture the victims' families, their relatives, their neighbors? If the end justifies the means, then where would you draw the line?"

And how does one define "coercion," as opposed to "torture"? If making a man sit in a tiny chair that forces him to hang painfully by his bound hands when he slides forward is okay, then what about applying a little pressure to the base of his neck to aggravate that pain? When does shaking or pushing a prisoner, which can become violent enough to kill or seriously injure a man, cross the line from coercion to torture?

Montell has thought about these questions a lot. She is thirty-five, a slender woman with scruffy short brown hair, who seems in perpetual motion, directing B'Tselem and tending baby twins and a four-year-old at home. Born in California, she emigrated to Israel partly out of feelings of solidarity with the Jewish state and partly because she found a job she liked in the human-rights field. Raised with a kind of idealized notion of Israel, she now seems committed to making the country live up to her ideals. But those ideals are hardheaded. Although Montell and her organization have steadfastly opposed the use of coercion (which she considers torture), she recognizes that the moral issue involved is not a simple one.

She knows that the use of coercion in interrogation did not end completely when the Israeli Supreme Court banned it in 1999. The difference is that when interrogators use "aggressive methods" now, they know they are breaking the law and could potentially be held responsible for doing so. This acts as a deterrent, and tends to limit the use of coercion to only the most defensible situations.

"If I as an interrogator feel that the person in front of me has information that can prevent a catastrophe from happening," she says, "I imagine that I would do what I would have to do in order to prevent that catastrophe from happening. The state's obligation is then to put me on trial, for breaking the law. Then I come and say these are the facts that I had at my disposal. This is what I believed at the time. This is what I thought necessary to do. I can evoke the defense of necessity, and then the court decides whether or not it's reasonable that I broke the law in order to avert this catastrophe. But it has to be that I broke the law. It can't be that there's some prior license for me to abuse people."

In other words, when the ban is lifted, there is no restraining lazy, incompetent, or sadistic interrogators. As long as it remains illegal to torture, the interrogator who employs coercion must accept the risk. He must be prepared to stand up in court, if necessary, and defend his actions. Interrogators will still use coercion because in some cases they will deem it worth the consequences. This does not mean they will necessarily be punished. In any nation the decision to prosecute a crime is an executive one. A prosecutor, a grand jury, or a judge must decide to press charges, and the chances that an interrogator in a genuine ticking-bomb case would be prosecuted, much less convicted, is very small. As of this writing, Wolfgang Daschner, the Frankfurt deputy police chief, has not been prosecuted for threatening to torture Jakob von Metzler's kidnapper, even though he clearly broke the law.

The Bush administration has adopted exactly the right posture on the matter. Candor and consistency are not always public virtues. Torture is a crime against humanity, but coercion is an issue that is rightly handled with a wink, or even a touch of hypocrisy; it should be banned but also quietly practiced. Those who protest coercive methods will exaggerate their horrors, which is good: it generates a useful climate of fear. It is wise of the president to reiterate U.S. support for international agreements banning torture, and it is wise for American interrogators to employ whatever coercive methods work. It is also smart not to discuss the matter with anyone.

If interrogators step over the line from coercion to outright torture, they should be held personally responsible. But no interrogator is ever going to be prosecuted for keeping Khalid Sheikh Mohammed awake, cold, alone, and uncomfortable. Nor should he be.

POMPADOUR
WITH A MONKEY
WRENCH

JUNE 2004

I wanted to write about the 2004 presidential campaign, and looking at it a year in advance it was shaping up to be uninteresting—a shoo-in for President Bush. Sharpton's candidacy was hardly vital, but I figured it would at least be colorful. Following his campaign would give me a less-traveled angle on the political year. As it happened, winds began to blow differently, the Democratic primaries turned out to be hotly contested, and, as of this writing, the general election was still very much in doubt. Sharpton's futile campaign proved to be very revealing about him, and demonstrated some significant changes in the nature of African-American politics.

"How does a movement-based political agenda sustain itself in the face of the success that it itself has wrought? It doesn't. It becomes farce."
—Debra J. Dickerson, The End of Blackness

The Democratic primary race was well under way last year when I went looking for Al Sharpton's national campaign headquarters. It was a hot late-summer day in Washington, D.C., and steam rose from the streets as I drove south from downtown toward Fort McNair, looking for the address given me by Frank Watkins, Sharpton's campaign manager.

I had met Watkins and his candidate two months earlier, on a day when they were shopping for office space. At that point they were just getting started. Sharpton had formally announced his candidacy only weeks before, and the primary season wouldn't begin until January. He strolled noncommittally behind Watkins through a spacious second-floor location over a big Greek restaurant off DuPont Circle, listening with his head tilted and his eyes at half mast as his campaign manager described how each space might be used, where phone banks and computers might be set up, where volunteers might stuff envelopes or unpack posters and pamphlets. I had pictured the place, months ahead, alive with the industry of democracy.

Now the race was on. The nine candidates had already met for several televised debates, in which Sharpton's cheerful pugnacity had made him an early audience favorite. He was clearly the most entertaining politician on the stump. His name showed surprising strength in some initial polls. Of course, no one really thought the notorious Harlem rabble-rouser could be elected president, but Sharpton was already an undeniable force in New York City politics; and if he could rally black voters nationwide, the way Jesse Jackson had in his two 1980s presidential campaigns (both involving Watkins), he might arrive at the party's convention, in Boston, with real clout. To accomplish that he would have to score big in the District of Columbia's otherwise insignificant January balloting. It was an unofficial and nonbinding event, but because it was the first actual tally and a majority of its voters were African-American, it would gauge Sharpton's core strength—or lack of it. This was one reason why he wanted his campaign headquarters here.

The address Watkins had given me was nowhere near DuPont Circle; evidently, they had decided on a different place. I found the street in a neighborhood lined with tall apartment buildings, but as I was counting down to the right address, the street abruptly ended. Before me was a small park, and surrounding it were blocks of two-story row houses. I parked my car and went looking on foot.

It seemed an unlikely place for a political office, so I stopped a man on the sidewalk and asked for help. He made a face that mirrored my doubts. "There are no offices here," he said. "Just homes."

When I found the right number, I was standing before a simple residence. A dusty old motorcycle, long unused, was parked to one side of the front door. There were no posters or festive bunting. I double-checked the address and rang the bell.

Watkins opened the door. A dour man with thinning hair, he wore shorts, bedroom slippers, and a red T-shirt over his small pot belly. Noting my surprise at the surroundings, he executed a slight bow and swept his arms wide. "Welcome to the Al Sharpton for President National Campaign Headquarters," he said.

For me, it was like the scene in *The Wizard of Oz* when Dorothy glimpses the man behind the curtain. I hadn't expected a juggernaut; Sharpton was at best a minor candidate. But even the most rudimentary campaign has an office and a staff. Watkins was running this one from his living room.

He wasn't happy about it. In fact, just a few weeks later, as the primaries were about to begin, he would resign. This would leave the Sharpton campaign moneyless, virtually staffless, organizationless, and—as the primaries would show—supportless. The campaign had only one thing.

A candidate.

BOOKER T. BELLBOTTOMS

Of all the details I learned about Al Sharpton while sifting through the alp of stories devoted to him since he bellowed his way to notoriety more than fifteen years ago in New York City, the one that struck me most was this: he was in grade school when he began calling himself "Reverend." After evincing a precocious aptitude for preaching, Sharpton was "ordained" by his pastor, a precipitate step in his Pentecostal church that required no education, training, or certification.

Picture him behind a classroom desk, a fat, imperious ten-year-old boy, inscribing his name at the top of an assignment, gripping his pencil mightily, practicing the dips and curves of his new honorific. Picture him standing his ground before a surprised teacher, or proclaiming his sudden eminence to the other children on the playground, where he excels at none of the contests that earn respect in a boy's world. These are the images that came to mind last June, when I saw Sharpton in person for the first time, a fifty-year-old man arriving to give a speech at a political conference at the Omni Shoreham Hotel, in Washington.

He briskly and commandingly crossed the lobby, head up, eyes forward, heedless of the fuss stirred by his arrival—camera lights, shouts of "Reverend!" and the sudden coalescence of a small mob. Sharpton in person is theatrically aloof. "Rev" (as he is called by his intimates) is said to have lost a hundred pounds in recent years; he once topped 300, and favored pastel leisure suits and a heavy gold cross around his neck. He is still a long way from passing through the eye of a needle. When he walks, bouncing slightly on the balls of his feet, he leads with belly. These days the gold cross is gone, and he's attired in conservative, well-tailored suits. His famous helmet of conked hair, which used to descend in stiffly contoured waves to his shoulders, is graying now, and has been trimmed to form a bob that protrudes a good six inches from the back of his head, a ballast for the great round expanse of his outthrust jowls and chin.

He was late. He is often late.

Awaiting his arrival in the hotel ballroom was an army of supporters: leftist movers and shakers; Winnebago-hipped block captains with megaphone voices; tangle-haired young anarchists with tattooed necks and bejeweled noses; gray-stubbled men with thinning ponytails in patched jeans and T-shirts that read IMPEACH BUSH and SOMEWHERE IN TEXAS A VILLAGE IS MISSING ITS IDIOT; big-armed unionists fed up with corporate power; confrontational lesbians; New Age grandmas; militant vegans; eco-guerrillas; international antiglobalists; fierce pacifists—in other words, the Democratic Leadership Council's nightmare, an agglomeration of fringe believers 1,500 strong from all over America, ready to act up in almost as many directions, any one of them guaranteed to make your average suburban middle-class white voter hastily lock the doors of her car. But these were the kind of people who live their politics, who really work: organizing, marching, phoning, fund-raising, cajoling. Assembled here for a morning session of the Take Back America conference, planned by the Campaign for America's Future, they were venting, plotting, and enjoying a three-day carnival of leftist affirmation, all calculated to drag the stubborn centrist donkey bequeathed to them by Bill Clinton back into the turbulent world of "progressivism" (the word "liberal" having been jettisoned after years of conservative abuse). If anybody could think boldly enough to imagine Al Sharpton in the Oval Office, it was the people in this crowd.

Six of the Democratic Party's presidential candidates were scheduled to address this conference in person, but for most of the field the event was dangerous. A mere nod in the direction of gay marriage or taxpayer-funded universal health care, for instance, would be ballot-box suicide. Of the then front-runners, the centrist candidates Joe Lieberman and Bob Graham had decided to avoid the event altogether, and Dick Gephardt had opted to speak from an antiseptic distance, by video. But what did Sharpton have to lose? It would take a strenuous act of God for him to win anything. Most people regarded him as a troublemaker and a demagogue, if not a buffoon. After swimming for more than fifteen years in Manhattan's media shark tank, Sharpton was both shameless and resilient; he had survived gaffes, betrayals, and attacks from all comers, including a would-be assassin who stabbed him in 1991. (Jesse Jackson unkindly commented that Sharpton's life was spared because the blade was so short and the flab so thick.) No, this candidate was damage-proof.

Outrage was Sharpton's milieu. He came wrapped in such a blinding aura of controversy that he could blithely make faux pas that would be disastrous for other candidates. For Sharpton this Take Back America crowd was pure opportunity. His root political argument, the rhetorical centerpiece of his campaign, was that over the past fifteen years the party had drifted disastrously from its ideals in its search for mainstream voters; it had been co-opted by centrists to the point that "real" Democrats—the folks in that ballroom—had been nearly pushed off the playing field. Two terms of Bill Clinton aping the conservatives, and then ... what? The party had lost the White House and Congress. It had become worse than powerless; it had become purposeless. On this sunny morning in June he planned to meet precisely the people who could help him change that. He needed people and he needed money. He still hadn't raised enough to qualify for federal matching funds, and he would need some kind of organization in the primary states, if only to get his voters to the polls. If ever there was a crowd he needed to work, this was it.

But Sharpton doesn't work crowds. He makes appearances.

His entourage that morning consisted of Watkins, dressed in black and looking typically glum. Together they camped in a large side room across the corridor from the ballroom. Sharpton paced in the empty space, hands clasped behind his back, gathering his thoughts for the performance, while Watkins shooed away the press and the curious. "Not now," he said sternly.

Sharpton entered the hall to a standing ovation. He moved with ease and purpose, seizing the energy in the room and revving it higher. He quickly showed how good he is at the fine political art of preaching to the choir. "Too many of us have been intimidated into apologizing for being right!" he said. Of the party's shift to the right, he said, "Not only is it morally wrong and politically cheap, but it doesn't even work!" Loud cheering. "We're coming out of a war that we still don't know why we went in," he said. "Where are the weapons that the secretary of state brought evidence of before the UN? . . . If you could find the weapons before the war, how come you can't reveal the weapons now?"

Laughter and cheering. He turned his full-throated scorn on President Bush: "He can't find [bin Laden]. He can't find [Saddam]. We have come out of a war with weapons we can't find. Everything Bush has gone after, he can't find. I shouldn't be surprised, because I can't find the votes in Florida that made him the president in the first place." Wild cheering and laughter. There are "too many leaders of the party who have been elephants running around with donkey jackets on," he said. "And they think we don't know what they are!" Laughter and applause. His speech jumped lightly from topic to topic, punch line to punch line, all stand-up comedy and no substance, but well honed and full of tested material. "Don't get confused; they may be the Christian right, but we're right Christians." Laughter and applause. "George Bush is talking about Iraq being our fifty-first state; well, I say, what about the fifty states that you already occupy?" Cheers. Sharpton summarized his vision for his campaign: "I'm not asking for your help now; I've always been there. We can't win unless we build a movement. We've got to go to the streets, go door-to-door, get the disaffected, the disenfranchised. We've got to get America back so we can take America back!" Then his voice suddenly dropped to a hoarse whisper. "My grandmother is from Alabama. And one time I asked her how to handle a donkey. She said, 'Well, a donkey is stubborn . . . but if you slap the donkey, you can make the donkey respond.' . . . I'm not here being divisive; I'm trying to slap this donkey!" More laughter and cheering. "If I can wake this donkey up, it will kick George Bush out of the White House!"

The finish left them still standing and cheering wildly. But instead of staying to shake hands, to move from table to table, to take names and phone numbers, to marshal some of this excitement for that "door-to-door" movement he had envisioned, Sharpton abruptly strode from the ballroom and the hotel. Those inspired to support his candidacy were left to fend for themselves. There was no Sharpton campaign outreach or follow-up. Lloyd Hart, an effusive and somewhat easily impressed activist from Martha's Vineyard, who had been swept off his feet by the speech ("I was amazed by his substantive grasp of policy!"), chased after the candidate. He wanted to corral him for a TV interview and to share an idea he had for raising money. Watkins tried to shoo him away, but Hart was persistent: he got his interview and he managed to leave his name and phone number. He was the only one who did. Sharpton was gone minutes after finishing his speech. He had enlivened, entertained, and even inspired some people, but when he left, all of that energy went with him.

The Take Back America conference was in Washington for three days, but Sharpton's appearance was the only effort there from his campaign.

As colorful, quotable, and provocative as he is, Sharpton is a lousy campaigner. A self-proclaimed man of the people, he doesn't appear to have much time for actual human beings. Writers enjoy writing about him because he's fun, unpredictable, and unafraid of being flamboyantly wrong. Cameras and crowds respond to him because he comes fully to life before an audience, his low growl blossoming into an orotund baritone. He lives for his moments onstage. But one-on-one it's as if he isn't there. A skillful politician working a crowd will make each three-second handshake seem like a deep and permanent connection. When Sharpton meets people, he tends to stare off into space. If his cell phone rings in the middle of a conversation, he'll abruptly walk away and take the call—more important business. When strangers approach, Sharpton's first instinct is to escape.

He is disorganized and inconsiderate. It is not unusual for him to simply not show up for a scheduled event. In Los Angeles in July he failed to appear after scores of people had gathered for a planned campaign stop at a soul-food restaurant. In Denver in August he stood up a panel discussion titled "Blacks in Government." He abandoned two scheduled events in Wilmington, Delaware, one morning in September when he decided at the last minute, and without informing anyone, to travel to Tennessee instead. About a thousand people were gathered to see him last fall at Friendship United Methodist Church, in Nesmith, South Carolina, a state where in February he would face his most critical primary test. He never appeared. In the spirit of Christian forgiveness, Pastor Leonard Huggins rescheduled the event, and this time the candidate came; but the crowd was only about a tenth the size it had been before. Sharpton pulled out all the stops in his speech anyway. Afterward, according to the *Washington Post* reporter Hanna Rosin, he accepted donations (a "love offering") from the audience but stayed aloof from the people who had come to see him, eating lunch on a dais with the pastor and church elders, speaking briefly to reporters, and then exiting "out the side door."

At rallies and picnics Sharpton will stick to his own small entourage—usually Marjorie Harris-Smikle, the head of his National Action Network;

Eddie Harris, a filmmaker (and Marjorie's brother); and one or two local contacts. No socializing, no pressing the flesh, no dialogue with actual voters. His campaign workers have asked him if he's afraid of people, or whether he even likes them. Sharpton dismisses such questions as criticism, which he does not take well. A veil of scorn descends over his face, and he turns away.

"It's just not in my personality construct to worry about others' reactions," he told *The Christian Science Monitor* last year. "It's kind of hard when you've been marching to your own drummer all your life, to start listening to other beats now."

Sharpton has been somebody since he was a child. At the 1964 New York World's Fair, he earned small-time fame as a wunderkind preacher. After his father, Alfred Sr., walked out on the family that same year, Sharpton started aggressively seeking father figures or mentors—some of whom, including Jesse Jackson, have on occasion resisted his embrace. On the list are his childhood pastor, Bishop Frederick Douglass Washington; the soul singer James Brown (whose hair inspired Sharpton's startling do); the boxing promoter Don King; and Adam Clayton Powell Jr., a skirt-chasing, high-living former Harlem minister and Democratic congressman—who, Sharpton says admiringly, once told the interviewer David Frost, "I'm the only man in America, black or white, who doesn't give a damn about what people think." Of all his acknowledged role models, Powell is the one about whom Sharpton is most enthusiastic.

It's an old loyalty, and reveals Sharpton as what few people recognize him to be: an anachronism. Powell was one himself. Even at his height, during the 1950s and 1960s, he was more like a character from the glamorous Harlem Renaissance of the Roaring Twenties, with his fine suits and immaculately groomed straightened hair. He certainly did his part for racial empowerment and social reform, but with Powell there was always the sense—which he encouraged—that ultimately he was in the game for himself. He was slick in an era of moral piety, an individualist during a broad awakening of racial identity, an establishment figure (albeit a rakish one) at a time of social rebellion. Sharpton attached himself to Powell when other young black men were drawn to Martin Luther King Jr. and Malcolm X.

"Adam had a defiance and self-confidence that were very appealing," Sharpton told me that day in June, before launching happily into the story of how, as a boy, he had gone with his sister to hear Powell preach. He was so taken with Powell that he dragged his sister with him back to the pastor's office, and demanded to be seen.

"Who should I tell the pastor is calling?" Powell's secretary asked.

"Reverend Alfred Sharpton," the boy said.

It turned out that Powell had heard about the World's Fair boy preacher. "He said, 'Let the kid ride with us,'" Sharpton recalled. "We went to Times Square and Sardi's Restaurant. I remember sitting at Sardi's with Lucille Ball at the next table. I felt like I was in a different world."

Latching on to Powell may have been a bold political move for Sharpton (his first mentor, Bishop Washington, was a Republican), but to the budding black revolutionaries in the schoolyard, Sharpton was a joke.

"This was in the days of the Black Panthers," he said. "We would have debates over tactics for the movement. I was always into nonviolence and integration. They used to call me Booker T. Bellbottoms."

His schoolmates saw him as a throwback then—and despite all the changes in the world and in him since then, he remains one today. He is a man with a megaphone, standing on a street corner trying to whip up enthusiasm for a protest march that ended thirty years ago. His pitch is pure nostalgia. His campaigns against police brutality have scored some important points in the struggle against the abuse of power, and have illuminated the risks inherent in arming some men and giving them the right to arrest and subdue others; but they no longer strike a deep racial chord in a country where the police chiefs of major cities are as likely to be black as white, and where the officers accused are often the same color as their victims. In 2003 Sharpton embarked on an ultimately futile "mission" to war-torn Liberia that echoed the naively romantic pan-African dreams of the sixties; he got only as far as Ghana before belatedly (and wisely) realizing how dangerous Monrovia was (and besides, no pilot would take him). His goal of uniting the fractious leftist fragments of social discontent in this country into a coherent political movement is the old pipe dream of post-Vietnam social revolutionaries, abandoned as impractical by the Democratic Party twenty years ago. Sharpton's political program is a fairly straightforward call for the redistribution of wealth, right out of the socialist movements of the early twentieth century. His five-year, $250 billion federal plan to "rebuild the nation's infrastructure," and his national health-care system, ignore ballooning deficits and widespread public disenchantment with huge federal spending programs—not to mention the disastrous history of such socialist schemes worldwide.

Rip van Sharpton is fighting wars already won. He said that he was running so that the voices of black Americans would be heard; but today—compared with 1965, when the Voting Rights Act was passed—there are four times as many African-Americans in Congress, three times as many in state offices, and twice as many in local positions. And those numbers don't include blacks in appointive office. When Sharpton piously hopes that his candidacy will show black children that they can imagine themselves in the White House someday, he forgets that black candidates have been running for president in every election cycle for the past twenty years; that the secretary of state, fourth in line for succession to the Oval Office, is Colin Powell, a black man; and that President Bush's national security adviser, one of the most influential figures in America, is Condoleezza Rice, a black woman. America has a long way to go before it is color-blind, but some of the important battles have been won.

As Sharpton hurried away from his rousing speech at the Take Back America conference that day last June, I tried to put my finger on what impression he had made. The words that came to mind were "blast from the past."

THE RACE MAN

Lloyd Hart, the spellbound Martha's Vineyard activist, had a good idea for how to raise campaign funds. He knew that among the well-to-do who summer on Martha's Vineyard are a substantial number of successful African-Americans from all walks of life, including the film director Spike Lee, the Harvard professor and author Henry Louis Gates Jr., the NAACP chairman Julian Bond, and Dave Mays, the CEO of the hip-hop magazine *The Source*.

On August 8, Hart threw a party for Sharpton at Spike Lee's summer house and invited all the prominent black vacationers on the island.

"I mean, I figured if Al could crack this nut, it could be huge," Hart said. "This group that summers here is significant. They have the means, and the clout. So I approached Spike, and he agreed to host it." But the plan proved harder than Hart had imagined.

"Getting these people to turn out for Al was like pulling teeth," he said. "People were very skeptical about his run."

Among those who attended that evening was Elijah Anderson, a noted sociologist at the University of Pennsylvania and the author of *Streetwise* and other books about black urban culture. "I had never met Sharpton before that night," Anderson told me. "Previously I was not a fan, but I went because I was curious. Cornel West was supposed to be there, and a lot of other interesting people. They asked me to go on TV, to in effect be one of his sponsors, but I declined. I went because I wanted to see who else would turn up and support him. It was a mixed crowd, mainly white liberals, but there were a significant number of black people ... people who were down with the community, but well-heeled."

Sharpton had high hopes for the party. These were people with deep pockets. Even if they gave only halfheartedly, he figured, it ought to add up to as much as $50,000, which his already debt-ridden campaign badly needed. After Sharpton gave his pitch on the lawn outside Lee's house, arguing that he could inject issues into the 2004 campaign that white candidates would not, people did pull out their checkbooks and wallets.

"This guy was not going to get a lot of support," Anderson said. "But most of us there decided he deserved to get some. I was surprised at how articulate he was, and who else was going to raise issues of importance to black Americans, such as the overwhelming number of young blacks in prison? This was an argument even those uncomfortable with Sharpton could buy—that and the fact that he was not going to be even close to a serious candidate. So most people kicked in something for his campaign."

Hart considered the party a rousing success. Watkins was disappointed. They'd raised a total of $8,000.

Sharpton's fatal problems as a presidential candidate, which became more apparent in the following months, are both general and specific. The general problem is that he is seeking a role in American life that is long gone; call it the Negro Spokesman—about which more in a moment. The specific problem boils down to the sad case of Tawana Brawley.

This is the incident that first gave Sharpton notoriety as an adult, and one that he will never live down. Brawley was a fifteen-year-old girl who in 1987 was found smeared with dog feces and wrapped in a garbage bag. She claimed that she had been kidnapped by a group of two to six white men, who tortured and raped her for four days in the woods near her home in Wappingers Falls, New York. She said that one of the men had worn a badge, which seemed to implicate local law enforcement. Sharpton embraced Brawley's case, and even as evidence mounted that her story was a hoax, his accusations on her behalf grew more and more grandiose, until he had accused virtually the entire state law enforcement system of complicity. He specifically named Steven Pagones, a Dutchess County assistant district attorney, as one of the rapists.

The charges quickly fell apart in every detail. There was no physical evidence to support them; in fact, the evidence painted a pointedly clear contradictory account of Brawley's lost four days. As for Pagones, there was no evidence that he had been involved in an assault, and (as one might expect of a man with a very public job) he could account for his whereabouts on the days in question very nearly minute by minute, with scores of witnesses, documents, and even photographs. A grand jury carefully weighed the evidence in the case and issued a report debunking Brawley's story so convincingly that a civil jury subsequently assessed a $345,000 defamation judgment against those who had publicly accused Pagones. Nevertheless, Sharpton has steadfastly refused to back down from his support of Brawley or to pay his $65,000 share of the judgment. Reportedly it was paid off in 2001 by a group of wealthy supporters. But the issue hasn't been defused; Sharpton is asked about the Brawley case everywhere, and every time he gives basically the same answer.

"I stood up on her behalf," Sharpton told an interviewer at the Washington radio station WTOP last June. "I stand up for people all the time. I disagreed with that jury . . . You take a position based on your firm beliefs and the evidence presented to you. We do believe that young lady, and I have a right to believe the young lady."

This puts a noble spin on the episode, but Sharpton did considerably more than "stand up" for Brawley. Without his intervention the case would most likely have been examined and quietly dismissed. Sharpton trumpeted the grotesque charges worldwide and enlarged the incident into a bruising racial issue that harmed everyone involved—particularly the innocent accused. He did this apparently without subjecting Brawley's story to the slightest scrutiny. And he refuses to admit he was wrong. He often says, "I will not say something just to please somebody else," which makes him sound like a man of unswerving conviction, admirable and true. When he says he "disagrees" with the grand jury, that, too, sounds reasonable enough. Sharpton points out that he was ultimately vindicated in his support for the young men accused in the 1989 Central Park jogger case, who, years after a jury declared them guilty of rape and battery, were found to be innocent. He cleverly turns doubts about O. J. Simpson's famous acquittal against his critics, asking why, if they feel free to disagree with a jury, isn't he entitled to do the same in Tawana Brawley's case?

All this makes it sound as though the Brawley matter is one over which reasonable people still differ. It isn't. To anyone who has read the grand jury's calm, devastatingly thorough report, believing Brawley is like believing that the moon is made of cheese. Sharpton has flailed around in his efforts to explain himself, at one point telling a reporter from *The Nation* that he often refuses to back down because he found it so humiliating when his father backed down before a white restaurateur who refused to serve the family—as though stubbornness when wronged, which we admire, somehow equates with stubbornness when wronging someone else. Sharpton's posture is more than stubborn; it is arrogant. It speaks to both his judgment and his intentions.

Debra J. Dickerson, the author of *The End of Blackness* (2004), a discussion of racism and stereotypes, thinks that Sharpton epitomizes a certain kind of black mind-set. "It believes Tawana Brawley, long past the point when any child gives up on Santa Claus," she writes. "Why? Because she accused whites of hideous acts, the kind of thing they 'would do.' . . . Anything 'black,' however odious, must be defended or denied, and anything 'white' attacked or dismissed. George Washington's slave-mongering matters, but O. J. Simpson's wife-beating doesn't. David Duke's racism signifies, but not the Nation of Islam's. Racial profiling of blacks is wrong, but feel free to throw Arab Americans up against the wall. Tawana Brawley's inconsistencies mean nothing, those of a testifying cop, everything. Why? Because whites got away with gang-raping and torturing nigger gals for centuries—big deal, they finally had to pay for one . . . It's Kabuki. It's a stylized acting out of unresolved trauma and revenge fantasies. It's neurotic. It's pointless. It's counterproductive. It's demeaning. It keeps blacks from looking in the mirror or finding better uses of their civic time."

So why would anyone—other than those so steeped in historical anger that they embrace this Kabuki—want to vote for Al Sharpton as president of the United States?

This brings us to Sharpton's broader problem: the death of the Negro Spokesman. I use this antiquated term because the concept itself is so dated. Throughout our history white America has recognized a certain few figures as "leaders" of the black community—a pattern that Michael Eric Dyson, a writer and a humanities professor at the University of Pennsylvania, has called "an old, abiding problem." They alone were considered able to speak for the whole race. This was true on a local level and also nationally, as prominent African-Americans from Frederick Douglass to Booker T. Washington to Martin Luther King Jr. stepped up to serve as spokesmen for people otherwise excluded from public life. Sometimes, as with King, these figures had the enthusiastic support of black Americans; sometimes, as with Washington, they did not. In a country that increasingly accepts itself as multiracial, where blacks are no longer even the largest minority, the role of the Negro Spokesman is as outmoded as the Victrola. Most black intellectuals, particularly younger ones, are glad to be rid of it.

With the success of the twentieth-century civil-rights movement and the rise of a strong black middle class, anyone looking for a "black leader" in this country needn't look far: blacks in most states have elected representatives of their own race, and academia now boasts many black scholars. Jesse Jackson, who actively sought the mantle of the Negro Spokesman after King's assassination (much as Sharpton is seeking it now), actually closed the door on this phenomenon himself by running for president in 1984 and 1988, and doing surprisingly well. In effect, Jackson's candidacy carried the traditionally nonpolitical role of black leadership into electoral politics.

Dickerson believes that Sharpton doesn't get this. Although she feels that he deserves a lot of credit for some of the work he has done against police brutality in New York, she told me, "Reverend Al is not very visionary or forward-looking. His presidential run seems predicated on the proposition that the civil-rights movement wasn't that successful. It was quite successful. Racism is still there, but it is much more subtle and organic; it plays itself out as interest-group politics today. The fight is no longer a fight for our race but a fight for justice . . . Black people are much more plugged in to the system today. The progress of the movement has made it very clear to all that it cannot be Us versus Them. Blacks today are more concerned about outcomes than color."

Mat Johnson, a novelist and a professor at Bard College, agrees. He told me, "Black people are way past the point where they think they will further their agenda just by voting for someone black. Voters today are more sophisticated than that. In that sense Sharpton is a dinosaur; he's a white liberal's idea of what a black leader is."

Civil-rights progress has desimplified black politics. African-American voters no longer come in one flavor. Today they find common cause in a yearning for continued racial progress, but they increasingly disagree—just as white voters disagree—over how to achieve it. There are still radical black activists, but there are also Clarence Thomas, the arch-conservative U.S. Supreme Court justice; J. C. Watts, the conservative congressman from Oklahoma; and many others who defy the old model of black leadership. There are similar divisions in the ranks of black intellectuals, who publicly debate the advantages and disadvantages of social-welfare programs and affirmative action, the murder trial of O. J. Simpson, the implications of gangsta rap, and the call for slavery reparations. The rise of an educated, ambitious black middle class has begun to alter the formerly predictable patterns of black voting. Young blacks are increasingly unimpressed by the choices the Democratic Party offers. A *New York Times* article by Lynette Clemetson last August reported that whereas 74 percent of African-Americans had called themselves Democrats four years ago, only 63 percent did so in 2003.

John McWhorter, an associate professor of linguistics at the University of California at Berkeley and the author of *Losing the Race* (2000) and *Authentically Black* (2003), believes that Sharpton is part of a culture of victimology. Like Dickerson, McWhorter sees traditional black protest politics as a kind of theater in which all blacks, under pain of being labeled a race traitor (as he has been), must play along.

McWhorter sees Sharpton as an "inveterate liar" and an "opportunistic cartoon" who sits, with Congressman Charles Rangel, "at the gates of Harlem like the lions at the library on Forty-second Street, more interested in trying to steer development efforts in the old Big City Boss style than in lifting Harlem out of its misery at all costs." His politics and even his goals are as anachronistic as his straightened hair, and—here's the farce—he appears oblivious. He has chosen to define himself as the Negro Spokesman, and by God, the rest of the world will have to come around. He proceeds on the principle that if you insist loudly enough that the

broomstick between your legs is a pony, eventually the thing will whinny
and gallop.

THE VIRTUAL CAMPAIGN

"Fund-raising is going badly," Frank Watkins said when I visited him at
"Sharpton National Campaign Headquarters," just weeks after the disap-
pointing Spike Lee event.

"The campaign is going to hell."

Watkins is a serious fellow. A lifelong Christian activist who has
devoted himself to left-wing politics ever since his hopes of playing for
the Philadelphia Phillies fell through, he worked on both of Jesse Jackson's
presidential campaigns. I traveled briefly with Jackson in Texas during the
1984 campaign, and saw the excitement he generated everywhere. Jackson is a born politician. On the road he attracted crowds wherever he
stopped, and usually spent time warmly meeting and greeting. He would
stop at the local high school and work out in the gym with the basketball
team—he still had a mean baseline jumper, and when he moved to the
paint, few schoolboys dared get in his way.

Watkins is the one who encouraged Jackson to run. If anybody knew
how to sell a black candidate with somewhat mixed appeal to the political
mainstream, he was that man. The strategy now was specific: If Sharpton
could win the District primary in January (Jackson had won it with 80 percent of the vote in 1988), it might bump his numbers in Iowa and New
Hampshire enough to surprise people. That would position him to possibly win the primary in South Carolina, where more than half the voters
were black, and where polls then showed Sharpton running strong. And
that would crown him a serious candidate, and put him in the game right
up to the convention.

But nothing was playing out according to the script. The money
raised so far was well short of that needed for federal matching funds: at
least $100,000 in contributions of no more than $250 apiece, and from a
total of twenty states. The target for each state was twenty contributors
and $5,000. In Alabama the campaign had raised only $45.

Watkins sat in his shorts and slippers in front of a computer in his
living room, notepads and folders scattered at his feet, wearing a telephone

headset, answering my questions, and fielding two or three calls a minute. It was hard to tell when he was talking to me. He would be telling me about his failure to secure a church after graduating from divinity school (the church elders objected to his activist methods) and then, without segue, would answer a question from someone on the phone; then he'd slide right back in where he had left off with me. He did this with ease. At that point he was campaign manager, speechwriter, researcher, receptionist, scheduler, chief fund-raiser, accountant, strategist... "You name it," he said, and took another phone call.

"Al is doing great in one sense," Watkins said, his attention focused on me again. "People love him in the debates—he's a terrific speaker. None of the other candidates can touch him. But we've raised about two hundred thousand [nearly all of it in a few contributions too large to meet the FEC (Federal Election Commission) requirements], which is next to nothing. It's already spent. We need a campaign structure, an organization in each of the states. We need a political director, a press person, someone to coordinate fund-raising, a research-and-issues person. I told Al when we started that we would need at least three million dollars for 2003, and double that for 2004." He considered those figures to be modest. Jackson had raised $11 million in 1984, and $21 million in 1988. But not even Watkins's low goals had been met.

"He should be spending three hours a day on the telephone," Watkins said. "He ought to have one hundred prospects lined up, and he should just move on down the list, one call at a time, asking for contributions. Every day. But he doesn't like to ask people for money. Who does? But you can't campaign without it."

He took another phone call. I noticed that he still had a large album collection from the sixties and seventies, and a turntable.

"I identify with people who identify with the left out," he said, to me again. "And Sharpton identifies with the left out. He polls highest in the black community, and I understood when I joined up that he wouldn't get a lot of pull beyond it. But my religious background says that God can take a crooked stick and hit a straight lick."

Watkins had big plans. He wanted to run a real campaign. The office he had wanted to rent over the Greek restaurant would have cost $11,000 a month—a bargain. He had envisioned a staff of twenty-five, although he could have managed with just twenty. He has a computer program to help him do targeted fund-raising and build an organization on the Internet, but without funds—perhaps $2,500 a month—he hadn't been able to make use of it. He wanted to prepare a fifteen-minute video-tape, something that campaign workers could use as the centerpiece for small gatherings or rallies. He envisioned twenty or thirty such gatherings around the country after each debate, raising maybe $1,000 per event. But he didn't have the money to prepare, copy, and distribute the tapes, or a list of people to receive them. He wanted to do a direct-mail campaign, soliciting donations from *Black Enterprise* and *Jet* and from thousands of elected black officials, but . . . His biggest frustration was Sharpton's idiosyncratic schedule.

"I tell him, 'Rev, every day counts,'" Watkins said. "'You are doing the schedule, and the schedule should be doing you.' His appearances should make political sense." Strategy, he told me, "is my strong suit." A yellow legal pad on the floor charted the number of days left until the District primary—158. Watkins had calculated how many days Sharpton needed to spend in the city and in each important state. The most impor-tant state was South Carolina. On his computer he showed me a graphic display of the state; using voting records from 2000, he had broken it down county by county. After fielding another phone call, he explained the color coding, which showed the counties where Sharpton could hope to run strong, those where he didn't have a prayer, and those where he might still make progress. With the days counting down rapidly now, Watkins thought his candidate ought to be working South Carolina the way a catcher breaks in his mitt, pounding it again and again. Instead . . . "He's off in California, preaching in Oakland and meeting with the mayor of San Francisco, speak-ing about the [Gray Davis] recall campaign."

Sharpton is irresistibly drawn to cameras and lights, and few of those were to be found along the hot, dusty back roads of rural South Caro-lina. Yet if he hoped to make an impact, a real impact, something more meaningful than those fleeting moments of TV time, that's where he needed to be.

Except . . . Sharpton was not actually campaigning in the real world. His run existed only on TV and radio, in newspapers, and on the Internet. Watkins never got that, or never accepted it. When he left, on the last day of September, along with Kevin Gray, the South Carolina coordinator (the only paid coordinator in any state), the last vestige of real campaigning vanished. The wheels had entirely left the road. Sharpton's run had become an idea of a campaign. It had gone virtual.

A ROLLICKING GOOD TIME WITH AL

Early in the morning on Tuesday, January 13, the day of the District primary, Pastor Melvin G. Brown was standing by himself, cradling a cup of steaming coffee from 7–Eleven, looking out expectantly toward the entrance to the Fort Totten Metro-station parking lot. According to Sharpton's daily agenda, the one posted on his cool Web site (www.sharpton2004.org), Rev was to have begun this important day greeting commuters before dawn at the busy station, the first event in a projected day of classic get-out-the-vote campaigning. Brown had showed up on time. The sun was just a dull orange glow over the treetops when I met him there, about a half hour after Sharpton was supposed to have arrived. The pastor, a broad-beamed man with salt-and-pepper hair and a big jeweled golden cross hanging around his neck, looked peeved but hopeful.

"He should be here in about fifteen minutes," he said.

Commuters streamed past us and through the subway turnstiles, hundreds of unshaken hands per minute.

Brown, too, had worked for both of Jesse Jackson's presidential campaigns. He had been asked days earlier by a local disc jockey, Mark Thompson, to help with Sharpton's primary push. So far he seemed only marginally impressed.

"Jackson had a few more connections," Brown said. "He was able to attract a little more enthusiasm and excitement. He also had more financial resources."

And he tended to show up. In the months since I visited Watkins, things had continued to go badly for the campaign. Representative Jackson had decided to endorse Howard Dean, then the front-runner—a decision that the congressman would most likely not have made without his father's approval. This was a blow. Sharpton had campaigned in Chicago for Jesse Jr.'s successful congressional run, and had long depicted himself as a political heir to the elder Jackson. His whole campaign had been conceived in that spirit. Sharpton lashed back with a bitter public statement to the effect that Jesse Sr. was over the hill and Jesse Jr. was an Uncle Tom. "You are not doing nothing but playing with yourself," he said, addressing the Illinois congressman. "These people are not discussing you; they need a few cosmetic pictures to add to their profile. I'm ready to put out ads telling all Uncle Toms, At least send me part of the money you get from selling out, because if I wasn't in the race they wouldn't be offering you nothing. I put a whole new generation of Toms in business." In the midst of this spat Jesse Sr. called Sharpton "over the top," "mostly inaccurate," and "ridiculous." There had been embarrassing stories just that week about how his penniless campaign was paying for him to stay at four-star hotels all over the country—a practice that Sharpton defended ("We're holding fund-raisers. Do they expect us to host them in a dump?") but nevertheless promised to curtail.

He had shone in his December appearance on *Saturday Night Live,* in which Sharpton demonstrated a strong singing voice, a willingness to poke fun at himself, and some mean dance moves. But an hour in the comedy spotlight was a far cry from having his candidacy taken seriously.

He was the only candidate whose strategy turned on doing well in this District beauty contest, and he was the only one in town for it. He had replaced Watkins with Charles Halloran, a veteran political manager, and claimed to have raised sufficient money to qualify for federal matching funds, although the Federal Election Commission had not approved his application. Wesley Clark had received $7.5 million, John Edwards $6 million; even Lyndon LaRouche had qualified for more than a million. Sharpton had borrowed $150,000 in anticipation of getting the funding. (Eventually the FEC would give Sharpton $100,000, and would then initiate an investigation with an eye toward taking it back, claiming that the candidate might not have played entirely by the rules.) He had finally opened a proper campaign office in the District, with much fanfare, just over a month earlier. The excitement was mostly manufactured. Michael Doyle, of *The Sacramento Bee,* noted the striking paucity of Sharpton supporters at the event, and quoted a drum major with the 120-piece marching band from nearby Bowie State University as saying, "To be honest with you, this is just a performance for us." The headquarters was a small room on the second floor of a brown brick building in Anacostia, over a hair salon and adjacent to a dentist's office.

A win or a big showing in the District was critical. Washington voters are 70 percent minority, 60 percent African-American. Five of the nine candidates had decided not to run here; with Sharpton, only Howard Dean,

Dennis Kucinich, and Carol Moseley Braun were on the ballot, along with seven obscure hopefuls. It was a chance—one of the only chances—for Sharpton to win something, to show that he could rally and inspire black voters as Jesse Sr. had.

A young woman entering the Fort Totten station eyed the waiting group of reporters and cameras and approached Pastor Brown. "What's going on?" she asked.

"Reverend Al Sharpton is going to be here," he said. "He's running a little late." The woman waited for a few minutes and then pushed on through the turnstile to catch a train. A half hour later there was still no sign of the candidate. "His schedule is kind of fluid," Brown said.

Eventually we got word that he wasn't coming. Brown made a few calls on his cell phone and determined that Sharpton's campaign day was actually going to begin about two hours later than planned, at a nearby polling place. So we all drove over there.

There weren't many voters at the Bertie Backus Middle School. "Most everybody has come and gone before they went off to work," said an elderly gentleman guarding an invisible line atop the steps leading down to the playground and polling place, which campaign workers dared not cross. A small group of reporters, some of the same ones who had been at the Metro stop, waited, bouncing from foot to foot and trying to keep warm. Mark Thompson, the DJ and Sharpton's point man for the day, arrived with a megaphone. He was a young man with a basketball-sized knot of dreadlocked hair bundled behind his head. Using the megaphone, he belted out a few amplified words to the empty alleyway behind the school.

"Come meet Reverend Al Sharpton, the only man to campaign in D.C.!"

The candidate finally arrived in a gigantic tan Lincoln Navigator. He stepped out into the cold and paced around for a few moments, scowling. This absence of voters to greet was evidently confirming his worst suspicions about the wisdom of visiting polling places early on a winter morning. With nobody around except a Dean volunteer, it was looking like an unfortunate TV photo op. He huddled with Thompson, strategizing. When a radio reporter approached to ask a question, the candidate growled, "We're talking!" She backed off.

A solution to the photo-op difficulty materialized when a herd of middle school students appeared below, walking across the playground. Thompson was after them like a border collie.

"All you students who want to meet Reverend Al Sharpton, come on up!" the megaphone barked.

None of the students stopped walking.

Again, the megaphone: "Y'all want to meet Reverend Sharpton?"

"No!" one of the students, a boy, shouted back.

Undeterred, Thompson and the eager candidate barreled right past the elderly guardian at the top of the steps and chased down the somewhat bewildered-looking students, most of whom got away. One or two submitted to having their hands shaken for the TV cameras, and then quickly scampered.

It was a little better at the next polling place, where Sharpton chatted with two voters. Then he moved on to Anacostia Senior High School for a prearranged meeting with Fredericka Freeman, an eighteen-year-old senior about to cast her first vote. Freeman was the only voter in sight. There was a little problem with getting all the cameras past the guards and metal detectors at the front doors, but (in brazen violation of polling-place rules) Sharpton accompanied the newly hatched voter down the aisle of the school auditorium and stood proudly by for the cameras as she filled in her ballot and deposited it.

"This is what my campaign is about," he said.

After that Sharpton broke for breakfast. When he got out of the Navigator at the restaurant, he gestured for me to join him.

Like many men used to being at the center of an entourage, Sharpton has a way of being with you without fully acknowledging that you are there. As I hovered in his space, he chatted on the phone, shook hands with the restaurant staff, picked out a table, huddled with Marjorie Harris-Smikle, and placed his order (eggs, turkey bacon, and grits). Not until his plate had been delivered and he had taken his seat did he turn his attention to me. There is something pugilistic about the way Sharpton sits for an interview. He squares himself in his chair, shoulders back, head up, gazing off into the middle distance, the heavy lids of his big eyes drooping. (His wife calls him "Eyes.") He rolled them balefully to me, as if to say, Okay, I'm ready—give me your best shot.

I asked him about Watkins's departure, and about Jesse Jackson Jr.'s decision to endorse Howard Dean.

He regarded them as the same betrayal. "I think the fact is, the day after Frank resigned, Junior went with Dean," he said. "I think that maybe

Frank's leaving had something to do with them deciding to go with Dean ... I was disappointed [about Junior's decision] more for him than for me, because Illinois is way down the road on the list of primaries. I would have thought that he would have wanted to continue the tradition that gave his name the validity it did in the first place. So I was disappointed for him. ... Politically, it meant very little to me."

Politically, it had been disastrous for him, actually. I asked him whether he thought black politics in America had changed since the civil-rights years, and he said no, in so many words. He felt it was still about young leaders' operating outside the system and battling the more entrenched mainstream blacks. The one difference he did see was that certain young elected black officials from the North (he did not actually mention Jesse Jackson Jr. by name here), who have had no experience with the movement, overestimate the significance of their "enfranchisement." He told me, "So they keep saying, 'Black politicians, it's a new day.' But their status is no different than those before them. So the question becomes, Is it their illusion or is it their reality? And I think in the gap between illusion and reality, a lot of times, they lose their constituents, and I think that's the problem. ... It wasn't about new. It was about whether they were 'establishment' party politicians."

He still seemed genuinely enthusiastic about his prospects.

"We'll do well in South Carolina. ... Let me just put it this way: If forty to forty-five percent of the voters in South Carolina are African-American, you have nine candidates. Let's say, theoretically, I get fifty percent of the black vote. If there's not a major go for one of the white candidates, you win just with that. I don't think anyone is looking at that. ... The next primary is the Michigan caucus, which is the same week. Then that Saturday is Virginia, where I'm the only person of color on the ballot. If we do the scientific delegate-processing that we intend, I could come into Super Tuesday with as many delegates or more than the front-runner ... and when you get to the convention, he who has the delegates has the leverage."

Sharpton won just 34 percent of the vote in the District primary that day, finishing second to Howard Dean (43 percent) and ahead of Carol Moseley Braun (12 percent). He could boast about finishing second, but it did not bode well for a man trading on the color of his skin to be bested on what might be called his own turf by a white former governor of Vermont—especially considering that Dean hadn't even bothered to campaign in D.C.

The "victory party" that night was an anemic affair at a nightclub. Notably absent were any of the "grassroots" supporters Sharpton was always talking about. Most of those present were from the press, waiting for the candidate to make a statement. In contrast, 150 Dean supporters were packed into another D.C. bar awaiting their candidate's victory phone call.

When Sharpton swept in, the TV lights switched on. He arranged his paltry entourage around him in a corner, which made the event seem crowded.

"The fact that I won one third of the vote where there were only four major candidates on the ballot speaks volumes about what we can do in South Carolina, Delaware, Missouri, and Virginia in the coming weeks with nine in the race," Sharpton said. "I am quite sure that the candidates not on the D.C. ballot will take away many more votes from the front-runner in the upcoming primaries in states with heavy minority populations. Our grassroots efforts and progressive message will continue to be a decisive factor in communities of color across the nation."

I was on the other side of the cameras, in a thin semicircle of reporters, aware that the real audience for this moment was millions of Americans at home—who were no doubt thinking they were missing a rollicking good time with Al in downtown D.C.

South Carolina

I was surprised to see a pretty good crowd of poll workers gathered around Sharpton's campaign office in Columbia, South Carolina, early on February 3, a chilly gray morning. It was the day of truth for Sharpton's campaign, whose bankruptcy few could fully comprehend. Where had poll workers come from?

With mounting debts (they would total nearly half a million dollars by spring), without a campaign staff, without an organization, without funding, and without any real popular support, Sharpton had, in effect, struck a deal with the devil. In a remarkable story that would run a week later, *Village Voice* reporter Wayne Barrett documented how the candidate had increasingly leaned on Roger Stone, a notorious Republican Party operative. Stone and Sharpton were kindred spirits on different ends of the political spectrum, in that neither man was a stranger to public outrage. Stone had been scheming for Republicans since the days of Watergate, when as a young functionary allied with Richard Nixon's "plumbers" he made a donation to the New Hampshire primary campaign of Nixon's rival Pete McCloskey in the name of the "Young Socialist Alliance." More recently he had been a leader of the effort that shut down the Miami-Dade County recount, a step on the path to George W. Bush's being awarded the presidency. Everyone has heard of politics and strange bedfellows, but why would Sharpton, who rails against Bush at every opportunity, be in league with a man who helped put Bush in the White House?

There would be plenty of speculation in the coming weeks that Sharpton had planned it all along. He certainly was not above playing spoiler, and his antipathy for the current national leadership of the Democratic Party was well-known. He had feuded with the party chairman, Terry McAuliffe, and had bragged about using his influence in New York to undermine the Democratic mayoral bid of Mark Green. But the timing of his alliance with Stone, who had been quietly bailing out the sinking ship of Sharpton's campaign, suggested that it had less to do with strategy than with desperation. Sharpton was flailing. He was accepting support wherever he could find it. At first he had just accepted Stone's advice. The old Republican prankster is said to have suggested the now infamous debate challenge to Dean about the dearth of African-Americans in Vermont's gubernatorial cabinet, and to have furnished Sharpton with an ax handle to wield as a prop in the July NAACP debate, when the candidate accused the party of harboring the old segregationist mentality of the former Georgia governor Lester Maddox, who had used an ax handle to roust blacks from his restaurant. The candidate had gone from accepting debating tips to, reportedly, accepting $200,000 from Stone to keep his campaign afloat. He still owed Frank Watkins just under $60,000, and Kevin Gray $38,000. Charles Halloran, Watkins's replacement, had managed the Stone-run independent New York gubernatorial campaign of the billionaire Tom Golisano in 2002. There could be only one plausible reason for Stone's helping Sharpton, and that was to undermine the mainstream appeal of the Democratic Party by forcing whoever became the front-runner to deal with Sharpton's ostentatiously leftist agenda. There was no plot—just a marriage of convenience, albeit one of the more bizarre in modern politics. Stone simply wanted Sharpton to be Sharpton, which coincided perfectly with the candidate's own plans. But the alliance would pay off for

neither man unless the candidate could deliver votes on this day in South
Carolina.

I wondered again where the crowd of poll workers at Sharpton's campaign office had come from. It was bigger than any I had seen at his rallies.
So I started asking questions. A tall, toothless man with gray hair and a week's
worth of gray stubble over a sallow complexion explained that he and most
of the others had been approached the night before at a homeless shelter
and promised $75 each for a day's work handing out Sharpton pamphlets.
Another man nearby said the same. They were a little disgruntled to learn
on arriving that the amount would be only $50, but they were undeterred.

"Are you Sharpton supporters?" I asked.

Both men rolled their eyes and laughed. "Hey, fifty bucks for ten
hours, that's five bucks an hour," the toothless man said. "I'd hand out
pamphlets for anybody for five bucks an hour. That'll buy me cigarettes
and a good meal."

"I got no political interests," the second man said.

With the others was a group of young women from Benedict College, where Sharpton had visited the previous Friday. They, too, had been
promised $50 to $75 for the day. One of them said that the candidate "came
to our school and … spoke about issues important to the black community"—but clearly the money was the draw. Eddie Harris, the filmmaker
who is part of Sharpton's traveling entourage, was shuttling cars full of these
workers out to various districts around the city.

It didn't look good. Sharpton had been bragging about his "grassroots"
strategy in this state for months, about the enthusiastic support he had been
finding here, especially in black communities, and this was supposed to be
the one place where he had a measure of organization. "I fully intend to win
primaries in the coming weeks," he had said in the South Carolina primary
debate, just days earlier. There was little evidence of this momentum.

The night before, he had held an impressive gospel rally at Reid
Chapel AME, a simple clapboard house of worship with a congregation of
about five hundred. The church was packed and rocking. Its own Voices
of Unity choir put on a magnificent performance, swaying, clapping, and
electrifying the overflow audience with cascading, rhythmic choruses of
infectious hymns. It was followed by the University of South Carolina's
Touch of Faith choir, and then by the main attraction, the gospel singing

star John P. Kee. Kee was the man most people had come to see, so Sharpton took over before bringing him out.

"We decided to end this campaign right where we started, in church, the black church in South Carolina," he said, rocking back and forth. "To-morrow we're going to make history! I believe in taking the possible out of the impossible. I started this morning at a slave market in Charleston, and I stood there in a place where a few hundred years ago black men stood to be assessed as slaves, and this morning I stood there to be assessed as a candidate for president of the United States. We're going from property to president!"

"Amen," said a voice in the congregation.

"Disgrace to Amazing Grace!"

"You tell it!"

"They can't poll us because they can't find us. To just vote for who they tell you to vote for is to waste your vote! … You know, I've been black all my life. I've been black three times. I've been a black baby, I've been a black boy, and now I'm a black man! I've been black three times!"

And on he went, warmly received. Then Sharpton asked for a show of hands. "How many of you all are going to vote tomorrow?"

About two thirds of the hands in the audience went up.

"Okay, now how many of you are going to vote for me?"

A much smaller number of hands went up, about a third of the earlier showing.

"Be honest now," Sharpton said.

It looked to me as though the congregation was being painfully honest. A clipboard was being passed around the church for people to sign up to work the polls the next day. When it had made the trip down every pew, two names were on it. Two.

"I was contacted about setting all that up only a week ago," said the church's pastor, the Reverend James R. Glover. "I think most people came out to hear the music."

The next evening, after the polls closed, I sat with Sharpton's South Carolina public-information coordinator, Cheryl Washington, at the bar of the Sheraton Inn during Sharpton's "victory" party, waiting for the early returns. Washington seemed tired, and was disappointed that the band that was supposed to come had not shown up. Most of the people at the party

were reporters. A few camera crews were setting up in one corner for the
ritual postprimary speech. The large room was mostly empty.

"There really was just a few of us volunteering," she said. "I would
love to get a job at the U.S. Capitol. I did an internship there with Congressman [James] Clyburn's office, and worked there for a few years. I'm
impressed with the way Reverend Sharpton handles the press. They are
always trying to trip him up and they can't ever do it."

The returns were not good. Sharpton had won only 9 percent of the
vote. The estimate on various TV channels kept swaying between 9 percent and 10 percent, but eventually settled down to the single digit. John
Edwards had won 45 percent of the vote, John Kerry 30 percent. Sharpton's
hopes—that white candidates would split the white vote at least four ways
and he would carry half of the black vote, or more—were dashed. I thought
of the paltry show of hands at the church the night before. That crowd had
demonstrated about the same level of support as South Carolina's blacks
as a whole. Sharpton had received only one of every five votes cast by
African-Americans. He had won exactly one of South Carolina's fifty-five
delegates. It wasn't just a loss—it was a repudiation.

I called up Lloyd Hart on Martha's Vineyard.

"This is a great victory for us!" he said. Then he said some other
things, but I confess I was too astonished to take notes. (Hart abruptly
switched his support to Ralph Nader three weeks later.)

The defeat was so resounding that the New York papers speculated
about Sharpton's having hurt his standing as a black power broker in the
city—something no one (certainly not Sharpton) would have imagined
when he dreamed up this campaign. He had been fond of saying to black
audiences, "We can't lose!" Well, maybe they couldn't lose, but he could.
The revelations of his ties to Stone broke a week later, and people all over
the country began questioning his motives.

In the following weeks Lieberman, Clark, and Dean bowed out. By
the end of the month the Democratic race was a contest between Kerry
and Edwards, with Sharpton and Kucinich flapping like scraps of colorful
cloth on the tail of their kite. The FEC had still not awarded Sharpton any
matching funds (there were suspicions about some of the reported donations), and the campaign was reportedly $500,000 in debt. Sharpton had
still not paid Watkins or Gray. Less than a month earlier he had outlined
for me his strategy of arriving at Super Tuesday, March 2, with "as many

delegates or more than the front-runner." When Super Tuesday rolled around, he had just 16 delegates, compared with 754 for John Kerry and 220 for John Edwards. Even under the terms Sharpton had set for himself, South Carolina was the end.

Or so it seemed. The crowd at the Sheraton Inn victory bash never filled out that night. Sharpton made his appearance in time for the eleven o'clock news, strutting in with his usual small entourage, resplendent, smiling, light gleaming off the sheen of his slicked-back hair. He squared himself in front of the array of microphones, and to the small clump of reporters and cameras declared, "Tonight we started a movement that will transform the Democratic Party.... This is an astonishing boost in the arm for the Sharpton campaign."

GORE'S STIFF COMPETITION

AUGUST 2000

As a reporter for The Inquirer, *I was assigned to help cover the GOP 2000 convention in Philadelphia. All the newspaper wanted from me were fairly standard daily reports, so I contacted* Salon *and talked them into this essay about the whole surreal experience, my first with a national political convention. It made me pine for the days of smoke-filled back rooms, the days when real decisions were made at the conventions, and when reporters could unearth real news.*

There was a moment on the second night of the great carnival of hooey held here last week, as I sat about two stories up in the shadows of the First Union Center looking out across the exuberant throng of delegates pouring forth a great tide of partisan affection for former President George Bush, when I experienced a flash of pure historical synchronicity.

The picture was familiar from old prints, black-and-white newsreels and TV broadcasts: one man standing before a crowded hall of cheering people, many waving flags and wearing funny hats. At intervals in the crowd there were placards with the names of states listed vertically. In that moment, I might as well have been watching another Republican National Convention a century ago in this very city when Teddy Roosevelt strode into Exposition Hall wearing his "acceptance hat," or have been a reporter in Chicago fifty-two years later when another war hero, Dwight D. Eisenhower, rose to receive his own ovation. George Bush's standing O was part of a continuum stretching backward and forward in time, a ritual that connects us to the whole sweep of American history and reassures us of its continuance. And in that moment I felt cheated. If I had been a reporter at those earlier conventions I would have had a real story to cover, real news to break, floor fights, backroom deals, delegate swapping and defections, appalling acts of betrayal, Turkish mazes of subterfuge . . . the whole pageant of hardball national politics and plunder. Instead, born too late, I was trapped in the world's most lavish, prolonged infomercial.

Even that synchronicity I felt was, of course, by design. I would feel it again with even more intensity two nights later when Bush II, George W., stepped out onto the stage to his own thunderous ovation, a thing so loud, long, and heartfelt that it seemed it might simply rend the vault of the arena, split the sky, and lift the anointed one from his spotlighted foothold on center stage straight to the ever-loving lap of the Christian (no, make that ecumenical) God Almighty. I felt the connection because it was what I was supposed to feel. Everything at the convention is by design. It is stagecraft preserved and perfected by people who know how to produce desired emotions and to make desired connections, just as surely as Steven Spielberg knows how to make you scream or cry on cue.

Where politics is concerned, we are blessed to live in boring times, and where there is no passion, there must be artifice. W.'s convention took the ritual of the national convention to a new level. It was salesmanship of the highest order, and it was attempting something particularly hard. It was trying at once to remake (in four days) the party of privilege into the party of diversity, while nominating for president the patrician son of a patrician president—And, lo! a Yalie shall lead us to the multicultural promised land!

No detail was overlooked. To give you an idea of how carefully scripted it was, how thoroughly thought-through (and socially inclusive): There was this little plot of grass off one of the vast parking lots outside the arena roped off and designated as the place for guide dogs (for the blind) to poop. All this masterful orchestration was designed to help us look past W.'s rather thin resumé, to forget the often harsh truths of modern Republicanism, and to see instead a Rainbow Coalition of corporate decency with lovable W. himself, with his playful wink and crooked smile, firmly in the current of historical inevitability.

The Republicans, tired of getting beaten by Bill Clinton, have turned the tables, have dropped their more divisive social priorities (or at least have agreed to soft-pedal them), expropriated the Democrats' "We Are the World" rhetoric and at least some of their issues (education, Social Security reform), and have nominated a charming, moderate, Southern governor who can beat up on the Washington establishment and promise a fresh start.

And why are we going to vote for W.? Because *his mother* says he's a good boy, that's why. And because unlike Al Gore, that stiffy, W. is a real fella, a bit of a reformed party animal who sowed some wild oats before he was tamed by good women—first his mother, the most popular white-haired woman in the world, and then his wife, by all accounts and appearances a paragon of conventional middle American (Midland, Texas) womanhood. In one of the best lines of his superb acceptance speech, W. said, "I know grace because I've seen it, I know peace because I've felt it, and I know forgiveness because I've needed it."

We are asked to vote for W. as a way of redeeming ourselves from the goofiness of our own youth, from the guiding hedonism of our age, captured by the old hippie mantra "If it feels good, do it"—not to mention, at least not directly, that popular overage flower child in the White House. If W. could straighten up, settle down (after Laura threatened to leave him and take their twin girls), and give up boozing and partying and who knows what all else, to embrace what conservatives like to call "core values," then we can, too.

W. asks us to rise to the standard set by Tom Brokaw's "Greatest Generation," the folks who helped win WWII, then built the suburbs, the interstate highway system, and the hole in the ozone layer, just as he is living up to the standards of his father, the WWII fighter pilot whose dignified service in the White House was interrupted by the first baby boomer president. It helps that the vast majority of baby boomers already have, living in their suburban homes, nurturing their retirement accounts, sending their oldest children off to college (as W. and Laura are), and paying whopping sums in taxes to Uncle Sam. We are asked to finally accept, as W. has, the fact that we're all grown up—and accept our tax cut as reward.

Coming up for air after a week of total immersion in this production, swimming upstream through what H. L. Mencken once called the "Niagra of bilge," it certainly looks to me like W. is the man of the moment. Next week I'll be holding my nose and diving into the Dem-fest in Los Angeles, into the ring cycle of the real pros out in Hollywood, no less. I might just surface believing the twenty-first century demands Al Gore. But I doubt it. The Republicans have zeroed in on the one thing the Democrats cannot defend, their kryptonite . . . that is, Bill Clinton's dick.

There's no nicer way to put it, which is the point. Content as I am with our national prosperity, in agreement for the most part with the current administration's liberal social agenda, a believer in abortion rights (although appalled by abortion), the election keeps coming back to Slick Willy's slick willy. Yes, I wish Ken Starr and the rabid right-wing Clinton haters behind him had never brought it up. Yes, the whole Monica Lewinsky scandal was trivial in the greater scheme of things, and Clinton is not the first commander in chief to discover the aphrodisiac of power. Yes, Republicans certainly share a large measure of blame for the poisonous partisanship in Washington, and had no business pushing the matter to impeachment . . . but what in God's name could Clinton have been thinking, playing sexual games in the White House with a ditzy, love-struck intern? What the Republicans realize is that no matter how high the president's favorability ratings, and no matter how angry people are at Starr and the GOP for their mad impeachment effort, America remains appalled by Clinton's behavior . . . both the scandal and his classic mealy-mouthed self-defense, which produced that one line for which Clinton is doomed to be best remembered: "That depends on what your definition of the word 'is' is." Not exactly Lincolnesque. And Gore will pay the price.

The enduring vision of Bill Clinton's dick was behind Gore's decision Monday to name Connecticut senator Joseph Lieberman as his running mate. Lieberman, something of a moral gadfly, was the first Democrat to publicly slam the president for his behavior in the Lewinsky episode, back when Hillary was blaming the whole thing on a right-wing conspiracy. But it's not going to be enough. If Gore had stepped out in those early days and chastised the president himself, that would be one thing. He who stands beside a giant is doomed to look like a dwarf. Give Gore points for loyalty, and a strong turnout of Jewish voters, but that will be small compensation home in Tennessee come January.

The smell of pending victory was behind the buoyant optimism at the FUC (an unfortunate acronym, but not without a certain Maileresque aptness). It stands with Philly's other sports arenas in the middle of nowhere, at the basement of South Philadelphia surrounded by acres of macadam, bordered to the north by the old Spectrum and Veterans Stadium, to the south by the Navy Yard, to the west by a smelly oil refinery and a vast auto junkyard, to the east by Interstate 95 and the Delaware River. It's a perfect location

for security, because a few high, temporary fences were enough to keep all
but the invited almost a half mile away. Inside the fence were byzantine levels
of further security, each with its own long, rectangular, color-coded pass.
Access to the press seats in the FUC was purple; to the floor, yellow. Green
passes allowed technicians access to the works backstage, gray passes were
for telephone workers, blue for security. There were nineteen categories of
media credentials, and fourteen for nonmedia, and to make matters worse,
new passes were issued for each session, so the yellow floor pass for Monday morning's session was obsolete by Monday evening.

Passing through the outer perimeter of security required the low-
prestige, red, limited-access pass, which also granted admission to the
bustling international media village camped outside the FUC itself. This
consisted primarily of four interconnected, blue-carpeted, air-conditioned
media tents, which were the size of airplane hangars, and a trailer park for
the more equipment-laden TV operations. CNN had a complex of trailers
just to house its catering needs, which says something about how far that
cable network has risen in the world (and started me wondering about job
openings). The spaces between these trailers and tents were roped together
by tangles of fiber-optic and power cables as thick in places as Dennis
Hastert's waist, like the exposed entrails of some emerging colossus. Inside the tents the various news operations were partitioned off with flimsy
curtains, so you could peer through at the portable newsrooms of *The New
York Times,* the *Los Angeles Times,* Knight-Ridder, Hearst, Gannett, and the
other big boys, each of whom imported not just dozens of reporters, but
editors, researchers, technicians, and clerks to tend their temporary computer installations.

Much was made at this convention about the cutback in coverage by
the major broadcast TV networks—ABC relegated its convention coverage the first night to a peek during halftime of *Monday Night Football* (a
preseason game, yet!) and CBS actually cut away from vice presidential
candidate Dick Cheney during his acceptance speech Wednesday night
to resume its normal inane weeknight schedule. Where CBS once had eight
reporters roving the convention floor with sci-fi headsets, only gray-haired
Ed Bradley roamed the aisles during this one, looking glumly forlorn.
Pundits ascribed this erosion in broadcast TV attention to the diminished
drama of the event. What was once rough-and-tumble politics in prime
time was now more akin to a coronation ceremony, sans any real royalty.

But the truth is that with cable channels like C-SPAN and MSNBC, and with the collection of streaming Internet channels, this convention was arguably the most thoroughly covered political event in history.

Everybody's favorite place in the media village was the carnival tent, the west end of tent 4, which housed the stage sets for cable TV stations, Internet alley, and rows of radio booths, where there was a steady parade of celebrities to feed the insatiable maw of new media. Carl Bernstein was there, looking like an elder statesman, pasty, chubby, and wrinkled, but still ready to pounce. There was the funereally dapper Senator Orrin Hatch, with his tiny well-groomed head perched atop his high-collared shirt like one of those African tribesmen who stretch their necks, and a pale, rotund Jerry Falwell, taking the decline of his Moral Majority's influence with hearty good cheer—"Now is the time for us to keep our mouths shut," he said, biding his time. There was Ollie North, leaning into his radio mike with the intensity of an infantryman storming a pillbox, like he was about to take a gap-toothed bite out of it. Sam Donaldson came over to do an interview, and sat perched on a stool under the bright lights, his perfect hair seemingly glued in place, looking like nothing so much as a smooth airbrushed Robert Grossman caricature of Sam Donaldson.

There was Ralph Nader, the Green Party candidate, cadaverous and grouchy, announcing that he'd come "because you have to see it to believe it . . . so grotesque is the carnival taking place here." The Republicans' most prominent nonperson, Newt Gingrich himself, came strolling down the alley between the media tents like he'd stepped right out of a Thomas Nast cartoon, his round frame and thick shock of white hair so familiar that the convention's volunteer workforce kept stopping him and asking for autographs, or to pose for pictures. In another country, Gingrich would by now have been taken off someplace and shot, but this is America, where after your image has been airbrushed out of the official party photo you become a high-paid commentator for a TV network—in Gingrich's case, Fox.

The very symbol of slash-and-burn Republicanism W. wants America to forget, Gingrich is cheerfully unapologetic about his short-lived revolution. We had a long talk about it, and when I suggested that the wheel of fortune had turned quickly for him (five years ago he was *Time's* Man of the Year; today he is a private citizen, banished from the official ranks of his own party), Gingrich corrected me in that am-I-the-only-one-bright-enough-to-see-this? rhetorical style of his: "It didn't happen fast,"

he said. "My becoming speaker was part of a twenty-year plan," where-
upon he summarized for me his steadfast climb to power, which he says
he conceived of from the beginning as a military-style campaign—"Politics is, of course, war."

In his case, as Gingrich sees it, the brilliance of his "Contract with
America" campaign spread him and his troops so thin that they failed to
adequately plot out the moves and countermoves needed to sustain their
momentum, and "events" (i.e., Bill Clinton) outflanked them. Realizing that
his army was now mired in a losing defensive position, Gingrich wisely
chose to retreat from the field. He is now embarked on his next twenty-
year campaign, which involves absorbing a lot of information about new
technology and trends, writing books, teaching courses on the Internet, and
positioning himself for the next wave of political inevitability. Gingrich
claims to have been talking about W. themes like diversity and education
years ago, but I must have missed that part of his old agenda.

Gingrich thinks big. You ask him a question about the international
space station and he talks to you about the failure of China's Ming Dynasty to take advantage of its overwhelming sea power. He reminded me
of a pudgy kid I knew in college who was so determined to impress with
the breadth of his knowledge that I once encouraged him to wear a beanie
with an asterisk on top—"because you're a walking footnote." Don't count
out General Gingrich. There are second, third, and fourth acts now in
American life.

On Tuesday night the Republicans squirmed through another prime-
time address by Colin Powell, who has achieved such unique status in
American life that the Republicans are obliged to listen to him even though
they don't like what he has to say. Twelve hours after Powell urged the
party to listen to the voices of all African-American leaders, no matter their
political stripe, as though to fulfill the GOP's worst fears, the Reverend
Al Sharpton marched into the carnival tent, an impeccable gray suit draped
over his ponderous belly and the rust-tinted waves of his helmet hair reaching to his shoulders, halted, and then watched wordlessly as the inevitable
knot of cameramen and reporters arranged itself around him like iron fil-
ings to a magnet.

"I'm an equal opportunity activist," he announced. "Inclusion is not
choreography, inclusion is real power sharing. Anyone can put minorities
onstage; the question is whether the Republican Party is ready to put them

at the table." By the look of him, before inviting the Reverend Al to the table they had best prepare a heroic spread. Sharpton was last seen jovially squaring off before radio mikes against Falwell, two men of God who won't be gliding through the eye of a needle anytime soon.

I say give the Republicans credit. The big parties get this one shot every four years to project their identity to the nation, and the GOP has suffered the consequences of having been on the wrong side of the civil-rights movement now for long enough. Somebody who matters (the party says it was W. himself) realized that the core values of the movement led by Martin Luther King Jr. have long been embraced by mainstream Americans. Those still holding out against ethnic and racial integration in this country are living in trailers and recruiting from state penitentiaries. So it was high time Republicans tried to work themselves out of that hole. The effort may have been a bit extreme, but then, wasn't it a prominent Republican who once said, "Extremism in the defense of liberty is not vice"?

"Are you looking for a black delegate to interview, honey?" asked Nora Reese, an orange-haired woman in a bright red dress festooned with buttons and ribbons from Warner Robbins, Georgia, on Monday afternoon, the Republicans' day of diversity. "All you reporters are looking for black folk today, and I think there's not enough of us to go around!"

Indeed, only 4 percent of the delegates were African-Americans. Inside of one ten-minute period last week there were two African-Americans, a Latina singer, and a rabbi onstage. About the time the Philadelphia Boys Choir opened with an African chant Wednesday it felt like enough already. But only a hopeless C-SPAN addict was seeing as much of the convention as I was, and I suppose the strategy was to guarantee that anyone in America who tuned into the convention, no matter how briefly, had a better-than-average chance of seeing a Republican of color at center stage.

The truth is that Republicans do have something valid to offer African-Americans: Condoleezza Rice. W.'s wunderkind foreign policy adviser and former member of the elder Bush's National Security Council, not to mention Russian scholar, concert pianist, and expert figure skater, put it succinctly when she said she had chosen to be a Republican because it was a party that "sees me as an individual, not as part of a group." It is high time that a black person not be regarded as a race traitor for believing that welfare is destroying African-American families or that vouchers might give urban black families an alternative to sending their children to failed public schools. It is patronizing to view African-Americans as a predictable left-wing, Democratic voting bloc, and as the ranks of America's black middle and upper classes continue to grow, so will diversity of political opinion. I surveyed the locker room of the Philadelphia Eagles on Election Day 1992 and provoked a bit of a scuffle between black players who were loyal to their Southern Democratic roots and those who, with their million-dollar bonus money, found the elder Bush's "read my lips, no new taxes" promise irresistible. The sociopolitical landscape was evolving right before my eyes. The fact that the Republicans are moving to take advantage of it is just smart politics, and certainly in keeping with the basic principle of "liberty and justice for all."

Contrast that with the colorful band of inept hooligans who gathered in Philadelphia to enact that now sacred adjunct to the ritual of our national political conventions: street protests. This traveling crew, straight from window-busting in Seattle, can now add to its list of accomplishments having been thoroughly outwitted by the Philadelphia Police Department, which until last week was most recently famous for whaling the bejesus out of a handcuffed perpetrator under the watchful eye of a TV news camera, and for having systematically falsified crime statistic reports to the FBI for decades—thereby claiming imaginary status as the American city with the fewest incidents of violent crime.

There wasn't a whisper of violent crime in Center City last week, as every member of the department was placed on duty, along with help from the state police and the feds. The cops were ready for trouble, but not in the old head-busting tradition. The protesters had issued invitations. By inviting reporters to their strategy sessions and working out details of their clever arrest-evading tactics on the Internet, the activists assured that everyone was well apprised of their intentions. They actually made the Philadelphia police look good.

My vote for hero of the week is John "Ten-Speed" Timoney, the pug-faced Philadelphia police commissioner, newly imported from New York, where he was a favorite with the literary crowd in part because of his devotion to James Joyce (although this may speak more of Celtic loyalty than literary inclination). It wasn't so many years ago that another Philadelphia police commissioner made national headlines by appearing at a street demonstration straight from some official function dressed in a tuxedo with a nightstick thrust theatrically in his cummerbund. Frank Rizzo went on to become mayor, a path conceivably open to Timoney now, after thoroughly disarming the polite majority of protesters by speeding from trouble spot to trouble spot on a bicycle, wearing short pants, a polo shirt, and a (safety first!) helmet. Even the image gurus on W.'s payroll could not have invented a more friendly but industrious way of presenting the police effort.

When a few hundred protesters assembled on Broad Street on Monday for an unauthorized protest march through the center of the city, daring the fuzz to respond in the old-fashioned, truncheon-swinging way, Ten-Speed showed up and politely cleared a path for them. And when the hardcore made their move to disrupt traffic Tuesday, Timoney's troops moved in with calm assurance, steering rush-hour traffic around the blocked intersection while systematically picking off the ringleaders of the event and escorting them into waiting vans—as if this sort of thing happened once a week. One protester was heard to shout, "This is what a police state looks like!" an inanity I will kindly chalk up to youth and inexperience overseas.

The cops were so well prepared that they even had special hacksaws to cut through the piping and chains protesters used to link their hands and make it hard to arrest them one at a time. Good detective work led the police to a warehouse where protesters were manufacturing props for their street theater, and, more important, to some of the intellectual masterminds (I use the term facetiously) of this farce. Once jailed, the protest leaders came up with the self-defeating strategy of refusing to leave jail until every case was processed, thereby assuring that the bulk of them would remain confined until the last GOP delegate had flown home, fulfilling Timoney's fondest wishes.

The commissioner's exploits grew to the status of legend when he plowed his bicycle into an anarchist demonstrator who was doing his bit against The Machine and Global Capitalism and all that by trashing the vehicle of one Reginald Case, a maintenance worker who had spent his day repairing an air conditioner in a high-rise. Inspecting his damaged Toyota Camry, Case complained, "I didn't do nothing to nobody."

I don't know, but are anarchists supposed to make sense? I spent some time in Somalia in 1997, a country with no government, and encourage anarchists longing for the experience to check it out. Don't carry with you anything of value.

Breaking up the vandals, Timoney ended up in the middle of a brawl and was left with enough scrapes and bruises to abandon his bicycle, and endear him to lovers of law and order everywhere. The Camry trashers were among 285 arrested that day, effectively clearing the streets of trouble for the remainder of the convention. By the end of the week Ten-Speed's department had even won approval from the local American Civil Liberties Union legal director, Stephan Presser, someone more accustomed to suing cops than praising them.

"It's probably smart tactics," said Presser, speaking of the way Timoney targeted ringleaders of the protests for arrest. "And it probably succeeded, if you look at the speed at which the city resumed to normalcy. I don't see that there's a constitutional question here. It just makes good sense on the part of the department."

It might be wise to cool the mandatory street protests at political conventions altogether, at least until some cause comes along that's big enough to make them effective. Taking to the streets has only one basic purpose: to advertise a message and rally people behind it. A march is a show of force and mass conviction. Our history shows that when enough people rally it can touch the national conscience and effect real change.

So many groups banded together to protest in Philadelphia last week that any message (other than a kind of adolescent rage) got lost. There were marchers for animal rights, abortion rights, welfare rights, gay and lesbian rights, and economic rights; there were anarchists, opponents of world trade policies, environmental activists, and death penalty abolitionists (many of whom confuse their abhorrence for execution, which I share, with admiration for one Mumia Abu-Jamal, a convicted cop-killer, which I don't). Any of these groups would have accomplished more by simply handing out leaflets at the entrances to the FUC complex. By joining forces they may have fleshed out their number slightly (at most they numbered maybe 5,000), but at the price of reducing their message to a Babel-like muddle.

I marched against the Vietnam War back in the early 1970s, at a time when a huge number of Americans were sharply opposed to continuing that war, and when the cause drew hundreds of thousands of people into the streets at a time. Any protest march that can't deliver more than a few hundred people for a given cause ought to be embarrassed enough to stay home and continue spreading the word on the Internet. The mostly civil proceedings of the Shadow Convention, hosted by Arianna Huffington across town at the University of Pennsylvania, was at least as effective at challenging the status quo.

I say "mostly civil" because fighting Senator John McCain was booed at the Shadow Convention, the audience disappointed by his decision to temporarily drop his heretofore passionate insistence on campaign finance reform. There was little talk about the issue last week, probably because everyone was too busy eating, drinking, and lining their pockets with gifts from lobbyists—so much money was floating around that two *Philadelphia Inquirer* reporters stumbled across a $5,000 check made out to the campaign chest of Representative John McHugh, of upstate New York. Other than one oblique reference in McCain's speech to the need to "reform our institutions," the straight-talker from Arizona ate crow big-time before a nationwide audience. Meanwhile, the party was busy stuffing its coffers at lavish affairs all over Philadelphia sponsored by monied interests buying access and favor. There were an estimated thousand events hosted by lobbying interests. The Union Pacific railroad laid a half-mile-long track and rolled in 30 vintage cars, quaint portable troughs, wherein they wined and dined politicians and delegates night and day throughout the convention. One fund-raising luncheon alone raised $10 million in soft money for W.

The same sort of thing will be going on in Los Angeles next week (Union Pacific will have its rolling troughs out there as well). For all the high-minded rhetoric spent deploring this state of affairs, I doubt anyone will change it soon. For all of the hand-wringing we do in this country over money's effect on politics, the truth is that money will always be close to power. Money is the distilled reward for innovation, hard work, and, in this day and age, shrewd investing (like, say, buying an interest in a baseball team for $660,000 and selling it a few years later for $33 million), and those who have it will always be working to protect their interests.

In the old days liberals equated money with evil because the wealthy were assumed to have earned their spoils on the backs of honest, ill-paid labor, and used their influence to buy politicians who kept the workers in chains. Some of that was true, and some big-time corporations still shamelessly exploit labor overseas, but it hardly defines the essence of American capitalism today. Bill Gates didn't make his billions by lashing programmers to their desks in basement sweatshops. We have every reason to insist that our political leaders operate on some principle besides quid pro quo, but it is unlikely we will ever eliminate money's influence altogether. It takes money to deliver a message and mount an effective campaign; there is no better proof than the marginality of Nader's effort. Despite the pervasiveness of soft money, it is just fashionable cynicism to rank the Republicans and Democrats with plutocrats of the ages because they aggressively court donations.

To do otherwise would be suicide. In the Oliver Stonian worldview, W. and Al Gore are just front men for the silent cabal of ruthless, wealthy power brokers who secretly rule America and the world. If you believe it you do belong in the streets, probably armed.

I don't. If our country was split by one great issue, as it was when Abe Lincoln won election seven score years ago, it would be easier to see how power in America turns on the will of the majority. Today, thankfully, the division on most important issues is small. Both candidates want to save Social Security, although they have different plans for doing so guaranteed to put most voters to sleep. W. probably wants to spend more money building up the American military than Gore does, but even that's an issue that no longer cuts down strict liberal/conservative lines, since nowadays it is generally the liberals who want to dispatch American troops around the world on missions of great complexity and subtlety, and the conservatives who think we ought to use military force more sparingly, but with violent authority. W. wants to spend gazillions more on a missile defense system that doesn't work and will make the world a more dangerous place, and he wants to cut taxes and shore up Social Security. Gore will have his own set of favorite boondoggles. There are plenty of issues that divide them, but in the end the one that will decide the election is Bill Clinton's dick.

W. managed to iron the impish smirk off his face for nearly an hour Thursday night as he delivered the speech of his life. It is essential that he do so, because he knows the election is fundamentally about dignity. We were assured again and again that the Texas governor was brought up right. His brother Jeb, the governor of Florida, casting his state's delegation vote for W., introduced himself as "the only delegate in this chamber who has had his mouth washed out by the most popular woman in America, been spanked by the president of the United States, and been given a wedgie by the future president of the United States." There, in a normal Rockwellian snapshot, was the picture of W. the convention was selling: a well-raised boy with a devilish gleam in his eye.

After a cunningly well-produced short film that showed him driving around his ranch in Texas and chatting happily with Laura on the patio, portraying him as quite simply the best guy in the whole world, lovable Dubya emerged in person at the center of an elaborate stage that took up the whole north end of the hall, equipped with three giant screens and designed to look like the world's largest home entertainment system. The FUC exploded into the kind of transcendent ovation that can only come from a sense of shared victorious destiny. W. invoked the founding fathers, Benjamin Franklin and Thomas Jefferson, and then leavened the presumption with humor: "And, of course, George Washington—or, as his friends knew him . . . George W." He saluted his father, his mother, his wife—who had assured us moments before on-screen how "loyal" W. is—and the entire WWII generation, and then sadly assessed the great national error in judgment that unseated the old man.

He spoke mournfully of Clinton in words that Milton might have used to describe Lucifer himself: "So much talent. So much charm. Such great skill. But, in the end, to what end?" What W. promised was a restoration of character and dignity to our national life, nothing short of the kind of president played by Martin Sheen in *The West Wing,* a president we can be as proud of as George and Barbara are of their boy. And as the ritual balloons ruptured their constraints, raining great blobs of red, white, and blue in slow motion through a shower of confetti and even a mini fireworks display, as the band fired up a victory song, W. all but rose right there from the stage in Philadelphia into the pantheon of the great presidents who managed to serve their entire terms without their penis making it into the headlines.

We could ask for more, but we certainly deserve no less.

THE GAME OF
A LIFETIME

DECEMBER 2002

I was born in Webster Groves, Missouri, and even though we moved away when I was very small, it has always been a special place for me. We visited my mother's family there every summer when I was a child, and it had always seemed to me the idyllic American suburb—big beautiful homes on shady lots, a busy Main Street, a high school which was the focus of the community's past, present, and future. I had cousins and uncles who had played in the annual Turkey Day game against nearby Kirkwood, and for years I had been promising my family there I would come back and write a story about the event, one of the oldest high school football rivalries in America. The idea fit neatly into a series Sports Illustrated *was doing in 2002 about high school sports. It is a story about more than a football game. It's about the joys of community, ritual, and tradition, and, in this case, the flexibility that is sometimes needed to keep it all alive.*

The word spread by electronic teenage drumbeat throughout the leafy St. Louis suburbs of Webster Groves and Kirkwood. Phone calls, e-mails, IMs, pagers—it was big news, and on the Sunday before last it flew: "Jim, did you hear?"

"What?"

"Jayvee is playing."

"Are you serious?"

"That's what Ryan Peterson said."

The call was from Jim McLean's friend Akyra Davis. She's a cheerleader at Webster Groves High, so she's plugged in. It must be true. The Game, the celebrated annual Turkey Day game, the nearly century-old high school football showdown between the Kirkwood Pioneers and the Webster Groves Statesmen, attended by thousands, broadcast on local radio and TV, mentioned from time to time during NFL Thanksgiving Day games, the biggest event on the calendars of both schools, a mutual homecoming, the game that Kirkwood High principal (and '67 graduate)

Dave Holley calls "larger than life itself," was going to be played this year not by the schools' varsity squads but by freshmen and sophomores, the scrubs, the jayvees!

Jim could hardly believe his ears. The freckly, fifteen-year-old Webster sophomore running back, a stringy fellow with ramrod posture still waiting for his teenage growth spurt, had been attending Turkey Day games all his life. In this part of St. Louis it was just how certain families spent Thanksgiving. You packed into the stands or joined the crowd that formed a ring on the track at either Webster or Kirkwood (the schools took turns as host), you cheered for your side, and then you went home to thaw out over turkey dinner, walking either a little taller or a little smaller, depending on the game's outcome.

"I always hoped I'd get to play in the game when I made varsity," said Jim. "Around here Turkey Day is the biggest deal there is." But if Akyra and Ryan were right, the future was now. Jim would get his chance in just four days.

Donald "DJ" Jackson heard it on the nightly TV news. It shook him up a little. The way he heard it, which was also how Jim heard it, was that the Webster jayvees were going to square off against Kirkwood's varsity. "I wasn't scared," says DJ, a sophomore who stands just over five feet and weighs less than 115 pounds. "I was nervous, though. Those guys are pretty big."

It might be daunting, but it made sense. The Webster varsity squad had unexpectedly won its state tournament semifinal game that Saturday in double overtime; DJ and Jim had been there rooting. Led by all-everything junior quarterback Darrell Jackson ("It's a bird, it's a plane, it's Darrell Jackson!"), who is not related to DJ, the Statesmen would play for the Class 5A Missouri championship the following Saturday, downtown in the Edward Jones Dome, where the St. Louis Rams play. This would be only the third time in twenty-three years that Webster had qualified for the state final, and it meant that Turkey Day was suddenly a problem. There were only two days between Thanksgiving and the state final, and both games were too big to skip. Something had to give.

"If it was up to me, speaking strictly as a coach, I'd call off Turkey Day and pick up the tradition again next year," said Cliff Ice, the Webster coach, a blond, square-jawed man who has something of the hard edge suggested by his name. "But you can't. The annual game has a life of its own in these two communities. Everybody around here looks forward to it all year long."

The superintendent of Kirkwood's school district was on the phone Saturday night, pleading with his Webster counterparts to do something. The same dilemma had arisen twice before. When the Statesmen qualified for the state championship in 1979, they played both the Turkey Day game and the final two days later, and won both. But in the same situation in '88, Turkey Day was called off. The Statesmen won the state championship that year, too, but the communities of Webster Groves and Kirkwood were outraged and unforgiving. "It was the most depressing week I can remember in all my years at this school," says Holley, a boisterous cheerleader of a principal. "In both of these towns, the whole week was like a funeral."

There are places in America where football is taken more seriously, and there are Thanksgiving Day high school football rivalries that are older than the ninety-six-year-old series between Webster Groves and Kirkwood, but nowhere is the tradition so ingrained in the lives of generations of two communities, and nowhere is it more redolent of America's all but extinct, small-town culture. Turkey Day has featured the sons, grandsons, and great-grandsons of players who battled for the black-and-orange-togged Statesmen or the red-and-white Pioneers. The local radio station, KFNS, sells tens of thousands of dollars in advertising for its broadcast of the event. Shops and restaurants cater to the football crowds and the hundreds of family reunions the game prompts every year. The friendly rivalry shapes relationships among the two towns' residents all year round, and not just among the teenagers. Turkey Day is the cornerstone of the two communities' identities.

"We had protests right and left," says former Webster coach Jack Jones, referring to the cancellation of Turkey Day in 1988. "I was summoned to a meeting with the principals and the superintendents. They told me that if Webster was ever in such a position again, there would be a Turkey Day game, even if we had to play our cheerleaders against theirs." Maintaining tradition, it seems, doesn't mean just dancing the same steps year after year. It sometimes demands, of all things, a willingness to change.

So on the afternoon of November 24, the day after Webster's state semifinal victory, officials of both schools plotted a solution. The Turkey Day game would go on, but it would be played by freshmen and sophomores from both schools. DJ Jackson, Jim McLean, and the other Webster jayvees got only half of the story from the teenage drums. They would learn the next day, to their relief, that they would play against Kirkwood's hastily reassembled jayvee, whose season had ended three weeks earlier. Webster's varsity could concentrate on its state championship game, and the annual rivalry would continue.

The Turkey Day game would be smaller and less polished, played on raw talent and emotion. "That's what it will have to be," said Kirkwood coach Mike Wade. "We sure don't have time to teach them anything." The decision would gladden the hearts of about seventy surprised fourteen-, fifteen-, and sixteen-year-olds in both towns, most of whom had grown up dreaming of playing someday in the Game, and it would satisfy the communities' appetite for Thanksgiving ceremony and hoopla—the annual breakfasts, luncheons, banquets, pep rallies, bonfires, and other game-related events. The only losers would be . . . Kirkwood's varsity.

The Pioneers hadn't had as good a season in Class 6A as Webster had in Class 5A. (Webster Groves High is slightly smaller than Kirkwood High.) When the Pioneers were eliminated in the first round of the state tournament, the loss was easier to take because they still had their biggest game ahead. If they could beat Webster on Turkey Day, local bragging rights would be theirs. In these communities, victory or defeat on Turkey Day lasts a lifetime. At the annual breakfast the morning of the game, alumni are invited back to break bread with the young men about to do battle for the Frisco Bell, the big brass symbol of Turkey Day victory that goes to the winner until the next year's contest. The elders stand up one by one, call out their years, and announce, "We took the Bell" or "We lost the Bell." For Kirkwood's seniors, who lost the Bell in 2001, this year's game was one final chance for vindication. And just like that, it was gone.

The Pioneers took it hard. Big Joe Mopkins, a junior lineman, was angry. "Websters are all cowards," he said. "How much would it take out of them to play one half, or one quarter? Then they could put in their subs." What made it harder for this suddenly sidelined varsity was that Turkey Day week was proceeding with all its usual gusto, but without them. They had become ghosts at their own party. The hallways of Kirkwood's sprawling orange-brick campus were alive with excitement, the profusely decorated hallways and classrooms filled with students, many with color-coordinated faces and hair in addition to their red-and-white clothes, buttons, ribbons, and hats. The Kirkwood pep rally on Tuesday shook the school as the cheerleaders unveiled elaborate new routines and students performed skits poking fun at their teachers and, of course, at Webster Groves. Meanwhile, Kirkwood's football coaches were scrambling to match helmets and pads with freshmen and sophomores who had finished their seasons three weeks earlier. They collared recruits in the halls.

One of them was John Lothman, a six-five sophomore who was already into his basketball season. He got permission from his coaches to take a week off and resume football practice. "I always pictured myself playing in this game someday," he said with the grin of someone who has been given a great unexpected gift. "Looks like it's going to be the day after tomorrow."

John would be the fourth generation of his family to play in the Turkey Day game. His father, Carl, played for Kirkwood in 1971. His grandfather William played for Webster Groves in the 1930s, and his great-grandfather Richard Kremer played for Webster two decades before that.

Coach Wade rallied his startled new team for its first practice on Monday afternoon in the gym. "We're going to go with about five passing plays and five running plays," he told a reporter. "Ordinarily we'd go into a game with a book of about eighty-five plays, but a lot of these kids haven't ever played with each other. But you know what? We're going to win this game. I don't think it's as important to Webster as it is to us. They're going to be focused on the state championship game."

Behind Wade, his demoralized seniors were draped over chairs and sprawled on mats, watching the underclassmen do calisthenics. A few varsity players led their proxies in exercises, but most just looked stunned and angry. "It's horrible," said Principal Holley. "I feel so bad for these varsity guys. Something important has been taken from them. But I think we made the best of a bad situation."

Two days later Webster's coach, Ice, was less compassionate. At a Lions Club lunch for his players and cheerleaders he said the sympathy for Kirkwood's varsity was excessive. "They started their season with the same opportunity you guys had," he told the players. "Bottom line? They didn't take care of business. You guys did."

Driving west on Interstate 44, away from the muddy Mississippi River and the giant silver Gateway Arch, you encounter the exits for Webster Groves about ten minutes from downtown St. Louis. Webster Groves is a leafy, stately suburb centered on a quaint train station and a thriving business district. The same description pretty much applies to Kirkwood, about five miles farther west. It was named after a railroad engineer, and its historic train station is still used by Amtrak. Both towns were founded in the late nineteenth century as stops along the Pacific Railroad, and in their older, tonier sections they resemble the gilded suburbs on Philadelphia's Main Line, shaded by towering elms, oaks, and maples, with grand houses that feature wraparound porches and the kind of rooflines and eaves that were dismissed as frilly by the more practical architects of postwar suburbia. Kirkwood, being slightly farther out, was hit harder by 1950s and '60s architecture, but it boasts three hundred acres of open space and a spectacular Frank Lloyd Wright house. Webster Groves has three hundred houses in the National Register of Historic Places.

What may be most remarkable about these two communities is their continuity. In the U.S. young people grow up and leave. Parents tend to move out of the old homestead when their children are gone, and every twenty years or so whole neighborhoods turn over. The very idea of the modern suburb is of something temporary. Most people today, returning to the blocks where they grew up, find familiar streets and houses with strangers in residence. Not in Webster Groves and Kirkwood. To a great extent, these two Missouri towns either keep or recapture their young, who raise their own children just down the street from their parents and send them off to their old schools to be taught, in many cases, by their old teachers.

Time hasn't left Webster Groves and Kirkwood untouched, but more than most modern suburbs they cling to an ideal of enduring community. An event such as Turkey Day symbolizes what has been lost by a society that so unquestioningly embraces motion and change: a sense of history and place, a sense of belonging, a communal memory, the idea of lasting values and accomplishment.

"Every year it is a reunion, not just of your old class, but of every class, of the whole town," says Andre Nelson, who quarterbacked the 1979 Webster Groves team to victory on Turkey Day and in the state championship game two days later. "When we won the semifinal game the Saturday before Thanksgiving, our coach started talking about skipping Turkey Day in order to get ready for the championship game. We all said, 'Skip Turkey Day? No way!' So we played both. We were young, and we didn't think anything of playing twice in three days. We ran up the score in the first half of the Turkey Day game and then put in the subs."

Nelson is a stockbroker in his early forties. He grew up in Webster Groves's sizable African-American community and says he never felt anything but included in the town. Today he lives in Ballwin, a nearby suburb, but he attends the Turkey Day game every year and says he may move back to Webster Groves. "I'd like to send my kids to Webster Groves High School," he says.

Similar sentiments abound in Kirkwood. "If we took you to Kirkwood High, then to Webster High, you wouldn't know the difference," says Jones, the old Webster Groves football coach, who now does substitute teaching at Kirkwood. "You couldn't tell the kids apart, or their parents. Turkey Day is just your basic bragging-rights game. Around here, the words 'Turkey Day' are a synonym for a big game or a big deal. If you say, 'This is my Turkey Day,' people know exactly what you mean."

The fact that the event revolves around football doesn't trouble Webster principal Pat Voss, who brags about her school's female teams and rattles off all the rallies, contests, awards presentations, and other activities the school organizes to involve students whose interests don't lean toward sports. "I've always had a great interest in student activities of all kinds, but the key at any school is to establish a positive culture," Voss says. "An event like this gives students a sense of ownership of the school. The event gives the students a spark of connection with each other and with the larger community, whether they are cheerleaders, band members, committee members, or just fans."

The Turkey Day game was already a tradition of twenty-eight years' standing when Harry Kaufman played in his first one, for Kirkwood, back in 1935. He played again the next year. He's now eighty-five and lives in University City, just a few miles away.

"We wore leather helmets, shoulder pads, canvas pants, and wool jerseys," Kaufman says. "I wore these big clodhopper cleats that must have been a half to three quarters of an inch long. I was a running back. We used a T formation, and the coach had me call the plays even though Fred Shans was our quarterback. Thousands of people came to the game even then."

Kirkwood lost both Turkey Day games in which Kaufman played; in fact the team failed in both games to score a point. Kirkwood was terrorized by a Webster player named Gale Keane, who was recently inducted into his school's Hall of Fame.

"We beat Kirkwood three times while I was playing," says Keane, who is also eighty-five. "We didn't have a quarterback. I was more of a running back, and the center just snapped me the ball. Sometimes I threw it. We had this one play where I would get the snap, turn around like I was going to hand it to someone else, and then just run backward through the hole up the middle. Worked like a charm. I also remember intercepting a lot of passes. I don't know how I did it, because I was half blind even then, and I couldn't play with my glasses on, and sometimes it would be almost dark by the time the game ended. But I was bigger than most of the other fellows, so it was pretty hard for them to stop me." Keane settled in Kirkwood, where he raised two sons and a daughter who attended Kirkwood High. Given the closeness of the communities, many people have switched loyalties over the years.

Elaine Jenkins remembers her husband throwing the dramatic winning touchdown pass to Kay Felker that won the 1939 game for Kirkwood. Harold Jenkins was also Kirkwood's quarterback in '38 and '40. He died thirteen years ago. He rarely missed a Turkey Day game once he returned from World War II, and his family treasures its scrapbooks of news clippings about his high school heroics. "Even back then, everybody went to Turkey Day," Elaine says. "You wouldn't even think about not going. It cost fifty cents to get in, and there would be thousands of people. I was dating Harold, but I think he was dating every other girl in the high school."

She lost track of him when he joined the Navy as a pilot after graduation. But after the war they met again at a Kirkwood swimming club, married, and had two daughters, one of whose sons now marches for the enemy. "My grandson Michael Barry marches in the Webster Groves High School band!" Elaine says. "I look at those colors, black and orange, and I can't get used to it. I never thought I'd live to see the day!"

In 1951 Robert Stone, vice president of the Frisco Railroad Company, contacted Kirkwood principal Murl Moore and offered to give the school the four-hundred-pound bell from an old steam locomotive that was being retired. They decided to make the bell a symbol of Turkey Day victory. Stone presented it to both schools at that year's game. The Pioneers trounced Webster, rang the Bell (as it came to be known), and then displayed it in the Kirkwood High foyer until the next Turkey Day. The Bell stayed put the next year, when the Turkey Day game ended 0–0. Webster first claimed the prize in '53 after walloping Kirkwood 33–13. During the game the Bell is rung repeatedly on the holder's side of the field. When it changes hands— which has happened thirty-three times—the winning team and its fans typically sweep across the field after the game to lay claim to it.

There is a loser's prize as well, the banged-up Little Brown Jug, which is supposed to be displayed by the defeated school until the next Turkey Day. This tradition actually predates that of the Bell by more than a decade. Both schools have a tendency, however, to misplace the Jug. "I think somebody spotted it in a closet earlier this year," said Mike Havener, one of the Kirkwood coaches, earlier this season. "I'm sure we'll find it in time to return it to Webster after this year's game."

Great pains are taken by both communities to stress the friendliness of this local feud. The first Turkey Day game was arranged in 1907, it is said, by school administrators looking for a constructive alternative to gang fights in the cornfields among teenagers from the two towns. The tradition used to include pranks. Webster students, the proud orange and black, would scatter the hallways of Kirkwood High with rotting oranges and pumpkins. Kirkwood students countered with tomatoes.

For many years in the 1970s, Carl's Drive Inn, a popular eatery on Manchester Road about halfway between the two schools, was divided right down the middle. Kirkwood students had one half of the restaurant and Webster students the other, and neither group would cross the invisible line, even if the other side was empty. Each group even had its own door. Sometimes food fights would erupt between the rival groups, and sometimes fistfights. In recent years, however, both schools have worked hard to eliminate the more unseemly aspects of their rivalry.

In keeping with the game's original intent, the schools have developed a calendar of cooperative events leading up to the game. They sponsor a Friendship Dance at the school that is not hosting the game. (This year it was Kirkwood.) There is an annual dinner, the Ray Moss Banquet, for the football teams and the cheerleading squads. There are interfaith church services for both teams, and on the morning of Turkey Day the cheerleaders from the schools gather for a communal breakfast.

This year the breakfast was held at the home of Leslie Marecek, a seventeen-year-old Webster senior whose younger sister, Jennifer, is also a cheerleader. "We've been preparing like crazy," Leslie said as the big day approached. "We've been spending two hours every day after school practicing, in addition to the hour we usually spend. We put on an original seven-minute building routine to music that we pick out and edit, and we do a four-minute original stomp."

The stomp is unveiled every year at the Ray Moss dinner. Kirkwood, being the funkier of the two communities, tends to dominate the stomp competition. Webster is a building-routine powerhouse. Each team performs both its routines before its school's bonfire on the eve of the game and then, of course, during the game itself.

"We also are assigned to decorate the lockers of several of the players," said Leslie, "and we make the big banner the team will run through at the beginning of the game." Leslie is a dancer, and she knows some of the Kirkwood cheerleaders from dance classes. "We tease each other about who's going to win the game all through the year," she said. "I was never a football fan before I started cheerleading. Now I love to watch the games. I go with my dad to the Rams game almost every weekend."

Any long and storied tradition like Turkey Day produces local heroes, such as Harold Jenkins, Gale Keane, Andre Nelson, and Dan Sprick, who is a salesman for a roofing company in Brentwood, Missouri, and whose pass to the diving receiver Kurt Kinderfather in the final seconds of the 1975 game set up the winning touchdown in Webster's 15–14 victory. But just as there are heroes, there are goats. It is rare in football for the blame for a loss to fall on a single player, but that's what happened in '87, when Webster went down by the score of 2–0.

John Dames Jr. knows he will never live it down. He is a big, cheerful, frank man of thirty-two who is a partner in a design business in St. Louis. His father played in the 1953 game for Webster, and his older brother Brian starred for Webster's '79 state champs. Johnny Jr. grew up attending Turkey Day games. As a high school junior he played in the '86 game, a Webster loss that he shared painfully with his teammates. But the '87 loss would be, in a sense, all his.

Dames played tackle on offense and end on defense, and he had a good 1987 season. He knew he wasn't enough of an athlete to play college ball, as his older brother had, but he was happy with his high school career. The '87 Turkey Day showdown was to be his swan song.

The game was a grinder. "Neither of us had a very good team that year," Dames recalls. "We just went back and forth, up and down the field the whole game without anyone getting close enough even to kick a field goal."

There was no score with just a few minutes to play when Webster's offense stalled at its own thirty-five-yard line. Coach Jones decided to punt, and Dames—who, in addition to playing on both sides of the line, was the Statesmen's long snapper—lined up over the ball. Counting middle school, Dames had played football for six years, and during all that time he had been his team's long snapper. He had never made a mistake. His job, once he snapped the ball, was to hustle straight downfield to take a shot at the punt returner. Earlier in the game Kirkwood's returner had failed to raise his hand for a fair catch, and Dames had nailed him. He ran downfield hoping to make another hit like that, maybe knock the ball loose.

But the punt returner just stood there. He wasn't looking up for the ball. Suddenly Dames was aware of cheering behind him. He wheeled around to see red-jerseyed Kirkwood players running jubilantly toward the opposite end zone. Dames had snapped the ball over the punter's head. The punter had chased it, retrieved it, and been tackled in the Webster end zone for a safety. "There was this weird pause," Dames recalls. "Safeties don't happen all that often, and it took a few seconds for people to realize what had occurred, and what it meant." The Kirkwood team and fans were dancing for joy. Dames walked back toward his own bench, beginning to digest the awful truth. As close to single-handedly as one can in football, he had lost the game.

Just about everyone on the Webster team tried to console Dames—everyone except Coach Jones. The Kirkwood coach, Dale Collier, sought Dames out and patted him on the back. "Don't feel bad," he said. "You played a helluva ball game, and you are a helluva player." It was small consolation. When Dames got home, his father handed him two cold beers. "Take a hot bath, relax," his dad said. He had never given Johnny a beer before.

Sitting in the steaming tub, sipping the beer, Dames made a decision. He wasn't going to hang his head. He was going to school the next Monday with a sense of humor and without missing his stride. And he did.

He was immediately slapped with the nickname Snap, and it stuck. He discussed the incident and what he'd learned from it in a speech to the senior class, which voted him to give his class's commencement speech.

"We were so proud of him," says his father. "It was horrible. Johnny was devastated, but he made something positive out of the experience. If you ask him about it today, he'll say, 'Yeah, it was tough, but after a lot of psychotherapy and drugs, I've gotten over it.'"

Dames still attends Turkey Day games. People call out to him, "Hey, Snap!" Enough time has gone by to make it a joke, and the nickname prompts a lot of laughter and reminiscence. But the wound hasn't completely healed. Dames hasn't spoken to Jones since the day of the safety.

Back in the leather-helmet era Turkey Day was unscripted and exuberant. Sometimes the game would last all afternoon, ending only when one side had had enough or the sun went down. Today football is choreographed to the second, and even high school games are as much contests between coaches and game plans as they are tests of brawn and grit. Teams scout each other for weeks, scour game films for tendencies and to plot counterstrategy. But events had conspired to make this year's Turkey Day game a throwback. Neither Kirkwood nor Webster knew what to expect from the other. Kirkwood was fielding an inexperienced, unpracticed squad with the kind of game plan—ten plays—that the kids could have put together themselves the night before.

Webster Groves had an advantage. Its freshmen and sophomores had not disbanded when their season ended; they had been scrimmaging almost daily with the varsity to help prepare it for the state tournament games. "For us this is just another game added to the schedule," said Yarmon Kirksey, the jayvee coach. "We usually spend only a day or two putting a game plan in place, so we're ready to go."

If Webster came to Turkey Day with a full playbook, well rehearsed, Kirkwood brought little more than its passion. In the four days the young Pioneers had to get ready, the sidelined varsity players (in many cases their older brothers) had fired them up. If Webster was going to the state finals, and if the Kirkwood upperclassmen weren't going to get their shot, then at least they were going to bring back the Bell. Webster Groves had won it the last two times, so Kirkwood's seniors were in danger of going their whole high school football careers without a Turkey Day victory. "It's not a question of *wanting* the Bell," said Big Joe Mopkins, the Kirkwood lineman. "The Bell is the only thing left for us. We *have* to have it."

Thanksgiving Day was cold and sunny at Ray Moss Field (named after an esteemed former Webster football coach). The soggy remains of the previous night's bonfire filled a stone pit beyond the east end zone, and the air smelled faintly of burning leaves and wood. The high school's grounds crew had painted a black-and-orange checkerboard pattern in both end zones and a giant Statesmen helmet at midfield, and the mood was festive. The competing marching bands were blasting warm-up tunes into the air, and crowds were already filling the stands on both sides of the field and beginning to form around the track. It looked and felt just like every other Turkey Day.

But there was Blake Earnhart on the Kirkwood sideline, looking forlorn, bare-armed against the chill in his white-and-red varsity jersey, hands thrust deep into his baggy blue jeans. The eighteen-year-old had been an all-conference center and defensive end for the Pioneers. This was supposed to have been his day, his last big football game. Instead, he was watching his oversized kid brother, Matt, a freshman, warm up. "It's painful," Blake said. "I started playing football in the eighth grade, and I've grown up dreaming about playing here. Now, not only do I not get to play, I have to watch our rival team go play for the state championship. On top of that, my little brother, a freshman who never even played football before this year, gets to play."

Varsity wide receiver Martin Drummond was out on the field helping to coax the Kirkwood underclassmen through warm-ups. He had rebounded somewhat from his depression earlier in the week but was still sad. He had watched his brother Greg play in this game in 1996 and lose. "He came home all upset," said Martin. "I couldn't understand why it was such a big deal—a bell. But as I got older I understood what it really meant. It's a memory you make for yourself. So far every year since I started high school, Webster has won that bell. This year I really wanted to win it back. I wanted to play in this game so bad. I went to the Webster semifinal game, and when they won in double overtime, my heart just broke completely down. After graduation I'm planning to go into the Navy, so I'll probably never play in another football game."

Martin predicted victory for Kirkwood's underclassmen. "Before we came over here, I told them, 'Promise me you are going to win back the

Bell.' And they looked me in the eye and promised they would. And I believe it."

Martin and his teammates, all of them in their white-and-red jerseys, formed a raucous cheering section that moved up and down the field with the action, bellowing encouragement to their proxies through a giant white plastic cone. On the Webster side of the field, a few of the varsity Statesmen watched the action, with a comparative lack of interest. Darrell Jackson tossed a football casually with a teammate. They had used the field all morning to practice for their big Saturday game. They looked like varsity players forced to attend a jayvee game.

Coach Wade had called it days before: Kirkwood had all the passion for this game. Football students, take note—in the contest between desire and preparation, bet on desire.

Kirkwood dominated from the start. A tall, fast freshman named Jeremy Maclin, whom Webster had never seen before, carried the ball on nearly every play. Lining up in a single wing, he would catch the snap from center and just take off—left, right, or up the middle. Webster couldn't stop him. With his long legs and quick cuts, Jeremy seemed to grow in stature with every snap. On Kirkwood's first two possessions he marched his team upfield for touchdowns. By the end of the first quarter the score was Jeremy Maclin 14, Webster 0.

Webster pulled together and kept him from scoring in the second quarter. Coach Kirksey laid into his players at halftime. They weren't playing with discipline! They were forgetting their assignments! The ends were failing to contain! "And the defensive line," Kirksey said, "you haven't shown me nothin'! Nothin'!"

In the second half one of Jeremy's long, skinny legs got hurt. Stripped of his pads and helmet, seated on the bench with the painful limb stretched out in front of him, tears streaming down his cheeks, Webster's nemesis was revealed to be a baby-faced fourteen-year-old boy. "Can you bend it?" the Kirkwood trainer asked.

"No!" said Jeremy. "It hurts too much!"

"Is your mom here?" one of the coaches asked.

"No, she had to work," said Jeremy. And his father lives in Florida, so the Kirkwood star sat by himself, a dripping bag of ice taped to his knee.

"It's just a bruise," said the trainer, looking back at the boy over his shoulder. "He'll feel better once he calms down."

Then, in the third quarter, Kirkwood kicker Andy Krapfl's little brother Matt, the young Pioneers' quarterback, launched a perfect sixty-yard touchdown strike. Andy ran out on the field to congratulate Matt, but the kid was already buried under his happy teammates.

Webster came alive in the fourth quarter, seemingly on the determination of DJ Jackson alone—"I set goals every day, and I try to reach them," the tiny sophomore had said. "My goals are: Every game I give one hundred ten percent, show leadership, play my very best." DJ kicked, ran the ball, and played strong safety for Webster. He was all over the field. In the final minutes of the game he broke loose twice for touchdowns.

On defense DJ saved a touchdown by executing a perfect open-field tackle on a Kirkwood back about twice his size who had broken free with a clear shot at the end zone. DJ hit him ankle-high near the Kirkwood sideline and took his feet right out from under him. Martin Drummond ran out to help DJ to his feet. "DJ, he's my cousin," Martin said happily.

Kirkwood scored again midway through the fourth quarter, and Holley leapt with both hands in the air. "The Bell is ours!" he said. The young Pioneers would win 28–14.

As the clock wound down, Coach Wade lined up Kirkwood's players on the sideline. "Nobody on this team goes for the Bell until you have shaken hands with the Webster players," he said.

John Lothman squeezed into the line. He had made several tackles in the game. His white uniform was dirty, and he was wearing a big smile. It looked like his six-five frame had grown two more inches. "It was great!" he said.

When the final whistle blew, a mob of deliriously happy Kirkwood varsity players led a mad dash across the field for the Bell. Wade's underclassmen dutifully trotted across the field to shake hands with the defeated young Statesmen as the Bell was hoisted aloft and carried by the crowd out to the parking lot, loaded in the back of a flatbed truck, and, followed by a caravan of honking cars, taken for an in-your-face tour of downtown Webster Groves.

"Hold your heads up," Coach Kirksey shouted at his team, which huddled on one knee in a disciplined semicircle around him as the jubilant horns faded in the distance. "You have nothing to be ashamed of. You all are just starting to learn how to play football, and today was a good lesson. Now let's say a prayer."

Darrell Jackson stood silently to one side. "All I can say is, we better win state," he said. "Otherwise we've got nothing." (The Statesmen would win 23–22 over Raymore-Peculiar High, and Darrell would be the star of the game.)

The last player off the field was DJ Jackson, who was pleased with his effort despite his team's loss. His father, Donnie, a former Kirkwood star, had in the past watched his son's games standing in the end zone, between the Kirkwood and Webster sides. "He came over to the Webster side today," said DJ, grinning.

The Bell was waiting outside the gym as the jayvee victors emerged from the locker room showered and changed, ready to head home for turkey dinner. The varsity Pioneers were still celebrating. They grabbed the younger players as they emerged from the gym one by one and insisted that each clang the Bell, stake his claim to it.

Kirkwood had the Bell, and Webster Groves would have its state championship. The young Pioneers would walk with a swagger for the rest of the year, and the Webster jayvees still had two or three years to avenge their loss. It was as close to a perfect ending as anyone could ask.

THE UNKINDEST CUT

FEBRUARY 1997

Anyone who ever tried out for a high school team remembers the emotionally grueling process of waiting out the coach's cuts. There were times in high school when I saw my name on the list and times when I didn't. Sports Illustrated bought the idea of letting me follow this excruciating process at Coatesville High School, one of the traditional basketball powers in suburban Philadelphia. The coach and the boys trying out were thrilled that SI was interested, even if it did mean that their success or failure would be acted out on a national stage. It was a reminder to me of how much things like making the team matter to teenage boys, and how hard it is to be that age. I fell in love with these guys, and on the day when Coach Smith posted the final list, it was almost too painful for me to watch.

It starts with the boys who cut themselves. They are a blessing. Take the freshman who trips in the first set of suicide sprints. Coach Jim (Scoogy) Smith whistles the start, and in a crisp volley of chirping sneakers the kid goes down. He promptly rights himself, but soon he is a full court behind the pack, his skinny arms and legs chugging, his buzz cut tucked deep in his shoulders, as if the gym were about to collapse on his head. Scoogy (rhymes with "boogie") loudly counts off the long seconds of the boy's humiliation.

He never recovers from the fall. Within days he is gone from the group of about fifty boys who showed up for the start of basketball intramurals, or preseason workouts, at Coatesville (Pennsylvania) Area Senior High. The two-day tryout from which the twelve-man varsity will be chosen is still six weeks off, but each of the hungry young hearts in the gym knows that it's in the intramurals that he will or won't make the team. And making the Red Raiders, wearing the red and black, is about as big a deal as there is for a teenager in Coatesville.

Mark Hostutler, a junior who has spent hundreds of solitary hours launching jump shots at the Y near his house in a suburban development, sums it up for many of the boys in the gym: "Basketball is my life. I have to make this team. It's all I think about."

Coatesville (pop. 11,038) is a worn-out steel town about forty-five minutes west of Philadelphia, where the land begins to riffle up toward the Piedmont Plateau, Blue Mountain, and the mighty Appalachians. The town bends like a gray scar along an old rail line between two wooded ridges that, as basketball season begins, are in full autumn flame. Coatesville High takes most of its 2,176 students from the upscale developments and small towns scattered across the surrounding hills, but it draws its reputation—and nearly all of its basketball players—from the hard streets of Coatesville proper, where most folks are poor and black.

These players grow up under the looming gray sheds and black stacks of Lukens Steel, in a hive of run-down row houses and bland projects around a derelict downtown strip whose only thriving retail trade is in crack. Here basketball is more than the biggest game in town. It's hope. It's often the only thing that keeps teenage boys off the streets. Basketball can be a ticket to college, to a *life*. This was true when Scoogy wore the red and black in the 1960s and was still true when his assistant Ricky Hicks was a Red Raiders star in the '80s. Coatesville is a perennial power in Philadelphia-area schoolboy basketball. The high school game is the town's intergenerational glue.

The boys who show up for intramurals are signing on for an ordeal familiar to every kid who ever chased a dream of sports glory: the sizing up of talent and the hazarding of ego called trying out. It's a process that began for most of them years ago with the choosing of sides on the asphalt at Ash Park or the Ninth Avenue rec center, where the nets hang in tatters and the backboards are gray from the smudges of a million caroms. Those who were chosen, who kept being chosen, who went on to star in rec leagues and summer basketball camps, have reached the ultimate reckoning at this new gym tucked against a leafy ridge east of downtown, where Scoogy's practiced eye decides who will become a Red Raider and who won't.

"It's hard," Scoogy says, sitting with the back of his plastic chair tilted against the wall in his office a few days before intramurals begin. He toys with his whistle. Scoogy, fifty, is a rangy man with pale copper skin, big hands, and a round face whose features are so large that they need an extra second or two to arrange into a smile or a frown. He got his nickname as a baby—it was his grandmother's word for an especially wiggly, insistent child—and it still fits. Mouth and man are in constant motion on the court, teasing, instructing, berating, howling with pleasure, or, more often, dismay. He's a cheerful tyrant.

Some parents don't much like Scoogy—who was a basketball assistant at Coatesville High for two years before being named head coach in 1995—because he's blunt and impatient and so demanding of their boys. But most of the parents do like him, and what the players feel goes way beyond that. They want to be his boys. The task of choosing only a dozen of them, of dashing so many tender hopes, gives Scoogy pause. He hums a sustained bass note and then repeats with emphasis: "Hard."

Intramurals run from late September through October and into November, three evenings a week of demanding drills and scrimmages. Official tryouts start Monday, November 11, and two days later Scoogy will pick his team. Some boys, like the hapless sprinter in the first suicides, will do him a favor and cut themselves. They will fall on their faces or simply size up the competition and go home. But most of the others who show up are infected with the dream. Each can see his career as a glorious progression from playground to state championship to NCAA Final Four to . . . the NBA! And the only obstacle to this megabucks, slam-dunk future is one man with a whistle.

SEPTEMBER

They come to the gym in groups of two or three and anxiously await his arrival. They wear jerseys that hang to mid-thigh. Their playing "shorts" billow to below the knees and are pulled down at the waist far enough to show off a full hand of Fruit of the Loom. They wear anklet socks under yacht-sized sneaks. Their sleeveless T's and jerseys advertise summer basketball camps and rec leagues.

Newcomers and former jayvees admire from a distance the joyful ease of returning varsity players, most of whom regard the intramurals as beneath them. They are an established elite. Counting one or two sure bets who are playing football and won't be out for basketball until after Thanksgiving, Scoogy has only five or six empty slots on this season's varsity.

Among the dozens vying for those slots are Mark Hostutler and three seniors: the short, tightly muscled Damon Watson, who considers himself, at least in spirit, already part of the team; the tall, talented, but dreamy Tion Holmes; and the lanky, at times clumsy Eric Kruse, who wants to play small-college ball. For the seniors, it's the varsity or nothing. Mark, a junior, can still play jayvee, as he did last year, though to him that would be another endless season in limbo.

"Making varsity is the best thing in the world, the best," says Clarence (Nin) Bacon, a sophomore with long dagger sideburns who is vying with Damon and six others for one of three point-guard spots. "It's everything. I was on the ninth-grade team last year, and we got in to see all the varsity games. The gym is filled, and it's so loud, and when the team comes out, the crowd goes crazy, man . . . it's . . . it's . . ." Nin just puts up his hands and smiles. "It's the biggest thing. If you're on the team, everything is great. Your problems are all gone. Even your schoolwork goes easy. Everybody looks up to you, because everybody would like to be on the basketball team. At the parties after the games, you're the man. The girls, like, line up."

Tion has a better chance than most. He's six-four, with long arms and big hands and a grace remarkable for a boy his size. Scoogy has already mentally penciled in Tion, not only on the varsity but also in the starting five—so long as he doesn't mess up. Tion has a history of defeating himself: he lacks discipline and direction. Predictably, he's not in the gym on the first night of intramurals.

Scoogy's arrival hushes the crowd. "All jewelry off!" the coach shouts. Then he lines the boys up at one end of the gym for suicide sprints and blows his whistle. The ordeal has begun.

OCTOBER

Five-on-five, shirts and skins. Ten guys on court and thirty or so who stand and wait. Getting noticed is your only chance. When Nin, a shirt, gets poked in the nose and starts to roll around on the court, Damon, on the sideline, sprints for his own T-shirt.

But before Damon gets back, pulling on the shirt as he runs, Scoogy has waved another boy in. Damon shrugs his thick shoulders and slowly pulls the shirt off. He stands all of five-five; his naked back is a taut black triangle. The other boys tease him for being so eager.

Damon wasn't going to try out. His desperate hope of making the Red Raiders survives alongside an almost certain knowledge that he won't. Damon didn't come out for basketball in his first three years of high school. He could kick himself for that. Scoogy is close to the other point guards who did play, guys like Lamar (Maury) Boyer, who started a few games last season, and Dennis (Doober) Holmes and his cousin Kris Bottoms, who were on the jayvee team. Maury and Doober wear their jersey numbers on their earlobes, having stuck tiny, white-numbered videocassette labels there. Maury is a lock to make the Red Raiders. Doober is a strong candidate, as is Kris, who a few years ago moved to Coatesville from New York—Poughkeepsie to be exact, but the boys aren't big on geography, and to them New York means, like, *Harlem.* "He grew up playin' on the playgrounds in New York," says Damon, unduly intimidated.

Then there's Nin (short for Ninja), perhaps the most skilled of the four. But he's just a sophomore. Scoogy will probably stash him on jayvee.

Even so, there's too much traffic at point guard. Damon feels that because he didn't come out in previous years, he has marked himself for doom. He always had a reason for not trying. As a sophomore it was a bum ankle. Last year it was his asthma; it started kicking up something awful. At least that's what he told his friends. "The real reason is, I was scared of gettin' cut," Damon says, offering up the worm in his gut. "I went out and saw how good the other guys was, and I just quit."

Quitting was better than getting cut: it preserved the illusion that he would have made the Red Raiders if he had tried. This was the fragile base that sustained Damon's ego. Until last summer, that is, when his mom found $275 that she could hardly spare and sent him to a one-week summer basketball camp in Reading, with Scoogy and the guys on the team. Damon played with them day and night and slept in the same dorm with them. They bonded. "I overcome my fear," Damon says. "It's like I'm on the team. I hang with the guys all the time. We always be playin' ball. I know all the plays. I hustle. Other people, they good, but when I hustle I can play with any of them. I decided I got to do it for my mom. If I get cut, I get cut. I can handle it. I think I'm gonna make it, though."

* * *

Two weeks into intramurals, Mark comes home in a funk. He dumps his books in his bedroom and emerges with a deep pout. His mom, Kathy, prods. "Scoogy's got me running with the third and fourth teams," he says. Mark knows that won't be good enough to make the varsity. He's a skinny six-one, with an Adam's apple so prominent that it gives a sharp angle to his long, thin neck. He ranks seventeenth out of 517 students in his class, but schoolwork is a secondary concern to him. Basketball is his obsession. He is an exception; whites make up 65 percent of Coatesville's student body, but the Caucasian boys have all but conceded basketball to the black kids. Mark and Eric are the only white guys at intramurals. Mark's friends call him the Great White Hope.

Mark lives in a redbrick colonial house with a basketball hoop in the driveway. His dad, Jim, drives him down to Ash Park in the summer so Mark can play pickup ball in the playground, where teams of high schoolers often take on teams of older guys, many of them former Red Raiders, and get whipped every game. Mark is often the only white person there.

He thinks he has a shot at varsity this year, but he's not sure. Scoogy doesn't like to load the jayvee with juniors, so there's a chance Mark won't make varsity or jayvee. "I don't know what I'll do if that happens," he says. "My dad said that if he has to, he'll send me to Bishop Shanahan [a Catholic school about sixteen miles away in West Chester], where I know I could play."

Later, out in the yard, Jim says, "I don't know if I can afford Bishop Shanahan. We're just praying he makes this team."

Scoogy is constantly annoyed by the boys' inability to dribble with both hands. He blows his whistle to interrupt play for a speech: "Can anybody here honestly tell me they worked on their weak hand? Anybody? Too busy trying to dunk"—he mimes a comical dunk—"tryin' to dribble between your legs, tryin' all this fancy shit. *Work on your weak hand!* That's what summers are for. The weak hand! The weak hand! The weak hand! You need to put your body between your opponent and the ball. You've got to be able to use both hands. That's the difference between a mediocre player and a good player. Which hand is your good hand? Put it in your damn pants! Play with yourself! I don't care! Just get rid of it.

"Y'all are lookin' at me with that coach-be-talking-shit look. Tell me I'm wrong. Because I know I'm right. Know why I know? Because I did the same thing when I was your age. Listen here"—his voice drops to a stage whisper—"this is wisdom talking. I'm trying to pass something along here."

Tion has shown up. It's a few days into the second week of intramurals. He's the tallest kid on the court. He can dunk from a two-step jump. He looks born to the sport. Anybody surveying the crowd of boys playing in this gym would pick Tion as the one with a future in basketball.

Scoogy runs the boys in teams of five. Though he doesn't say which is the first team and which the second and third and fourth, the kids can tell. On one of his first days out, Tion is asked to replace Glenn Gray, the six-three center who played varsity last season, on the first team. "Tion, we'll give you a break," says Scoogy. "This'll be interesting. You ought to be dead by the time you run up and down the court twice."

Tion plays hard, and well, for about ten minutes. Then he poops out. "What, hurt again?" Scoogy asks scornfully as Tion shuffles upcourt. Tion says nothing. Scoogy motions for someone to replace him. Tion skulks off the court and eases himself to the floor, grimacing as he slowly stretches his long, slender legs. "My hip," he says. "I had it x-rayed. Doctor said there's no damage. But it hurts."

When Tion came out for intramurals last season, he left in the middle of the first session. Just walked off the court and out of the gym. "I had a problem with the coach," he says. "I can't stand to have nobody fussin' at me."

When Eric screws up, he balls his fists at his cheeks and mouths a silent scream. He doesn't get in that often, and he plays timidly. "I do better when I'm just playing pickup, you know, not running all these plays," he says. "When I get out here with these guys, I tense up."

Eric has the kind of size Scoogy needs. He's six-two, and he's solid enough to stand his ground under the boards, but he's got flat feet and moves like a caricature of the thick-legged white guy. As a sophomore Eric made the junior varsity under Coatesville's longtime coach, Ross Kershey. But last season, when Kershey retired and Scoogy took over, Eric was cut. He thinks Scoogy has already dealt him out this year, too. "You can tell by the way coaches talk to you," Eric says, "and by the players they like to put into certain situations. They always leave me out. I know that I'm not as fast as these guys."

Eric probably wouldn't have come out if he hadn't received a letter from a Division III college recruiter who saw him in action last summer at a basketball camp. The letter convinced Eric that he could play, even though he didn't grow up breathing basketball on the Coatesville playgrounds. He's grimly determined. What he lacks in gifts he tries to make up for in heart.

"I hate this part of coaching," Scoogy says. "No, don't say 'hate.' I don't like to use that word. There's too much of that in the world already. Say I 'extremely dislike' this part of coaching."

Scoogy is off to one side of the gym with jayvee coach Nick Guarente, taking a break from all his strutting and hollering. His long legs are stretched flat on the floor before him, his big feet drooping to the side. In a few weeks he will have surgery for a ruptured disk between two cervical vertebrae, but the real pain in his neck right now is deciding which boys to leave behind.

Last season be got lucky. He had forward-center Richard (Rip) Hamilton, a player with talent and determination. Rip was one in a million, and he led Coatesville to a 26–4 record. He's now a freshman at Connecticut, where he's starting at guard-forward. This season Scoogy has a group of boys who . . . well, let's just say "state championship" doesn't spring to mind. At one extreme are the gifted who won't work; at the other, the inept who will walk through walls. Scoogy will keep twelve who fall in between and make them run, run, run. The rest must go.

Last year Scoogy cut a big player with megadreams and slow feet. Scoogy put up the cut list at 7:15 a.m., and the kid's parents were at his office before noon. "It was one of those love-is-blind situations," says Nick. "In that case, stone blind."

"They called me everything but the N-word," says Scoogy. "As much as said I cut the kid because he's white. I hated to cut the kid. I've got a rainbow mind. I'm out here looking for talent. The kid's mom told me her son was going to go on and play in college and prove me wrong, and I told her, 'Good, I sincerely hope you're right. I wish him nothing but the best.'"

The kid did not speak to Scoogy again. Just walked past him in the halls without a look. Scoogy could feel the boy's hatred. "Some of these boys, I have them in my phys-ed classes," he says. "I came up with their parents. Some go to the same church as me."

Damon, the muscular little point guard, is inserted into a scrimmage. He plays like a dervish. While playing pressure defense, he ties up two men by himself. They pass back and forth at midcourt, but Damon keeps up with the ball, finally slapping it downcourt and then outracing everyone to it. He dribbles back toward half-court, allowing his teammates to set up on offense, and then, with a flurry of fakes, he makes a suicidal drive into the key. The ball ends up across the gym.

"I got one word for you guys who love all that playground razzle-dazzle shit," Scoogy scolds loudly. "It's a four-letter word. Most of you haven't heard it. It's 'pass.'"

Late in October, Mark is regularly playing in the first five. He's so blond and pale he could be a film negative of the other boys on the court. His torso glows pink with exertion. Mark was the best player on his Catholic school team in the eighth grade, but the first time he came out for basketball at Coatesville, he says, "It was, like, *whoooah*. I was getting killed. The black kids were just way quicker and had more skills than I had."

Jim Hostutler says many white parents in the area discourage their kids from playing basketball. "I've seen kids with talent playing with Mark and heard their fathers say, 'Why waste your time?' Because they just assume their kids can't compete with the black boys from the playgrounds. The white parents steer their kids to football and baseball." Coatesville's football team is 58 percent white, 42 percent black. Its baseball team had one black player last season.

Asked who he thinks Scoogy's final twelve will be, Mark picks out players intently. Among them are two from the football team who haven't come out yet. Mark does not pick himself.

On the court, meanwhile, Scoogy is amazed. Doober puts a particularly good juke on two men in the key, faking a move to the foul line and then cutting back to take a nifty pass from Nin and casually drop in a layup.

Scoogy leans his head against the gym wall and howls. *"Aaaaaooooohhhhh!* That was the first person groaning," he shouts, both saluting the offensive play and chastising the defense. *"Aaaaaooooohhhhh!* That was the second person groaning. I *can't* believe it! That was so wide open!"

Tion walks through the door of his aunt's house on Coates Street, a block of ancient row houses on the East Side, several blocks uphill from Main Street. He lets his backpack slide to the floor, moves to the leather couch without saying a word, slips one big hand under the warm belly of his sleeping two-month-old sister, and gently lifts her to his face. He nuzzles the sleeping baby, delicately fixes the pink blanket around her, and speaks to her softly.

This house is his cousin Doober's place. Doober and Poughkeepsie Kris are upstairs in a tiny attic bedroom. Its slanted walls are decorated with pictures of girls from magazines and with drawings and photos of Coatesville High basketball players. Doober's mom, Roxanne, videotaped all the jayvee games last year. Doober has quite a stack of cassettes. He likes to hang out upstairs with his buddies, running the tapes over and over. Roxanne's voice provides loud, hilarious, emphatically one-sided commentary.

"I get so tired of hearing my voice on those tapes," Roxanne says. She's a cheerful woman whose long hair is woven into hundreds of thin, shiny braids. She and her sister, Cassandra, Tion's mom, who is expressing milk for the baby, practically share their children. Tion spends most weekends in this house and often comes here after school. This is also where a lot of basketball players congregate. "They come over because they like to see themselves on the tapes," Roxanne says.

Damon drops by, breezing through the front door without knocking. This is home. There are dangers on the streets of Coatesville, but there is also an emotional network connecting these boys to one another's kin and friends from one end of town to the other. Scoogy is famous in this world, and infamous.

"Scoog ought to praise these boys, not be ragging on them all the time the way he does," says Cassandra. "Other guys this age? They're already out on the corner selling drugs. These are good boys. If they're out there playing basketball and trying hard, he ought to praise them all the time. They deserve it."

* * *

Scoogy is always telling the boys, "If I ain't giving you a hard time, it's because I've pretty much given up on you." There's an example of this toward the end of the month. Tion has been coming to every intramural session, but he just sits. It's the hip. This evening he's draped in a chair a few yards behind one basket.

"Tion, get on your feet!" shouts Scoogy when a couple of players come crashing down near him. Tion stirs, stands up, and moves over a little to the side. At half-court Scoogy reconsiders, stops, and shouts, "I don't care if you sit, Tion, just don't sit there." It doesn't penetrate, but in the code of the gym, the coach has told the player, *You might as well go home.*

Eric can read his own subtext. Scoogy never gives him a hard time. He says only nice things to him—when he speaks to him at all. Eric, whom the other boys have taken to calling E, is the opposite of Tion. He has gotten the message, but he won't stop hanging in there under the boards.

Scoogy regards his surplus of capable point guards with dismay. There's the hard matter of choosing among boys with similar skills. Scoogy could make one or two into shooting guards and bump his bigger shooters to forward, but he would be left with no size underneath. His only hope for rebounds this season is the hefty Glenn, whom he calls Bubba and rides constantly about being out of shape. Glenn never answers back. He has thick round shoulders that slump when he's tired or depressed. He's lugging twenty extra pounds. His belly rolls over the top of his drawers. Seeing the boy's soft edges provokes Scoogy, who loathes off-season complacency.

"Some of you guys think you've got it made," he says. "Just because you played varsity last year, you think it's going to be handed to you. You come out here all lumpy and out of shape. Well, believe-you-me, nobody is giving away jack. You got to be hungry. You should have been running all year long."

In the suicides Scoogy stands at midcourt counting off the seconds while the boys sprint. If one of them fails to finish the run in thirty seconds or less, they all have to do it again. Trouble is, Scoogy kind of *scooges* his count. After about ten sprints, Glenn is galumphing up the rear. His late finish dooms everyone else to another round. "Did not make it!" the coach shouts. "Come November, those are the four ugliest words in the English language."

November

"I don't know," Damon says. "I'm not a hundred percent. My chest been hurting me. It started about three intramurals ago. I don't know if I'm gonna come out or not." Damon is getting cold feet. It's the last week of intramurals. Official tryouts start in four days. "I'm having a hard time keepin' my hopes up," he says. "I ain't even gonna be mad if I don't make it."

But he'll be embarrassed. "'You didn't make it, you're not as good as me,' that's what people be sayin'," he says. "I don't think I can handle that." Then he sees another possibility. "If I don't make it, maybe I'll be manager. Sometimes Scoogy, he let the manager suit up, be a backup. He did that twice last year."

It all comes down to two days of deciding. Snow falls on the fateful first morning, the second Monday of the month. "Intramurals are over, boys," says Scoogy with a giant grin as he greets the players in the chilly gym. "Now you're mine!"

He makes them run a mile outdoors in the freezing air, a torture whose advent was rumored for weeks but fervently disbelieved. Some of the boys are pleasantly surprised by their times. Scoogy is not. He makes all of them run a mile again the next day, indoors this time.

On the second day of tryouts, even some boys who should have an idea of where they stand don't. Despite what he senses, Eric remains stubbornly hopeful. "I don't know," he says. "Ask me after this practice."

Damon, who has come to the formal tryouts after all, just shrugs and smiles sheepishly. "I'm tryin'," he says.

There are more than forty boys in the gym. Twelve will play jayvee. Twelve will play varsity. A yellow legal pad lies on the floor, off to one side of the court. At one this morning Scoogy sat with the pad at his kitchen table, sipping a glass of iced tea, and wrote out sixteen names in pencil. He wrote down the returning varsity players: Maury, Glenn, Carl Cannon, Ty Legree, Johnny Miller, Robert Taggert, and Brian Ward. He also wrote down Nin, Mark, Poughkeepsie Kris, Doober, Maurice (Cup) Peterson (a six-two senior guard-forward who has shown ferocity under the basket), Dante Buchanan (a gaunt junior forward with terrific skills but a brooding personality that troubles the coaches), Preston Jones (a dignified senior guard with good moves whom Scoogy cut last year), Keenan Chase (a forward from last season's jayvee who's a prodigious leaper), and Ramzee

Stanton (a promising junior forward-center who recently transferred to Coatesville High from a school in Philadelphia).

Already axed are Damon, Eric, and a number of other seniors hustling through the second day of tryouts, desperate to make an impression. They are as oblivious to their fates as Tion, who is still lounging in the corner, holding a big blue winter coat over his long legs. It's as though he believes that making the team is simply a matter of showing up. His hip is fine now, but he's in danger of flunking one of his classes and becoming ineligible. "My teacher gonna talk to Scoogy about it," he says. Asked about Tion, Scoogy just shakes his head.

Scoogy had planned to hang this list of sixteen outside his office tomorrow morning and take one more day to make the last four cuts. But after practice the list is further trimmed. The coach stands in the middle of the gym with Nick, Ricky, and a third assistant, Mark Bailey. Most of the boys have gone home. A few wait for rides in far doorways.

"I don't know why you have him on this list, the way he drags himself up and down the court," says Mark, pointing to Dante's name. "I'll never forget what he did to me in that jayvee game last year, after I pulled him out. When I sent him back in, he just sat there on the bench staring at me. Just flat-out refused."

"He's got talent, but he hasn't showed us anything," says Ricky.

Scoogy draws and redraws a red line through *D. Buchanan.*

The next target on the list is Poughkeepsie Kris. His skills are on a par with those of the other top point-guard candidates, but he missed two weeks of intramurals when he was suspended for fighting, and he's in academic trouble. "If he stood out a lot from the other guys, maybe you'd consider it," says Mark, "but with these other things . . ."

"You've got too many point guards as it is," says Ricky.

Scoogy draws another red line through *K. Bottoms.*

The discussion turns to Preston. "He's a great kid, a super kid," says Ricky. "But you can't have that many guards. Why drag it out for him?"

Scoogy has Preston in gym class, and he likes the kid a lot. He slowly draws a line through the boy's name.

"You're going to have to get rid of Doober," says Nick. "You can't keep that many point guards."

"Yeah, but Doober, he's the smartest kid on the court sometimes," says Ricky.

"I'll give him another look," says Scoogy.

When they finish, Ricky ribs Scoogy: "Man, you are gonna be un-popular around here. You ain't even gonna be able to go to church! People gonna be throwin' Bibles at you!"

WEDNESDAY, 7 A.M.

The cold morning sky is streaked with orange and purple clouds. The school is stirring to life. A few boys come wandering down the hallway leading to Scoogy's office.

"Where the list at?" one says.

"List ain't up yet?" asks another.

Scoogy strides in at 7:10. Overnight, sitting up at his kitchen table, he decided to keep thirteen players on the varsity, something he vowed last season he wouldn't do, because it means more disgruntled guys without enough playing time. He'll deal later with the players coming from the football team. By then at least one of these boys will have difficulty with his grades or will miss a practice—in other words, will cut himself. For now, though, Scoogy has his team. He opens his office door, thumps his briefcase on the desk, and withdraws a white 8½" × 11" lined sheet of paper on which he has written in bold pencil:

The following individuals should report for boys varsity basketball practice today at 2:45:

B. Ward

R. Stanton

J. Miller

C. Bacon

R. Taggert

T. Legree

M. Peterson

L. Boyer

M. Hostutler

G. Gray

C. Cannon

D. Holmes

K. Chase

He tapes the list to the brown tile wall outside his office. "I just thought to myself coming in here, Technically I'm fifty years old," Scoogy says. "Now I'm fifty-one. I like to just put it up and get the hell out of here."

Which he does. Quickly, boys in bulky winter coats crowd around the list.

"Cup!"

"No! Cup made it!"

"Nin."

"Ooh, Dante's not on it."

"Keenan made it, and Ramzee."

"Kris ain't on it!"

"Kris not on there?"

Cup emerges from the crowd overjoyed. He is embraced by one of his friends.

Nin, the little sophomore with long dagger sideburns and big varsity dreams, approaches alone. "You on it," a friend tells him. "You on the list."

"Don't play with me, man," Nin says. The crowd parts for him as he approaches the wall. He makes two fists and leans up close. "Oh, my God!" he shouts.

Ty, one of the returning members of last season's varsity, saunters down the hallway wearing a white stocking cap that sticks up five inches from his head. "I ain't got to look," he says. "I know I'm on it."

Mark, the Great White Hope, arrives with a friend. He stands before the list silently for a moment. No more worries about transferring to Bishop Shanahan. He turns away from the list with a broad smile. As he walks off his friend asks, "That isn't the varsity list?"

"That's varsity," says Mark.

"You kiddin' me? You made *varsity*?"

Poughkeepsie Kris has gotten the word. He comes down the hall, his head down, his face a mask of anger and disappointment. He looks at the list briefly and then heads into the adjoining boys locker room.

Next comes Damon. He's afraid to look. "Am I on it?" he asks a friend. "No, I know I'm not on it." He walks up, studies the list for a moment, and then steps into the locker room. Inside, Damon and the starting point guard, Maury, try to console Poughkeepsie Kris. "You got all year to work on it, man," Maury tells him. "Next year, you come back, it'll be your year to shine."

"That's right, Kris, you still got a year, man," says Damon. There will be no next year at Coatesville for Damon.

Eric comes down the hall alone. He approaches with the same grim determination he showed standing on the sideline during all those intramural sessions. Eric does not dress in baggy jeans like the other boys. He has on straight-legged pants and a sweater. He stands at the back of the crowd around the list, craning for a look. "Let me see," he says.

"You ain't got to see," says one boy, teasing. "You cut, man."

Eric leans in, blushes, and then turns to walk away.

"No, no, wait, E!" shouts Ty, pushing clear of the crowd, chasing Eric with his hand outstretched. "You did good, E. You did good."

Ty stops, hand still outstretched, as Eric walks slowly away without turning back.

EPILOGUE

When Scoogy went home the day he posted his list, he found an angry note from the grandmother of a boy he had cut. During the season the team struggled, as the coach, who turned fifty-one in December, had feared it would. The Red Raiders ended the regular season last Friday with a 10–14 record, good enough for the Ches-Mont League championship, and will go to the state District One playoffs, which will begin this week. Coatesville's most consistent scorers were Maury Boyer and Glenn Gray. Nin Bacon was a spot player and, according to Scoogy, "got some good experience." Mark Hostutler came off the bench in one game and scored 18 points. "It was the best night of my entire life," he says.

Eric Kruse didn't attend any of the Red Raiders' games. He played on two rec league teams and plans to throw the javelin for the Coatesville track team in the spring. Damon Watson, meanwhile, helped out the Red Raiders part of the season as team manager. He attended almost all of the home games.

SCHMIDT'S MISFORTUNE

MAY 1982

The Phillies' great third baseman had a prickly relationship with the sports reporters who chronicled his amazing career, but he was generous with me when I asked for his help in writing this story. The idea was to follow him through the first few games of the season, wait for a game when he clobbered a few good hits, and then write a detailed account of each at bat. I wanted to get inside his head during his duels with pitchers. As you might expect, Schmidt was a serious student of hitting, and routinely studied videotapes of each at bat after every game. I was privileged to sit alongside as he did this. He got off to a slow start in 1982, but kept working graciously with me game after game. It got to the point where he would grimace when he saw me coming to interview him after each game. Then, with one swing in Shea Stadium, he broke a rib and brought his new season to an abrupt halt. I felt like I had jinxed him, and told him so in the locker room afterward. "I wasn't going to say it," he said, and then apologized to me for ruining my story by not getting more hits.

*A*pril 13, 1982. Opening Day at Shea Stadium. Mets vs. Phillies. Top of the second inning.

Mike Schmidt eases into the batter's box with ritual, a lifetime of accumulated tics. This rectangle of soft soil bordered with lye is his realm. He grooms it with the spikes of his right shoe, then steps out to knock dirt off the spikes with his bat. He takes two slow practice swings. With two deep breaths he attempts to clear his mind completely, of the hostile fans arrayed in steep walls of seats all around him, of how he has been hitting lately (badly), of the pain of the broken toe on his left foot, of the thousand whispered images that float uninvited across the still pool of his concentration.

Then he steps back in, digging his right foot into the back corner of the box, the corner farthest from home plate, and planting his left foot closer in, about two thirds of the way up.

Standing this way, legs spread wide, slightly bent at the knees, leaning forward from the waist, his left shoulder and back are turned toward Mets pitcher Randy Jones. Schmidt tugs at the brim of his batting helmet, takes two rhythmic half swings, and then steadies the bat, holding it up and back and bolt upright. His hands in tight batting gloves work at the bat's grip as Jones goes into his windup.

Schmidt wiggles the bat ever so slightly. He is watching, not the pitcher's gyrations or the ball, but Jones's *slot,* the place over his left shoulder where Schmidt knows from long experience this left-handed pitcher habitually releases the ball. As the ball is thrown Schmidt's bat goes stock still and in that instant he sizes up the pitch and decides, *Let it go.*

He drops the bat slightly and strides forward with his left foot as he watches the ball all the way into the catcher's mitt. It passes through the outside corner of the strike zone. The umpire, crouching, turns to his right and juts his hand out sharply as he calls the pitch. *Strike One.* The walls of Mets fans shout their approval.

Again the ritual: smoothing the dirt. Rapping the spikes, the practice swings, very deliberate, the deep breaths, then planting first the right foot, then the left, tugging the helmet, the rhythmic half swings. Bat back. Watching . . . watching . . .

Jones releases a spinning pitch, an off-speed breaking ball to the outside corner. Something clicks right with this one.

Schmidt moves toward it instantly, striding forward, concentrating on keeping his left shoulder turned in so he can reach the bat across with enough strength to hit the outside pitch into right field, swinging smoothly, not violently, *just meet it,* reaching out . . . Smack! . . . but wait . . . in the same instant of sweet connection pain flashes through Schmidt's body and mind, terrible pain—pain that explodes through his torso and chest and emerges finally in a wrenching scream. . . .

The ball is well hit. It rises in a slow high arc toward deep right field and curves toward the foul pole, away from sprinting Mets outfielder Ellis Valentine, who is not going to catch it. . . .

Schmidt, limping slowly toward first base, clutching his back with his left hand, watches the ball, hoping for once in his life that it *won't* clear the fence for a home run. He felt muscles along his rib cage tear away from bone—X-rays would later show he had cracked his lower left rib. He doesn't think he can get around the bases. . . .

The ball falls just at the base of the right field fence, well over 300 feet out, dead in the corner. Schmidt stands on first, doubled over, holding his back.

Just like that, one swing, one base hit, one freak twist, and Mike Schmidt's 1982 season came to an abrupt halt.

He had been eager to play, to get started. He was convinced greatness would be his this season. His performance, by most measures already the best in baseball, has been improving steadily over the past three years. An intensely cerebral ballplayer, Schmidt believes he's finally got this game figured out. He *knows* more each time he walks on the field.

He is thirty-two years old, a millionaire several times over. He has two lovely children and a loving wife. His spirit is ripe and full with Christian fervor. He has it made.

"Do you believe this?" he asks later, down in the visiting team's clubhouse, the muffled sounds of the Shea Stadium crowd overhead. Schmidt has stripped to his underwear and has a big pack of ice wrapped around his torso under a Phillies T-shirt. He can't quite stand upright. His steady, serious blue-eyed gaze is troubled.

"I mean, I was afraid it would clear the fence because I didn't think I could make it around the bases. I was hoping the ball wouldn't go out. What's the rule on that? Do I have to run around the bases myself? Can they substitute somebody for me in the middle of the play to run for me? I don't know what the rule is on that."

Breathing hurt. Walking hurt. Sitting hurt. Mostly thinking hurt. Right away Schmidt was thinking a month and a half. For a man whose success depends upon run totals, hit totals, and home run totals, slicing off a sixth of the season is like exacting a pound of flesh. The damn thing hurt like that, too. Game five of the Phillies season. He hadn't even gotten started and now he was out. Just like that.

Schmidt knew only one way to take it. "It's the will of God," he said quietly. But the look on his face said *Why?*

Two months earlier. Monday, February 13, 1982. Innisbrooke, Florida.

Schmidt is hitting golf balls and he is perplexed. His standards are all out of whack. Just because he's arguably the best hitter in baseball, winner of the National League's Most Valuable Player award for two consecutive seasons, that doesn't mean he ought to be a great golfer, too. But tell Schmidt that. Here he is with his two-iron and a big wire-mesh basket full of golf balls, wincing with displeasure every time he swings.

It is a dazzling morning, a warm winter day to break the hearts of folks up north. Just back from taping a segment of the television program *The Baseball Bunch* and a weeklong cruise in the Caribbean, Schmidt is pleased to be in his winter golf-haven near Clearwater. Spring training doesn't officially begin for a week, and he's looking to squeeze in as much golf as will fit. Sporting his usual leathery suntan, he's got on a blue sun visor, a bright red Phillies polo shirt, and a pair of lumpy blue bell-bottom trousers. Sandy brown hair falls in neatly cut layers over his ears to the bright gold chain around his neck.

Baseball's premier slugging third baseman somehow seems smaller than you might expect, out of uniform here in Florida. He's six feet two, about two hundred pounds, but the physical presence is still shy of the legend.

Mostly Schmidt is just built wide. His shoulders and arms, right down to his thick wrists and his upper legs and buttocks, seem too big for his torso, as if they belonged to someone else. He has high, prominent cheek-bones from which his face cuts down sharply in two angled lines to his chin. What must have been a difficult case of teenage acne has left scars along these chiseled features, softening them somewhat, adding to his weathered complexion a curious blend of ruggedness and vulnerability. He's got a wad of Skoal pressed into his right cheek and a knot of concentration on his brow.

Thwack! One after the other he strokes the balls cleanly. They zip off at one angle or the other, falling down toward a target flag about 200 yards away across the hazy green field. *Thwack!* There is power and even a hint of grace in the brute swing, but it seems wrong. It lacks the fluidity of a truly gifted golfer's. He hits in the mid-80s and aspires to much, much better. *Thwack!*

"You know what kills me about this game?" Schmidt offers unsolic-ited. "You only get one chance, you know what I mean? In baseball you get three strikes or four balls, but in golf you get just one swing. You spend the whole time walking down the fairway looking at the ball and sizing up exactly where you want to hit it. And then you get one chance. When you blow it, man, it makes you feel like throwing your whole golf bag in the lake."

Thwack! The ball spins off on a slow slice away to the right of the flag. Schmidt turns with a frown to an Innisbrooke golf pro who has stepped out of his cart to watch. "I've tried everything," he tells the pro. "I've tried baseball grip, crossing hands, locking fingers. It doesn't seem to make any difference."

Schmidt's problem is control, not power. To demonstrate, he steps back a bit from the ball, gripping the two-iron like a baseball bat, bending at the waist and taking a vicious cut. "Aaaaugh!" he grunts, and he slams it perfectly. The golf ball rises in a straight line from the tee and just keeps on going up, up, and up over the long grass fairway, still up as it passes over the distant target flag, up over the slope beyond and over the fence atop the slope and over the tennis courts past that. There is a moment of stunned silence. Even Schmidt is surprised.

"Of course, I can't always do that," he says.

If there is a way, though, Mike Schmidt will probably figure it out. Excellence dogs the man. Gifted with extraordinary strength and athletic ability, he is also possessed of (and by) an analytical mind, a mind that grabs a problem like a bull terrier grabs a throat. He approaches the game—any game—with enormous physical talent, filtered through layer after layer of pure thought.

"Did you ever *think* about baseball for just a minute, about how perfect it is?" he asks. *Thwack!* He is talking while he strokes, head down, reaching over with the iron to roll the next red-striped ball into place. Setting, swinging, *Thwack!* "I have. It's one of the only sports where the players are not overtaking its dimensions. You take basketball. The players are so big now that scoring points is like nothing. The baskets ought to be higher. And I was watching football this year and it occurred to me that the kickers were regularly kicking the ball completely off the field, over and out of the end zone. It never used to be like that.

"But baseball—take a ball hit between the second baseman and the shortstop. A hard-enough-hit ball is going to go through, no matter how quick the fielders are. There is just enough space between them so they can't cover it all. The same thing is true between the third baseman and the shortstop, and the outfielders. A home run is just far enough away so that a plain old hard-hit fly ball won't make it. The dimensions of the game are, like, *perfect.*

"Now you know when ole Abner Doubleday set down ninety feet between the bases and sixty feet between home plate and the pitcher's mound that he couldn't have known all that, but it works out that way. Incredible."

Great baseball players have this in common. To the thoughtful baseball fan, the game can serve as a rich metaphor for life, but to a professional ballplayer, baseball *is* life. Schmidt lives to play baseball well, and playing badly just about kills him. But the intensity with which he plays is different from, say, that of Pete Rose.

Rose's obsession is outward-directed, combative. Rose is in a battle with *the other team,* and he is unrelenting. You can see it in his slide, which is not so much a slide as a banzai lunge—bombing himself at the bag head-first, as if it were the only way to arrive, launching himself at a dead run a good five paces off, hungry, hard, and fast.

Schmidt plays with equal intensity, but with him, the passion is directed inward. He is battling himself. Sure, the other team is there to be beaten and his teammates are there to help, but the key to victory is performance, and the secret to perfect performance is locked somewhere deep inside, soul deep. Schmidt knows how much of the game is instinct. He knows that success or failure in that instant after a ball is thrown or hit rests as much in a realm outside his conscious control as inside it, just as his golf swing stubbornly resists his will to make it perfect, to blend that extraordinary power with proper technique.

When he plays badly he is often accused of thinking too much, which is probably true. Even he acknowledges it. But, you see, that's Mike Schmidt. His way is to think his way out. Master those instincts. That's why the man so often seems perplexed with himself. Why can't he get those goddamn neurons in the deepest part of his brain to fire exactly as he wants? Why not?

Roger Angell, noted baseball writer for *The New Yorker* magazine and a man who has spent almost five decades watching major league baseball, mused in an article on hitting last year about the chances a batter has of making contact with a ball thrown by a wily, strong, big league pitcher, and concluded that it simply *ought to be impossible.*

Think of hitting as a duel, fought between two circular patches of dirt sixty feet, six inches apart, one with a bare rubber slab at its center, the other divided into two rectangles on either side of a rubber pentagon—home plate. The pitcher's mound at mid-diamond is raised about ten inches, an elevation that can seem mountainous when the pitcher is well over six feet tall with arms as long as most people's legs. Up on that mound is a man with a body seemingly designed especially by God to hurl a small, hard, leather-bound, stitched sphere at high speed past the waiting batter, whose job it is to hit the moving ball with a long, cylindrical wooden bat.

Today's fireballing big league pitchers can throw the ball at speeds of 95 m.p.h., which is to say 140 feet per second, which means their opponents in this duel have less than half of a second to decide, first, whether the damn thing is going to hit them; second, whether it is close enough to the strike zone to try to hit; third, gauge where the ball will pass before them; and, last, swing the bat quickly enough in the right place to hit it.

Little League coaches are always telling their charges to keep their eye on the ball until it makes contact with the bat—which is a physical impossibility. The ball moves too fast. While it isn't a bad idea to try to watch the ball all the way in, to make contact a hitter needs to almost instantly intuit where it will be when it reaches him, and to swing to that spot. Ultimately it is as much a matter of *feel* as eyesight or technique. It is, as most boys or girls learn early, something you either can or cannot do, no matter how much you may want to do it.

At least for most people. Schmidt believes he has turned himself from merely a good hitter into a great hitter solely by the application of technique.

He talks of two breakthroughs. The first had to do with controlling fear, the bugaboo that roughly separates the several dozen truly great hitters in baseball from the rest of humanity. The second had to do with controlling desire, ego, and natural exuberance, a battle he is still waging today.

By the time Schmidt was playing college ball at Ohio State in the late 1960s, he figures he had progressed about a far as natural ability would take him. He was a switch-hitter then. The change began when his coach, Paul Wren, persuaded him to stick with hitting right-handed only.

"I had a big swing and I could hit it out of the park either way—I can still hit them out of the park left-handed—but I still felt like I wasn't getting the most out of the talent God gave me," Schmidt says. "The reason hitting left-handed appealed to me was that I hated curveballs.

"You stand there watching the pitcher and he throws the ball and it's coming straight at your eyeball. You can see it spinning. At the last moment it breaks over the plate. I didn't like it. Watching the ball speeding straight at my head was tough. I'd be doing this," and Schmidt demonstrates by assuming his batting stance, holding his golf iron instead of the bat, and then pulling sharply away from the imaginary ball, jerking his head back over his left shoulder.

"I just didn't like it. I'd watch my buddies and I just couldn't understand how they did it. They'd just follow that sucker on in until it broke over the plate and then *smoke it*! They could even hit it to right field! I was just in awe of it. I thought, God, how do you do that? When I hit these home runs right-handed they were fastballs, of course. Anytime I got a curve I'd be bailing out, or just freezing up completely. Still, I was having more success batting right-handed because that was natural to me. Hitting right-handed all the time forced me to deal with that fear, and made me a better hitter."

Still, Schmidt says, when he began playing pro ball in the early '70s he had not overcome fear. It was a lesson he had to learn in the pros, because in the big leagues good pitchers use fear. It is an essential part of their arsenal in the duel. Schmidt says the main difference between top-quality amateur baseball and the pros is that, in the pros, the pitchers really do throw at you. Deliberately.

"Back in 1973, as a rookie, I hit a home run to beat Bob Gibson 2-to-1 in the eighth," he recalls. "It was 1-to-1 in the eighth and I hit a slider out. Gibson was a big mean-lookin' guy. He just stared at me all the way around the bases, like he was saying, No fucking rookie is supposed to hit me like that. Well, the next time I faced him he threw me another slider and I hit a cue shot, you know, off the end of the bat, that squiggled like this"—Schmidt wiggles his fist—"right up the middle between his legs. Again I got this look from him, like an evil eye. Gibson—that's just the kind of pitcher he was—he just figures at that point that I'm hittin' him *too* good.

"So the next time up he just drilled me right in my left arm. Zinged me. It came at me so fast I don't think I even had time to move, just barely saw it coming. Hurt like a mother. And he just stared at me as I trotted down to first. He had this self-satisfied expression, like he was saying, Hey, kid, I'm Bob Gibson and I just threw that ball at you and if you don't like it well then go ahead and do something about it. That's why he was a great pitcher. A lot of pitchers lack that killer instinct."

Over the years, Schmidt says, he has taught himself simply to *not fear getting hit*. He knows sometimes he will; it has happened to him often enough. He knows how much it hurts, and how quickly the pain goes away. He is used to it. Getting hit isn't something he likes, but he accepts it. It's one of the reasons he is paid more than a million dollars a year to play baseball. Usually he gets hit in the left upper arm or high on the fleshy part of his back. He assumes a batting stance, holding his golf iron like a bat, and demonstrates how he turns to absorb the blow.

"Now, you take Nolan Ryan, there's a different story," he says. "His pitch gets there about a good foot ahead of everybody else's. I'm scared to death sometimes when Nolan is pitching. If I thought *he* was throwing at me, well, then you're talking about life and limb, you're talking a man with a family. With Nolan, if just one pitch hits me in the wrong place, that could blind or kill me. I don't want to be blind or dead. But I not only go up to bat against Nolan Ryan, I get hits off of him.

"I *like* to have the ball thrown at my head every once in a while. It exercises that reflex for getting out of the way. You have to have confidence that you can get out of the way when it comes, so it's good to prove it to yourself every once in a while. I've earned my reputation in this league. Pitchers know I ain't gonna back down, even if I know they're throwing at me. That's why I make more money than just about anybody playing baseball."

Last year, he says, a rookie pitcher threw a fastball right at him that just missed hitting him in the ribs.

"I made it a point not to move a muscle," he says. "I just stared back out at the guy and spit, and set up for the next pitch. They want you to at least get riled, so maybe you're trying too hard to clobber the next pitch. But the key is just to not let it intimidate or bother you."

There are two aides to the intimidation game. Opposing pitchers know how important Mike Schmidt is to the Phillies, how a healthy home run hitter is money in their pockets. Throwing at Schmidt is an invitation for retaliation. In the National League, pitchers still have to take their turn at bat.

And there is the direct reaction. If Schmidt feels strongly enough that a pitcher doesn't respect him, he'll retaliate himself. In a Sunday afternoon game at Three Rivers Stadium in Pittsburgh three years ago, Pirates pitcher

Bruce Kison hit Schmidt with what the hitter took to be a deliberate assault. Schmidt calmly started walking toward first base until Kison turned away, and then he charged the mound. He says he got in a few good shots before both benches emptied and pulled them apart. In the ensuing confusion, someone stepped on one of Schmidt's fingers and fractured it. But he considers it to have been a necessary thing.

He smiles just thinking about it. "I was out to inflict the maximum amount of physical damage to the man in the shortest length of time," he says. "From my perspective, I want the pitcher to know that if I think he's throwing at me, he can expect to see me, if not then, then in the parking lot after the game."

Schmidt's second big breakthrough as a hitter is still happening, the way he sees it. He talks about having arrived at a new level of the game, one where he deliberately targets his performance for the good of the team, suppressing his own desire to play dramatic baseball, to swing from the heels all the time the way Reggie Jackson does, so hard that the force of a mighty miss knocks him over.

The great revelation in this—which Schmidt sees as profoundly connected with his concurrent spiritual awakening several years ago—is that by suppressing his desire for personal glory he achieves not only better team performance but also, like some kind of heavenly bonus, better *personal* performance.

"In my first few years in the majors, I was a guy who did nothing but pull the ball," he says, miming with his golf iron a swing at an inside pitch. "I was hitting thirty or more homers each year, driving in more than one hundred runs, but batting about .270. I wanted to hit like Roberto Clemente," who consistently hit for a high batting average and could hit the ball to any part of the field with power. "My coaches and teammates laughed at me. They told me to relax, to settle down, that I was already good enough. The thing is, I really *wanted* to be better. I was determined to be better than that."

Pull hitters rarely have better then a .270 batting average because they are too predictable—fielders know where to play them and pitchers know how to pitch them. So Schmidt did the unthinkable. He experimented with success. He changed his batting stance, moving farther away from the plate, and he began deliberately swinging the bat with only about 70 percent of his strength.

At the same time—he demonstrates this with the golf iron, flexing his muscular forearms—he concentrated on driving the bat *down* at the ball, attempting to hit at precisely the point in his swing where he turns over his wrists.

"Bam!" he says as he strokes down at the imaginary ball. "Hitting down at the ball like that gives it backspin when you hit it right. It will carry ten or fifteen more feet with spin like that on it. A lot of my home runs hit the fence in center and just bounce over for a home run. I'll take ten like that and sacrifice the one towering blast that everybody talks about all year."

In the last three years Schmidt's batting average has gone from .253 to .286 to .316, and in each of those seasons he hit home runs at a greater rate than ever before (though last year's home run total reflects the shortened season caused by the players' strike). He now hits a home run, on average, every fifteen times he comes to the plate, an astonishing percentage that has been bettered or equaled by only five players in the history of the game: Babe Ruth (who averaged a homer every 12 at-bats), Ralph Kiner, Harmon Killebrew, Dave Kingman (all with an average of one every 14 at-bats), and Eddie Mathews (15).

"I'm lucky, because I'm one of those guys who has enough strength so that I can afford to slow down on my swing without giving up home runs," he explains. "I hit *more* homers by slowing down my swing. Swinging with all your might is a hitter's nemesis. It is the standard flaw. Fans get down on me at the Vet every once in a while—not so much anymore—because they never see me really swinging so hard my batting helmet falls off. It looks like I'm not really trying. But I've discovered, and the stats prove it, that by relying on technique more than brute strength I hit for a better average *and* I hit more home runs."

Last season was Schmidt's best ever. Standing under the Florida sun, hitting the last of his golf balls two months before the 1982 season begins, Schmidt is confident the ascent toward his goal of excellence has just begun. After nine years of major league play, he expects to reach his peak during the next five seasons—at a point in most baseball careers where players must cope with decline. He works out easily, no weight lifting or heavy running, just an elaborate series of stretching exercises daily and an occasional run of a mile or so.

"At this point in my career, I've got all the strength I need," he says. "I work out primarily to keep fit and prevent injury, not to bulk up. My goal is to play 162 games"—the complete schedule. "I'm no good to anybody if I'm built like a gorilla from the waist up and I snap a hamstring muscle at midseason."

Friday night, April 9, 1982. Veterans Stadium. The Phillies' second game of the season. Top of the second inning; the Montreal Expos lead, 1–0.

Schmidt stands off behind home plate swinging his bat with a lead doughnut around the end, loosening up as he watches Expos pitcher Steve Rogers finish his warm-up tosses. It is a cold, cold night, and Schmidt is freezing. No night for baseball.

Standing on the playing field at the Vet when the stands are full, it is hard for a player not to feel that he has arrived at the exact center of world attention. The green plastic rug is made up of a zillion plastic squibs, soft and crinkly underfoot. Balls bounce off it uniformly, with a dull thud. Walls rise up all around, moving multicolored walls of people, thousands of them, so high that you have to turn your head straight up to see sky. It is like being at the bottom of some Olympian bowl.

But tonight most of the seats are empty, rising in thick bands of red, orange, and yellow. Only about 7,000 fans have braved the cold and dampness for this game, though it is only the second of the year. It has been snowing all day.

The Phils had lost their opening game the day before to the New York Mets, after having two games called off earlier in the week because of snow. In the opening game, Schmidt batted four times. He hit well the one decent pitch thrown to him by the Mets' Randy Jones, but the ball flew on a line directly into the glove of the third baseman for an out, which is the way things sometimes go in baseball. But Jones had taken notice. The next two times Schmidt batted Jones simply refused to throw the ball near the strike zone, walking the Phils' cleanup hitter twice. Schmidt had taken advantage of the gifts by stealing a base and scoring a run.

Now, watching Rogers warm up, he knows it's unlikely he'll get a good pitch to hit tonight—even if he felt warm and flexible enough to swing the bat well. Rogers is a skinny guy with a moustache who has been playing major league ball for eight years, only one year less than Schmidt. He pitches more with brains and finesse than power. Schmidt sees him as a sort of opposite number to himself.

Rogers is a tactician. He's got everybody in the Phils' lineup figured out and he knows how he's going to pitch each of them. Schmidt has this little imitation he does of Rogers, as a way of explaining how the guy approaches batters. The big hitter stands with both his feet pressed together, leaning forward from the waist and fingering a baseball out in front of his face; then, in a high, nasal voice, he'll say, "Now let me see, how'm I gonna pitch to Michael Schmidt?" Then Schmidt laughs.

But he's all business now. Schmidt discards the lead doughnut and strides deliberately to the batter's box. The plastic turf underfoot squishes with each step. Schmidt's name is announced, echoing high off the empty arena walls. As he performs his standard ritual and steps into the box, the widely dispersed crowd is cheering. A fan behind the first base dugout bellows, "Give us one, Mike!"

Rogers is standing just the way Schmidt says he does, peering in at his catcher, Gary Carter, and fingering the baseball inside his glove. He's thinking, *I've* got *to keep my pitches away from Schmidt, pitch him low and outside, don't give him anything he can really tag.*

Rogers doesn't wind up fully the way most pitchers do. Instead of bringing both hands over his head as he rocks back on his left foot, he continues to hold the ball in his right hand inside his glove out in front of his chest. He justs turns his body to the right as he shifts his weight and lifts his left leg, then propels himself forward with the throw. He has this little hitch in his delivery, when he kicks and throws, that makes it seem, to Schmidt, as though he's holding on to the ball too long. It's unorthodox, tricky, and it's one of the things that makes Rogers hard to hit.

Schmidt starts at the first pitch and then pulls the bat back, watching it for a called strike. Fastball, outside corner. Schmidt is a bit rattled. He's uncomfortable hitting tonight. He doesn't like the way he jumped at that pitch and then pulled back. It's as though he wasn't ready to hit it but he wasn't ready to take it, either. He steps out of the box and takes a deep breath to try to clear his mind.

Rogers gets the ball back from Carter and stoops immediately to deliver the next pitch. He's always a fast worker, but especially so in the cold. He needs to stay in motion to keep warm. Schmidt doesn't hold him up. He sets up immediately to receive the next pitch. *If you're ready, I'm ready.*

Rogers rocks back quickly in the same way and throws the same pitch, fastball low and outside. Schmidt starts to swing at it, striding forward and launching the bat, but then he changes his mind again, checking the swing just in time. The pitch is too far outside, beyond the strike zone. Ball one. The next pitch is another ball, this one a breaking ball to the same place. The count is now two balls, one strike. Schmidt has the upper hand. He steps out of the box to repeat his ritual, knocking dirt from his spikes, tugging at his helmet, taking a deep breath, two practice swings, then he eases back in and sets as Rogers rocks back to throw the next pitch.

Leaving the pitcher's hand, the ball looks to Schmidt like an inside fastball, one of his favorite pitches. It makes sense because the first three pitches have all been low and outside and Rogers likes to mix things up. Schmidt strides immediately forward and swings, but just as he does he picks up the spin on the ball, *Damn!* a slider. In midswing he tries to make the necessary adjustment as the ball breaks out and away from his bat—"I was screwed once I saw the ball move," he says later.

Schmidt's demoralized swing is now just a pitiful, uneven thing that happens to catch the ball right off the bat's tip—a tribute really to the hitter's quickness but just a pathetic little squibbler that thuds wetly off the infield rug and dribbles politely down the first base line into the waiting glove of Al Oliver, the Expos' first baseman, who flips it to Rogers, hustling over to catch the throw and then step on first base. *Out.* Schmidt runs all the way down to first base, even though he is out three fourths of the way there, and then strides silently back toward the dugout.

It is an omen for the night.

Schmidt comes up again in the bottom of the fourth. A beer vendor up in the stands hands a full cup of frozen brew to a customer and quietly suggests, "Honey, why don't all you people go home now." The cold seems to be bothering everyone except Rogers, who, until giving up a single to Phils' left fielder Gary Matthews on the previous pitch, had not allowed a hit. The Phils trail by two runs, and Schmidt would like to do something about it.

As the league's best home run hitter steps up to bat, Rogers eyes Matthews on first base and knows he'll have to pitch Schmidt very delicately—*Negate his power by pitch selection,* he thinks. *Don't give him anything he can drive. One wrong pitch here and he could tie the game.*

Schmidt is cold. His toe, which he broke in batting practice in the last week of spring training, hurts. Rogers first fires him a fastball on the outside corner, which Schmidt watches for a strike—"Why?" Schmidt says later. "Because sometimes you just walk out there with your head up your ass, that's why. When you're that cold it's like your brain doesn't really believe your body can move fast enough to hit the ball, so you hesitate."

Rogers next throws a fastball high and way outside, almost a wild pitch, but Carter leaps up to catch it. The next pitch is another fastball strike to the outside corner, which, again, Schmidt takes. He is now angry with himself. *How could I just watch it?* Now he's feeling stiff and uptight, down in the count. He steps out of the batter's box for two deep breaths and then climbs back in.

Rogers has decided to try a fastball low and inside. So far all of his pitches to Schmidt this at bat have been outside. *Mix things up, mix things up.*

He does his little half windup after pausing to check Matthews on first base over his shoulder—"Gary wasn't really a threat to steal," Rogers says later, and smiles; "the old legs just don't work that well anymore in the cold"—and throws, wildly. Instead of traveling down, the ball starts right off heading up, up practically to Schmidt's eye level. The hitter feels a sudden blast of adrenaline. A high pitch! *High and inside!*—just the kind he loves to hit.

In that split instant when the decision is made the batter's mental signals all flash green—"God, it looked like a pitch I could hit!" Schmidt says later, exuberantly—and so he swings, hard, and manages only to tick the ball with his bat before it snaps into the catcher's mitt. *Strike three.* It is his first strikeout of 1982.

Later, Schmidt says, laughing, "The pitch was too high to hit. Hell, I was pretty satisfied with a foul tip."

Schmidt faces Rogers again in the sixth inning and draws a walk, a semi-intentional walk. The Expos are still ahead by two runs; there are two outs and a man on base. In this situation, there's no way he's going to give Schmidt a pitch to hit. He'd rather pitch to the next batter, outfielder George Vukovich, than risk delivering Schmidt's first home run ball of 1982. Rogers's caution is rewarded when Vukovich raps a little grounder back to the pitcher's mound for the third out. End of threat.

There is drama in the bottom of the ninth inning when Schmidt comes up to bat for his fourth and last time. Twice fooled, once walked, stiff, cold, and a bit angry with himself, he strides up with another shot at tying the score. *Stay calm, just meet the ball. Think hit, not homer. Control the situation. Don't fall behind in the count.* Matthews has just drilled his second hit of the night, a double, so with no outs Schmidt represents the tying run. He is nervous. The crowd is cheering for him big, as big as what's left of 7,000 freezing fans can. He takes twice as long as usual to step into the box, drawing heavy, deep breaths and exhaling thick clouds of steam.

Rogers has had good luck pitching low and away to Schmidt all night, so he decides to stay with it. The first pitch is a fastball, low and away. Schmidt starts to swing and checks himself too late; the bat passes through the outside edge of the strike zone. Strike one. He steps out, adjusts his helmet, spits, grooms the dirt with his spikes, and takes another deep breath. Then he steps in for the next offering. Rogers kicks and throws a high-outside fastball. Ball one.

That high pitch worries Rogers. He knows Schmidt can step into a high pitch and drive it over the 371-foot marker on the right field wall. So he's determined to keep his next few pitches low. The next pitch starts off just like the first one. It looks like a fastball, low and outside, which is right where Schmidt is looking for it, but as he steps in to swing the ball breaks. Rogers has thrown a slider and Schmidt has not picked up the spin. On his swing he just tips the ball with his bat and it pops up foul into the upper deck behind home plate. Strike two.

Rogers is delighted. Schmidt is angry with himself again—"I was not hitting like a good hitter and I knew it," he says later. "I was doing exactly what I would tell anyone *not* to do. But that's baseball. I walked up there afraid of falling behind in the count. It's a tough situation: bottom of the ninth, man on second, down by two runs, you're telling yourself to make sure you get your cuts in, don't give away any strikes, and *don't fall behind in the count.*

"But a good hitter doesn't worry about things like that. I wasn't in control. Rogers was. So right behind that fear of strike one is the fear of strike two. I swung at a bad pitch the first time because I was too eager to wait. Then I did it again. If I had been in more control of the situation, like I should have been, the count would have been two-and-oh, not oh-and-two."

Strike three came with the next pitch, another slider that broke away from Schmidt's lunging swing. Again he was looking for a low-outside fastball and Rogers fooled him with a low-outside breaking ball. He turns abruptly on his left heel and strides straight back to the dugout. A loud voice from the stands demands, "Hold your head up! Hold your head up!"

"I just call it a panic stroke," Schmidt says. "Three panic swings and I went in and showered with shampoo and conditioner. There's always tomorrow."

In the visiting team clubhouse after the game, Rogers is seated on a folding metal chair before his locker with the standard postgame wad of ice packs strapped around his right shoulder and elbow. Reporters are crowded around him. He has thrown a two-hit shutout, with ten strikeouts, two of them against one of the best hitters in baseball. Rogers is doing his best to acknowledge his pleasure without gloating. Water from the ice packs drips down to a growing pool at his feet.

"Schmidt? I've watched him circle the bases around me a few times, so I know how it feels to have him get the better of me, too," he says.

The next day, Saturday, April 10, 1982. Veterans Stadium. Phillies vs. the Montreal Expos.

Earlier this afternoon, the segment of *The Baseball Bunch* that Schmidt taped in February was shown on network television. In it, the third baseman talked to a group of youngsters about The Game, touching upon some of the important lessons of life it has to teach. He counsels one little boy who is introduced as a good player who is nevertheless given to terrible tantrums when he strikes out. Striking out is something Schmidt has done often. He holds the major league record for the most consecutive seasons leading both leagues in strikeouts—from 1974 through 1976. In the program, he draws the child aside, and with warm, fatherly words explains that even the best baseball players must learn to live with recurrent failure.

"If I hit .300, then I'm a *great* hitter, but that still means that seven of every ten times I come to bat I don't get a hit," he says. "Seven of ten times I fail."

Now, several hours before game time, Schmidt is down inside a huge net batting cage in the tunnel under the Vet living with last night's failure. Dressed in a bright red warm-up suit, he is patiently stroking baseballs off a stationary tee, swinging almost in slow motion, trying to impress on his inner brain by repetition the smooth, perfect swing that is his goal. Rogers had gotten the better of him. Tonight Schmidt will face Bill Gullickson, another right-bander, but one with an entirely different style.

He will get his first hit of the season off Gullickson, a big, twenty-three-year-old kid with a thick shock of brown hair and a heavy dark brow. Gullickson has had only one year in the major leagues, but Schmidt already considers him one of the strongest right-handers in baseball.

"But Gullickson is just a bear," Schmidt says, his blue eyes peering out intently from behind the netting. "He can blow it right by you up at the letters"—chest-high, past the letters on the front of the uniform. "Rogers figures me as just a cog in the Phillies lineup, a special kind of problem. A guy like Gullickson has no idea how he's going to pitch one guy to the next. But he sees me as a special challenge to his manhood up there on the mound. If he's going to be bearing down on anyone out there with everything he's got, it's me. He's out to prove something when he pitches against me."

And, sure enough. Schmidt's first time up against Gullickson he strikes out—a called third strike on what the hitter calls "a nasty slider that just nicked the strike zone on its way outside." He walks straight back to the dugout, head down, but he's not angry. He feels as though the at bat was not a total waste.

"I felt like I was seeing the ball okay," Schmidt says. "I wasn't reacting to Gullickson's motion. I was really seeing the ball. Now I felt like all I had to do was swing at the ball to make good contact. I felt good."

The hit comes in the bottom of the fourth. The Expos have already scored four runs, and Gullickson still looks strong, despite having given up a homer in the third to Phils catcher Bo Diaz and allowing a run to sneak in on a wild pitch. Gullickson has started this half of the inning by striking out Gary Matthews on a bad pitch, a wide, slow breaking ball that Matthews will dream about for several days in disbelief.

Schmidt had stood in the on-deck circle watching Gullickson dispatch Matthews. He has said he admires the way Hank Aaron used to wait his turn at bat with serene confidence, plopped down on one knee, motionlessly watching the duel before him. Schmidt figures that aplomb like that has got to unsettle pitchers. But it's too cold to sit still tonight. Schmidt is stretching, swinging the leaded bat, limbering, limbering, limbering. He can't wait to step up and hit. He can feel a hit in his hands.

Gullickson's first pitch to Schmidt is a fastball, low and too far away. Ball one. He decides to go inside with the next pitch, to keep Schmidt guessing. He doesn't want the hitter to discern any pattern in how he's being pitched, which isn't hard because Gullickson confesses he has no plan. *Just mix 'em up.* The next pitch is inside, but too high. Ball two.

Now Schmidt feels good. In control. But he quickly loses the composure on the next pitch, a slider to the outside corner that he chases with a wild, reaching swing for strike one—"I just waved at it," he says. "The damn ball bounced, I think. It was a slider in the dirt. I was just overanxious, I guess. I did just what I hoped I wouldn't do: opened my shoulder, jumped at a bad pitch. I knew right away I should have taken it. So you end up with that half . . . little swing." Two balls, one strike.

The next pitch is in the same place—Gullickson liked the way the first one worked—but Schmidt has gathered his composure somewhat and lets it go for ball three. Gullickson now has to throw a strike, but without giving Schmidt a pitch he can hit well. He decides on a fastball, his best pitch, to the outside corner, away from Schmidt's real power. Schmidt spots the pitch instantly and goes for it. He swings badly, turning out his lead shoulder again the way he hates to see himself do, but he makes contact anyway and the ball sails over the shortstop's head for a single.

"It was a lucky hit," Schmidt says. "But I loved it. It's the reason I have a batting average." His first hit of 1982. On first base, Schmidt smiles. Two batters and two Gullickson wild pitches later Schmidt slides across home plate with the Phillies' third run of the game.

Afterward, Gullickson, the winning pitcher this time, has only one comment about his duels with Mike Schmidt.

"Sometimes I get him," he says, "but mostly he gets me."

Sunday, April 11, 1982. Veterans Stadium. The Phillies have just defeated the Montreal Expos, 1–0, for their first win of the season.

Big Ray Burris, the Expos' losing pitcher, is seated silently before his locker in the visiting team's clubhouse under the Vet. He is peeling off his powder-blue uniform and bombing pieces of it accurately across the room into a white laundry container.

The whole locker room is silent, unlike the boisterous, cheerful place it was after the two Expos victories this weekend. No one is really upset though, except maybe Burris, who pitched well the whole game and then lost. The quiet is just protocol. One reserves respectful silence in the presence of defeat, as for the passing of the angel of death. It was a good game. They played well. Two out of three on the road against a team that has been one of the toughest in the division ain't bad.

Burris gruffly agrees to talk, after he showers, about pitching to Schmidt. He plods off looking somewhat comical, naked in his white plastic sandals, a tall, broad-shouldered black man with a white towel in his left hand. He is in the shower for about a half hour.

Around the clubhouse, players are generally trying to ignore the sportswriters seeking interviews. Lacking anyone better, ballplayers enjoy venting their frustration in defeat on reporters, those annoying creatures huddled on the fringes of the game with pens and pads and cameras and microphones and questions, questions, questions.

Always they want to know why. Why? Who knows why? A thousand factors are wrapped up in the tight fabric of the game. Blaming teammates or the manager (even if it is clearly warranted) is bad form. Blame anyone but yourself and you just sound like a whiner, making excuses. So professional athletes must learn to regularly blame themselves before large audiences, even when they don't feel at fault. They don't like doing it.

Toweling off when he returns, Burris listens to a list of the pitches he threw Schmidt. The third baseman batted four times, drawing two more walks, popping out to the shortstop, and striking out again. For his part, Schmidt is growing impatient with himself, but knows that four games into the season is no time to start thinking slump. Burris is content with the way he pitched Schmidt. At least he didn't give him anything to hit. As each pitch is described, he nods, remembering it.

. "Fastball," he says. "That was my fastball." Or, "Slider, that was an outside slider." But Burris is unwilling to comment in detail. At one point he catches himself on the verge of explaining why, in the fourth inning with no outs and no one on base, he wasn't worried about walking the cleanup hitter.

"Hey, this isn't for publication, is it?" he asks the man who has introduced himself as a reporter and who has been jotting notes ever since he started talking.

"Of course it is."

"Hey, I don't think I want any of this printed," Burris says.

"That's why I'm asking you questions, to write an article for publication."

"Well, look," Burris says, a dark look coming over his face. "This has to do with strategy, man. I got to pitch to Schmidt again this season. I don't want him knowing how I pitch him."

In the Phillies' clubhouse, Schmidt is standing stark naked before his locker, surrounded by about fifteen reporters and an assortment of handheld cameras and klieg lights, which reflect sharply off the gold cross dangling in the hairs of his chest. Schmidt is holding a towel in one hand and a plastic bottle of shampoo in the other—a none-too-subtle hint, as if his nakedness were not enough, that *this is a man on his way to take a shower, guys.* But the questions keep coming, and the third baseman, the old pro, keeps fielding them with an edgy mix of candor and impatience. The sports columns will be filled for another day.

Finally, he escapes to shower. But when he returns, fifteen minutes later, one stray television reporter is waiting with his cameraman for an interview.

"Come on. Schmitty. Just one question," he begs.

"But I'm naked," Schmidt protests.

"We'll shoot you from the shoulders up, you know that."

Schmidt shrugs, resigned. "Okay, *one* question," he says, and of course it is The Question—"Are you concerned that you haven't been hitting well, Mike?"—which the reporter knows Schmidt wants least to hear, especially after just granting this small favor, so he rallies quickly with an ounce of empathy—"Is it the toe?"

The ballplayer has to laugh. He shakes his head, then looks up at the camera with mock seriousness, "Yeah, Frank, it's the toe," and he grins. The reporter signals his cameraman to stop taping.

"Come on, Mike," he pleads . . .

Later, Schmidt is seated in a back room of the clubhouse. His left foot, the one with the double-sized shiny red second toe, is in a yellow bucket of ice. He is wearing a white T-shirt and a pair of gray Phillies gym trunks. The lower parts of his legs and ankles are crisscrossed with thick blue veins, and there are wicked U-shaped scars on both knees—souvenirs of surgery for serious high school football injuries. One of Schmidt's knees is pinned together artificially inside.

He is watching black-and-white videotapes of his at bats this game, images recorded by a Phillies employee who sits each game with a small camera directly behind home plate under the stands, protected by a Plexiglas screen. Schmidt doesn't like what he sees. He has the cameraman roll the tape back again and again to take a closer look at a few crucial swings, and complains to himself as he watches—"Look at that, see the way I'm pulling my lead shoulder out and away from the plate as I swing? When you open up the shoulder like that you sacrifice all the power in your swing. . . ."

Watching the tape of his one strikeout this game, Schmidt winces as he sees his wild swing at an outside breaking ball for strike three.

"I missed because I didn't see it good, didn't pick up the spin," he says. "It's a day game, it's cloudy . . . in that split second in the swing where it matters I was swinging at where I thought the pitch was instead of where it really was. It was a good pitch to hit. I just missed it. The same pitch another time I'll *crush.*"

Midway through the screening, Schmidt lets go of his basic complaint, a frustration that applies to every strong hitter in the big leagues.

"Look at the way Burris was pitching me today," he says, agitated. "It's what you call pitching around a hitter. Look at that!" he shouts, watching another pitch on the screen. "Look at that!"

Then he grabs a black dustpan off the shelf behind him and lays it on his lap to serve as home plate. "They pitch me almost exclusively out here," he explains, holding his hands about eighteen inches apart, one hand just over the edge of the dustpan, the other well outside it. "The man had no thought for the inner three quarters of the plate," he says of Burris. "He's working the outside almost exclusively. Ain't nobody going to be mad at Ray Burris for walking Mike Schmidt. So he doesn't care if he misses. Just keep it outside and away. Burris is strictly a sinker, slider pitcher. Sinker, slider. And every one of them is way out here," again indicating with his hands the zone well off the dustpan.

"I have to deal with that all year," he says. "I can deal with it better when I'm hitting like a good hitter. But I'm not a good hitter yet this year. Not yet. If I don't get a hit off Randy Jones in New York Tuesday, then you'll know I'm in trouble."

*   *   *

*Again it is Tuesday, April 13, 1982. Opening Day at Shea Stadium. Phillies vs. the
New York Mets.*

It is a cool day of intermittent sunshine. For the traditional Opening
Day spectacle, the entire Phillies and Mets baseball clubs are standing
single file along the first and third base lines. As a dark-haired waif, star of
a hit Broadway musical, fills the whole U-shaped arena with her gutsy ren-
dition of "The Star-Spangled Banner," a jet passes overhead, descending
to nearby La Guardia Airport, roaring down—in competition or affirmation? Across the colorful celebration the plane's shadow flits quickly, omi-
nous somehow.

The Phils had their own Opening Day at Veterans Stadium against
the Mets last week. It has been a bad five days. They have lost three of
their first four games. They are like an automobile engine balking at ignition in the early-morning chill.

A big part of the problem is Schmidt. He has batted sixteen times
now and has gotten only one hit. He stands fourth in the row of Phillies
players along the third base line, legs apart, stretching slowly to the right
and then the left, limbering. He pulled a little something in his torso during batting practice, but he doesn't feel it now. In about fifteen minutes he
will.

After the Mets make three quick outs in their half of the first inning,
Schmidt trots back to the dugout with a knot of excitement at the center
of his chest. Now. He can't wait. He remembers how he ripped that pitch
off Jones last week. He wants another hit badly.

Grabbing his bat, he dons a red batting helmet and stands off behind
home plate limbering up slowly as Jones finishes his warm-up throws.
Schmidt feels confident. Time to feel again that electric surge of bat on
ball.

Then it is time. Mike Schmidt eases into the batter's box with ritual,
a lifetime of accumulated tics. . . .

THE GREAT POTATO PICK-OFF PLAY

OCTOBER 1988

This story is one of the most widely reprinted of my magazine articles. It resulted from a small item on the newswire about a "Potato Day" at the ballpark in Williamsport, Pennsylvania, in honor of Dave Bresnahan, who had pulled off a stunt with a potato in a game the previous year that had gotten him kicked out of baseball. I attended Potato Day, and got Bresnahan and his teammates to reconstruct the stunt, which I think captures both the fun and frustration of playing out a career in the minor leagues.

Now, some say there is no more than a hair's difference between minor league baseball and the bigs. Most who say so, admittedly, are minor-leaguers, whose dreams often dine at the table of delusion. The idea is also promoted by bush league team owners, who have been known to float an occasional lie in promoting 140-odd second-rate ball games every summer. But in the late summer of 1987, *nobody* was making that boast about the Bills of Williamsport, Pennsylvania.

Twenty-seven games out of first place in the Class AA Eastern League, two organizational rungs and an equal number of light-years away from the majors, their season was an embarrassment of near-epic size.

It was the time of year when shadows in late innings stretch long on the infield grass, and when ballplayers languishing on the lower rungs of the baseball ladder come face-to-face with youth's end. It was on a night like this, August 31, 1987, that the Bills met the Reading Phillies at Williamsport's quaint Bowman Field to play two of the last three games on their schedule.

Ball games had long since become grim duty for Orlando Gomez's squad. In fairness to Gomez, the Bills' manager had started off at a disadvantage. Most members of that year's team had been led to a Class A championship the previous year by manager Steve Swisher, a gung-ho leader who owned their loyalty and esteem. As a reward, Swisher and most of the team had been moved up to Class AA ball in Williamsport and were holding their own in high spirits through the first month of the season until Swisher got promoted. The Cleveland Indians, the Bills' parent organization, gave Swisher the club's higher-level Class AAA team, which had been struggling under Gomez's management. The Bills got Gomez.

Orlando Gomez is a swarthy, moustachioed Puerto Rican gentleman with a round face, who had been coaching in the minors for ten years. He is an emotional man, and his feelings about the demotion showed. The Bills, having lost their boisterously confident manager, now found themselves managed by a sensitive, sad, volatile fellow. Gomez might react to a loss one day with a compassionate postgame lecture, complete with a tearful "I luff you guys," and the next day challenge team members to a fistfight. That, coupled with a certain language barrier (Gomez spoke fluent Spanish and most of his team did not), made for a troubled managerial transition.

One of Gomez's least-popular moves that summer had been to send the Bills' catcher, Dave Bresnahan, back down to Class A ball. In every tight group of young men, whether they are convicts, soldiers, schoolboys, or ballplayers, there is a character like Bresnahan.

He was a short, blond-haired kid of twenty-four with a pink complexion and traces of a blond moustache. Brez, as he was known to team members, had torn up the Little Leagues in Phoenix, Arizona, had been an all-state catcher in high school, and all-conference in junior college. When he broke his right throwing hand one summer, Bresnahan taught himself to throw left-handed so he could play winter ball. He played that winter catching and throwing with the same hand and, emboldened by the feat, had taught himself to hit left-handed as well. When he was drafted by the Seattle Mariners in the eighteenth round in 1984, Bresnahan had made himself into potentially one of baseball's rarest finds, a competent switch-hitting catcher. But like so many blazingly talented youngsters, Bresnahan's promise ran afoul of baseball's relentless leveler—professional pitching. It was the same from both sides of the plate; every once in a while, Bresnahan would go on a two- or three-day tear, but over the long haul, he couldn't hit water if he fell out of a boat.

By the summer of '87, he was still playing on the strength of his catching ability and winning personality. Released by the Mariners, then picked up by the Indians, Bresnahan clung to his dream of a big league career with inspiring intensity. An avid fan and amateur baseball historian, he approached the game with an irrepressible fun streak that endeared him to managers, coaches, fans, the media, and, above all, his fellow players. When, in a fit of anger over a loss, Gomez outlawed drinking beer on the team bus during the long trip home, Bresnahan led the squad in rousing tuneless renditions of inane TV sitcom theme songs, such as *The Dick Van Dyke Show* or *The Brady Bunch*. Beneath the chorus one could just discern in the back of the bus the faint but unmistakable swish of tabs popping off cans of smuggled suds.

When the Bills started to lose, and lose they did after Gomez's arrival that summer, sending Bresnahan down to Class A ball seemed a logical step. The team needed a change, Bresnahan was hitting under .200, and there was a catcher in Kingston whom the Indians considered a prospect. What the new manager could not have known was how important Bresnahan was to the team in less measurable ways. He could not have known, for instance, how Brez, despite his anemic bat, had driven in four runs in a crucial playoff game the year before. Gomez couldn't have known the countless goofy ways Brez motivated his teammates daily. The Bills took the field the day after Brez left town that summer with the right sleeves of their blue-and-red jerseys rolled up as a gesture of mourning.

A month later the Bills' starting catcher got hurt, and Bresnahan was back, but by then, in early August, the season was already a write-off. Bus rides seemed interminable. Everyone was sick to death of each other, of ballpark hot dogs, of the faintly nauseating odor of stale cigarettes and spilled beer in the team bus, and of Gomez's vexed Hispanic lamentations. It was about then that Bresnahan first started talking about the potato.

One evening in August, Bresnahan was drinking beer at Joey's, a popular hangout in Williamsport, with his roommate, Rob Swain. Swain was a short, crewcut infielder with a muscular frame and such tiny feet that his teammates used to say his shoes were small enough to drape over a rearview mirror. The roommates were watching the bar's giant TV screen when a piece came on about big league pitchers scuffing baseballs.

"This is a kooky, crazy game," said Bresnahan, whose pensive musings on The Game tended to flow with a few beers. "People are always trying to get away with stuff. I read once that a player used a potato in a baseball game."

A potato?

He told Swain that he couldn't remember where he read it, or how the potato was used, but there was something about the idea that intrigued him.

No one knows how greatness comes to a man. For some it is a gift at birth, for others it comes with a struggle.

For Dave Bresnahan, it came in a moment of blind inspiration on a team bus in junior college. He thought: *Wouldn't it be funny to use a potato in a baseball game?* But through his school years and early years in the minors, the games had all seemed too important.

Now, the time had come. The potato haunted Bresnahan the way a cliff seems to beckon those who fear heights.

"I've always wondered if it would work," he said one night to Mike Poehl.

Bresnahan explained that the trick would be to make a runner on third believe the ball had been overthrown into left field. Then he could be tagged out at home. "You would have to have a guy on third and a potato shaped just the right size . . . ," Bresnahan explained.

Poehl laughed, but not heartily. The Indians' number-one draft pick in 1985, Poehl was a passive, pampered, towering Texas thoroughbred with a big league fastball and a tragically fragile arm. More than the Bills' wins and losses, Poehl worried about his earned run average. He told Bresnahan he thought it would be real funny so long as it didn't happen in his game.

But most of the Bills loved the idea. The potato got to be the one thing they looked forward to more than the end of the season.

Since a second-string catcher can be sure of playing only during a double-header, and the season had only one double-header left, it was decided that the game would be Monday, August 31. Sitting around a Reading hotel room Saturday afternoon, two days before, Bresnahan was chewing over the idea with Bills first baseman Bob Gergan, a power-hitting preppie with a bad back. Bresnahan said he had one reservation:

"What if they let the run count? I talked to Poehl about it, and he doesn't want the run to count against him."

Gergan said he was sure that the run wouldn't count.

"There's nothing in the rule book about a potato," he said with certainty.

But for Bresnahan this wasn't good enough. So Gergan phoned a friend who worked as a major league umpire and explained the proposed scenario. His friend said no clear rule would apply. This meant the ump would be on his own. If it happened to him, Gergan's friend said, he would most likely send the prankster to the showers and move the runner back to third—no harm done—and have a good laugh about the whole thing later.

When Bresnahan got a chance to play that night, he tried to pick a Reading runner off at third base. Reading would be back in Williamsport for the Monday double-header. He wanted them to note that, on occasion, this Bills catcher tried to pick runners off third.

Just in case.

On Monday morning Bresnahan visited the produce section of the Weiss market in Williamsport, seeing fruits and vegetables in a new light.

As he walked past the onions he had a fleeting thought . . . but, no, an onion might come apart.

Then the cantaloupes . . . but, no, too big. He stopped in front of the potato display, removed the twist-tie from the top of a plastic sack of Idaho spuds, and began rummaging through.

"Can I help you?" asked a produce clerk.

Bresnahan was so startled he jumped back and stammered a reply.

"Yeah, uh, I'm looking for some potatoes . . . My parents are coming over. They like really *big* potatoes."

Bresnahan couldn't believe how foolish that sounded, but the produce clerk seemed unfazed. He reached in and sorted out four choice spuds.

Back in his kitchen at home, Bresnahan set a baseball on the counter next to the potatoes to serve as a model. First off, the color was wrong. So he walked next door to borrow a potato peeler. He scraped the four potatoes bare. Next, their shape was too oblong. He whacked off the ends with a butcher knife and whittled away until they were round and white. Then he tried to draw on the seams with a red ballpoint pen, but the shaved potato was moist, and the ink wouldn't take. He squinted at his handiwork and began to worry that the stunt might not work.

"What if the guy on third can see right away that it's not a baseball?" he asked Swain.

So they took one out to play catch. To Bresnahan's delight, the potato in flight looked more like a baseball than it had on the kitchen counter.

Now, if Gomez would only schedule Bresnahan to play the second game. Poehl was scheduled to pitch the first game, and he had already made his feelings about the stunt clear. Besides, during the second game it would be dark and they would be playing under the lights . . . it would be perfect.

Bresnahan went to the ballpark that afternoon with a knot in his stomach. On the lineup card in the locker room, Gomez had penciled him in as catcher for the first game—Poehl's game.

That was that. Bresnahan set the carved potatoes on the shelf over his locker and began dressing for the game, half depressed and half relieved. But when the rest of his teammates saw the carved tubers on the shelf, there was real excitement in the locker room for the first time in months.

"It's Potato Day!" one shouted, playfully tossing one of the spuds across the room.

"Are you really going through with it, Brez?" one asked.

Bresnahan leaned over to Poehl, who was getting dressed before his locker.

"If I decide to throw the potato tonight, is it all right with you?" he asked.

"No way," said Poehl. "I don't want a run counting against me."

Bresnahan shrugged to his teammates, as if to say, *What can I do?* They started ragging Poehl.

"Lighten up, Mike," said Swain.

"Look, this is serious business for me," said Poehl. "If that run counts, it counts against me, not all of you."

Gergan then told Poehl about the conversation with his friend the major league umpire.

"There's nothing in the rule books about it, Mike," he said. "The run can't count."

Poehl felt himself outnumbered.

"Do whatever you want," he said, reluctantly.

Poehl pitched three good innings that night before Reading outfielder Steve DeAngelis singled in a run at the top of the fourth. The Bills failed to answer it.

So the Bills were down 1–0 at the top of the fifth. The sky had begun to darken behind the small stands at Bowman Field. The infield was mostly illuminated by the overhead lights, but the wooden outfield walls were still in sunlight, the two effects mingling to create a setting that seemed eerie, unreal. The large wooden panels of the outfield wall were painted with advertisements: "Singerland's Lawn & Landscape Service," "Knight Confer Funeral Home Inc.," "WNEP-TV—Channel 16," etc. A crowd of 3,258 was watching.

Reading's big catcher, Rick Lundblade, singled to left to open the inning. Then Phils pitcher Mike Shelton moved Lundblade to second with a sacrifice bunt. One out, man on second. Behind the plate, Bresnahan had butterflies in his gut. He knew the moment he had been waiting for was near.

With a left-handed batter, Bresnahan signaled to Poehl that he wanted a low breaking ball inside, a pitch calculated to produce a grounder to the right side of the infield that would be perfect to move Lundblade to third.

Poehl's pitch worked like a charm. The batter grounded out to second base, and the scene was set. Two outs, Rick Lundblade towering there on third base, glowing with earnest, unsuspecting ambition for home.

It's now or never, Bresnahan thought. He stood up before the next batter could step into the box and waved his catcher's mitt at home plate umpire Scott Potter.

"The netting's busted," Bresnahan said.

"Go ahead, get another one," said Potter, waving Bresnahan to the dugout.

Down at third, Swain put his head down, kicked one of his spikes at the infield dirt, and turned away to keep from laughing as he saw Bresnahan waddle off purposefully toward the dugout. Poehl had profound mixed feelings. He gazed over at Lundblade at third base and just shook his head. He did a quick mental calculation to see how the run would affect his ERA.

In the dugout, Bresnahan dropped his mitt and reached into his bag for another. All the other players on the bench watched with a mixture of disbelief and hilarity. Only Gomez was oblivious to the catcher's intentions.

As Bresnahan trotted back to home plate with the potato cradled in his new mitt, he worried how he was going to catch Poehl's pitch without anyone spotting the potato. He would have to take it out of the mitt somehow . . .

Crouched down behind the right-handed batter, Bresnahan signaled Poehl to throw a slider low and away. Then he gingerly removed the potato from the mitt, cupping it in his right hand, which he draped over his right knee.

Out on the mound, Poehl shrugged off his reservations, reared back, and fired the pitch low and outside.

Bresnahan watched the pitch come in, pleading silently, *Don't hit it!*

As umpire Potter shouted "Ball!" Bresnahan speared the pitch in his empty mitt, leapt to his feet, and threw the potato hard, aiming just over Swain's head. The third baseman was startled because the damn thing was bearing right at him—Brez had made a near-perfect throw! For a fleeting second Swain noted that Lundblade was far enough off third that he wasn't going to get back in time . . . but, of course, this wasn't a ball!

Swain lunged at the potato and deliberately missed it.

Lundblade stood off third, momentarily frozen, as the throw sailed off toward left field.

At home, Bresnahan threw his catcher's mask to the ground and swore theatrically.

Reading third base coach Joe Lefebvre was screaming, "Go! Go! Go!"

Lundblade started home. Bresnahan had turned and was kicking the dirt, looking dejected. At third, Swain watched as the big Dominican left-fielder, Miguel Roman, sprinted in to scoop up the ball . . . and then stopped dead in his tracks.

Roman, who had not been in on the planning for this moment, gave Swain a look that said, What the hell is this?

Lefebvre stared out to left, wondering why Roman was just standing there looking confused.

And just as Lundblade was about to lumber across home plate, Bresnahan turned toward him with a grin and tagged him with the ball.

"Hey, Rick, you're out," he said.

Then Bresnahan turned, rolled the ball back out to the mound, and started trotting off the field.

The whole stadium was silent for a moment, bewildered. Lundblade stood at home plate, looking back out toward the third base coach.

"Brez!" shouted umpire Potter, breaking the spell. "What the hell did you do?"

"It's a fucking potato!" shouted Lefebvre, who had sprinted out to left field to examine the contents of Roman's hand. He was striding back with the offending object to show the umpire. Reading manager George Culver had run out on the field to have a look.

"You can't bring another ball on the field!" stormed Potter.

"It's not a ball, ump, it's a potato," said Bresnahan.

Potter was fuming.

"You're trying to show me up," he said.

"I'm not trying to show you up," said Bresnahan. "And that run doesn't count."

Gergan, who had trotted in laughing from his position at first base, towered over Potter, who was flustered and angry.

"Hey, lighten up, ump," he said. "It's only a joke."

"This is professional baseball; you guys can't be out here showing me up like that," said Potter. "That run counts."

"You can't do that, ump," argued Swain, who had run in from third. "It's just a joke. Just do it over."

"No, the run counts!"

"Come on, ump."

"The run counts!"

Orlando Gomez took it personally. While Bresnahan and the rest of the team retired the last Reading batter, the manager called Jeff Scott, head of player development for the Indians' farm clubs. For the time being, Bresnahan stayed in the game, but Gomez was angry.

The manager knew how much the team liked Bresnahan, which he had always seen as a vague threat to his own leadership. He knew the second-string catcher was no prospect but felt there was a chance Bresnahan could end up with a coaching job. He hadn't liked sending Bresnahan down to Class A ball, and he suspected that the catcher resented him for it. Now this! This was just too damn much. As far as Gomez was concerned, there was nothing funny about it. He saw it as Bresnahan's way of thumbing his nose at the manager.

When Bresnahan headed to the dugout after the inning was over, Gomez told him to take off his gear.

"You're out," he said. "I'll talk to you after the game."

Rob Swain was the first Bills batter up in the top of the sixth. From beneath his catcher's mask, Lundblade grinned up at Swain.

"Man, that was *awesome!*" he said.

The episode fired up the Bills. They came back to score four runs and win the game. Mike Poehl ended up with a five-hitter. He stayed mad for a few hours, but then he cooled off. He still doesn't laugh about it as hard as his teammates, but he has no hard feelings.

After the first game, Gomez called Bresnahan into his tiny office under the stands.

"What you do, Brez, is very embarrassing to the team," he said, placing the accent on the third syllable of the word "embarrassing" in a way that tickled Bresnahan so that he could hardly keep from laughing.

Gomez fined Bresnahan $50. His teammates took up an immediate collection.

The next morning's newspaper failed to see the humor in Bresnahan's prank. "BILLS SPLIT BILL WITH PHILS, FINE THEIR POTATO-THROWING CATCHER" was the headline on a story that called his caper "a foolish stunt" and quoted Gomez as saying, "Bresnahan did an unthinkable thing for a professional."

In the story, Gomez was also quoted as saying that Bresnahan would never play for him again.

That morning, the manager summoned Bresnahan back to his office and fired him.

Bresnahan never expected his baseball career to end when he threw the potato. He figured he'd get tossed out of the game and probably get fined. But Gomez's decision just floored him. When Brez talked to Jeff Scott, the Indians' head of player development, after Gomez had given him the bad news, even Scott had to admit the prank had style.

"Brez, what are you trying to do, get on *Letterman?*" Scott asked, chuckling. But Scott, who had real affection for the catcher, said he would have to back the manager on this one.

Bresnahan drove home and broke the news to his teammates, who were flabbergasted. For all of about an hour he was depressed, thinking maybe the stunt had been a bad idea after all.

But that feeling passed when he called his dad later that day to tell him what had happened, and his father laughed and laughed. Brez ended up coughing and crying with laughter at the other end of the phone.

Bresnahan went back to the ballpark on Wednesday to clean out his locker. He stopped at Weiss market on his way and bought a bag of potatoes. In the locker room, he placed one potato on the shelf of each of his teammates' lockers. Then he dumped the rest on Gomez's desk.

As an afterthought, he went back and wrote the manager a note:

"Orlando—You really do not expect me to pay the $50 fine levied on me. However, I will oblige you by paying you these fifty potatoes. This spud's for you.—Brez."

EPILOGUE: *Dave Bresnahan now works as a real estate agent and a broker in Phoenix. Despite the sour initial reaction to his practical joke, the legend of the potato-throwing minor league catcher has been warmly embraced by baseball fans all over the country.*

Within two days, the Williamsport Bills received inquiries about the incident from more than thirty newspapers and radio and TV stations. The Chicago Tribune *last year named Bresnahan its "Sports Person of the Year" for "attempting to have a little fun with life, to inject some lost levity into sports."*

Spurred by this groundswell, the Williamsport Bills braved the disapproval of their parent organization to hold "Dave Bresnahan night" at Bowman Field on May 30. Dave was flown back to town to autograph baseballs and potatoes and to have his number retired. It's out there now, No. 59, on the wooden fence in straight-away center.

"Baseball purists ask, Why? He made a travesty of the game," said Bills general manager Rick Mundean. "But we think Dave did something that is the essence of the game—he had fun with it."

Orlando Gomez, who was demoted this year to Class A ball in Kingston, North Carolina, still thinks Bresnahan's stunt was "unprofessional."

"I can't believe all the attention he's gotten over this thing," complained Gomez. "I love this game. What he did was to make a joke out of it."

Precisely.

A BEAUTIFUL
MIND

JANUARY 2004

In the three years I covered the Philadelphia Eagles for The Inquirer, *I used to write a weekly story called "Inside the Game." The idea was to pick a player, watch him carefully during a football game, and then interview him in depth about that game the day afterward, usually a Monday. The "Inside the Game" story would run on Tuesdays, and each week it offered an insider's perspective that illuminated the game, the featured player, and his position. It always struck me that the players were the ones who really knew what happened during a football game, while writers were just watching from a distance. Why not let the participants tell the story? I am particularly fascinated by the mental aspects of the game. In my years of writing about pro football, I have never met a stupid player, and the most consistently bright and articulate are offensive linemen. The "Inside the Game" stories had to be reported and written in a day. The Atlantic gave me a chance to do the same kind of piece, only with more time to report and write it, and more space to tell the story. Hank Fraley couldn't have been nicer. As it happens, when this story ran in 2004, the Eagles were just one game away from playing the Patriots for a second time in the Super Bowl—which would have made both the magazine and me look amazingly prescient. Alas, the Eagles lost the NFC championship game to the Carolina Panthers.*

If you take a walk half an hour before game time around Lincoln Financial Field, Philadelphia's new football stadium, you will find a summary history of the city's seventy-year-old NFL franchise in the jerseys worn by its fans. Many old-timers still wear the team's traditional kelly green, a cheerful shade that matched the infamous synthetic turf in Veterans Stadium—the much-reviled gigantic concrete bowl, home to Philadelphia's pro baseball and football teams for thirty-one years, that sits brooding, empty, and forsaken across Pattison Avenue, awaiting its date with implosion. Marking that old era you'll find jerseys bearing the numbers of retired heroes such as Harold Carmichael (17), Bill Bergey (66),

Ron Jaworski (7), Randall Cunningham (12), Seth Joyner (59), Jerome Brown (99), Reggie White (92), and a multitude of others. Nine years ago the team's current owner, Jeffrey Lurie, began remaking the franchise, and one of his first changes was to chuck the cheerful green for a more à la mode shade. (We live in a period that disdains bold colors.) So now a dark metallic shade of green predominates among the masses who move into position before a game. Just about every starting player on the current Eagles roster is represented, from the obvious ones—quarterback Donovan McNabb (5) and running back Duce Staley (22)—to receivers, defensive backs, kickers, linebackers, and even linemen. The scarcest jersey numbers are those of offensive linemen, but even they are here. Pro Bowl tackles Jon Runyan (69) and Tra Thomas (72) are represented, as are guards Jermane Mayberry (71) and John Welbourn (76). But search as you might, and I have searched high and low, you will be hard-pressed to find one among these thousands sporting the number 63, worn by Hank Fraley.

This despite the fact that Fraley has started almost every Eagles game for the past three seasons, and has handled the ball on at least three fourths of the team's offensive plays during that period—the most successful stretch of football the Eagles have played in more than twenty years. He played a critical role in orchestrating most of those plays. He was rewarded for his skills last year with a $1.4 million signing bonus and a five-year, million-dollar-a-year contract extension—precisely the kind of deal sought in vain by Staley, the Eagles' star running back.

Fraley is the center. He is the guy who squats and offers his wide rear end to the quarterback before almost every offensive play, who snaps the ball into the star's hands and then braces himself to be run over. He has never scored a touchdown. He has never passed, kicked, caught, or carried the football in a game—not in high school, college, or the NFL. Not once.

He doesn't look like a professional athlete. He weighs more than three hundred pounds. Even when he's wearing shoulder pads, his middle is the widest part of his body. He looks soft. His midsection spills over the stretched elastic waist of his skintight white-and-silver uniform pants. It is not a pretty sight. Even in the ever-rounder, oversized, overweight world of football linemen, Fraley seems especially doughy. And the impression comes from more than just his physique. He has a mildness, a sweetness of character, that goes with the apparent softness of his body. His teammates dubbed him "Honeybuns," or "Buns," after a practice session in his rookie season when he was beset by a stubborn bumblebee, which prompted Tra Thomas to joke that he must be "sweet as a honeybun." He has small, narrow eyes of pale green, a pug nose, and pouty lips. These features are all pinched at the center of a broad, flat, pink landscape of cheeks and neck. His chin is little more than a lightly cupped shadow in the great roundness that rises from the neck of his jersey. Even his wan stubble of fair beard fails to suggest so much as a hint of jawline.

Fraley likes to come out to the field early on game day, hours before kickoff. It calms him. There is something cathedral-like about the empty stadium in the pregnant calm before game time: the lush flat rectangle of pampered, perfect grass, carefully manicured and lined, is surrounded by towering walls of silent seats. It is thrilling to stand at the center of such a monumental space, and humbling. Small flocks of pigeons soar in sudden graceful fits in the empty enclosure. High above, the big gray undersides of commercial jets slide low across the framed patch of sky on their approach to nearby Philadelphia International Airport. The new stadium has an airy feel, as though it were constructed from ropes and cloth instead of concrete and steel. It is the boldest achievement yet in Lurie's ongoing makeover of the Eagles, and is such an aesthetic triumph that many locals worry it may be *too* nice—that it doesn't feel like blue-collar Philly and could ruin the team's surly, working-class image. Fraley has no such worries. He spends much of his time on the field crashing into that turf, and he appreciates the more yielding texture of real grass, even if it is threaded with millions of green-plastic strands to make it more durable.

On September 14, the Eagles played the New England Patriots in the second regular-season game at Lincoln Financial Field. The Eagles had christened the new facility the Monday before, with a gaudy celebration before a national ABC-TV audience, and then had executed a humiliating swan dive, losing 17–0 to the reigning Super Bowl champions, the Tampa Bay Buccaneers.

The loss sent the team's local critics, on radio and TV and in print, into awful spasms of doubt and blame, but it didn't especially rile Fraley and his teammates. They always hate to lose, but it was, after all, only the first of sixteen games. They had been defeated by the league's top-ranked team, and the game had actually been close the whole way. Fraley was concerned mostly about three passing plays in which he had found himself disastrously out of position.

Three times he had left a wide opening off his right hip for Tampa's star defensive tackle, Warren Sapp. The first time he was out of position, he had gotten lucky. Sapp had had an opening to Fraley's right but had gone left. But the second and third times, Sapp had shot right past him, charged into the backfield, and disrupted the play. Mistakes like that can lose a close football game—and if uncorrected, can end a career. He knew Sapp was fast enough to beat even the league's best blocker sometimes; but for it to have happened three times meant that there was something wrong with Fraley's technique. He left the locker room that night wondering what it was.

Two days later, after devouring a small alp of food in the cafeteria of the Eagles' practice facility, Fraley filled another plate and retired to a classroom to study the game tapes in slow motion. In each of those plays he was supposed to have snapped the ball and then stepped back immediately with his right foot, pivoted left, and prepared to absorb Sapp's charge. But in all three plays, he noticed, after snapping the ball he had taken not one long step back with his right foot but two short steps—the first more like a little hop. Despite their manly job descriptions, offensive linemen are a bit like the dancing hippos in *Fantasia*. Footwork is as careful and deliberate for them as for a ballerina. Fraley tries to perfect his footwork every day, in practice and at home. So it was frustrating to watch himself unconsciously ad-libbing a hop into the movement. Where had that come from? He hadn't even been aware that he was doing it, but it had been enough to give Sapp the advantage. In the week leading up to the Patriots game, Fraley practiced at home to restore the proper rhythm: snap, long step back with the right foot, pivot left, brace.

Playing center is one of the most important jobs in football. It involves a lot more than just hiking and blocking. In the seconds between leaving the huddle and snapping the ball, the center must evaluate the defensive formation he sees in light of the play just called. He must anticipate what the defense is going to do—say, blitz a linebacker or a safety, or try some stunt—and then adjust the blocking assignments to cope with it. Donovan McNabb, the Eagles' star quarterback, studies game tapes all week with Fraley, and the two work together closely on the field. "Hank and I work as a team," McNabb says. "Everything that people see me do starts with Hank." While the center is making adjustments to the blocking scheme, shouting out changes in code, the quarterback is shouting out his own

changes to running backs and receivers—or he may change the play altogether. Each must listen to the other. Fraley has to be alert to the changes
called by the quarterback, and vice versa. All of this takes place in the seconds before every offensive play, often in a stadium roaring with noise,
before a defense that is deliberately trying to disguise its intentions. "Hank's
calls influence a lot," says McNabb. "Suppose I see that we don't have
enough blockers to handle everyone coming at me. If Hank makes a check
to counter that, and I miss it, I'll ending up throwing hot"—dumping the
ball quickly to a predesignated "hot" receiver—"when I'm protected." In
that scenario McNabb's hot pass not only aborts the called play but will
also probably go to a receiver who is not expecting the ball.

But as important as the center's position is, it is also peculiarly invisible. The eyes of everyone watching a football game move away from the
center the very second he snaps the ball, and except for the linemen who
battle with and against him, hardly anyone notices where he ends up when
the play is over. Usually it's in a bruising heap. His is arguably the most
difficult and least rewarding role in all of sport. What center is ever featured in a highlights reel unless he makes a big mistake? What center has
ever been carried off the field by his triumphant teammates after a big win?

In recreational football the offensive line is a repository for boys too fat,
too slow, or too awkward to be trusted with the ball. Many an aspiring
footballer has quit the game forever after a few days of getting ignomini-
ously knocked around in practice. Once you become a blocker, the only
glory you will ever taste is team glory.

Dave Alexander, who played center for the Eagles a decade ago, now
coaches his two sons in recreational football back in Tulsa, Oklahoma. They
are big, like their father—"destined for the line the day they first walked
on the field," he says with a fatherly chuckle. "And the thing that strikes
me is, when the team scores a touchdown, there's nobody on the field who
is happier than they are. For linemen, it's not about people slapping you
on the back or having your name announced on the loudspeaker, it's about
making the numbers change on the scoreboard. It's weird, but even after
all the years I played, I never fully appreciated that until now." A quarterback, a running back, a receiver, a linebacker, a cornerback, a safety, or
even a defensive lineman can dazzle the crowd, even in a losing effort.

Players in these other positions can amass all-star statistics: touchdowns, sacks, interceptions, tackles. Not an offensive lineman. If the team loses, he loses. And of all the jobs on the offensive line, center is the least desirable, at least when one is starting out. Among other things, don't forget, the center is the guy who has to let the quarterback lay hands on the underside of his butt—a matter whose awkwardness for teenage boys cannot be overestimated. So the job attracts big, sturdy boys who aren't easily embarrassed, or who are willing to swallow a little ridicule in order to make the team. Many a star football player pays lip service to the principle of Team First; but for the big man at center, the team is all there is.

The terms "offensive" and "defensive" are misleading when they refer to linemen. Along the line of scrimmage, defensive linemen essentially play offense, in that their job is to attack, to go after the man with the ball; offensive linemen play defense. On the snap of the ball defensive linemen cut loose with everything they've got, using strength, speed, and cunning to avoid blockers and make the tackle. Defensive linemen tend to be intimidating men—loud, fast, and emotional. They live by furious blasts of effort, launching themselves toward the opposing team's backfield. Offensive linemen have a more placid, controlled nature; they tend to be neither glory seekers nor hotheads. Their job is to absorb the onslaught. The keys to their success are not fury and cunning but footwork and balance. Because he is in charge, the center usually epitomizes these traits. On most football teams he is the least mercurial man on the roster. And, in contrast to the stereotype of the big dumb football player, at the pro level the center's role demands a high degree of self-possession and analytical skill.

Of all pro football players, offensive linemen are the least likely to be taken for athletes off the field. Fraley likes to wow pickup players on the racquetball court, where he proves surprisingly nimble. He doesn't always tell his humbled opponents what he does for a living.

Stan Walters, the Pro Bowl tackle in the Eagles' one Super Bowl appearance (1981, a loss to the Oakland Raiders), was the same. He moved with his family to a suburb of Atlanta years after he retired, and was washing his car one weekend afternoon when a group of men from his neighborhood, with no idea of his past, invited him to join them in a game of touch football.

"It was the first time I had played football since I played for the Eagles," Walters told me recently. "I had a ball. I hadn't had so much fun playing football since I was a kid. I was running the ball, kicking it, knocking guys on their asses, throwing touchdown passes, catching touchdown passes. And on the way home a couple of guys were walking up the road from me when one of them turns to his buddy and says, 'Man, that fat guy can really play!'"

None of Fraley's old coaches—from his high school team, in the Maryland suburbs of Washington, or from his team at Robert Morris University, a small school near Pittsburgh, where he played Division I-AA college ball—envisioned him as a future pro. Neither did the NFL. He wasn't drafted by any pro team out of college. In the highly specialized world of professional football, at about three hundred pounds he was considered too small to be a guard, and at six-two was considered too short (and short-armed) to play offensive tackle—a job that requires handling the outside rush of defensive ends, some of the fastest and most powerful big men in the game. He made it onto the Eagles by impressing the coaches with his intelligence and work ethic, qualities that especially appeal to the team's head coach, the massively rotund Andy Reid, himself a former offensive lineman. The team reflects Reid's personality, which is—well, bovine. He is a resolute nonconductor of electricity. Winning for Reid is strictly method, not magic. When he was interviewed for the job, he arrived with a three-ring binder that spelled out in precise detail his method for building a championship team. He had been working on it for years. Reid likes players who share his calm, workmanlike approach—and no one conforms better than Fraley, who even looks like a younger version of his head coach.

Fraley stays late to study tapes with both the offensive line and the quarterbacks, and then takes the tapes home at night. He memorizes formations and tendencies, and scours the images for clues to his opponents' intentions. Players often develop subtle habits that give away what they intend to do; sometimes linebackers will set their feet differently if they plan to blitz, or linemen will lean slightly in the direction they intend to charge. Fraley knows from personal experience how unconscious this is. In his rookie year he had the habit of drumming his fingers lightly on the ball during the snap count until it was time to hike it. Hollis Thomas, one of the Eagles' defensive linemen, had kindly pointed it out.

"Look, kid," he told Fraley. "As soon as those fingers stop, I know you're going to hike the ball. It gives me an extra second on every play."

*   *   *

On his ritual visit to the field before the Patriots game, Fraley spent a few minutes stretching in the end zone with Jon Runyan, and then the two sat and talked a while. A light drizzle was falling. When Runyan headed back to the locker room, Fraley walked, as he always does, to one of the end zones. He tapped the metal goalpost twice and repeated a personal incantation: "It's going to be a great day, a great game."

By game time the swirling clouds and drizzle had given way to a sunny, steamy afternoon. The stands were filled with stomping, cheering fans. The loudspeakers blared music and pregame announcements as Fraley did his last-minute footwork drills and went through a couple of snaps with McNabb.

From a media booth high above, Phil Simms, the CBS-TV color man, surveyed the playing field with Greg Gumbel, the play-by-play man. Setting up the context for the game, noting that both teams had lost their opener, Simms said, "The week of suffering is almost over for both teams."

Fraley's assignment against the Patriots was to block the giant nose tackle, Ted Washington, who is listed at three hundred and sixty-five pounds but weighs closer to four hundred. It's hard to imagine a three-hundred-ten-pound man looking overmatched, but when Fraley squatted for the first snap with Washington leaning directly over him, he looked small.

All his nerves settled down after the initial crash of pads and the first hard tumble. Fraley likes the feeling of hitting and getting hit. It wakes him up. His team's opening drive faltered on a couple of dropped passes, and it wasn't until the second Eagles offensive series that the team made a big play. On the third down, with nine yards to go, Eagles tight end Chad Lewis caught a pass for a big gain and a first down on New England's half of the field—but there was a flag.

Emerging from the huddle before the play, Fraley had seen Patriots linebacker Tedy Bruschi sneaking up to blitz. Fraley had shouted out a protection scheme that called for him to pick up the linebacker, and for the left guard, John Welbourn, to slide right and pick up the nose tackle, now Jarvis Green (giving Washington a break). But on the snap of the ball Green had charged to his right, into Fraley, who, turning to block Bruschi, was caught off balance. He rolled his ankle, and went sprawling backward. When Fraley fell, Green crashed down on him like a man who has been charging a door that is suddenly flung open.

Fraley heard the roar of the crowd as Lewis made the catch, but then spotted the yellow flag alongside his knee. He knew how the play had looked to the ref: as though the center had grabbed Green's jersey as he fell, yanking the nose tackle down with him—which might actually have been a smart move. He pulled himself up on one knee and pleaded with the ref, "I wasn't holding!"

To no avail. In the mess of action on the line of scrimmage, appearance is always reality.

"Looks like it's going to come back," Gumbel said.

The penalty wiped out the first down and any sense of momentum, and left the team with nineteen yards to go for a first down. The loudspeaker boomed out Fraley's name as the offending player, and the CBS camera, for the first time in the game, zeroed in on the center, his hands on his hips, seething.

"That's the center, Hank Fraley," Simms said—one of only two times Fraley was recognized in the broadcast of the game.

CBS ran a replay that clearly showed Fraley had not grabbed Green, but neither Simms nor Gumbel noted it. On the field, Patriots safety Rodney Harrison shouted across at Fraley, "Cheap-shot artist!"

"Fuck you," Fraley said.

The Eagles failed to get a first down and finished the first quarter trailing the Patriots 3–0. The hometown crowd was starting to boo. But the Eagles came right back in the second quarter, driving the ball down the field sixty-five yards in eight plays, to the Patriots' two-yard line. Fraley helped steer the drive with furious effort, orchestrating the grunt work that most often makes a play succeed or fail: reading New England's defenses; shouting "Jam! Jam!" to alert the line to an overloaded defensive front; designating the "mike," or middle linebacker (which, given the various ways New England's defense lines up, can be a different player each time); shouting "Fan!" to signal a scheme of sliding blocks that might send the two players on his left in one direction and himself with the two players on his right in another. On this drive everything seemed to work, even a missed block. When Eagles running back Brian Westbrook swept around the left end, Hank slipped his block and raced after him. He lunged in vain at a linebacker, who deftly sidestepped him, and crashed emptily to earth. He was struggling to his feet when another Patriots player accidentally ran smack into him and went flying several yards farther upfield, landing upside down.

Fraley's fellow lineman Welbourn helped the center to his feet. "I saw you down, so I ran my guy right into you," he explained, grinning.

The downed Patriots player pointed at Fraley menacingly, as if to say, *That was an unfair hit, sixty-three, and I'm going to remember you.*

The drive led to a critical third-down play just two yards from the goal line. This is where offensive and defensive linemen are suddenly the most visibly important players on the field. The CBS cameras now focused and lingered on big Ted Washington.

"It's hard to run up the middle when you play the New England Patriots when Ted Washington is inside," Simms said. "Number ninety-two. Bill Belichick [the Patriots' head coach] says he's just a boulder. You got to double-team him at least. So that's why when you see the Eagles run it, most likely when he's in there, they're gonna try to go outside."

"He's a classic nose guard," Gumbel said.

"I think what people don't understand is that this is not a fat guy," Simms said. "He's six-foot-five, three hundred and sixty pounds, he's pretty athletic, and he is tremendous at stopping the running game up the middle."

As is often the case, the announcers were dead wrong about what was coming. Reid, speaking by radio to McNabb, called a running play right up the middle, and it proved to be the perfect call. New England's defense had guessed wrong. Betting that the Eagles would not run right at Washington, they planned to execute an "out charge." Fraley spotted it instantly. The Patriots' two nose tackles, Washington and Ty Warren, at the center of their six-man front, slanted outward in opposite directions, leaving only the middle linebacker, Roman Phifer, to handle whatever happened to come straight up the middle. The Eagles' play called for fullback Jon Ritchie to precede Duce Staley into the hole, knocking the linebacker out of the way so that Staley could sail into the end zone.

At the snap Washington lunged, as expected, to Fraley's right, and Warren to his left. Fraley threw himself at Warren, knocking both of them to the ground. Washington went down, hit by the two blockers on the left side of the line. Ritchie nailed Phifer, but the Patriots linebacker managed to break free and grab Staley before he crossed the goal line. The running back and the linebacker collided and were stymied, a meeting of equal and opposite forces. They teetered near the line. Fraley rose to one knee and threw himself into the two men; they all fell over the goal line.

The referee's arms shot straight up. On the ground in a pile of tangled players, Fraley heard the crowd erupt with joy. "Touchdown!" Gumbel shouted. "The Eagles put some points on the board for the first time this season, and take the lead."

Fireworks exploded overhead, and a great guttural roar shook the stadium. The state-of-the-art sound system blasted out the Eagles' fight song. Staley danced off with the ball, and the cameras and announcers celebrated him. Fraley pulled himself off the pile and got ready to block for the extra point. The kick sailed between the uprights, and the center trotted off the field, unnoticed and elated. He was greeted with high fives on the sidelines, and McNabb slapped him gleefully on his helmet. The team knew Staley hadn't scored by himself.

This proved to be the high point of the afternoon for the Eagles and their fans. The Patriots went on to score two touchdowns in succession, taking a 17–7 lead by halftime. As the sun began to set behind the upper tier of the stands, its light replaced by the gentler glare of stadium lights, the Eagles' hopes were fading. Their offense not only wasn't scoring but was continually failing to manage even a first down. The boos grew louder and louder.

On one third-down play late in the game Fraley hit his man, fell to the ground, rolled, and saw the ball drop a few feet away; an attacking linebacker had knocked it from McNabb's hands. Fraley leaped for it. Deep in a pile of wrestling big men, scrambling for the loose ball, he grabbed hold of something and pulled. It turned out to be the helmet of a Patriots player. In the melee he did finally get his hands on the football. It's not unusual for the ball to change hands several times at the bottom of such a seething pile before the referee can untangle the players and declare which team has legitimate possession. Often possession falls to whoever has the ball last. Fraley gripped the ball tight. Patriots defensive lineman Richard Seymour reached under Fraley's jersey and grabbed a fistful of his ample flesh (he would have a purple welt after the game), trying to force him to release the ball. There was punching, kicking, gouging. "You don't want to be there," Fraley would say later. By the time Fraley saw daylight again, the referee had concluded that the rightful owner of the fumbled ball was Patriots defensive end Willie McGinest, and was shouting "Blue ball! Blue ball!"

"Aw, ref," Fraley complained. "He never even had it."

It was an omen. The Patriots scored another touchdown. The Eagles managed a field goal in the fourth quarter, closing the gap to 24–10, but all hope died when a McNabb pass was intercepted by Bruschi, who ran it back eighteen yards for another New England touchdown.

Down by three touchdowns with only five minutes left to play, the Eagles were still battling. Their pride was on the line—as were their jobs. When a player stops trying, even in the hopeless final moments of a loss, it will be obvious on the game tapes. To be branded a quitter is a quick ticket to waivers. Very few pro football players feel any sense of job security. For all the affection of his coaches and teammates, and despite his generous contract extension, Fraley always feels he's only one or two bad games away from being on the bench—or even out of football altogether. Letting down also brings the risk of injury. In the final minutes of a blowout the winning team's defense often turns up the intensity, seeing a chance to run up its stats. A sack, a tackle, or an interception in the final minutes of a rout looks just as good on the score sheet as one earlier in the game.

Reveling in success, seeing the disappointment on the faces of the Eagles, some of the Patriots tried to further demoralize them.

"You suck!" one linebacker repeatedly shouted at the Eagles' offensive line. Others joined in: "You guys are overrated!" "Y'all have lost a step—you're getting old!"

The incorrect holding call at the beginning of the game continued to haunt Fraley. "Cheap-shot artist!" a linebacker shouted at him again. At the end of one play the whistle blew in time to stop a charging linebacker from blind-siding Fraley at the knees. "Hey, sixty-three, you know I was coming for you," the player taunted.

Long before this, Eagles fans had started leaving, and wide expanses of empty seats expressed the hometown's disgust. The final minutes of the 31–10 disaster were attended by only a few thousand spectators, most of whom appeared to be staying in order to heckle and jeer.

After the game a cloud of gloom hung in the steamy twilight of the Eagles' locker room. The team's big-name players lingered in the showers, hoping that the waiting horde of reporters and cameras might thin or give up entirely. In a corner Fraley slowly pulled on his big boxer shorts and then his blue jeans. He was bruised, stiff, and tired. His thigh hurt, he had a purpling welt on his side, and he had strained something in his ankle when he fell over in the first quarter.

"I've got to get that checked out," he said glumly.

After a victory offensive linemen can get trampled in the locker room by packs of reporters chasing down the players who made the big plays. But though the star players speak for the team in victory, in defeat sometimes the big, easygoing linemen are the only players willing to stare down the cameras and take the questions without rancor. By the time Fraley had his pants on, the pack had gathered. His face was still pink from the shower, and he squinted in the bright camera lights.

"How does it feel to start off losing two in a row?" one reporter asked.

"I don't think we're doubting ourselves," Fraley said, stiff and serious. "If you doubt yourself, you start to panic, and if you panic, you don't play well. We just have to execute on offense."

He was asked about the poor offensive showing, and about the second subpar performance by Donovan McNabb. More lights flicked on. Fraley mopped the sweat off his brow.

"I'm just going to have to look and see what I can do better," he said, diplomatically avoiding passing judgment on his teammate.

When the reporters realized that Fraley was too self-possessed to say anything remotely newsworthy, they abruptly clicked off their lights and headed for Chad Lewis, who had dropped a couple of big passes.

Fraley was left to finish stuffing his bag with his gear. After glancing up over his big shoulder at the reporters, he winked at me and smiled.

"Man," he said, "am I ever hungry."

(*Despite the depths of doubt and disbelief reached by the team's fans and the media after these two opening losses, the Eagles won nine of their next ten games.*)

RHINO

FEBRUARY 1982

*Gene Roberts just wandered up to my desk in the newsroom one afternoon and said,
"I want you to write me some stories about the rhino." He let that sink in, and then
added, "I want you to go where the rhinos are." That was all he said, but it launched
me on a project that was my first international assignment and the most ambitious
reporting and writing project I had ever undertaken. Roberts had been to Africa on a
vacation safari, and while there had learned that the black rhino, the World Wildlife
Fund's "Animal of the Year" the previous year, was considered the most endangered
large mammal in the world. He was concerned about the animal's plight, but he was
also curious to find out what had happened to the millions raised by the WWF all over
the world. Ever since these stories ran, they have been cited, usually disparagingly, as
Exhibit One of Roberts's eccentricity and excesses, and are unvaryingly referred to as
the "White Rhino" series (drawing on the analogy to a "white elephant"). When my
friend Paul Taylor wrote an article about* The Inquirer *for the* Washington Journalism Review, *he referred to the "six-part" rhino series. I wrote to him that it might
have seemed like six parts, but was actually only four. I think the rhino series is Exhibit
One of what made Roberts a great newspaper editor. It certainly is a prime example of
how he changed my life. For many years I was convinced that it would be the lead in
my eventual obit. This is my favorite of the four parts.*

Luangwa Valley, Zambia—They are twenty men. They have been
at their dangerous, impossible task for two years, patrolling for
poachers in this pristine African valley. They expect to be at it one
more year. After that, the World Wildlife Fund money will be gone.

Led by Phil Berry, a sturdy former Zambian game warden, this force
received almost 40 percent of the $2.3 million raised in the fund's 1980
"Save the Rhino" campaign. They are a brave crew, waging a losing battle
in one remote location to stem the slaughter of the rhinoceros.

Ten years ago, estimates of the rhino population at Luangwa went
as high as 10,000. Today, Berry's men hope to save the fewer than 4,000

that remain. This is believed to be the largest black rhino population left in the world.

Until Berry's men went to work, Zambia was a free zone for elephant and rhino poaching. Government game guards went unsupervised and often unpaid. The old colonial wilderness parks were ravaged by poacher gangs who lived unmolested in large camps throughout supposedly protected areas. Often, government game scouts acted as middlemen in the brisk elephant-ivory and rhino-horn trade. The country's rhino population was falling at the rate of one per day.

Berry's rhino-protection force is hopelessly small. Combined, the north and south Luangwa National Parks cover 6,000 square miles. The whole valley, a largely unspoiled wilderness in northeast Zambia, is closer to 20,000 square miles.

"That's one man for every 1,000 miles," Berry said with a bitter smile.

Despite this, he and his men have slowed poaching rates in the valley. They have given Luangwa's rhinos perhaps a few more years. Poaching gangs no longer squat brazenly inside park territory, stringing up skins to dry, stacking their haul of horn and ivory in the open. Berry's patrols average about ten arrests per month. Another small antipoaching unit in a different part of Zambia, funded from other sources, has a similar record.

But the gangs still prowl Zambia's national parks, moving with stealth and speed. Berry's men encounter slaughtered elephants and rhinos more often than poachers. Even poachers they catch have little to fear. Many draw fines far below the value of the horns and tusks they sell.

"What we're doing is, at best, a way to buy time," said Berry. "The only way to really stop the rhino killings, even in this valley, is to stop the rhino-horn trade. But we can't do that here. What we can do is make it bloody difficult for these poachers. And we'll be doing that as long as the money holds out."

One morning in August, five of Berry's scouts assembled for a typical four-day patrol. Each scout took a bolt-action, World War I–vintage rifle and ammunition. Their five bearers, barefoot young men clad in tatters, packed food and bedding into big canvas sacks they would carry on their heads. The food consisted of *mshima,* or "mealie-meal," the airy white maize powder that is the staple of the Zambians' diet, and twisted strings of dried elephant meat.

It was dry season, African winter, when the air smells of dust through 90-degree days and long, cool nights. Berry huddled over a faded map with Abraham Phiri, who would lead the patrol.

Abraham would march his men north for two days to the Luwi River and then south into higher, rockier ground where grasses were shorter, trees more numerous, and the nights much colder. On the fourth day they would walk out of the hills, down to the Mushiyashi River, where Berry would retrieve them in his Land Rover.

Berry's men spend as much time in the bush as in their home camp of round, tin-and-mud huts. They walk in corners of the vast valley where paid informants send them, keenly sensitive to signs of a poacher's presence: a distant swirl of vultures, a vaguely defined footprint in the dust, a pattern of snapped branches or reeds at man-height.

Walking through the bush for years accustoms the ear to soft sounds of birds, water, and wind, so the sudden slam of a rifle shot jars these men many miles away. Patrols often find abandoned poacher campsites. What they seek are direct confrontations.

Two years ago a squad of Berry's men was ambushed by poachers. The attackers grabbed one of the scouts, Tryson Mwandila, a clever, cheerful young man, and paraded him before the others with the barrel of an automatic rifle pressed to his temple.

"Poor Mwandila was trembling in his boots," Berry recalled. "Thought he was dead for sure. But one of my other boys shot his rifle off into the air and the poachers, including the one who held the gun to my bloke's head, took off running. They exchanged fire, but nobody hit anything. That was before I'd had time to really work with my boys. That sort of thing wouldn't happen today."

Poachers are not the valley's only dangers. The scouts always carry a loaded rifle, their only protection against Luangwa's lions, leopards, and cheetahs. And they are alert for the sudden charges of elephants or rhinos. Last year a charging cape buffalo rammed one of Berry's men, fracturing his hip and tearing off part of his ear. He was left with slight paralysis.

"The buffalo appeared unhurt," Berry wryly noted in his report of the incident.

This land is among the unique natural wilderness areas left on earth, a kind of lost valley protected from human encroachment by annual floods and the tsetse fly. Luangwa is a branching fracture of the Great Rift Valley, a long break in the continent that stretches from Mozambique north to the Dead Sea. Snaking through the center of this wide, sunken region, far below the cliffs on either side, is the Luangwa River, a fast-flowing torrent when water spills down from the escarpments during rainy season but a river of sand spotted with still, pea-green pools during the long dry season. Stagnant lagoons, formed by the river's ever-changing course, support the valley's rich variety of wildlife.

In just one year, Berry and his men have won a reputation throughout the valley and Africa that far outweighs their numbers or means. George Mubanga, an admiring wildlife expert in the Zambian capital of Lusaka, said, "Phil Berry? There are great men who live out their lives working in almost complete obscurity. He is one of them. Berry is a man of action. He puts the lie to the notion that one man can't make a difference. We need ten more just like him."

The men set off in a Land Rover, leaving Berry behind at the patrol's blockhouse headquarters, and rode north on dirt roads and fire trails until they ended. Eventually, the sturdy four-wheel-drive truck could proceed only in short hops, each turn of the wheels plowing into one deep rut or climbing out of another. There were miles of this pitted black clay, preserving the prints of elephant and hippo and rhino that slopped through it in the rainy season, when it was muck. Finally, walking was the only way to go on.

Abraham led the column at a walking sprint, the rifle under his right arm suspended from a shoulder strap. With short, quick steps, shoulders erect, Abraham, who is fifty-one, moved over the scarred terrain so nimbly that the taller, younger men in single file behind him—four armed scouts and I—stumbled and half ran to keep up. Behind them walked the five bearers with the big bundles balanced on their heads.

Each man concentrated on the next place to set his foot; a misstep on this uneven ground at Abraham's rapid pace could snap an ankle. No one spoke. Poaching gangs are always afoot. They usually are heard before they are seen.

After a half hour's hard pace, the men were in a full sweat. As the sun rose, the day grew hotter. The pitted clay gave way to sand that shifted slightly underfoot with each step, slowing them. The patrol climbed down a small embankment to the surface of a dry streambed. Gnarled remains of trees, washed along during the February floods, lay sunbaked and withered on the sand. Dusty air dried our mouths and throats.

Abraham halted before a slight impression on the sand. Bending, he traced with one black finger three curved prints arrayed in a tight arc.

"Rhino track," he said. "These are the three toes. One day old." The spoor led to a narrow path up the embankment into grass. A poacher who wanted this rhino's horns would only have to wait by this place. Judging by the worn footpath, the animal trudged by daily.

Around a tight bend on the wide sand highway we saw an elephant standing under a tall winter-thorn tree on the opposite bank. It was an old gray female with small tusks, rhythmically thrashing against the ground a clump of long grass clutched in its trunk. There were many elephants in this area, although this was the first the patrol had seen. Deep holes marked the sand where their trunks had dug down two feet or more for water. This gray old lady, upwind, appeared oblivious to the passing men, but Abraham, an old elephant hunter, took few chances. He led us back up the embankment into the cover of high grass.

Five years ago, Abraham was nearly killed by a charging elephant. It bellowed and lunged full tilt.

"If a man tries to outrun an elephant, the man will die," Abraham said in his flat, matter-of-fact way. "The elephant runs very fast, but he sees very bad. A smart man does not run fast when the elephant comes. He runs slow. He watches to see which way the wind blows and which way the elephant runs. To escape he must run the right way. If the man runs with the wind on his back, the elephant will not know where to find him."

In Abraham's case, the elephant was too close and the attack too fast for him to think of running. He leveled his rifle and put a bullet between the charging beast's eyes. The elephant fell dead only a few yards in front of him.

"I nearly died," Abraham said.

Elephant-control and antipoaching work, even with its hazards, is relatively tame for Abraham. When he was young, and Zambia was still a British colony, he served in the Queen's African Rifles, a regiment that fought the Chinese in Malaya from 1948 to 1951. He recalled with genuine appreciation how the British had spread the word to the Chinese that black soldiers were cannibals.

"The British soldiers smeared charcoal on their faces before battle to scare the enemy," he recalled mirthfully, still taken with the joke.

After he left the army, Abraham worked as an elephant hunter for the game department, shooting elephants that strayed from wilderness areas, destroying crops and frightening villagers. It was in this job that he had his near-fatal brush with the charging elephant.

Abraham was one of the first men Berry requested when the Zambian government gave him permission two years ago to recruit a crack Luangwa antipoaching unit. Now he is one of Berry's two patrol leaders.

When his men's shadows fell in small pools at their feet, Abraham stopped in a clearing of msolo trees, each with straight boles and a thin canopy of leaves overhead. The leaves had just begun turning to the bright reds and oranges of the late dry season. Because the driver had taken them far beyond the park's dirt roads, the patrol had reached Berry's predesignated first campsite early. We would rest there until morning. The carriers dropped their heavy bags in the shade and began setting up camp.

The scouts sat together at the base of one tree, laying their rifles on the ground at their sides, chanting and laughing softly. They spoke *Nyanja*, the indigenous language (one of the seventy-two in Zambia) that prevails in the northeastern province.

There was John S. Phiri, who is not directly related to Abraham. The name Phiri is very common in Zambia, like Smith, John S. explained. So Abraham Phiri was known simply as Abraham, but John preferred being addressed by his full name, John S. Phiri. A handsome, cocky fellow of twenty-nine, he jokingly introduced himself as "king of kings." John S. Phiri has also proved to be courageous to a fault and, if anything, a bit too eager for an encounter.

There was David Mulanga, at thirty-nine the oldest except for Abraham on the patrol. A compact man in a full field uniform, Mulanga had worked for years as an assistant to a game department botanist. Though he had no formal education, he knew each of the myriad varieties of trees, shrubs, and grass in the valley by name in both Latin and *Nyanja*.

There was Matteo Mwanza, twenty-five, recently married, the newest of Berry's recruits. Mwanza did not yet have the green uniform of the other scouts. His cotton shirt was loose and torn, his khaki pants the same. He was a bright, introspective man with an especially gentle manner.

There was tall Prospa Myatwa, twenty-eight, a hardy, joking fellow who spoke better English than the others. His uniform was new and clean, natty on his lanky frame. Myatwa's smile came easy and often, exposing a mouth of wide gums and small teeth.

As these men relaxed, the carriers scavenged beyond the msolo grove for firewood, bringing it back in great twisted heaps; enough to keep a circle of fires burning around the camp through the night. They set fires by arraying several long, dry branches radially, with one end of each touching at the center. In a large pot over one of these they cooked their *mshima*.

"*Mshima* in the morning, *mshima* in the afternoon, *mshima* in the evening," Abraham joked: "*Mshima* is what makes the African strong. The *muzungu* [the white man] is weak because he doesn't eat *mshima* like us." His scouts all laughed. When the powdered maize is stirred in water and cooked, it becomes a heavy white paste utterly without flavor.

After lunch, Abraham left the scouts and strolled out to the nearby Luwi Lagoon.

"We will wait here this afternoon and listen," Abraham said.

He positioned himself at a spot overlooking the water with a wide clearing behind him—"to see lion coming," he explained. Below, a family of fat hippos grunted and whooshed as they floated peacefully, only their eyes, ears, and round snouts above water. Their sudden roars echoed up from the water, breaking the stillness sharply. A crocodile lay dead still, sunning on the opposite bank, its mouth open wide, alert to opportunity.

Only the graceful arrival and departure of big gray-and-black herons altered this scene through the afternoon. At sunset, Abraham walked back to join the others for dinner. As the reds and golds of dusk faded to black, the carriers set fires blazing around the camp perimeter. The men sat around a central fire for several hours, telling stories, laughing. Then they stretched out fully clothed under blankets, rifles at their sides, to sleep.

When lions roared from the darkness beyond the fires that night, Prospa Myatwa stood up in the warm glow and urged his fellows to move their grass beds closer to me. He had sensed my uneasiness.

"It is normal for you to fear the lions," he said, with his wide, gummy smile. "Facing the lions is not something you do often. It is our job to do it."

* * *

On the day before this patrol started, Berry had made a run to Chipata. His big Land Rover blasted flat-out over dirt roads on the four-hour round trip, an explosion of dust in its wake. Before leaving, Berry had spent nearly an hour driving from village to village picking up those of his men who wanted to go along.

Berry repays his men's respect by looking after them with paternal interest. A general fighting a small war in a faraway place, he makes the concerns of his "boys" his own.

Berry once held an important job in Zambia's wildlife department, and though he has lived most of his forty years here, his whiteness and his British birth were enough to target him for "Zambianization" several years ago. He was replaced by a black Zambian and went to work for a safari company in the valley, as a guide on walking tours. He was overjoyed when the Save the Rhino Trust, a cooperative public-private group administering the wildlife fund's grant, asked him to head the antipoaching unit. It was a chance to resume the work his race and nationality had denied him.

When not in the bush, Berry is usually taxiing his men and their families back and forth to Chipata. The only other way for these villagers to make the hundred-mile trip is to walk, a journey of three or four days, the nights spent camping by the roadside. The crowded Land Rover roared past many walkers, men in loose dirty clothes with walking sticks and battered hats, women in drab olive shifts with babies slung in colorful wraps from their backs, serenely plodding, loads balanced easily on their heads. Most of the walkers would stop and turn to watch the more fortunate pass on wheels. Most waved.

Chipata is a dusty town with several paved roads at its center, dominated by the bright red-and-white onion-shaped domes of its mosque. Up dirt paths off the main roads are row after row of squat houses, stone boxes with slanted roofs, so many that they seem to sprout up from the soil, their outer walls stained the same color as the dust. Laundry flaps from a thousand lines strung over dirt yards, and everywhere are running children and small dogs.

"There are so many children," Berry said. "How do they manage to have so many children? You wonder what things are going to be like when these grow up. I don't like to think about it."

At game department headquarters, Berry learned that the government paychecks that were due the previous month still had not arrived.

But this was routine. Abraham had come along because he needed money to buy his son a bicycle. The boy had been walking for hours to the Catholic mission school and back each day, Abraham said, and had been promised a bike. His son would not be disappointed because Berry had promised to advance his patrol leader money if no checks were in. But his other men were downcast. They had hoped to have something to spend on their day in town. Berry had warned them before leaving that he would not give them all advances.

Game scouts earn much less than successful poachers. Senior scouts like Abraham can earn two hundred and sixty *kwachas* each month (one *kwacha* is worth slightly more than a dollar) if they spend eighteen days on patrol. Of that amount, about one hundred and thirty *kwachas* per month is their normal salary as government game scouts. They receive a supplementary payment of up to seventy *kwachas* from the Rhino Trust and small bonuses for catching poachers. Younger scouts earn about seventy *kwachas* total per month.

In order to have the men's supplementary money for payday three days later, Berry stopped at the crowded Barclay Bank and withdrew enough bundled *kwachas* from the Rhino Trust account to fill his briefcase.

Abraham and the other men climbed out of the truck. Berry was going off for lunch with a friend; the others had their own places to go for a few hours. But they lingered by the truck quietly. Berry knew they wanted him to advance them their pay from the bundles of money in his briefcase. Faking weary impatience, but actually pleased, Berry turned to his patrol leader.

"Ab'ram? How many days on patrol this month, Ab'ram?" he asked, reaching for his briefcase. Abraham turned to face him, threw his shoulders back, pulled his feet together, and thrust his hands to his sides at attention. Berry returned the military protocol, an exaggerated formality that typically ends, between Berry and his men, in laughter. But at this moment Abraham's brow was knotted intently.

"Eighteen, er, seventeen, no, eighteen days, sah," he said.

"Okay, that's seventy *kwacha*," Berry answered, unlatching the case. He started unwrapping the crisp pink bills. "And how much did I say I would advance you for the bicycle?"

"Ninety-seven *kwacha*, sah."

"Okay," Berry said, counting out the money and handing it over, "that's twenty-seven *kwacha* you owe me, right?"

"Right, sah." But Abraham looked worried. "But, sah. Bwana Berry?" he asked, still standing at attention, a pleading grimace on his face. "It is one hundred seventeen *kwacha* for the bicycle, sah. The price went up."

"One hundred and seventeen!" Berry bellowed. "What's that? Twenty more *kwacha*? That's bloody robbery!"

Berry retained his mock annoyance as he counted out the extra bills, and then proceeded to advance the other scouts' money, too, despite his earlier warning. The happy group trotted off down a dirt path. Besides the bike, Berry guessed, they would spend their pay on whores and beer.

"They're good men," he said. "They know their business and I can count on them. Besides, it's not often they get to Chipata."

On the second morning of the patrol, Abraham strolled back to the Luwi riverbed before breakfast to look for signs of the lions the men had heard during the night. He also hoped to see rhinos at the nearby lagoon, early morning being the best time. The sun had not yet risen, but the sky glowed bright gray in the east.

Abraham took pride in his talent for judging with accuracy the distance and direction of sounds in the bush. He wanted to see if the lions had been where he had heard them. On the sand were water holes dug by elephants and a deeply worn narrow path—"Hippo Highway," Abraham said—where the Luwi Lagoon's hippo family walked from the water each night to browse on vegetation. There were also fresh rhino tracks, but the rhino that had left them had already vanished into the grass.

Abraham found tracks of one lion in the sand, four gentle impressions left by the pads of the forepaws, each pad topped by the point of a claw. On the other side of the campsite he found the tracks of another.

"Lions hunt together at night," he explained. "They will wait on both sides of their game, then one will roar. The game will then run away from the sound, but it will run toward the second lion waiting in the grass. We were the lion's game last night. But we did not run. But lion are very clever. Animals are very clever. They know the bush better than a man."

After their *mshima* breakfast the carriers doused the campfires and spread the ashes. With his cap back on, rifle over his shoulder, field glasses hanging around his neck, Abraham inspected each of the doused fires as

the carriers bundled their burdens. When all was ready, he led the column off again with the same quick, short steps, straight into the tall grass.

The night had been cool but by mid-morning the air was again swel-
tering, skies a blank, faded blue. The men followed the path of the Luwi
north, staying away from the river's sandy expanse, which widened as they
went on. Abraham preferred to keep his men invisible in tall grass. Away
from the riverbed was better footing because the ground was firm, but the
men had to extend one arm before them as they walked to keep the sharp
edges of grass from cutting their faces.

Downwind was a large herd of cape buffalo, powerful black animals
with wide, curved horns that shone a dull blue in the sunlight just above
the weeds. Catching the column's scent, a big bull was the first to react. Its
head jerked up as it turned its gaze toward the patrol. Buffalo have good
eyesight. This one grunted alarm and then all the herd was startled, thick
snouts suddenly up. Then they ran, a black thundering clump of animals
passing through the grass about two hundred yards ahead. They ran to a
distant clearing near the riverbed, where they stopped and resumed graz-
ing. The bull was the last to bend its head back to the grass.

Just beyond where the herd had crashed through, trampling a wide
swath of high grass, the men came upon the scavenger-picked bones of a
cape buffalo. They stood in silence for a moment around the white, sun-
bleached limbs and bare vertebrae until Abraham, the joker, slid one thick
horn off the skull. It pulled off easily, like a sheath sliding off a knife, exposing a short, pointed protrusion of bone underneath. Abraham drew his
feet together, bent at the waist, and, placing the pointed end of the horn to
his lips, pretended to sound a funeral dirge. He and the other men shattered the silence with their laughter.

Starting patrols in the Luangwa Valley was not easy. Experts might debate their usefulness in the long run, but there is no question that it took
skillful efforts by the World Wildlife Fund to put Phil Berry's group to
work.

Most of the tricky bargaining was done in two weeks of May 1980,
when a fund representative named Peter Murphy visited Lusaka to see
about investing the fund's "Save the Rhino" money in an antipoaching

project. After Murphy's first day of meetings, he wrote in a confidential summary for fund executives back in Switzerland, "It quickly became evident that the overall situation was more complex and difficult than had previously been imagined."

An hour's flight southwest of the Luangwa Valley, Lusaka is the proud center of this new nation, granted independence by Britain in 1961. Despite its 559,000 inhabitants, it still has the feel of a frontier city. The taller buildings rise up from dirt. There is little to buy in the modern stores downtown. Most of the available products are imported from South Africa, but because that nation's racist policies are offensive to Zambia, retail items are repackaged and labeled to disguise their origin. Huge pockets of slum communities lie on the city's outskirts, distant multicolored clusters of laundry lines, tin roofs, trash heaps, and plastic shelters.

It is forbidden to take photographs of government buildings in Lusaka. A local businessman explained that this was to discourage a coup d'état. By seizing a few key locations, an enterprising general with a small skilled force could turn things around in Zambia quickly, or at least make trouble for several weeks. The president's residence, the parliament, the airport, and the local radio and television station (which the government controls) might suffice. This sort of thing has been tried more than once in Lusaka, so authorities do their best to keep the city's official layout obscure.

Guided by President Kenneth Kaunda's vague but friendly philosophy of "humanism," Zambia, a country of 5.6 million people, is seen by admirers as a nation attempting a brave compromise between the high social ideals of Marxism and the hard realism of the capitalist West. To critics, who have no voice in the government-controlled press, it is an essentially benevolent despotism that uses its ideology as an excuse to seize 51 percent of every prospering enterprise and manage it into the ground.

What Murphy learned quickly was that the politics of wildlife protection in Zambia was governed by the same uneasy compromises and suspicions as everything else in such small, developing nations. There were petty gripes among the predominantly white conservationist groups, none of which trusted the government game department.

They had reason to be wary. Zambia's game guards were often involved in poaching the animals they were supposed to protect. The game department was poorly managed and funded. Guards in the bush went for months without their meager pay. Many had taken to farming on park lands as well as poaching. Despite the sensitive wildlife-protection policies voiced by Kaunda, efforts to enforce those policies were notoriously lax.

But it was clear that any effort inside Zambia's borders would need the blessing of Kaunda's "nonaligned," one-party socialist state. In his first meeting with government officials, Murphy received formal notice of Zambia's displeasure that the wildlife fund was dealing with "third parties," that is, with the private wildlife groups.

For nearly two weeks Murphy crafted a cooperative effort to spend the rhino money. He left Lusaka after pledging to Zambia about half the $2 million the fund hoped to raise for its "Save the Rhino" project. The government agreed to match whatever the fund contributed. Additional money was to be raised by the Lusaka wildlife groups through solicitations of local industry. These funds were to be administered by the Save the Rhino Trust, with an understanding that eventually this authority would be transferred to the government—though no specific terms were set for the transition.

Things did not work out that well. The wildlife fund raised only $1.3 million of its $2 million goal. So Zambia got only $490,000, or about 40 percent of the total raised, from that source. Contributions from industry were also disappointing.

Berry and his men are hard at work in the Luangwa Valley, but on a sharply restricted level. They have no radio communication with teams in the field, something Berry said would improve their effectiveness more than any other single thing. So far, a special detective team to follow up on information obtained from poachers about ivory and rhino-horn middlemen, the real profiteers in this business, has not been established or funded by the government. There is no camp for Berry's men, only the blockhouse headquarters near his house.

"One would even pray for a helicopter," Berry said, rolling his eyes heavenward.

In addition to these shortcomings, many of those involved with the anti-poaching project are dismayed by the apparent indifference of Zambia's judges in dealing with poachers. Most penalties are so mild they just encourage more poaching. Chronic offenders are often fined the equivalent of sixty dollars to one hundred twenty dollars, less than what they earn on one poaching trip. Since Zambians arrested for minor crimes can be jailed only for one day after being charged, accused poachers have been known to head directly back into the bush upon release. It is the easiest way to raise money for the anticipated fine.

A notorious example of such lenience is the case of Dingiswayo Banda, the former minister of labor and social services. In 1980 a Lusaka policeman, acting on a tip, stopped then-Minister Banda in his official government limousine, flags flying from the hood, at a roadblock. Searching the trunk, the policeman found six pairs of poached elephant tusks. Elephant hunting is illegal in Zambia without a permit, and the ivory trade is banned.

Banda lost his government job and was eventually fined five hundred *kwachas* ($610). He appealed the fine, and a sterner appellate judge lifted it but substituted a twelve-month jail term at hard labor. But Zambia's Supreme Court reduced Banda's sentence to a fine of about one hundred twenty-two dollars, far less than the black-market value of one elephant tusk. Then the court decided to return Banda's confiscated elephant rifle.

A case closer to the antipoaching unit involved Partson Mjobvu, one of Berry's game scouts, who was arrested by Zambian police and charged with murder after killing a poacher in an exchange of gunfire in the valley. Murder? So far as Berry and his men are concerned, there is a war going on in the valley. They are not eager to exchange fire with poaching gangs, who usually are better armed, but they maintain that they would hardly be taken seriously if they did not return fire when it came. Mjobvu languished for months in a Chipata jail before the Rhino Trust succeeded in having the charge reduced to manslaughter.

This lack of government support for their efforts was demoralizing to the extreme for Abraham Phiri and the other game scouts.

"It's damn discouraging," said one Lusaka conservation activist.

Early in the afternoon of the second day, after the patrol had stopped to lunch and rest between noon and 2 p.m., the hottest hours of the day, Abraham spotted a poacher's footprint. Just a single footprint, unmistakably human, implanted on the short downslope of a gully about a mile south of the Luwi riverbed. The patrol had turned away from the Luwi toward the hills after its break, and the ground underfoot had turned from sand to hard brown soil. There were clumps of trees and rocks, and the terrain was uneven. There was a mild scent now of blossoms in the air. Most of the walking was uphill.

Abraham's face under the crooked brim of his hat grew stern as he bent for a closer look. The other scouts fanned out around him looking for more prints. In an instant the group had been shaken out of its walking reverie. Now the mood was crisp, tense, exciting.

"Poachers here two days ago," Abraham said, to no one in particular.

When no other footprints could be found, the patrol began walking again, but the tension remained. These men knew that poachers were always moving in the valley, but spotting recent evidence put a new edge on that knowledge. Their marching seemed to grow quieter. Each man listened intently to the valley's quiet sounds: the distant screech of a hawk, the honk of a hornbill, the sound of the patrol's footsteps and breathing, the wind in the thorn bushes.

They passed trees growing from the tops of huge anthills, ancient anthills whose formation predated the trees. Here and there in the open stood a huge, solitary baobab tree with a wide, wide trunk that looked like the flexed thigh of some giant weight lifter.

There were more insects that afternoon, their annoying buzz growing louder around the ears before the sharp prick of their bite. There was the danger of contracting sleeping sickness from the tsetse fly, or malaria from the bite of a mosquito. Now and then there was a sharp slap as one of the men lashed out at a bug on his arm or the back of his neck. Berry had sent along enough chloroquine (antimalarial) tablets to wipe out the chills and sore joints that presage the onset of malaria. Most of the men would want doses that night at camp.

As the patrol moved ahead, David Mulanga occasionally fell behind to pick edible berries from the bushes he knew by name. He would hastily grab a handful and then sprint back to his place in line, popping the treats, which tasted like sour candy, into his mouth one by one.

The patrol came upon a herd of twenty elephants on the side of one hill. The men stopped cautiously because the herd, including a bull with tusks worth a year of poaching penalties, was downwind and certain to sense their presence. The elephants responded quickly and with alarm to the scent. "Big Tusks" trumpeted loudly, his cry echoing across the vale, and the whole herd fled as daintily as ladies caught at their bath. With remarkable speed they went high-stepping over the hilltop, ears fully extended and flapping, tails up.

It was mid-afternoon when Abraham saw the vultures circling high in the distance. He stopped the column abruptly.

"Dead animal," he said, and without another word the group was off in that direction at a run.

Jumping down ravines, scrambling up the other side, rushing through the tall grass, all former caution disappeared in their haste to cover the mile or two uphill toward the circling scavengers. More vultures were visible now. They had found something big, a feast. The game scouts had their rifles in hand. The carriers, with their burdens, had fallen behind.

Again, Abraham jerked to a halt. In his haste at the head of the column he had burst upon two elephants, a large female with her nearly full-grown calf. The huge animals, only ten or twenty yards away, stared directly at the men, who had stopped running and who had begun to slowly back away. All eyes were on the elephants. Would they charge or run?

After agonizing minutes of standoff, the elephants abruptly turned and fled. The scouts began moving uphill again toward the circling birds.

Approaching the hilltop, they slowed again and moved forward, bending at the waist in the grass. The bolts of their rifles clicked as cartridges were moved into place. The scouts fanned out in the grass as they continued up the hill with rifles pointed and ready. John S. Phiri, a look of feral intensity on his face, rushed to be the first to enter the clearing. Prospa Myatwa was right behind. Matteo Mwanza had moved wide to one side, and David Mulanga to the other. Abraham stayed in the middle, directing the others with quick gestures. They braced to hear the first shot.

The silence broke, not with gunfire or the cries of startled poachers but with a sudden, awful chorus of whoosh and squawk as hundreds of big, black vultures jumped back into the sky, so many they cast a shadow over the patrol, whirling and crying in anger at being chased from their banquet. As if fanned by the flapping of their wings, the odor of their meal swept over the men all at once in a putrid wave.

"Elephant," Abraham said.

He and the others now had their weapons at their sides and were standing upright. The poachers were long gone from this. The stench was so horrid it was nearly visible.

"Four days dead," Abraham said.

Few animals in death could feed so many vultures. The three elephants lay together in a heap directly at the top of the hill, bodies bloated and thick round gray legs bent stiffly up in rigor mortis. As the scouts approached, millions of flies lifted like a shining blue drape and settled on the other side of the oozing carcasses, their collective sound a high-pitched whining engine.

The elephants' heads had been chopped off and evidently carried down into thicker bush. It would be easier to remove the valuable tusks from the facial sockets after a few days. Discarded to one side were the amputated trunks, flaccid decaying lumps of flesh. The stretched gray skin of the huge bodies was coated with a dull sheen of dried blood. These three had all been dropped with the same burst of automatic rifle fire. Bullet entry wounds tracked across their sides, the dried holes clogged with flies. A male, a female, and a calf. The vultures had already mostly devoured the calf. Bloodstained white ribs projected from the black pool of its entrails. In another day the calf would be eaten and the ripened bigger corpses would be ready. The earth underfoot was stained a deep brown by the dried blood.

Abraham stood leaning on one leg, rifle at his side. His men circled the scene, taking it in. He scowled.

"This is just *careless*," is all he said.

Because the valley is so big, it takes a fortuitous collection of coincidences to catch poachers at work. When poachers are found in the valley, it usually is because paid informants have told the game scouts where to look. Berry considers it vital to maintain a constant presence in the valley itself, but his most effective antipoaching work is often done in the human communities around the park.

Inhabiting the northern hills of the escarpment are the Bisa people, a large, prosperous tribe whose hunters have been descending into the Luangwa Valley to hunt elephant and rhino for centuries. Bisa communities

of small brick houses are more modern and comfortable than the grass-
and mud-hut villages that typify the region.

It is the Bisa, many of whom resent Zambian restrictions on what they
consider their God-given way of life, who are Phil Berry's biggest problem. No matter that the valley's once-teeming wildlife are being killed off
faster than they can reproduce. Cultural traditions are not easily argued
away, even with the strong logic of numbers. Top Bisa hunters are still
admired and respected in their communities. And though they are more
likely today to be carrying sophisticated automatic rifles than spears or
bows and arrows, they still are esteemed for bravery and skill.

In November, one of Berry's patrols captured a Bisa poaching gang
in the valley. After some forceful coercion, several of the poachers revealed
the names of the Bisa's foremost hunters. One of the names extorted from
them was Brown Chiwantila Muchose, or simply Chiwantila. One of the
poachers captured had been carrying many rounds of cartridges for a
Soviet-made Kalashnikov automatic rifle, but no rifle was recovered. The
man said he had been carrying the ammunition for Chiwantila. Berry's men
had just missed nabbing one of the biggest threats to rhinos and elephants
in the valley.

"We started asking around about this Chiwantila bloke and even set
a few traps for him," Berry recalled. "But he was very cagey and he eluded
capture on a number of occasions."

But once he had learned the name, Berry was determined to catch
his man. Aside from removing a potent poacher from the valley, he knew
it could have a psychological effect. It would make a strong impression on
the Bisa, perhaps stronger even than his presence in the valley warranted,
if Berry could catch one of their top hunters and bring him to task. Eventually, the information Berry needed was pried from another captured
poacher.

Chiwantila was arrested in bed, sleeping in one of the five residences
he kept in the Bisa communities. This was in July. Berry had filled two of
his Land Rovers with armed scouts, and from 11 p.m. until dawn they raided
one community after another until they found him.

At first Chiwantila would say nothing. He denied owning the Kalashnikov rifle—a far more serious offense in Zambia than poaching—and he
insisted he was not a hunter or a poacher. But Berry's men were able to
wrest information from him in time. Faced with the threat of prosecution

for possessing an illegal weapon, Chiwantila admitted to having poached some elephants. Information he provided about the rifle enabled Berry's men eventually to recover it. Zambian police were interested enough in the rifle to track down and arrest the dealer in Ndola who sold it. Now they are trying to trace the deal back one step further to find out who imported it.

Meanwhile, Chiwantila had become so helpful that he was pleasant to have around.

"These Bisa chaps are fatalists," Berry explained. "Once you catch them, once they know they are at your mercy, they tend to just surrender completely."

At a recent beer-making gathering in the game-scout village near Berry's house, Chiwantila sat quietly and happily drinking with the men who had captured him. An oddly effeminate man to have such a fierce reputation, he had been living comfortably with the scouts while awaiting trial. He was older than the man the patrol had expected to catch. He looked about sixty, weathered and gray, a slight, windblown creature who appeared quite at home wherever he landed. Berry, in return for Chiwantila's cooperation, had succeeded in having the weapons charge dropped, so all the Bisa hunter faced now was six months' imprisonment and a fine. He was resigned to that.

Sipping the foul-smelling, brown milky mixture of home-brewed beer, a faded blue turban wrapped around his gray head, Chiwantila smiled and laughed. He fit right in. Dressed in a flimsy yellow short-sleeved shirt, dirty brown polyester slacks a bit short in the ankle, gray socks, and black leather shoes missing laces, he clapped as two of the game scouts reeled playfully to the band music from their portable radio.

Chiwantila spoke no English. Tryson Mwandila, the scout who had been held at gunpoint on the patrol two summers ago, translated Chiwantila's Bisa dialect. The poacher evaded questions about his work. Yes, he was a hunter. This was followed by a big yellow-toothed smile, eyes averted from the questioner, limp-wristed hands folded on his knees. No, he never hunted rhino. Yes, perhaps he had killed elephant, but very few. Only the ones he had confessed to Bwana Berry. No, he did not make good money killing the animals.

Berry and his men laughed out loud at Chiwantila's answers, and the poacher laughed with them. He was playing a comic scene. Yes, he knew the animals in the valley were being killed so fast none would be left, just as the bwana said. With a look of utmost sincerity, Chiwantila vowed he would never take up his rifle in the valley again. This elicited the most laughter of all.

"He's lying, of course," Berry said. "He still has to be wary. His case hasn't come up to trial yet and he's counting on getting only those six months. He's confessed to killing a few elephants and swears he's learned his lesson. Don't you believe it."

Berry respected Chiwantila. He understood that hunting in the valley was part of the Bisa people's life. He knew that Chiwantila was a brave man who had started hunting as a boy with a muzzle-loading rifle, a frightening device that, if overloaded, could easily blind the shooter or blow off his hands.

"They may have better weapons now, but hunting elephant and rhino in that valley is still a tricky and dangerous business," Berry said. "In the old days a hunter would go off after an elephant only once every few months. Nowadays they're at it day after day. They no longer hunt for meat, but for ivory and horn. It used to be that one elephant kill would provide enough meat to last a village for some time. But they are paid very little for tusks and horn, not like what the middlemen will make down the line. So they have to keep at it. It takes courage to stay out in the bush like that stalking dangerous animals. And for now they have me to contend with, too," he added with a satisfied little smile.

Hunting and camping full-time in the valley is a way of life not altogether different from Berry's own. He has real empathy for the men he hunts.

"I don't know but if I were one of them I might be doing the same thing," he said.

Before Berry left the village that afternoon, Chiwantila had a request. Mwandila approached Berry's Land Rover to translate. The old hunter kept his eyes averted to the ground as the question was asked.

"He wants to know if you will give him a job when his six months in jail are up," Mwandila said.

Berry grinned and shook his head with disbelief. "Oh, he'd like to work with us, all right," he said. "He'd like to work with us so he could tell all of his friends about our movements. Tell Mr. Chiwantila that he will have to do better than that." Berry hesitated for a moment, and then added, "Wait, tell him I will not have a full-time job for him but that we will employ him as an investigator. I will pay him for information: twenty-five *kwachas* for information that leads to the recovery of elephant tusks, fifty *kwachas* for information leading to the arrest of poachers with rhino horn. Tell him that. But the information must be good. He will only be paid if we make the arrests."

Mwandila turned to translate all this to Chiwantila, but the old man had already wandered back to the boiling kettle of beer.

On the third day of the patrol, near noon, the men found a young crocodile lying in a shallow pool on the wide, mostly dry bed of the Mushiyashi River. Prospa Myatwa and John S. Phiri yanked the snapping young croc, only two feet long, by the tail and capered around it happily, teasing. The little croc lunged at them in vain and tried to hide in the trickling stream of water.

Later on the same afternoon, the striding column of men nearly smacked headlong into a huge rhino hidden in shadow and tall grass. Stock-still, it stood directly facing the men, a one-ton specimen at least, only its horns and the round gray outline of its shoulders visible above the grass in direct sunlight. Though the patrol had come within twenty feet of it, the rhino had not spotted them. Sensing threat, but unable to precisely determine the direction of its approach, the rhino waited motionlessly, its head and horns held high. Abraham slowly backed the column away from this encounter, easing backward, downwind from the animal. The rhino never bothered to move.

On the last night of Abraham's patrol, sixteen hours before the rendezvous with Berry, the men camped in a grove of trees near the Mushiyashi. The carriers dug holes in the sand for muddy water, which they boiled before drinking but which remained muddy. Though they had walked out of the hills, the night was cold again. Some of the carriers, who were not dressed as warmly as the scouts and whose job it was to keep the perimeter fires burning through the night anyway, forsook chilly slumber to sit around the flames until dawn.

It was a moonless August night, brilliant with stars. Up through the clear night shone not just the familiar constellations but sweeping milky bands of nebula, fuzzy swaths of interstellar gas and the arms of galaxies, accumulations of stars so numerous and distant as to defy imagining. The bright night chirped with insects and shook, from time to time, with the deep reverberant roar of a lion, a sound so primal it registers fear even before one is awake enough to know, consciously, what it is. The roar reaches deep into a sleeper's dream and yanks him from it. He awakens to find himself sitting bolt upright, already alert to the undefined threat nearby.

The scouts dined on *mshima,* of course, and dried elephant meat. They had continued happily to eat the elephant meat, undeterred by the similarity of its odor to the heavy stink of dead elephants they had encountered earlier. This would be their last night of camping. After their meal, John S. Phiri rolled pencil-thin *chamba* (marijuana) cigarettes, and the men smoked for the only time in their patrol.

"I only smoke *chamba* one time each month," Abraham said, smiling. Buoyed by the beauty and crispness of the evening, and, perhaps, the *chamba,* the men talked softly long into the night.

Matteo Mwanza, the thoughtful twenty-five-year-old who recently had married, was interested in American marital politics.

"What present must an American make to the father of the woman he would marry?" he asked me.

In the custom of his tribe, the gift a bridegroom makes to his wife's family is meant to demonstrate his worth and means. It is what makes him, ostensibly, the acknowledged leader and provider for the new household. Mwanza found it most peculiar that the custom in America was for the bride's family to pay the wedding expenses.

"Does that not make the woman boss of the house?" he asked.

"Sometimes that is so, Matteo."

He and the others shook their heads gravely, genuinely sympathetic to the hardships imposed by such an ill-considered cultural tradition.

Paulo Mwale, a twenty-one-year-old carrier who was alternately sullen and mirthful throughout the patrol, entered this line of questioning by approaching the campfire with clownish fanfare. He stood very erect, tugging at the lapels of his blue jacket, once a sportcoat in some previous incarnation, but now just a loosely fitting, torn, flapping rag with barely enough shape to stay on his skinny frame. His pants were equally tattered, and his feet were bare.

"Bwana, Bwana," he implored, "what am I to do? What American girl will marry me? I have no nice clothes."

The others laughed. Abraham rebuked him. "Do not worry, Paulo," he said. "No American girl will marry you. You are too ugly."

Paulo Mwale was a favorite with the scouts. Several months ago he had dropped his burden to help chase a fleeing poacher and had brought the man up short by aiming a set of field glasses at the man like a weapon and shouting, "Freeze!" The poacher thought he was being threatened with some exotic new weapon. The scouts laughed and laughed about the incident. Ever since, they have considered Mwale exceptionally clever. Before becoming a carrier for Phil Berry, Mwale had worked in a textile mill. He was earning only about two *kwachas* a day for each long, hard day of patrol work.

"Why did you leave the job at the mill?" I asked.

"I was dismissed," Mwale said with a bright smile, "for loafing and absenteeism." He announced this cheerfully, as though his move from the factory to hauling a heavy burden through the bush barefoot was a promotion.

Scientific David Mulanga had his own interest in America.

"Did those men, those astronauts, really walk on the moon as it is said?" he asked, and expressed pleasure and surprise to hear that this was true.

"And are these men still alive?" he asked, as if the astronauts might have been expected to perish by the sheer magnificence of the deed.

Finally the men discussed their own work in the valley. Mwanza had the most to say. It worried him what was happening, he said. It was not just the poaching, but the apparent involvement of officials in the Zambian government. Berry's men have arrested a number of government game scouts for poaching, and they are demoralized by the lenient penalties given to the men they risk their lives to catch. Matteo Mwanza said he believed the killing of rhinos and elephants was a serious crime against Zambia, because the country's wildlife was worth money to the nation in tourism. But he was bothered by it for another reason.

"And what will the Americans and Europeans think of African people if all the rhinoceros are killed?" he asked.

Abraham, who had seen more of the world, answered.

"The Americans and Europeans already think that Africans are a stupid people," he said. "To kill all the animals, all the beauty in our land to sell for twenty *kwachas* or fifty *kwachas,* this, they will say, is just what you would expect these Africans to do. The African knows nothing. This is what they would say."

THE URBAN
GORILLA

MAY 1982

*I think it was my experience in Africa that prompted my curiosity about animals in
captivity. The Philadelphia Zoo is the oldest in North America, located on a sliver of
land between the railroad tracks and the Schuylkill River. Its most famous resident
was Massa, an ancient gorilla who had lived his entire life in captivity. He was a
magnificent creature, although much diminished by age, and a familiar character to
generations of Philadelphians. When I heard that the zoo was planning a state-of-
the-art facility for its apes, I thought Massa's long life would be a good way to examine
changing attitudes and philosophies in zoos. Massa died three years after this story
ran. His lifespan is still the longest ever recorded for a gorilla.*

Day settles softly down from the skylight over Massa's bare confinement like some dim memory of sunshine. Alone he squats day
after day, the old ape, the ancient ape. Massa is like no other gorilla
the world has ever seen.

He has lived too long. Gone is the monster frame, the hairy arms thick
as trees, the torso that bulged like the bronze relief on a medieval suit of
armor. Age has withered this old brute to almost half his youthful bulk, a
transformation that intensifies the alarming resemblance to his slender
cousin, Homo sapiens. His jet-black skin hangs in long loose folds at each
joint and in chevrons down his shrunken chest and belly. His gray coat is
tattered from decades of hair-plucking, a habit long ago identified as a
symptom of pathological boredom.

At fifty-one, Massa is the oldest gorilla in the world. He is older, quite
likely, than any other gorilla has ever been.

In his cage at the Philadelphia Zoo, this ragged and toothless figure
waits out the steady procession of days and nights with implacable, gruff
dignity. He is the zoo's most famous exhibit, still one of its premier attractions. Massa's longevity pays silent tribute to the skill of the keepers who

have nurtured and fed him through his lifetime of captivity. When he arrived in a crate on December 30, 1935, captive gorillas rarely survived longer than six months. By the standards of his day, Massa is a supreme triumph. But the standards have changed. Massa, beloved senior resident of America's oldest zoo, is an embarrassment.

Especially now, as the zoo's new management is poised for a total transformation, one they hope will make their institution at Girard Avenue and Thirty-fourth Street a model for small, urban zoos everywhere. They are working at fashioning a new kind of zoo, one that reflects the sensibilities and concerns of a planet in ecological crisis. Instead of collecting exotica, they are building an ark.

Survival for many threatened wild species already depends upon captive management and breeding programs, and the tragic acceleration of pressures on wildlife the world over will make such programs even more important in the future. The newly defined goals of the Philadelphia Zoo mostly concern developing techniques to enable rare animals to thrive in captivity. Zoo officials see themselves as part of an international network of zoos and parks, a conspiracy to save the Earth's wild heritage from the crush of civilization.

The other part of their mission is to give city-dwellers, on whose concern depends the world's wild places, a taste for the exquisite joys and mysteries of the natural world.

Today, almost all of the zoo's forty-three acres are for people—animals are caged in only about 5 percent of the space. The new zoo will gradually, over the next decade, turn that ratio around. Plans call for a smaller number of animal species to be displayed, but for vastly improved living conditions for those that remain. Cages will be replaced by spacious, creative "habitats," naturalistic enclaves that instead of displaying animals like exotic museum pieces on a shelf will allow tigers to be and behave as tigers, and apes as apes. Massa's sharply circumscribed, unnatural lifestyle contradicts the whole approach.

Yet each year Massa's record-setting birthday draws more attention to the zoo than any other event. The zoo's publicists aren't sure whether to be delighted or dismayed. At the same time that Massa makes the zoo look good, the surly old fellow makes it look bad.

"Look at it this way," says Bill Donaldson, the zoo president. "If a group of little green men from another planet asked to learn about human

beings and were taken to see an old, old man who had lived his entire life
in a dimly lit cave in solitary confinement . . . what would they learn about
men?"

Massa's stark quarters, where he has lived on display now for more
than forty years, are in the Monkey House, which sits precisely on the site
of the zoo's planned $4 million Primate Center (the terminology alone is
revealing). The Monkey House was built in 1895, and represents state-
of-the-art for what one zoo official described as "the old Capture-the-
Savage-Beast-and-Put-It-Behind-Bars philosophy of zookeeping." Even
the more modern Rare Mammal House, where the zoo's active, breeding
family of young gorillas romps behind a glass wall in relative felicity, is
hopelessly outmoded by New Zoo ideals. Robert Snyder, the zoo's research
director, disparagingly refers to displays in the Rare Mammal House as
"the bathroom cages," because they were designed with what he considers an undue and single-minded preoccupation with sanitation.

The Primate Center and an innovative new Children's Zoo are the
first big steps into the institution's brave new world. Half of the money
needed for the Primate Center has been donated by the Glenmede Foundation, and preliminary plans have been drawn. It is described in the zoo's
project proposal as follows:

"The facility is envisioned as consisting of a gently sloping green vista
bordered by the lake. . . . Animal housing will consist of a series of twelve
to fifteen separate, but potentially communicating living units associated
with servicing facilities for food preparation and cleaning. Wherever possible, these maintenance and other non-exhibit facilities will be located
underground. The living units can be thought of as condominiums, each
designed according to one of perhaps four or five different plans, all in a
'soft' unobtrusive architectural style. Each pattern will be designed to satisfy a very specific set of environmental and spatial needs shared by several of the primate species chosen to be their inhabitants. . . ."

Not for old Massa will life be this way, unless gorilla heaven corre-
sponds with the zoo's master plan. Even if he is still alive in five or ten
years (which is only slightly less likely an assumption today than it was in
1972) when the Primate Center is ready, Massa is just too old and fixed in
his solitary ways to adjust to such a liberal lifestyle.

Besides, Massa doesn't know how to get along with other apes. He exists
in a kind of suspended position on the evolutionary scale, certainly not man

but not exactly ape, either. Raised by a devoted rich woman in Brooklyn, cared for all his life by human keepers, Massa is a true urban gorilla. He no doubt finds other apes as curious and threatening as people do.

"Ole Massa'd just die of a heart attack if they tried to change the way he lives now," says Ralph McCarthy, the keeper who has cared for Massa these last twenty years. But it hurts to see him there, intently picking at a wad of hay held between two fingers directly before his face, rolling his baleful black eyes vacantly around the familiar edges of his world. The image says zoos are bad places, cruel places, places where creatures of profound beauty are caged in bleak isolation from the glorious landscapes of their creation.

"The ideal thing would be to somehow preserve Massa's cage and routine exactly as it is today, and just incorporate it into the new facility," mused Mary Scott Cebul, a young wildlife researcher who wrote the zoo's new philosophy and master plan. "It would be a good way of showing how far we have come from the old idea of a zoo. But there would be a lot of expense involved, and I doubt Massa will be around to see it anyway."

Massa usually sits on the lower of the two levels of his indoor cage. His cell is about ten paces long and five wide. His water pan is on one side of the upper level in the rear. On the opposite end of the lower level is a pile of hay. Straight up from the center of the cage, up from where the gorilla's regular urination has badly rusted the metal front of the back platform, a support beam connects to the slanted bars below the skylight. Suspended from a chain tied to these bars is a tire. Ralph, his keeper, hung it up there because it seemed like the thing to do—"you know, just somethin' to occupy his mind a little." But the tire is a failure. Massa ignores it except to swat it every now and then in what Ralph interprets as disgust.

Sometimes, aggravated, he will still do what Ralph calls "his Jackie Gleason shuffle," a sort of sideways dance across the cage, slapping the tire and ramming the bars. Time was that the full force of his three hundred and fifty pounds would rattle the whole Monkey House, but the shuffle ain't what it once was. He has resorted to more subtle gestures of contempt. After forty-six years in this same cage, Massa still hasn't gotten used to people staring at him. When visitors squint in at him too intently through the heavy glass pane and the wire fencing and bars, Massa will gravely stand and turn his back on the gapers to greet them with shriveled, calloused, gray buttocks. He will stand there like that until they leave.

* * *

Left to their own quiet ways, gorillas are good at minding their own business. Native to the equatorial forests of central Africa, these giant primates live in small bands led by one dominant male. They are extraordinarily shy creatures, vegetarians who pass their days in search of food, building new nests each night on the ground or in trees. Contrary to the old *King Kong* image of ferocity, gorillas are creatures who frighten easily and would almost always prefer, when threatened, to run away.

The book *Inside the Animal World* relates the following story of an attempt at capturing a wild gorilla:

In the days when gorillas and other great apes were hunted for zoos and other scientific institutions, a handful of scientists engaged a group of local African hunters to net a gorilla. It was a task that Africans were used to carrying out in the adjacent rain forest. The time chosen was night, at a point where the local hunters were confident a family of gorillas would pass the following morning when they awoke.

The long net was in position, held up by stakes pushed into the ground. The scientists had little to do but wait, and they were astonished at the way the local hunters carried out the task in complete and utter silence.

By daybreak all was ready and complete silence still reigned. Then the gorillas could be heard crashing through the undergrowth and calling, heading straight for the net. Suddenly, they were silent. They had evidently noticed something suspicious and the suspicion had been communicated by some means to every member of the family, judging by the suddenness with which all sounds ceased.

The hunting party waited and waited. Nothing happened. Then they spread out to search for the gorillas, who had escaped as skillfully and silently as the hunting party had set their trap.

Wildlife researchers who spend extended periods observing gorillas in the wild typically come away with a deep reverence for the reclusive gentility of this gravely endangered species. Scientists generally recognize two types: lowland gorillas (like Massa) of west Africa from Cameroon to the Congo River, and the mountain gorillas of the highland forests of east-central Africa. Demand for samples of these rare creatures by zoos and scientific laboratories was a major factor in tragically decimating their numbers in the wild. There are now thought to be fewer than eight thousand remaining.

The story of Massa's capture and journey to America as an infant has been told so often and is based on such hearsay that the specifics of it long ago lapsed into the realm of the apocryphal. It is enough to say that the lowland gorillas of Cameroon are often killed by farmers when they are caught raiding plantation crops. It is likely that Massa's mother was killed in such an incident, and that area natives took him in as an infant—it was well-known in that part of the world in 1930 that a baby gorilla would fetch a good price on the animal market.

Little Massa arrived in the United States in 1931, an exotic cargo shipped with six baby chimpanzees aboard the West Key Bar, a trading vessel. According to an account of Massa's early years in a book about the famous circus ape, *Gargantua,* by Gene Plowden, the baby gorilla was crippled with pneumonia and near death when the ship's captain sold it to Gertrude Lintz, a Brooklyn animal-lover whose marriage to a successful physician gave her the financial and medical support to pursue her fascination with wild animals. She named Massa and nurtured him back to health, spoon-feeding him and even chewing his food herself before feeding it to him. She rigged an exercising device to strengthen him when he suffered infantile paralysis. Gradually this pitiful, nearly hairless little creature regained its health and strength.

Massa spent four years in the Lintz household, growing into a robust, one-hundred-and-forty-pound young gorilla. He and his childhood companion, a gorilla whom Mrs. Lintz named Buddha, lived in basement cages in the spacious Lintz household. Mistaking Massa for a female (gorilla genitalia are too small to be readily distinguished from even a short distance, and they do not readily submit to a more careful examination), Mrs. Lintz often dressed him in little girls' clothing.

It was this mistaken identification of Massa's gender that originally brought him to the Philadelphia Zoo—that and the realization that mature gorillas cannot make tame house pets. Mrs. Lintz, a heavyset woman who cared for a menagerie of wild pets throughout her life, faced up to this inevitable truth only after Massa attacked and seriously injured her. As the story goes, Massa was on loan for display at the Chicago World's Fair in 1933. He was visiting Mrs. Lintz in a house in that city when his kindly stepmother got in a tugging match with him over a kitchen mop. Massa apparently lost his temper and lunged at her viciously, inflicting wounds that took sixty-five stitches to close.

After that, Massa was for sale. Advertised as a female, Massa interested the keepers of Philadelphia's zoo because they already owned an impressive, healthy young male named Bamboo. Gorillas had never before been successfully kept in captivity for long, much less bred, so the purchase of Massa for $6,000 five decades ago was an act of high ambition.

The Philadelphia Zoo then, more so than today, was one of the most celebrated in America, and one of the most successful. The zoo was simply one of the most famous things about Philadelphia. It was the oldest zoo in this country, and had one of the most extensive and valuable zoological collections. The zoo's staff of experts enjoyed—as they do today—high prestige throughout the world. Imagine how embarrassed they were when they found out about Massa.

Massa's arrival in Philadelphia was one of the hottest stories that cold winter. Local newspapers played up the story cleverly, announcing the arrival of Bamboo's blushing bride. Newsrooms dispatched their prize feature writers for the story. *The Philadelphia Record* ran a formal announcement of Massa's betrothal with all the stylistic ornament of a Main Line event. There was Massa's five-year-old face, looking very much in childhood as it does today, the same slightly sunken cheeks and bushy jowls scowling out over a caption that read "Miss Massa." A particularly sanguine reporter for *The Bulletin* recounted Massa's introduction to "her" mate:

"She looked him over and started beating her chest, an apparent sign of complete approval. His admiring eyes took in his future Missus and he okayed her by smashing his hairy fists against his manly bosom."

So it went. On the fateful day when keepers decided to open a passageway between the cages of the two "lovers," Massa, who was smaller and faster than big Bamboo, slipped quickly into the groom's cage, belted him on the chin, cuffed his ears, pulled at his hair, and then quickly retreated through the passageway—which was too narrow for Bamboo—into the safety of his own cage. This was not the way male and female gorillas were supposed to behave together. For the first time zoo officials began to entertain the dark suspicion that they had made a basic reproductive error. News like this was bound to leak out.

"GORILLA NO LADY; WEDDING IS OFF" was the headline in the next day's *Daily News,* which detailed the embarrassment of zoo experts with typical populist glee.

"Actually, it wasn't an inexcusable error," explained Wilbur Amand, one of the current zoo directors. "It isn't easy to tell the difference between a male and a female gorilla without taking a close look. You can't get that close to them safely, and they're hairy. At the time they didn't have the squeeze cages and the knockdown drugs we use today. There was a period there even after the unsuccessful introduction of Massa and Bamboo when not everyone on the staff was in agreement that Massa wasn't female. Mrs. Lintz felt certain he was. There were some top-level meetings where it became the topic of serious debate. At one point they even established a committee to figure out the truth."

Eventually the truth was established, perhaps because of the committee's efforts, and Massa settled in to the monotonous routine that has been his lot ever since. He and Bamboo barely tolerated each other in opposite cages. Their posturing and threatening entertained generations of city zoo goers. Massa was particularly fond of tormenting his rival by splashing water at him. During Bamboo's lifetime—he died of a heart attack in 1961 at age thirty-four, then the oldest captive gorilla in the world— Massa was the lesser attraction. Bamboo was always a bigger ape, was older, and had arrived first. It took many years for Massa to live down vague public suspicions that he was something of a failure.

While Massa began his confinement at the zoo, his childhood cage mate, Buddha, was fast becoming the most famous gorilla in the world. Sold to Ringling Bros. and Barnum & Bailey Circus in 1937, Buddha was rechristened "Gargantua" and made the star of the circus's extravagant promotions. Posters depicted the Brooklyn-reared ape—whom Mrs. Lintz had decided to sell after he began behaving too affectionately toward her—as a giant, snarling beast ten times the size of a man. In one lurid advertisement, Gargantua is clutching in one oversized hand a doll-sized dead African tribesman.

He was a fearsome sight. Overfeeding pushed his weight well over five hundred pounds. Owing to a grotesque facial disfigurement that happened when an irate merchant sailor threw acid on him as an infant, Gargantua's features were frozen in an expression of awful anger. His value to the circus as an attraction ensured the best care circus money could buy. Despite this, Gargantua lived for only twelve more years after Mrs. Lintz sold him. He was less than twenty years old when he died, and had lived what was then considered a long life for a captive gorilla.

Massa, in his cage in Philadelphia, was just approaching his youthful prime. A photograph of him published in *National Geographic* in 1940
shows him as a broad, virile beast with full, wide features and a thick coat
of black and silver.

Zoo officials point with pride to two innovations that led to the extraordinary health and longevity of their captive apes. The first was a decision to erect glass barriers between zoo goers and the primates housed
in indoor cages. Tuberculosis was a major killer of apes at the zoo before
the barriers went up. Animal primates also are extremely sensitive to respiratory viruses that tend to afflict humans less severely. Today, zoo workers who tend Massa and the other apes are routinely tested for the disease,
and anyone who hasn't been tested is not allowed near them. The second
innovation was the introduction, in 1936, of a carefully monitored diet of
fruits, vegetables, and "zoo-cake," a healthful mixture of vegetable nutrients
that was formulated by zoo researchers over years of experimentation.

It was not unusual—and still isn't—for gorillas in captivity to reach
six hundred pounds or more because of over- and improper feeding. With
obesity come the usual medical complications of high blood pressure and
cardiovascular disease. Many captive gorillas die of heart attacks. Massa's
peak weight of three hundred and fifty pounds, which was quite impressive, was much more in keeping with the size of wild gorillas. He has grown,
matured, and aged under skillfully controlled circumstances.

These achievements took place over many years of prosperity at the
Philadelphia Zoo. Every year for thirty-five years after Massa arrived, zoo
attendance increased. Revenues at the turnstiles and the refreshment and
souvenir counters account for 70 percent of the zoo's operating budget (the
rest comes from city government and private donations). It was an unquali-
fied success story in the era before the dominance of TV, the entertainment industry, and professional sports. On warm sunny weekends, the zoo
was the place to go.

"All that changed rather suddenly in 1970," said Thomas Gilmore,
who has been the zoo's business director since 1978. "The zoo had its first
major downturn of attendance that year. Everyone was stunned. The de-
creases continued year after year for the rest of that decade. In the first
few years they were content to identify the problem as too many rainy
weekends—one bad weekend and you can lose a hundred thousand

dollars—but as the trend continued over a few more years it was clear that bad weather wasn't the only factor. . . . Finally the board of directors sat down and decided to take a closer look at what was happening."

What they found, Gilmore said, is that zoo attendance is unavoidably linked with children. By the mid-sixties, the last members of the baby boom generation were leaving childhood behind, and were taking fewer and fewer trips to see Massa and his friends at the zoo. At the same time, competition had intensified for Philadelphians' leisure money. The zoo was competing with the Phillies and the Eagles, with theme parks like Great Adventure and amusement parks like the one in Hershey. Tradition-minded zoo managers, accustomed as they were to effortless popularity, were simply not meeting the challenge.

In order to meet deficits each year that attendance slipped, administrators began dipping into the zoo's building construction and maintenance fund, which meant that the zoo stopped building and changing. Instead, it had begun to fall apart, to took like a place where people *used to* spend weekends.

"They stopped maintaining the facility," Gilmore said. "Their vehicles were old, their buildings were falling down. What happened was that the zoo began to look old and run down. And the zoo wasn't marketing itself well. In the long run those things just start to hurt you worse."

By 1977, Ronald Ruether, then the zoo president, told the City Council that unless Philadelphia gave an additional $250,000 the zoo would close during the winter months. Closing down the zoo was even less of a solution than a threat. Animals must be fed and cared for, buildings must be heated and grounds maintained whether the zoo is selling tickets or not. Closing the zoo would just mean its main source of revenue would be gone. Ruether himself was gone before the end of the year.

The zoo was being hurt at a deeper level, too. The average person in current times knows a whole lot more about wildlife and the world than his grandparents did in 1935. Television and film have exposed millions to the thrill of a cheetah on a dead run or the sudden strike of a venomous viper. By comparison, seeing the same animals displayed in a cage had become a flat, static experience. The zoo seemed sad, in a way it had never been before. It looked and felt like an anachronism.

* * *

Age had begun to take its toll on Massa, too, as he entered his fifth decade. By mid-1969 he was already the oldest gorilla in captivity, and he was starting to look it. The winter before, he had contracted a bad case of sinusitis, and he couldn't seem to shake it. Finally, after months of his discharging large amounts of mucus through his wide, flat nose, there appeared inside the flared left nostril a large, pink polyplike growth. Massa had developed a serious problem that demanded drastic action.

In April of that year Massa underwent surgery. Canvas was draped over the bars of his outside cage to shield the operation from public view. The old ape was slipped a cup of orange juice laced with a drug called Sernylan. At first, his natural gorilla suspicion prevailed, but Massa was coaxed to drink it by an appeal to his notorious sweet tooth. With a green Life Saver floating in the cup, the offer was too good to refuse. Massa downed the mixture and was soon groggy. A supplementary dose administered through a needle at the end of a long bamboo pole knocked him out completely. He lay in helpless, unconscious repose for an hour and a half as the vets doctored him, cleaning his sinuses with antibiotics, and altering slightly the inner structure of his nose to improve drainage. Afterward, the 300-pound sleeper was carried on a canvas stretcher back into his indoor cage.

"He remained in a stuporous state throughout the night," wrote Kevin Fox, a zoo researcher who participated in the unusual procedure. "He would occasionally rise to his feet, stagger about his cage briefly, and then collapse in the straw that padded his cage floor. Several times when he arose he appeared to be wrestling with demons and flailed out angrily at those imagined enemies."

Massa recovered fully within several days. He underwent another operation several months later because during the first procedure the vets had noticed that many of his teeth were beginning to rot away. Tooth ailments are potentially deadly to apes because of their acute sensitivity to sinus and respiratory infections. So in July, veterinarian Wilbur Amand extracted seventeen of Massa's teeth, including one of his giant canines. Ever since, the set of Massa's jaw and mouth has had the decided look of a senior citizen's.

Bill Donaldson is the same age as Massa. When he left his job as city manager of Cincinnati to assume the presidency of Philadelphia's zoo three years ago, he inherited an institution in a bad state of decline. With his white beard and snowy hair, he is, in the words of one of his women staff assistants, "the kind of person who attracts attention when he walks into a crowded room, a real Alpha-plus male"—zoo talk for the dominant male in a primate social group—"if you know what I mean."

Working for twenty years as manager of a large city bureaucracy would tend to deeply imbue stoicism even in a person with no natural inclination for it. Donaldson seems to have been that way all his life. While taking the zoo job meant accepting a considerable professional challenge, Donaldson's approach to the new position was almost childlike. "How many forty-eight-year-old men get a chance to run away and join the circus?" he asked in an interview at the time. His style is relaxed and easy; in the midst of a detailed discussion of the zoo's financial status he will stand suddenly and cross the room to his bookshelf to reverently take down a small glass aquarium in order to show off one of his pet salamanders, displaying the motionless, slimy little yellow-spotted creature with all the wide-eyed wonder of a ten-year-old who's just scooped it out of a creek.

"We recognized Bill as an able administrator who was used to working with city governments, who understood how to get things done," said Samuel H. Ballum, chairman of the zoo's board of directors. "He is also an adroit person in dealing with people."

And animals. Donaldson likes to visit the zoo at night, after it is closed to the public. Then he can walk around in silent communion with his own urban slice of the natural world. Massa is one of his favorites. Donaldson prides himself on being one of the few people who are really close to the great old ape.

"He has the most extraordinary eyes," Donaldson said. "You get the feeling he would tell you so much if he could. You know, Eric Berg—the artist who did that magnificent sculpture of Massa out in front of the Monkey House—he is quoted as saying that Massa seemed to him like a Zen monk. I get that feeling."

When he arrived in 1979 Donaldson waded directly into the zoo's miasmic financial straits. He laid off sixteen employees—"eight from union ranks and eight from management," he said. Admission prices were raised on a sliding scale that would permit economy-minded zoo goers to pay considerably less at off-peak times, but would capitalize on those sunny Saturdays and Sundays that always draw good crowds. He instituted an energy-saving program and began advertising and promoting the zoo aggressively. Attendance has gone from 990,000 in 1979 to 1.1 million in each of the last two years. Since Donaldson arrived, the zoo has paid back all the money it took from the building funds during the previous decade. It's currently operating slightly under its 1982 budget.

Donaldson praises his staff for these accomplishments, while it seems that every man and woman he employs credits him. Clearly, something is working right these days at the zoo. Perhaps the best thing is the change in attitude. Stories from the zoo are no longer problem stories, though the zoo certainly still faces problems. There is a feeling at the zoo that zoos themselves are not a thing of the past, as it might have seemed during the lean years of the seventies. With its new master plan for an almost total redesign of the facilities, with its $12 million fund-raising effort success-fully under way, the oldest zoo in America is positively *fired up*.

"When I got here this place needed a philosophy," Donaldson said, relaxing with a pipe on the couch in his office at the zoo administration building. Out the window traffic hurried past on Girard Avenue.

"Early zoos were motivated primarily by two things: first, learning the physiology of animals, and, second, the least noble aspect, the desire to come and look at the funny animals. Some of the older zoos in this country took a lead from the circus and made it a matter of policy that all animals had to perform in some way. Showtime! Lions and tigers jumping through flaming hoops! They had this German guy at the St. Louis Zoo who insisted that every animal at the zoo *do something;* he wanted them all to pay their own way. To its credit, I think, the Philadelphia Zoo has always been a more serious place. Right from the start there were rules against using the collec-tion for research or performances. I thought the zoo needed to redefine it-self, to get a clearer picture of what they are trying to accomplish here."

To help do that, Donaldson hired Mary Scott Cebul, a Yale-educated ethologist. Cebul is one of very few young Ph.D.'s around to go directly from such prestigious training into zoo work. She mentions her graduate school colleagues one by one—this one is in the Philippines, this one is in South America or Africa. Cebul is in the wilds of Philadelphia.

"Donaldson talks about how hard it was as city manager in Cincin-nati to get academics involved in actually working on the urban problems they studied," she said, "get them to talk the same language as the people who were out there dealing with the issues day after day. Here you would have academics with all this insight into the causes of urban crime, and a police chief dealing with the effects of it every day. How do you get these people to work together?"

Cebul doesn't finish the thought, but clearly she's the academic Donaldson has lured into this real-world fray. Going straight to work in a *zoo*, a place most wildlife scientists regard as a sort of abomination, as at best a *necessary* abomination, was a step that took courage—but one with a bit more practical appeal for a young woman with a husband and an infant. Cebul still isn't all that certain she took the right step. Her green eyes turn away for a moment at the question. "Maybe they're right," she said thoughtfully. "Maybe zoos are an abomination. I don't know." But, as she sees it, zoos are definitely there, they can serve a vitally important conservationist role, and she's been given a chance to remold one of the best ones around.

After nearly a year of interviewing zoo staff members, of studying problems and mulling over solutions, Cebul wrote a philosophy for the Philadelphia Zoo. It forms an ideological basis for all planning—which she is now coordinating. The philosophy defines the zoo's lofty, conservationist mission, and spells out what kind of zoo it can and cannot be.

"Back when things were really bad, there was a lot of talk about moving the zoo out to the suburbs, where there would be more space for more dramatic exhibits," Donaldson said. "So long as that debate went on, very little was going to get accomplished here. We decided at the outset to accept our status as an urban zoo. Once we acknowledged that, we had to accept that there were some things we could do, and other things we couldn't do."

The main thing the zoo couldn't do was continue to maintain such a large and varied collection of animals. The cost in dollars and space was simply too high. In 1971, for instance, it cost about $1,100 a year to house, feed, and care for Massa alone. In 1982, the estimated cost is $6,257. In planning for the Primate Center, it was clear that some of the zoo's current collection of twenty-five species would have to go. The list was trimmed to fifteen. The rules for which animals would stay were set by two priorities: retaining a representative sampling of primates from different families and different parts of the world, and helping those species that are the most endangered. By those criteria, gorillas, orangutans, and chimpanzees were all too similar and safe—at least in captivity. But the Philadelphia Zoo is famous for its gorillas and orangutans—and *chimps*? Why, chimps are big favorites at zoos everywhere. Get rid of chimps?

It was an issue that prompted some soul-searching and debate at high levels inside the zoo. It was solved with one compromise—orangs would stay. And with one tough decision—chimps would go. No chimps?

"Look, there are chimps all over the place," said the zoo's director of mammals, Dietrich Schaaf, reflecting the hard-nosed posture of the zoo's new breed. "We can't be all things to all people. There would be no educational purpose served by having another chimp exhibit here. With the gorillas and orangs on display, the other great apes can be incorporated into the exhibit through films and lectures."

Cebul's first project, her pride and joy, is the new Children's Zoo, which will attempt to draw children into the experience of being an animal with walks in exhibits that make the child feel the same size as an animal, with special lenses to look through that will, quite literally, allow the child to see the world through an animal's eyes. Her approach to remaking the zoo, aside from the management and breeding considerations of giving animals more room and more naturalistic settings, is to give zoo goers something much more than the passive, static kind of experience that zoos usually provide. She talks about a dolphin exhibit at the New England Aquarium where visitors watch a film about dolphins on a large screen, and when the movie is over the screen rises and real dolphins swim out from behind it. She wants zoo goers to learn, and to teach them, she wants to find ways to give them a thrill.

Donaldson calls Cebul "one of the best things that has ever happened to the Philadelphia Zoo." Asked to summarize the zoo's new outlook, the initial fruits of Cebul's labor, he explained: "I see a threefold purpose for the zoo. First, it gives us a sort of laboratory to learn how to manage wild animals in captivity. Second, it can preserve at least a few endangered species. And, third, the most important role and one that we so far aren't doing well, is to help convince the average person that wild animals are worthwhile, that the wild world is connected to them and worth preserving. I think that what we hope to accomplish is just starting to happen here. In five or six years, then we'll really be somewhere. It's exciting."

There was a period last fall when Massa's keeper, Ralph McCarthy, and the higher-ups—who have grown used to local journalists' premature predictions of Massa's demise—really thought *themselves* that Massa was finished. He wasn't recognizing people the way he usually does. Ralph would climb up on the wooden ladder behind Massa's cage and call him—"Yo, Mass!"—the way he usually does, with the kind of friendly, growling tone that usually works, and old Massa would just ignore him the way he ignores the tourists who file past the front of his cage, more than a million a year. This was bad.

Massa displays a kind of affection for most of the zoo people he recognizes, and reserves a particular fondness for his buddy Ralph. Most times he'll stir his stiff, arthritic bones and slowly, with supreme economy of motion, stand to grasp the center pole of his cage and swing Tarzan-like up to the top level, then park his hairy back up against the bars so Ralph can give him a good scratching.

But one day, for reasons he kept to himself, Massa wasn't interested. It might just as well have been some complete stranger flagging him—"Yo, Mass!"—up in back. He responded with surly indifference, with the kind of profound arrogance God gave only to primates. This lasted for a few weeks, during which time quiet alarms went out among Massa's extended family on the Girard Avenue property. Then, just as suddenly and inexplicably, Massa came out of it.

He just keeps plodding along at his generally healthy pace. Since no gorilla has ever lived this long, there's no predicting how long Massa can last. There are those who feel that gorillas, with proper feeding and medical care, should be able to live as long as human beings. Their physical structure is very similar, after all. If anything, gorillas seem stronger. Old Massa just might still be around to amuse our children's children. Still, it doesn't seem likely. You can almost hear his old bones creak every time he moves.

For almost two decades, it is said, local obituary writers have been poised to report Massa's passing with the sentence "Massa lies in the cold, cold ground." That won't be the case.

"Massa has become an important animal in the study of geriatrics," explained zoo research director Robert Snyder. "He's led a life under very controlled circumstances, controlled diet, and very predictable lifestyle, to put it mildly. When he dies, a lot of people are going to be interested in taking a close look at him."

For an animal who hasn't traveled more than about thirty yards during the last forty-six years, old Mass is going to do some big traveling when he dies—in about five different directions. When the regretful day arrives, Massa's withered carcass will be lovingly dissected in Snyder's lab. Snyder is particularly interested in how well Massa's diet has controlled the build-up of fatty tissue in his arteries. He suspects the results will shed some light on the role diet plays in causing or preventing heart disease—in all primates, including man.

But the process only begins there. John McGrath, professor of pathology at the University of Pennsylvania's veterinary school, plans to scarf up Massa's brain.

"Probably the spinal column, too," McGrath said. "I'll be interested in looking for some of the physiological manifestations of senility—not that Massa shows any real signs of growing senile. He seems to be as clear-headed as ever. We'll be interested in looking at it both from the standpoint of gathering information about aging in apes as well as to compare it with aging studies on humans. Both are primates, after all. We've never seen the brain of a gorilla Massa's age—there's never been a gorilla of Massa's age. There are also some people up in New York who are doing some really elegant studies with an electron microscope of the effects of aging on the brain. They've expressed interest in a few slides." He'll prepare a sample for the folks in New York, and parcel out bits and pieces to interested colleagues here and there.

Massa's final resting place, or at least the end of the line for most of him, will be on the sixth floor of the Smithsonian Institution's natural history museum, up with the collection of a hundred or so great-ape skeletons kept there. Snyder plans to ship Massa's scooped-out carcass to Jay Matternes, an artist in Fairfax, Virginia, who has done many technical illustrations for the Smithsonian's publications and exhibits, for Time-Life books and magazines, and for *National Geographic*. Matternes, who also "hopes the day is a long way off," plans to do a very detailed dissection of Massa, carefully measuring all his parts.

"It will be extremely useful in just gathering more information for comparative purposes," Matternes said. "We'll get as much information from the cadaver as we can. There are a lot of specific, technical questions about gorilla anatomy that right now aren't answered in the literature. You really have to go directly to the source for some answers."

Taking Massa apart will be a sort of labor of love (if a dissection can ever be one) for Matternes.

"Massa is a great sentimental favorite of mine," Matternes said. "I grew up in Lancaster, and in high school I used to spend nearly every weekend in the Monkey House doing drawings of Massa and Bamboo. Those two apes formed my idea of what a gorilla is. At the time, they were the only two adult gorillas on the East Coast. I've still got reams of old drawings of Massa; they were my first works."

These days, Massa is back to his old self, grunting appreciatively when Ralph slips him a pretzel or candy bar or gumdrop—things he's not supposed to have, but even gorillas have friends, you see. Massa will peer intently into the eyes of a visitor standing in the concrete corridor behind his cage. He will lean hard forward, laying his right arm down on the floor of the cage, resting his chin on his forearm and draping the other long arm over the top of his head, and fix his curious gaze on the human face just inches away. There is still a touch of red in the wiry mane of gray hair that stands up straight on the high crown of his forehead. His brow curls thick and coal black over wide, inquiring eyes, eyes with big blackish-brown pupils and with whites that are mostly bloodshot and brown.

Massa will stare only for a few seconds at a time if you meet his gaze. He will avert his eyes and then quickly look back for a moment, then avert them again, then steal another look. Beneath the brow and eyes, his facial structure descends in a series of broad, inverted V-shaped rims to the wide hollows of his nostrils. He works his gums just like an old man, but the gaze is more like that of a child.

You want to ask him something, somehow penetrate the biological wall.

Is it worth it, old man, living this long? They say your old companion, Buddha, your only real friend, died of distrust and viciousness, but we know better, don't we, Massa. He died of a broken heart. Missy Lintz went to visit him just before it happened. She said he came as close to her as he could inside his air-

conditioned circus cage, and pulled out his lower lip to show her a big gumboil over one of his teeth. It must have meant constant pain, so bad it added to the things that killed him. But he wouldn't let any of his keepers know about it. He hated them all. Instead Buddha just suffered it out and died. Poor Buddha. And what about you, old boy? What keeps you hanging on? Have you triumphed over it all or just given in?

BREEDING THE BETTER COW

MARCH 1980

My first job at The Inquirer was in the suburban Wayne bureau. Because Philadelphia's outlying areas were still primarily rural, we got a lot of farm publications at the office in Wayne. One day I noticed an ad for udder supports, with an illustration that made it clear such devices were, essentially, cow bras. Now, why on earth would a cow need a bra? The search for an answer to that question led me into the strange world of animal husbandry. The story won the first national award I had ever received, given by the American Association for the Advancement of Science, which was proof positive that you didn't need to know a lick about science to conquer science writing.

In the beginning, a cow was just a cow. Sloe-eyed, dumb but benevolent, she produced prodigious amounts of milk and a few heifers, and perhaps won a ribbon at the state fair.

Then man intervened. Employing an insidious arsenal of breeding devices, such as artificial insemination, superovulation, and embryo transfer, man has produced a cow that is little more than a gigantic lactating machine with four legs, a head, and a tail.

Take Alice, for instance. Alice is a motherly Holstein on the Oxford, Pennsylvania, farm of Dale Hostetter. She is a good milker, but Alice is, you might say, overequipped. She keeps stepping on her teats.

"Then her udder gets infected, and we can't milk her," Hostetter complains. "It gets damned expensive."

So Alice wears a bra. She is a walking, somewhat sore example of the revolution that is under way in American barnyards, and she is not alone. There was a tenfold jump in the last decade in sales of Tamm Udder

Supports, absurdly oversized nylon cow bras that keep mammoth modern mammaries from dragging underhoof.

Mass consumption demands animals designed for mass production. So today's sophisticated farmer thinks of his animals as little factories. Portly, friendly breeds of yore have become stripped-down, scrawny creatures enslaved to an artificial, sexless, joyless regimen of controlled breeding, eating, exercise, production, and slaughter. Prospects for their future are even more grim and bizarre.

But the system works. By accelerating the lazy progress of evolution, new selective breeding techniques have halved the number of dairy cows in the United States in the last ten years, while actually increasing total milk production.

Other barnyard breeds have shown similar improvement.

Chickens that once, in a wild state, laid about fifty eggs a year today produce two hundred and fifty or more and eat half as much feed. Ten years after standardbred horse associations endorsed artificial insemination, the number of trotters and pacers that have run sub-two-minute miles has increased dramatically.

First, the Dairies

But the revolution has been felt most profoundly in the dairy industry. Because dairy herds are small and regimented, they are the first to have been thoroughly enslaved by the syringes and chemicals of veterinary medicine. With 75 percent of American dairy farmers inseminating their cows artificially, the syringe has replaced sex as the most common method of reproducing the breed.

"The widespread use of artificial insemination is the most significant development in the history of animal breeding," said Dr. James Evans of the University of Pennsylvania's New Bolton Center veterinary school in Kennett Square. "It has vastly accelerated the pace of breeding progress by enabling farmers to breed a multitude of animals from the top ten or twenty bulls of their time."

Mating dairy herds today is a bit like department store shopping. Breeding firms publish catalogues that list, on the basis of records accumulated from thousands of offspring, the genetic makeup of their bulls. A farmer can match his cows' traits with those in the catalogue and pick bulls that best complement his herd.

The overwhelming majority of bulls lack the pedigree or outstanding characteristics to mate. They are castrated, fattened up, and trucked off for meat before they ever see a cow, other than the one that weaned them. But it seems that the ten or twenty bulls that have what it takes spawn offspring, like biblical Abraham, as numerous as the stars.

350,000 DESCENDANTS

Half the seven hundred thousand Holsteins in Pennsylvania today are descended from the same sire, a massive, three-ton bull named Osborndale Ivanhoe (otherwise known as 118970).

Ivanhoe was born in 1950 at Osborndale Farms in New England. He was six before he had sired enough offspring in the natural fashion to be considered marketable for mass insemination. He was sold for $10,000 to Atlantic Breeders Cooperative (ABC), a firm in Lancaster that is one of the two largest bull semen distributors on the East Coast.

"Ivanhoe was the largest bull we've ever had here," recalls Harry Roth, ABC operations director. "He stood about six feet, two inches at the withers; most of our bulls stand about five-ten. He weighed about seven hundred pounds more than most prize bulls.

"Ivanhoe was exactly what the Holstein breed was looking for in the sixties. He produced big-boned, angular, strong heifers, and his daughters were champion milk producers."

At ABC, Ivanhoe lived seven more years inside a narrow stall about twenty yards long, ten feet wide. After his semen was tested on thousands of cows, exploring just about every genetic possibility in his makeup, his excellence as breeding stock was proved.

He became far too valuable an animal to graze freely or exercise—a leg injury, for instance, could have made it impossible for him to mount teaser steers (castrated males that are used so no copulation can take place) in ABC's semen-collecting lab. So leviathan Ivanhoe spent his days confined, pampered, and chained to a demanding sexual regimen.

To the Mating Stall

Three times a week he was led by the ring in his nose to the mating stall, where a steer was strapped to the cage in front of him. If Ivanhoe performed as expected, his valuable seed was collected in a plastic tube. If Ivanhoe was reluctant, he got the "electro-ejaculator," a device that jolted out his semen with a carefully applied, mild electrical shock.

One way or the other, Ivanhoe was milked for enough semen in his lifetime to impregnate roughly two hundred thousand cows. Packaged in short, thin glass straws and stored in a supercold vat of liquid nitrogen, Ivanhoe's sperm is still being used today, for about $4,250 a shot.

Although dead for seventeen years, Osborndale Ivanhoe lives on. His semen has already sired 1,980 heifers and is expected to continue to do so for several more years.

Ivanhoe left a genetic stamp on the Holstein breed far greater than any other bull in history, far greater than nature would ever have allowed. He is one of only two bulls that ABC decided not to send for slaughter when age finally stilled his sexuality. In an uncharacteristically sentimental gesture, the breeding cooperative laid Ivanhoe's enormous carcass to rest outside the lab that stores his sperm, under an impressive tombstone.

Roth is mildly embarrassed about it today.

"We'll never bury another one, that's for sure, no matter how spectacular he is," the breeding expert said. "We don't need a graveyard out there. There's no value in that."

New Technique

Artificial insemination has drastically inflated the value of popular bull sires, but a newer breeding technique—superovulation and embryo transfer—has injected a strain of female equality into today's barnyard breeding labs.

In the past, cows were limited for breeding purposes by the pace of their reproductive cycle. Gestation takes an unalterable nine months. So a cow, no matter how superb, could only produce one calf a year (twins if the farmer was unusually lucky) for the six or seven years it was reproductively mature.

Superovulation and embryo transfer have changed that, like the miracle of the loaves and fishes. Hormone injections produce dozens of eggs at one time. Once artificially inseminated, the tiny embryos are flushed out and surgically inserted in the wombs of separate recipient cows. Each operation takes about fifteen minutes.

Using this technique, a clever farmer can get twelve calves from his prize milker each year instead of only one. The New Bolton Center last year produced twenty-eight healthy calves in nine months from a cow named Miss Catalyst. The world record belongs to a seven-year-old Pierouge Simmental cow named Castile-156, which engendered eighty-five heifers in eleven months.

Magic Cow

Wilmer Hostetter, Dale's uncle, is a prosperous Oxford farmer who owes his success in large part to this technique. Fifteen years ago, he bought a magic cow. He paid $1,250 for the animal, a doleful Holstein named Millie, and drove her home in the back of his covered pickup.

These days, Hostetter drives a Cadillac. He had a hunch about Millie that paid off. She was a one-in-ten-million cow, a daughter, incidentally, of Osborndale Ivanhoe. When Hostetter bought Millie, he owned thirty-five head of cattle and was looking to expand.

"Millie had what you'd call good dairy character," Hostetter recalls, "a well-formed and attached udder, good legs, and a nice general shape. I thought she might improve the quality of my herd."

Millie proved to be the nucleus of a top-grade Holstein herd so valuable that it may end up supporting several generations of Hostetters. Her milk production put her in the top 0.1 percent of the country's dairy cows. But, more important, she produced four daughters in the same category. Superovulation and embryo transfer did the rest.

Working with semen from top bulls, Hostetter has built a herd of more than thirty cattle directly related to Millie, carrying her valuable genetic traits. In her stall, Millie is surrounded by daughters who closely resemble her in size and coloration. Working with Millie and these daughters, Hostetter hopes to double the size of her immediate family in the next two years.

"We sold one of her bull calves for twenty thousand dollars," Hostetter said.

$4 Million Business

Today his herd numbers two hundred and seventy, and he runs a $4 million grain and dairy business.

"I never planned on getting into the breeding business, but Millie just sort of led me there. If our plans for her work out in the next two years, we'll sell most of her immediate family and just keep the offspring. I figure about three hundred thousand would be a good price.

"We'd keep the newer offspring and start over again from there, after taking a good long vacation and enjoying a nice slow year."

Stories like that of Wilmer and his magic cow have dramatically increased the value of individual cows. At a recent auction in Kennett Square, a local breeding syndicate paid $71,000 for a cow, an amount that still baffles older dairy farmers, who are not attuned to the newest developments. But cows have a long way to go before they are worth what breeders will pay for a proven bull stud like Osborndale Ivanhoe. A bull like that is worth millions.

A Drawback

All of which explains the sad story of Wayne Spring Fond Apollo, a prize Holstein stud whose semen was, two years ago, among the most sought after in the industry. His career collided with a simple genetic principle: the same breeding methods that have so improved milk production can also play havoc with the breed.

A normal, happy herd of Holsteins reproduces itself with an almost infinite variety of chromosome match-ups. But when all the cows in the same herd are bred with the same bull, and when many of the offspring issue from the same cow, there are fewer genetic combinations possible.

Although farmers select desirable traits to be multiplied by selective breeding, undesirable ones are sometimes magnified in the bargain. Several years ago breeders began noting significant increases in the rate of bovine birth defects.

"The numbers are by no means alarming, but the rates have gone up enough for the industry to begin watching it carefully," said Roth of ABC, who sits on the executive board of the National Animal Breeders Association.

Roth chaired an association committee last year that studied a number of common Holstein birth defects. The study concluded with a recommendation that all defects be recorded, along with the pedigree that produced them.

Two years ago it was discovered that Wayne-Apollo, owned by Select Sires, a major bull semen–distributing cooperative based in Ohio, had sired calves with birth defects. Somehow the prize stud had made it through Select Sire's elaborate screenings without displaying his birth defect potential.

"Mule-Foot" Arises

Wayne-Apollo's unexpected gene produced calves with "mule-foot," by far the most prevalent Holstein anomaly in recent years. Calves are born with a misshapen hoof, one that is more like a solid mule's hoof than the normal bovine cloven foot. Mule-footed calves rarely live out their first year, and those that do are so hobbled that they are worthless to cattlemen.

The likelihood of any one farmer experiencing the problem in Wayne-Apollo offspring was very small, and the immediate advantages afforded by the bull's superior traits were obvious. But the mule-foot trait could have been disastrous for the breed.

"Somewhere down the line, if a bull like that stays in service, you are going to have a serious and damaging rise in the number of mule-footed calves," said Evans of the New Bolton Center. "His chances of siring a mule-foot calf are small, but if he has ten or twenty thousand daughters, you can see how fast the potential grows.

"But, as with most things, the almighty dollar has its own priorities. Scrapping a bull with the potential of Wayne-Apollo would be a serious financial blow."

Select Sires opted to leave the bull in service. Wayne-Apollo is alive and well. Bernie Heisner, director of information for the co-op, estimates that Wayne-Apollo has so far produced enough semen to impregnate 140,000 cows artificially.

"There are two schools of thought among geneticists about that bull," Heisner said. "One would scrap him right away. The other would leave him in service, because of his other exceptional traits. Select Sires thinks so highly of Wayne Spring Fond Apollo's proven genetics that they have authorized bringing his sons into its program.

"We have a group of mule-foot-carrying females to test the sons on. Statistically, about half of them will be clean. He may go down as one of the great sires of the breed."

Heisner insists that the mule-foot danger Wayne-Apollo poses is relatively minor. Fortunately, Roth says, knowledge of Wayne-Apollo's mule-foot trait has kept "responsible breeders" from using the bull's semen. A dose of Wayne-Apollo's seed today sells for only $15 to $24.

LIMITS ON HORSES

Birth defects are only one of the less desirable consequences that could result from narrowing the genetic pool of a breed. Another is a phenomenon best illustrated by horses.

Ten years ago, standardbred horse associations permitted their animals to be artificially inseminated for the first time.

Before 1974, only 4,862 trotters and pacers had ever run a mile in less than two minutes, according to figures kept by the U.S. Trotting Association. In the first half of the '70s, the total increased by almost half again—2,298 horses broke two minutes. In the last half of the '70s, when the impact of artificial insemination would have been most fully evident, 10,572 horses broke two minutes.

Those numbers are impressive, but despite the multiplication of speedy standardbred horses, breeders did not produce a trotter or pacer that could improve records set in 1969 by Study Star (1:52:00) for pacers and in 1971 by Nevelle Pride (1:54:04) for trotters.

By selecting only top animals for breeding, the industry got offspring equal to the best of the previous generation. But what breeders could not get from those select parents was a horse significantly better. A horse that shatters world records is, in a genetic sense, a mutant horse. It is, by some surprise combination of chromosomes, a strikingly better animal than those from which it issued.

This is the theoretical dead end for selective breeding. As the genetic pool narrows, the possible combinations of chromosomes decrease, and the animals are more and more alike. It is partly for this reason that thoroughbred horsemen have refused to permit artificial insemination of their animals.

"It would wreak havoc on the economics of our industry, for one thing," explains a top official in the Jockey Club, the central governing power in thoroughbred horse racing.

"An example is Bold Forbes, a horse that won the Kentucky Derby and Belmont in 1975. Bold Forbes was sired by a horse named Irish Castle, a horse that was never outstanding in any way. If the standards of artificial breeding were applied to our industry, Irish Castle would never have had the chance to stud.

"What happens is that you reduce the possibility for surprises like Bold Forbes. Thoroughbreds are already pretty well inbred; most knowledgeable breeders shudder to think what would happen to the breed if artificial insemination was allowed."

In the dairy industry, this genetic dead end means that there is only so much drastic improvement to be expected from artificial breeding methods. By selecting top bulls and top milk-producing cows, the industry should end up with a multitude of closely related, similar animals. All will produce miraculous quantities of milk, but the chances of any one coming along that significantly improves upon the standard will grow smaller and smaller.

"That is quite a long way off though," Dr. Evans said. "Theoretically, it is possible that will happen. I'd say that the number of farmers like Wilmer Hostetter, farmers who selectively breed their animals intelligently, scientifically, are still comparatively small.

"Many farmers are still looking at the shape of the cow's head for a clue to its productivity, instead of looking at its rear end. So the improvements we've seen are really just a beginning."

LIMITED POTENTIAL

And the theory of the dead end discounts the potential for further advances in breeding techniques.

The Food and Drug Administration recently approved the use of a drug called Prostaglandin, which, when injected into a cow, brings her into heat. This capacity could enormously benefit beef cattlemen, who have so far only been able to use artificial insemination on a small scale because of the size of their herds.

"By using Prostaglandin, a rancher could put all the cows in his herd on the same schedule," Evans said. "He could inject them, and they would all come into heat at the same time. He could then inseminate them, and all of them would calve at roughly the same time."

Cloning and developing embryos in test tubes offer other bizarre possibilities for the future. Cloned embryos could duplicate prize cow after prize cow. Artificial wombs would conceivably enable scientist-farmers to grow herds of animals like tomatoes, reaping crops of newborn test-tube animals on a rigid laboratory schedule. Scientists such as Evans believe that such advances may be necessary to feed the world's mushrooming population.

But for the cattle and chickens and pigs and horses of the future, life looks grim indeed. They have become cows like Dale Hostetter's Alice, with udders so large that they need bras; they are little factories, four-legged crops. There is little room left in the barnyard for the kind of sentimentality that Atlantic Breeders showed when it buried Osborndale Ivanhoe.

When Wilmer Hostetter's Millie reaches the end of her line any day now, when she stops producing fertile eggs and can no longer get pregnant, can no longer be milked, what will Hostetter do? How will he treat the magic cow, the cow he has parlayed into a small fortune?

"I've given that some thought, you know," Hostetter said. "And I've decided to pack her off to the slaughterhouse for meat when she's through. Yep, that's what I'm going to do."

BATTLING "THE BADDIES" IN FANTASYLAND

JULY 1982

This story still haunts me. It is one of the only ones I have ever written where I appear as a character, and the only one that featured any of my children. I was, at the time, a single father, and the ordeal Donna was going through with her little boy just broke my heart. Billy died some months after this story ran, and to this day I think about him whenever I see my strapping, grown son.

It was my son's fifth birthday. *Five.* Five years since a nurse handed me a crying infant slick with afterbirth in a soiled white sheet and said, "Here is your son."

We were in Disney World in Orlando, Florida. I had come to write a story about fourteen kids from St. Christopher's Hospital for Children who were on a short holiday in this kiddie heaven. All fourteen had cancer. My son, Aaron, was along because the trip fell on his birthday and I didn't have the heart not to take him.

I was eating a late dinner on the balcony of my hotel room with Donna Schanel, whose son, Billy, was asleep inside on a bed with Aaron. The two boys had become fast friends. Billy, a precocious child just a few months younger than Aaron, has leukemia. Donna was explaining how the desperate battle for Billy's life demanded not only the latest drugs and medical procedures, but all of her hope and will and all of Billy's strength. Left unsaid was that even all this might not be enough.

The conversation helped shake my paternal contentment as I stepped inside the room to check on the boys. They were asleep back-to-back, my blond son turned to the right and Donna's brown-haired son to the left. There was only the sound of their breathing. Whatever pride I had taken in my own boy's passage from infancy to boyhood seemed suddenly fatuous and vain. Here was one child with every prospect of a long life before him, and another, a boy just as bright and lovely, just as sweetly nurtured, just as open and simple and yet already so full of that mystery *self,* whose very childhood was being strangled from within. And here was this mother whose loving expectations for her son had turned so cruelly to grim statistical odds on survival. I felt frightened. I wanted to scoop Aaron up, remove him from the threat I could feel cold in the room. And though I knew that the causes of Billy's disease were not contagious, I questioned in that moment my judgment as a parent, to have brought my boy so close to this.

This was no place for a child, I thought, but then watching Billy sleep, breathe, I shuddered at the absurdity of the thought and felt as powerless as a parent like Donna who must stand over her sleeping child at night and wonder if death would *dare rob* so much life.

The children from St. Christopher's were off to Disney World because a wealthy young woman had decided to liquidate her family's forty-year-old charitable foundation and set aside $10,000 to send them on a three-day wish trip. I went along to see how parents and children coped with it all: the grim battle with medical odds; the terrors of uncertainty, of having to rely on doctors who aren't sure how to proceed; the dreary regimen of hospital and home, hospital and home.

But these were not families burdened with grief; these were people living intensely, each day, every hour. Facing a nightmare of protracted illness and painful treatments, these children and their parents were dealing with *life,* life at a high-voltage level—not death, though death was certainly waiting nearby. I learned soon that their daily struggle demanded bonds between parent and child that would put to shame the relationship between a father and his healthy son.

They had found, in the shadow of ultimate loss, ultimate gain.

A week before the trip, I visited the hematology clinic at St. Christopher's. The clinic is on the second floor of this small hospital complex, in a Hispanic neighborhood in North Philadelphia amid blocks and blocks of dilapidated and abandoned rowhouses. Glass and garbage litter the sidewalks, and the street life lasts all day and night.

Inside, the clinic is crowded with toys, children playing, and parents waiting. The mood is busy but somber, and while there is laughter and conversation in the waiting area, there are occasional cries and screams from the treatment rooms. Pain—children rarely take it in silence—is part of the furniture here.

On the morning I visited, Anthony Mancini was in pain. He is a robust, tawny boy of eleven whose natural garrulity has taken on sharpness during his two-year bout with leukemia. Anthony is old enough to know what's going on in his body, even if he can't understand why. He isn't happy about it and he doesn't pretend to be. After nearly a year in remission, the disease has returned, and so have Anthony's treatments, brutal doses of cell-killing drugs. He had received his first injections just over a week ago, and already his thick brown hair was falling out in patches. But the pain resulted from a more insidious side effect: Anthony had been unable to move his bowels for six days. The pain had started Saturday and now it was Wednesday. The doctor asked Anthony if the pain was like a knife or more like somebody punching him in the stomach.

The boy groaned. "Like a punch," he said.

It pressed especially hard every few minutes. Prone on an examining table, Anthony would rock to his right side when it happened, rest his fingers lightly over the pain, roll his eyes back, and loudly moan.

"Oooooh, Mommy, Mommy, make it stop, make it stop," he pleaded, but whenever Mary Mancini moved to stroke his belly or back, the boy would complain harshly. "Don't touch it! Don't touch it! It hurts, Mommy, it hurts." His mother could do little but hover over the boy with futile concern.

"He has been looking forward so much to this trip," she said. "I just hope he'll get better in time to go. Maybe talking to you will cheer him up. He's been looking forward to meeting the reporter."

Anthony's powder-blue *Dukes of Hazzard* T-shirt was hiked up over his round brown belly. His blue jeans were unbuttoned at the waist to ease the pressure. The right side of his face was pressed into the pillow, and he did not look at me when he spoke.

"You the reporter?"

"Yes."

"Go ahead, ask me questions. I'm ready. What do you wanna know?"

With little prodding, Anthony began to talk. He talked in a torrent to take his mind off the pain and the place. He directed his mother to show off the scabs on his back where the doctors had only days before performed painful spinal tap and bone-marrow tests. He told me he wanted to be a paramedic when he grew up.

"Ask me about the leukemia," Anthony demanded.

"Tell me about it."

"This same thing happened to me last time when they gave me the drugs, but it was worse," he said. "It hurt so bad that one night when I stayed at the hospital I screamed all night. They kept coming over to me and asking me if I would just try to calm down, but I couldn't. It *really* hurt. Finally, they just gave me a shot of Demerol that took the pain away. But they won't give me that strong stuff very much. At first it made me mad, but now that I'm older I understand it. Yeah. You see, if you keep taking it, then eventually it has no effect on you. So when you hurt real bad, they can't help you anymore. That would be rough. Now I don't expect to get it. I only had it that one time . . ."

The doctor walked into the room and cut short Anthony's monologue. He spoke to the boy's mother, not to him. He explained that the constipation was typical of Anthony's response to the drugs, that after feeling the boy's stomach he didn't think it posed a serious problem.

"This is the reaction we expected with that large dose of meds we gave him last week," the doctor explained. "We could give him something to ease the pain, but the pain is a good indicator of what's going on. If we knock that out, then we don't know what's happening inside."

"I wanna go home," Anthony announced abruptly, starting to sit up, having heard in the doctor's hard reasoning an echo of his own explanation to me. Bent a bit at the waist, his mother's arm around his shoulder, Anthony lingered outside the examining room long enough to down a small plastic cup of Tylenol before boarding the elevator to wait out the pain at home.

As the elevator doors closed, Anthony said confidently: "I'm gonna make it."

The same morning, Donna was visiting the clinic with Billy. He was in a small treatment room sitting on his mother's lap, worried. His mood was in conflict with the cheerful cartoon animals on the wallpaper.

Billy is an especially beautiful child. He has his mother's oversized, oval green eyes and prim lips that purse tightly when he's troubled or angry but which usually grace an unrestrained, tiny-toothed grin. Even without the side effects of his treatments, Billy has the rounded belly of a four-year-old whose body has stretched into boyhood without shedding the budlike luster of infancy.

This was to be the second in a long series of injections, spinal taps, and bone-marrow tests. After leukemia was diagnosed in December of 1980, the first round of treatments put the disease in remission. Billy had resumed a normal existence, except for monthly blood tests and painful bone-marrow tests every third month. Then in May, just two weeks before the Disney World trip, the leukemia had come back. The relapse meant Billy's chances of surviving were drastically reduced.

The treatment—there's no way around it—is plain torture for a child. On this morning, Billy was to get two needles, one to draw blood from his left forearm and the other to inject drugs into his left leg. The leg shots *hurt.*

Billy was already an old hand at this, but fear showed in his face. Under a film of moisture, his eyes followed every move of nurse Dotty Golasa as she prepared the two syringes. Then, as Golasa picked up the first of them, Billy blurted, "Can I go to the bathroom? I have to go to the bathroom."

Donna and the nurse looked at each other over the boy's head, rolled their eyes, and smiled in sympathy. "Okay, Billy," Donna said, lifting the boy off her lap. The two hurried out the door and down the hall.

"I get that a lot," Golasa said, turning to me with a smile that summed up the sadness of her dilemma, how she must hurt these children to help them.

Donna and Billy were back in a few moments. "He wasn't kidding," Donna said. Then she positioned Billy on her lap for Golasa to begin the shots.

"Why don't we yell 'Ow!' when you get the shot; sometimes that makes it feel better," Donna suggested. "Maybe Mark will yell, too."

"Right," I said. "Why don't we see who can yell 'Ow!' the loudest. I bet I can yell louder than you."

Billy's eyes widened happily.

"You tell us when to yell, Billy," Donna said as Golasa leaned forward with the needle. Billy watched with knotted brow as the needle entered his arm.

"OW!" he shouted, and we all joined in, "OW!OW!OW!OW!"

"I yelled the loudest!" Billy said.

"People are going to wonder what's going on in here," Golasa said, and she laughed.

Donna had been notified earlier this year, out of the blue, that Billy was an alternate for the Disney World trip. Joan Taksa Rolsky, the clinic's social worker, asked her whether Billy had ever been there, and Donna said no. In March, she got a letter saying that because several of the children chosen were too sick to go, or had already been to Disney World, she and Billy would definitely be making the trip.

It was the only nice surprise Donna ever got from St. Christopher's.

That was two months before Billy's relapse, which put Donna "in a state of shock of some sort." The ordeal of the first year of treatments had been shoved way back in her mind. "I hadn't even considered that it would come back, which was dumb, I guess. But it really just wasn't in my mind at all. He was doing so well; he looked so good."

Donna said she found herself oddly incapable of emotion. She listened to the doctors, to the bad news, able only to absorb it.

"Before the relapse, they had made it sound like if the leukemia came back, then there was almost *no chance* Billy would survive," she recalled. "But then right away the talk shifted to possible treatments, and suddenly there were still chances, even though they were smaller. Billy was sitting in the chair next to me and he was asking me to read him a book, he was pushing it on my lap, so I took the book and tried to read to him, but no words came out. I just couldn't get myself to speak. When I left the hospital that day I was just numb. I said good-bye and walked out the door. I took Billy to the zoo. I remember thinking that the doctors must have gotten the impression that I didn't care about Billy at all. But I was just numb."

Billy's treatments started two weeks later, and this time she knew what to expect. The drugs would make Billy sick and irritable. His hair would fall out—those soft, silky baby locks. His belly would swell because the drugs would enlarge his pancreas and his appetite. His legs would hurt so much from the injections that he would hardly be able to walk. It would break her heart.

She remembered musing, at some point after learning of Billy's re-lapse, "I guess that shoots the trip." But the doctors, seizing upon some-thing they *could* guarantee, promised her that Billy could still go to Disney World. Suddenly, though, the joy of it took on a tinsel quality.

Miragelike across a sun-dappled lake, the green shores of The Magic King-dom rise gently, broken only by patches of perfect trees and sculpted bushes of dancing bears, elephants, camels, and birds. Beyond the tree line, the village rooftops of Fantasyland lean with the grace of innocent imagina-tion toward the familiar blue and silver spires of Cinderella Castle. There it rests like gumdrops on acres of meticulously groomed, blue-green Or-lando swamp . . . *a dream made real.*

Anthony Mancini wasn't along. When the pain was still with him the day before our departure, he decided on his own not to go. But the chil-dren here were in ecstasy. On the ferry to The Magic Kingdom, they ran and laughed and hung on the railings. We were on a *boat!* which was only slightly less fun than that morning's trip on the *airplane!* or the *TV cameras!* at the airport, which were at least one fun notch above the *neato electronic games!* in the lobby of the TraveLodge Hotel or the *bus!* that brought us to the ferry.

Inside the front gate, the theme park erupted with color and excite-ment, people and events, oversized costume animals who sign autographs for throngs of thrilled children, rides and marching bands, submarines that somehow dive in only four feet of water, and rocket ships that sweep be-lievers to Mars without ever leaving the ground. It would be more than a child could take, if not for exhaustless energy reserves of joy.

We parents spent a long, hot day just keeping up. By darkness, when the group gathered for a bus back to the hotel, most of the children were half asleep. Once aboard, they quickly dozed off on the plastic seats, clutching their new dolls and balloons and other Disney souvenirs. Par-ents swapped stories about the afternoon, then fell to talking about their children and cancer, treatments and side effects, *hospital talk,* compar-ing notes and the burdens, complaints, and little triumphs that only they understand.

As they talked quietly, an elderly woman, not one of our party, walked back to hold the rear handrail. A sturdy woman with a red suntan and cropped white hair, she seemed delighted to see so many children and started right in asking questions.

"Where are you all from? Are you here together?"

"We're all from St. Christopher's Hospital, here just for three days," said James Carroll, his son Jimmy asleep on the seat next to him. The word "hospital" registered immediate concern with the woman. She began to take in young Stephanie Schwartz's frailness and head scarf, the tracheal tube in the neck of Bruce Lee Zayas . . . and then there was a husky trace of sympathy in her voice.

"What's wrong with your boy?" she asked Carroll.

"He has cancer."

The woman groped for what to say next. "Is he going to be all right?"

The question caught Carroll short for only a second. "Yeah, he's been doing fine," he said, his answer calculated to ease them both out of a difficult conversation. But this was not a woman to turn back. She spoke to all the parents sitting around her, asking what was wrong with each child, inquiring sympathetically about each one's prognosis. By the time she turned to Bruce Lee's mom, a flamboyant young woman sporting purple-tinted glasses and tight-fitting, leopard-print short-shorts and tight top to match, Marianne Zayas had had enough of the whole scene.

"And what's wrong with your boy?" the old woman inquired.

"EVERYTHING!" Zayas exclaimed, and the crowd broke into laughter.

That night was when Donna and I dined on the small balcony, eleven floors up. Lamps from the TraveLodge parking lot cast a soft light. Donna is a good talker, an open, earnest woman. The slenderness of her face exaggerates the size of her hazel eyes, all lending to her look of innocent intensity. At the clinic, only a week before, this open gaze seemed stricken and weary.

Billy is her only child. It was not long after she separated from her husband and moved from northern New Jersey to Philadelphia that Billy's cancer was diagnosed. Divorce makes life hard enough to sort out, but add a child's leukemia, and it seems especially hard to bear.

"He was still a baby then almost," Donna said. "He spends weekends with Bill, his dad . . . Billy just worships his father. All through that period when we first broke up, Billy was running low fevers and was irritable. It always seemed as though he'd come back from his father at the end of the weekend like that and I'd get mad at Bill, the poor guy. 'What are you doing to him to always make him sick?' I'd complain. Bill would shrug and explain that he had taken him on a picnic or something or to his mother's. He wasn't doing anything wrong, of course, just the normal things. I suppose I was really blaming Bill for other things at that point. . . ."

Donna spanked Billy one night for being difficult and ornery, then put him to bed. When he woke up in the morning his bottom was blue— "not black-and-blue," Donna recalled, "just blue. It was horrible. I was frightened and torn. On one hand, I thought right away I should take him to the doctor—it was weird. But I didn't want anyone to see him looking like that! I felt like a child abuser. But I'm a rational person," and here Donna forced a comical, self-deprecating grin, "and I knew I hadn't abused Billy, that I hadn't hit him that hard. So I took him to his doctor that day."

Billy's pediatrician was concerned when he saw the bruises. The boy's history of fevers had puzzled him for some months. Now he wanted more tests, blood tests at the hematology clinic at St. Christopher's. Donna grew worried.

"You know, on the night after I took Billy to the doctor with the bruises, that was the first time I put all the pieces together. You'd think . . . I mean, I think of Bill and I as being people of above-average intelligence, we both have good educations . . . you'd think that we might have been able to deduce something after months of seeing Billy's fevers and bouts of nausea and easy bruising. You'd think we might have been able to reach the conclusion sooner that something might be seriously wrong. But that day was the first day I saw it all together, and I was really shook up about it. I had been talking on the phone to relatives all night, and then, very late, my boyfriend called and we talked about it for a long time. He could tell how upset I was, so to console me, you know, he says, 'Well, Donna, think what's the worst thing it could be.' And do you know what I answered? Right away I said 'leukemia.' That was the first thing I thought of, even though it hadn't occurred to me until then. Of all things. . . . Of course, for us, it turned out to be the worst thing."

When they told her at the clinic that Billy had leukemia, Donna "freaked out." She was there with Bill and her boyfriend, Carl. "I went right over and cried on Carl's shoulder—I feel guilty about that now. . . . Whose shoulder did Bill have to cry on? Billy is our son." When she wasn't crying, she was shouting at doctors. She was a stranger to cancer, and she recoiled at the sight of these sickly children who wore scarves to hide their baldness, of parents who dragged in and out of the clinic, so worn and weighted down by frustration and fear.

"I will not be like these people," she shouted that day, over and over again. "I will not be like these people!"

But over the next year and a half, Donna Schanel was ushered into clinic life. She became acutely empathetic to Billy, his illness draining her own vitality. She lost weight and started smoking more cigarettes. But when his condition took a turn for the better, there was such *elation*. During the year of Billy's remission, Donna's own health improved.

She developed a strong interest in holistic medicine and began consulting a chiropractor who specialized in nutrition. When the boy's leukemia returned, Donna started a nightly routine of confronting—with the combined force of their imaginations—the demons that had beset Billy's blood and bones.

Already she had given so much—like the teaching career, abandoned the first time Billy got sick. Later she started an exciting job as a sales executive, and that, too, would now have to be abandoned. Donna accepted that. But the relapse seemed to demand that she accept something else: *You cannot make Billy well with love.* Donna didn't want to hear it.

Just a few days before the trip, she and Billy drove into Center City from their Northeast Philly apartment to sit in the television audience of *The Jane Whitney Show*. A guest on the talk show was Gerald Jampolsky, an advocate of "attitudinal healing," which stresses the importance of surrounding sick children with the kind of loving, constructive attention they need to bring their own inner resources to bear in combating illness.

After the program, she had breakfast with Jampolsky and a representative of the TV station.

"They asked me what I thought of the show," she said, "and I had to tell them the truth. I told them I was disappointed with it. I explained that I was interested in hearing about Jampolsky's philosophy of attitudinal healing, but they hadn't actually talked very much about that. On the show he had talked mostly about dealing with the process of dying. Jampolsky—he's really a sweetheart of a man—told me that I should abandon curing Billy as my main goal, that I should concentrate instead on living every moment with him more fully, making the most of life from day to day, minute to minute.

"Well, I believe in making the most of every moment with Billy, but his message wasn't what I wanted to hear. My main goal is to get my boy well."

The sudden rush of feelings that came over me that night, watching my healthy son sleep alongside Billy, had much to do with the ties that Donna and these other parents had formed with their children. They had much to teach me about caring for my own.

Earlier that day, a mosquito had bitten Aaron just over his left eye, and his eyelid had swollen nearly shut. "If you don't have Dotty look at that, I'm not going to speak to you," Donna had said.

And though I had known the insect bite was hardly serious—Aaron hadn't even complained—I sought out Dotty Golasa, the clinic nurse, and asked her to check it. I was beginning to realize how much I took for granted: not just that Aaron would remain healthy, but that he would know how much I cared. The lesson these parents had learned at such cost—to live each moment with their children as fully and lovingly as they could—belonged not only to them, but now to me. It did not need to wait for deadly disease.

By late afternoon on our second day in The Magic Kingdom, Billy wasn't feeling well. Donna had been wheeling him around all day in a stroller, carrying him wherever the stroller wouldn't go. Now he complained of feeling chilled. On our way out of Disney World, she decided to buy Billy a jacket. His lower jaw was shaking.

She emerged from the gift shop with Billy in her arms. He was wearing a brand-new red Mickey Mouse windbreaker. He looked peaked. The spaces under his eyes were darker than usual, and he had fallen uncharacteristically silent. I asked him how he felt. As mothers will, Donna started

answering for him, offering her expert assessment of her son's situation.
Billy turned and interrupted her sharply, speaking so pointedly that both
of us were left momentarily speechless.

"You don't know how I feel," he said.

When we returned from The Magic Kingdom that night, Billy immediately fell asleep. He awoke refreshed and happy some hours later, but
Donna still detected a slight fever when she felt her son's belly. With the
second round of chemotherapy under way, the boy's immune system would
be weak, leaving him highly susceptible to viral infections—even to normal body bacteria that would cause no problem in a healthy person. Twice
during his first round of treatments, Billy had suffered pneumonia, and
Donna had learned to be cautious.

Because Billy's temperature was higher than normal, Golasa wanted
to call Billy's doctors and ask their advice. "They might want him to come
in as soon as we get back," the nurse said. "At this stage we don't want to
take any chances."

The next morning, Billy's temperature was slightly higher, but at breakfast he seemed to be feeling all right. Donna didn't have the heart to keep
him from joining the other kids for a quick dip in the swimming pool. They
would have to leave in an hour for the airport.

It was there she regretted her lenience. Billy's fever was rising, and
his lower jaw was shaking from the chill. He sat upright in the waiting area,
in a chair next to his mother's, stroking the worn orange puppet that ac-
companies him everywhere. He was wearing his new windbreaker. His
mother's purple jacket was draped across his legs, and his feet stuck out
from underneath. They were fitted in new Nike tennis shoes laced with
the alligator-print shoelaces his dad had bought him.

"Do you want to make a bed?" his mother asked, inviting him to lay
his head on her lap.

"Yes . . . I mean, no," Billy answered. "I just want to sit right here."
The boy spoke with such crisp authority that a woman seated across from
Donna caught her eye, smiled, and chuckled at the scene. Donna made a
face and laughed along with her.

"Stop it!" Billy demanded, startling both women. "I don't like people to laugh at me."

"We weren't laughing at you, sweetheart," Donna said sympathetically. "It's just that you looked so cute sitting there . . . we were laughing *with* you."

"I wasn't laughing," Billy said sternly.

"Oh," Donna answered, clearly out-argued this time.

"He has such lovely hair," the other woman said, changing the conversation.

"He's going to lose it soon," Donna said sadly, reaching over to gently stroke Billy's locks. "The drugs will make it all fall out again."

"Does it bother him?" the woman asked softly.

"Him? No," Donna said. "*He* could care less." Then she mouthed from behind him, "*I* care."

Carl came to meet them at the airport, but Donna and Billy didn't make it home that day. While they were waiting for luggage at Philadelphia International, the nurse took Billy's temperature. It had risen to 104. He was withdrawn and pale; the darkening under both of his eyes had deepened. He was still shivering.

"At first I was just going to take him home," Donna said. "Part of me just hoped all he needed was rest. Whenever he has to go in the hospital, I have this little denial stage I have to go through. Carl said to me, 'Aren't you going to take him in?' And I told him that I was afraid if we took Billy by for the doctors to look at him, then they would want him to stay—you get to the point where you just *know* these things—but, of course, as soon as I'd said it, I realized how ridiculous *that* was because obviously if they wanted him to stay, he needed treatment. Carl said, 'Donna, Billy's your boy and I'm not telling you what to do, but if he were my kid, I'd take him to the hospital.' So we came here right away."

She was dressed now, three days later, a Saturday, in faded jeans, a blue T-shirt, and powder-blue track shoes. We talked in the lobby at St. Christopher's. She had slept Thursday night in Billy's hospital room, on a folding bed alongside his. Billy's father had driven down from North Jersey to spend Friday night and most of Saturday. Now it was Donna's shift until late Sunday. The boy's fever had been going up and down; he was weak and irritable. His white blood cell count was, medically speaking, nil—the anticancer drugs kill good cells along with bad cells. In the absence of these microscopic guardians, some virus had seized his system.

And now, in addition to his leukemia drugs, Billy was getting antibiotics, nutrients, and other chemicals intravenously, through a tiny plastic needle in the back of his right hand.

"I was crying when they inserted the IV—you know, the crying where you make no sound, but tears start rolling from your eyes? You know how brave Billy is with needles. Well, they had to poke him three times to find a vein this time. For some reason, they would insert the needle and start probing around, but the veins kept just rolling away. Billy was hurt and crying. I was almost sick to my stomach."

In a darkened hospital room, Billy lay naked under a white sheet. His right arm was taped to a board so he couldn't move his wrist and accidentally dislodge the IV. He looked pale. There were blue plastic pans filled with water and wet cloths on a rolling table beside the bed—Donna had been bathing him periodically with cool water to help keep the fever down. All the shades were drawn despite the beautiful afternoon because Billy complained the sunlight hurt his eyes. He was watching TV.

Beside Donna's cot was a stack of books, most about health and nutrition, and the shelf under the window was lined with canned fruits and fruit juices and healthful snacks. Billy's Disney World keepsakes—his toy gun, Mickey Mouse ears, and other brightly colored souvenirs—were scattered around the room. Their small space had acquired a lived-in, rumpled look.

I asked Donna how she passed the hours.

"I watch TV. I read. I talk to the doctors and nurses here on the ward or on the telephone. I sleep. I take care of Billy. I'm usually busy."

"Mom?" Billy asked.

"Yes?"

"When do I get the IV taken out?" With what must have been quiet envy, he had been watching Aaron, along for the visit, run and climb around the room.

"Let's see," Donna answered. "In three days."

Billy took that in for a moment and then asked, "Mom?"

"Yes, dear?"

"How long is three days?"

"Well, today is Saturday, so tomorrow is Sunday, and then the next day is Monday and then comes Tuesday. So it will come out most likely on Tuesday."

Billy nodded without expression and looked down sadly at the arm taped to the board.

"A long time," he said softly.

Billy didn't get the IV out of his arm until the next Saturday. By then the fever had gone, and doctors felt he could safely go home.

It had been nine days since the group had returned from Disney World. One of the children on the trip, fifteen-year-old Kimberly Wildonger, had developed a brain tumor and died. She had stayed her last days in a hospital room just down the hall from Billy's. Donna was shaken.

"My last memory of Kim is of her father lifting her up out of the wheelchair so she could look in the window and wave to Billy," she said, choked with sadness and dread.

Another of the children, fourteen-year-old Stephanie Schwartz, had checked into the hospital that week. Her leukemia had returned. But Anthony Mancini, the eleven-year-old who was too sick to make the trip, was doing better. His leukemia was back in remission.

Life and death had resumed their routine at St. Christopher's.

Despite the pleasure Donna felt that Saturday in getting Billy out of the hospital, she was worried and depressed. She had the boy propped up on the couch, watching TV, because his legs hurt so badly he couldn't walk. There were purple bruises all over them.

The pain might be muscular, caused by the injections he had been getting. But it might also originate in Billy's bones, which would indicate a more deadly form of leukemia. She planned to take him back to St. Christopher's on Monday for more injections. She and Billy's father would then give some of their own blood to determine whether either's bone marrow might be suitable for a potentially life-saving transplant.

On top of all that worry, Donna had just spent a long day moving out of her apartment in Northeast Philly. She and Billy were staying temporarily with a friend, but she had not yet sorted out exactly where they'd go from there. Her mother and stepfather in North Jersey were urging her to move in with them, but that would mean quitting her job and leaving behind much that is important to her here. She was emotionally exhausted.

"Living with this is . . ." Looking across the room toward her son, she completed the thought by drawing her lips together and exhaling a long and confounded sigh. Then she smiled.

Donna and Billy work together every night to bring to bear on the disease whatever psychic healing energy the boy has. She makes it a game, but it is not a game. Billy lies flat on his back, and Donna sits next to him on the floor.

"Let's imagine you are lying down in your favorite place in the world. It might be under a tree or in your bed on a beach. I think my favorite place would be on a beach with the sound of the waves in the background. Now you're lying there, quietly, and you're totally relaxed, completely relaxed. And the way we do that, remember? The way we do that is to first tighten up all of the muscles in our legs and arms and tummies, tighten them up *real hard*"—Billy tenses his body stiffly, gritting his teeth with exaggerated effort—"and then we relax and let everything go loose. Completely loose." The boy settles back into the pillow. He has a slight smile. "Now that we're quiet and completely relaxed, it's time to fight the battle. Imagine stretching off in front of you is a big hill, and on top of the big hill is a castle, a giant dark castle. And inside the castle are the Bad Guys—we call them the *baddies*—and the baddies could be anything, they could be germs that give you a cold or they could be those bad blood cells. Now it's time to summon your armies. Imagine a great white light just over your head, shining down on the hillside in front of you, and what do you see there in the great bright white light? Your army, a huge army with jets and weapons of all kinds, light sabers and guns and everything. And when you're ready, this army is going to attack the castle. They begin moving up the hill and sweep up to the castle, and you are leading the charge, you are the leader, the boss of the armies. You show them the way. They storm up to the walls and break down the doors—the baddies are fighting them every step—but the good guys, your army, is killing them all. You just keep on fighting. Imagine the great battle waging right there before you. And all the baddies must be killed—you can't leave a single one. If they are hiding in the corner, you have to drag them out and kill them. None of them can be left alive. Then the battle is over. All the baddies are dead. Their bodies are lying all around you. Now you have to, one by one, have your armies carry the dead bodies down the hill. At the bottom of the hill is a big pool, or like a giant toilet, and when you bring the baddies' bodies down there, you dump them in and when they're all in, you *flush them away!"*

On this night, when the game that is not a game was over, Billy opened his eyes happily and sat upright.

"How were your armies tonight, honey? Were they strong?"

The boy nodded.

"How strong were they?" Billy didn't say. He just held up both arms, flexed his muscles, and grinned.

FIGHT TO
THE FINISH

SEPTEMBER 1994

This story resulted from a death notice, those small, agate-type items that run like classified ads alongside the obit page that ordinarily just recite the barest details about the deceased. Janet Jones, Mike McConnell's widow, had written instead a long tribute to her husband, in which she spoke frankly about his death being a suicide—something almost never done. At the time I had been assigned to a beat at the paper called "Behavior," which was general enough to allow me to write about anything I wished. I flew out twice to Yakima, Washington, to spend some time with Janet, to meet Mike's family, and to learn about how he had struggled in vain against bipolar disorder. The tangle of emotions he left among the loved ones in his wake, feelings of anger, guilt, and suspicion, were enough to give any potential suicide pause, but ultimately the story concludes that the disorder can be too powerful to resist, even by someone so in love with life.

On a small road on Ahtanum Ridge that turns north from where, on a better day, he and his wife had gathered rocks for terracing, they found Mike McConnell's body in the front seat of his silver Nissan station wagon, motor running, soft jazz still playing, the waning sun throwing long shadows eastward down the dusty slope.

He had run white vacuum cleaner tubing from the exhaust up to the passenger-side rear window. Sections of the tubing had been joined with metal clamps to make it long enough. Duct tape sealed the window around the tube. The one set of footprints in the loose dirt outside the car showed how methodically he had done all this and then stepped back behind the wheel and shut the door to die.

He looked asleep. All the pain that had so hardened his face had drained away. He was forty-two. He was an accomplished physician, beloved husband, father, brother, son. He played the saxophone. He wrote moving, searching, sometimes hilarious letters. He relished wine and foreign films and making love. He went sailing in the Caribbean, backpack-

ing in Yosemite, and hard biking up and down the Cascades, the mountains he could see from the hot tub on the deck of his hillside ranch in
Yakima, Washington. He loved to catch trout and ride horses.

In an ebullient letter he wrote home from college as a young man, Mike
said, "I just want to be swept up by life, surrounded by it, filled with it!"

Except when the cloud came. Mike McConnell was one of roughly
three million Americans who suffer manic depression, or what medicine
now calls bipolar disorder, a disequilibrium of the brain that provokes wild
periodic mood swings from euphoria to despair. It is an evil inheritance,
an ongoing family nightmare, a suicide gene that stalks the McConnells
from generation to generation. Eleven years ago, Mike's mother, Jeanne,
shot herself in the forehead. Other family members struggle with it now.
His three sisters watch their children with fear.

For all the remarkable progress of science and medicine in this century, mental illness remains poorly understood. Depression, one of its most
common forms, is often seen as a character flaw, a lack of stamina, or just
morose existential angst. Yet it is as concrete as cancer. Researchers can take
pictures that show striking differences between a normally functioning brain
and one in the grip of depression. Just last spring, researchers at Thomas
Jefferson University in Philadelphia, where Mike was once an instructor,
identified a specific sequence on chromosome eighteen of the human ge-
nome that appears to make certain people predisposed to the affliction.

"The thing about Mike is, he really was such an extraordinarily gifted,
beautiful human being, it makes you appreciate that what happened to him
is a disease, that it reflects no failing in him, no poverty of spirit or will, it
was just this thing," says Dr. Michael Baime, who supervised Mike through
a residency in internal medicine at Philadelphia's Graduate Hospital. "It
came over him like a cloud."

"This thing" amounts to cyclical bouts of utter, blank despondency.
Author William Styron borrowed from Milton's *Paradise Lost* to describe
his experience: "darkness visible." Mike said he felt as if his mind were
"cannibalizing itself." As if someone had thrown a switch, all the joy was
gone. He would awaken mornings then, swing his feet off the bed to the
floor, stop, and weep. All the ordinary issues of life would be blotted out
by the single, oppressive, ultimate crisis. "Why? Why bother to get up?
What's the point?" he would ask his wife. He wouldn't eat. Nothing reached
him, not even the smile of his six-month-old daughter.

Most bipolar patients recover. They respond to counseling and to lithium, carbamazepine, valproate, or other drugs. In the most extreme cases, many are helped by electroshock therapy. They learn to manage highs and lows. But for a small minority of bipolar victims, nothing works.

It is hard to track the numbers precisely, because most suicides suffer depression, and most sufferers (particularly those who eventually kill themselves) never get treatment, but it is estimated that 15 percent of depressives commit suicide. Suicide is the eighth-leading cause of death in this country. More people kill themselves in America each year—31,230 in 1993—than are killed by others.

Mike McConnell tried everything. In May, during the weeks before his suicide, he had undergone seven electroshock treatments. "When it works it's a wonder," says his wife, Janet Jones, "but it's basically just a medically induced grand-mal seizure."

The sessions left him reeling. They blew big holes in his memory. Mike the wit, the intuitive one, began missing subtleties in conversation, struggling to make simple connections. It was like bartering for sanity with pieces of his soul. He knew the pathology for hopeless cases. He had watched his mother. The breakdowns would accelerate, each one mining a new black depth.

Early on the day he took his life, he stood at the kitchen sink with his wife and broke down with anger and sadness: "You know, I know, everybody else knows! I'm going to have to face this again and again and again and again!"

Mike came to believe that there was only one way out. Those closest to him in the last months understood.

Janet left him alone the afternoon he killed himself. She knew the state he was in. She had stayed home with him all morning. Their arguments over suicide were constant. Janet would insist she needed him, she and the baby couldn't make it without him. She would fight until she was emotionally spent, and then, sometimes, she would lash out self-protectively, telling him she couldn't take it anymore, that if he was so damned determined to do it, he should just get it over with. Then, seeing her distress, he would apologize, weeping, somehow sadder still, and Janet would realize she had been turned around. No matter how hard she fought, suicide had come to seem inevitable.

"Just promise me you'll go peacefully," she said one day last June.

On the afternoon of June 14, Mike was supposed to go riding. His neighbor, an old cowboy, had promised to teach him how to break horses. So instead of leaving the baby home with Mike as she usually did (Janet saw it as a hedge against the worst; Mike would never harm or abandon the baby) she took her daughter with her to the office.

"Don't do anything rash," she told him before she drove off.

"Don't worry, I won't get any rashes," he teased, a glimpse of the old Mike.

They kissed.

Part of her, she says now, knew it was for the last time. "I thought love would be enough to save him," she says. "I learned different."

Marilyn McConnell was a little girl in Princeton, New Jersey, on the night her mother woke up screaming, the night the family remembers as the beginning of this long nightmare.

There was commotion down the hall in her parents' bedroom. Marilyn's older sister, Annalee, crept down and looked in. The family doctor was there. He and their father, Ed, were sitting on the bed talking to her mom, Jeanne, who was laughing hysterically. But nothing about the scene was funny. Annalee didn't know what to make of it. In the morning, Mom was gone.

"She's in the hospital," their father said, without further explanation.

"Who could explain?" asks Ed McConnell now. "She was a perfectly lovely, normal wife and mother until that night. She woke up screaming and incoherent. This was back in 1957. She was thirty-two years old . . . They gave her electroshock. That was about all they had to offer then. She worked her way back to almost normal, but every six months or so from then on she'd fall off the wagon."

Explanations for mental illness were hard to come by in those days. People just had "nervous breakdowns," they went "over the edge" or just "cracked up." People assumed that something must have gone wrong in Jeanne's childhood, or that she just wasn't strong enough to cope with life. There was the unspoken assumption that, somehow, *it was her fault.* She just needed to *pull herself together.*

She tried. Over and over again. Jeanne was a musician, a fine pianist and singer. Even with four young children, and then a fifth, she taught piano and founded and managed the fifty-member Hopewell Valley Chorus. Many of the old family pictures show her at the piano with children alongside. In periods of calm, she was clear and fine and a full-time loving mother. She would teach and bake bread and make meals and clean the house. That was when she was healthy.

When she "fell off the wagon," as Ed puts it, she lost interest in everything and everyone. She would lie in bed all day. It was embarrassing and scary. Ed would come home from work and ask the children, "Well, is she out of bed yet?" It could last for weeks. An older cousin came to help out for a while, and an aunt stayed with the family during one stretch. Mostly the kids learned to take care of themselves. The older girls took charge.

"It was always a little awkward when she came back from the hospital," recalls Annalee, who was eight when her mother had the first episode. Marilyn and Mike were, in turn, younger by a year. Barbara was still a baby. Bill was born in 1960. "We'd have settled into a routine that would start to feel normal, basically taking care of ourselves when Dad was at work, and then Mom would come home again, usually a little spacey from the electroshock, and it wasn't always easy to just work her back in."

Jeanne would come home altered. At one point she was diagnosed as paranoid schizophrenic. That was after she started following people around the streets of Princeton. She would scribble down the license numbers of passing cars, convinced they were clues to the plot against her. More common were memory lapses, like the time she packed up the kids and drove them to the store and, once there, was suddenly bewildered.

"She kind of blanked out," remembers Marilyn. "She couldn't remember why she was there."

There were suicide attempts. Numerous overdoses were followed by hurried trips to the hospital, stomach pumps, and long absences. One time Ed wrestled a large knife out of her hand in the kitchen where she stood ranting, threatening to stab herself. Another time she crashed the family car.

Barbara has no clear memory of the early episodes. But as a child she had a recurring nightmare. In it, she would see her mother covered with blood, her throat slit. Barbara would awaken terrified. She had the dream one night when she was staying with a cousin, and told the cousin about it.

"Barbara, that's not a dream," he told her. "You know that big scar on your mom's neck?"

Later Mike would say that during those years he was looking hard all the time to find the right words to say or the right thing to do. If he only could, he was convinced, his mom would pull out of it and be okay. But he could never find the answers.

Later, of course, he understood.

On June 20, 1984, Jeanne McConnell crawled into the bathtub of her apartment in Williamsburg, Virginia, and shot herself in the head.

She had been living alone for years. She was fifty-nine. Her children were grown, and the illness had driven her husband away. She had long since given up leaving her apartment. She paid a boy to bring groceries and run errands. She killed herself the day she got notice that the divorce from Ed was final. She left a letter downstairs, telling where she was to be found, and noting apologetically that the bathtub probably would have to be replaced.

Shortly after that, Mike McConnell stopped showing up at work.

Michael Baime, his supervisor, was shocked. Mike wasn't just a dependable performer in the residency program at Graduate Hospital, he was a star. He'd been "Best Intern of the Year" the year before. At thirty-two, he was older than most residents, older by four years than Dr. Baime. He was a striking character, fair-haired, square-jawed, athletic, brimming with confidence, enthusiasm, and personality.

There was no edge to Mike's confidence, no hauteur. To the contrary, he acted as though he had made mistakes, seen hard times, and had been both strengthened and drawn closer to others by the ordeals. He was a skilled listener.

If Mike had a problem as a doctor, Baime thought, it was caring too much. He gave patients his mind and his heart, which can wreck a physician. The same quality endeared him to his colleagues. If Baime hadn't liked Mike so much, he would have been intimidated by him.

"He wasn't just talented, he was brilliant," Baime recalls. "He was always breaking the rules, but in ways that made you step back and scratch your head and say, Now, why didn't I think of that?"

The road to medicine had been longer for Mike than for most. Out of high school in 1970 he had gone to Cornell University, uncertain of his bearings. Those were days of protest against war and a corrupt establishment. Mike moved in with a group of students and ex-students who shared his idealism and impatience for change, and after two years of spotty attendance in classes, he dropped out. The decision was more personal than political.

"I am not interested in stepping out of life, freezing it, analyzing it," he wrote to his sister Barbara. "I want to learn by doing, by tasting, touching, feeling what's in the world. In short, I want to learn to live in the real world by living in the real world."

With that, Mike's family lost track of him for almost two years. He surfaced in Chicago, living with a Guatemalan named Yolanda Heller, who had two sons. They married in 1973. Mike was twenty-two, working in a Ford factory, reading the works of Chairman Mao, and helping to raise two young boys.

"He was pretty close to being a Weatherman," says his father.

"Mike was never really as radical as Yolanda, but he was into it," recalls Barbara.

As Mike's zeal for revolution waned, however, his relationship with Yolanda grew strained. One of their arguments turned violent when Yolanda was pregnant, and she was injured seriously enough to require surgery on her spleen. Months later came an even more severe reckoning. Their daughter was born sickly, and failed to thrive. She lived only six months.

Mike was shattered.

Yolanda called Barbara from Chicago, complaining that Mike had locked himself in the walk-in closet he used as a study, and was refusing to come out. He'd been there for days. That's where Barbara found him when she flew out. He had lost weight, and his face looked like a tragic mask.

"All he could do was cry," Barbara recalls. "He couldn't seem to shake the overwhelming feeling of sadness and guilt. At the time, I didn't associate any of what he was going through with mental illness, or with my mother. It seemed to be a rational response to losing the baby, even though the mourning was so severe, and lasted so long. Eventually, he pulled himself together and came back out."

His marriage never recovered. Yolanda and Mike went through a bitter divorce. Determined to salvage something from the sad experience, Mike decided to go to medical school. He had been inspired by the doctors who tried to save his daughter. He reconciled with his family and returned to the East Coast, enrolling at the University of Pennsylvania, and accepted a National Health Service Corps loan to help pay the tuition.

He thrilled to his classes at Penn. By the time he began his residency at Graduate Hospital in 1983, he was an admired young doc with a promising future, ruddy good looks, and abundant charm.

"I met him walking down the hallway at Graduate one afternoon," recalls Janet, who was working as a neurological intensive care nurse. She was a star in her own right, a woman with a sharp mind and a warm, patient manner. She was also slender and blond, with big blue eyes.

"With me, it was love at first sight, although, with Mike, I always say it was more like lust at first sight," says Janet, who kept her last name, Jones, after they were married. "Mike would just come by my nurses' station after that and just sit there and watch me, saying nothing. So I just started talking to him. It was wintertime then and I was wearing these big yellow boots in every morning, and I started finding these romantic little notes stuffed in them at the end of the day."

After dating for a while, though, they stopped seeing each other because, as Janet recalls, "Mike was not ready to stop seeing other women then."

That June, Jeanne McConnell committed suicide, and Mike stopped coming to work.

When Baime couldn't get Mike by phone, he and a few of the other docs went looking for him. They found him lying in the bathtub after the landlord let them in his apartment. He refused to even make eye contact.

Baime had never seen such a transformation. Here was the brightest star in his medical class, this man who inspired everyone he met, reduced to someone emotionally and intellectually inert.

Janet found out about Mike's state at a party. She hadn't seen him in weeks, and when she was told, she walked to a back room immediately and phoned him. Mike always said that ring was one of the only ones he happened to answer during that dark time.

He wasn't exactly thrilled to hear from her, but Janet was determined. She stopped by every day, whether he wanted to see her or not. She got the phone number for Mike's nearest sister, and Marilyn flew to Philadelphia the next day.

"He got really angry when I walked in," recalls Marilyn. "He was lying in bed. He looked terrible. He told me he didn't want me there. He refused to get out of bed. I was hurt, and angry, and I expressed some of that. But none of it connected. He just kept telling me to get out. It was the first time I ever made the connection between Mike and Mom, and it scared me."

It scared Mike, too. The 1975 depression after his baby daughter's death had not been the only episode. He had been through another bout of depression in 1982, and had sought medical treatment. Now the cloud was back, worse. He grew convinced that what had happened to his mother was now happening to him.

He told his friend Stephen Ackers, another resident at Graduate, that he had been practicing sticking his head in the gas oven. Eventually, Mike's friends ganged up on him and talked him into a stay at the Institute, Pennsylvania Hospital's psychiatric division.

Mike was never sure what pulled him through that time. Neither the drugs nor the counseling seemed to reach him at first; then, suddenly, he was better.

A few weeks later, Janet got a call.

"Something lifted," Mike said.

In their first three years together, Mike and Janet took glorious vacations. On advice from his doctors, Mike had abandoned his specialty in internal medicine because of his tendency to grow too attached to patients, and concentrated on emergency room work, where he could work regularly scheduled hours, swoop in, save lives, and send patients upstairs for long-term treatment.

At Graduate they called him "Vacation Man." He and Janet planned adventures, sailing trips to the Caribbean and on Lake Champlain. They learned to scuba dive, took skiing trips, hiked, biked, and climbed.

Mike launched himself at life. Activity and adventure were antidotes to poisonous thoughts. He and Janet bought two houses in Manayunk and rehabbed them. They helped revitalize his grandfather's family campground in Vermont.

Mike confessed to Janet an ambition to turn his adventures into his lifestyle, to "live on a mountain and not work a nine-to-five job." Janet had a fantasy of living on a farm, raising animals, maybe starting a business. They began to scan want ads in the back of his medical journals and note exotic locations. In 1987, there was an ad seeking an ER doc for Yakima. "This one sounds good," said Mike.

They got out a map. Up in the high desert in the eastern foothills of the Cascades, it was a city of 95,000 or so, just a scenic ninety-minute drive from Seattle and Puget Sound. They took a trip west, rented a big, black Caddy, and drove it into the mountains. Mike accepted the job at Yakima Valley Memorial Hospital, and they found the perfect house: on a mountain, wraparound deck, lots of windows, a hot tub, stables. It looked over hundreds of miles to the north and east, an expanse rimmed in the distance by snow-capped Cascades. You could sit in the hot tub and look down on hawks swooping over the valley. They moved in 1988, and celebrated by getting married.

Mike worked in the emergency room, and Janet raised sheep and started a health-care consulting business, which took off. Mike bought a forty-two-foot sloop, and they explored Puget Sound up to the San Juan Islands. They were young, beautiful, well-to-do, energetic, and in love—the envy of everyone they knew.

If anything, Mike's deep depression in '84 appeared to have altered him for the better. He was extraordinarily empathetic. He seemed to see every new day of his life as a triumph of light over darkness. His energy was infectious.

One morning he called his sister Annalee, who was working in Anchorage, Alaska, as the city budget manager.

"I want you to meet me in Yosemite," he said.

"When?"

"Tomorrow."

Annalee laughed. She had meetings all that day and the next, loads of work to get done. Mike wouldn't buy it.

"Okay, I'll let you go to your meeting tomorrow, but I want you to get on a plane the day after tomorrow, meet me in Yosemite, and we'll go backpacking together for a week."

Hooked by the sheer whimsy of it, Annalee couldn't refuse. They met outside the park, loaded up on groceries, and hiked up into the mountains. They moved so fast Annalee got altitude sickness and couldn't eat dinner. Then a bear ransacked their provisions as they slept.

Determined to reach the famous Halfdome peak the next day, they hiked without food, and made it. They snapped pictures of each other in front of the otherworldly view, Annalee's blond hair brightly catching the sun, and Mike in flannel shirt and shorts peering out with binoculars. When they got down to civilization that night, thirsty and starving, Annalee put some coins in a soda machine and punched up, of all things, a Diet 7 UP.

"My God, Annalee, you haven't eaten in two days!" Mike said, and they laughed until it hurt.

Months later, when Annalee was going through a hard time, she got a card from Mike with an Ansel Adams print of Halfdome on the front and, inside, their pictures at the summit. The note read:

> *I remember hiking with you to Halfdome, hypoglycemic; and your diet soda before dinner at Mono Lake.*
> *You're on the trail now, hungry and tired. Mourn but do not despair because you will see Halfdome again. And dinner awaits.*
> *Make it a regular soda this time.*
> *Love, Mike*

"You can see why we all loved him so much," says Annalee.

On sailing adventures with Marilyn's husband, Peter Miller, Janet and Mike spent long hours talking about life—and death. Peter remembers how moved Mike would get at the beauty of a sunset, of a dazzling night sky, or the way moonlight softly rounded the wave crests of the ocean. The sudden appearance of a school of porpoises thrilled him as if he were a small child; it meant chucking all plans to follow them for hours, with Mike hanging off the bow of the boat. At such times he seemed "like a force of nature," Janet says, "something wild."

The cloud descended again in the fall of 1992. Mike was still under obligation to the National Health Service Corps, and it was threatening to force him to relocate. He would have to quit his job at the hospital and drag Janet, whose business was just getting on its feet, to some distant locale.

Janet noticed Mike start to slip, then slide headlong. He didn't want to get out of bed. He wouldn't eat. He obsessed about what a mistake it had been to take the NHSC loan in the first place. How his poor decision was destroying their lives.

It had been eight years since the depression in Philadelphia. It was back.

Janet called Annalee, asking for help. She was worried Mike would kill himself. His doctor had prescribed Prozac, but it would take weeks to take effect. She didn't want to put Mike in the hospital because it was where he worked. The humiliation might push him over the edge.

Annalee flew to Yakima the next day. Mike met her at the airport.

"He was not pleased to see me," she recalls. "I mean, in the past, when Mike saw me he'd sweep me up off my feet with a hug. This time he just stood there glaring at me. He was about forty pounds underweight. His face was just blank. Sadness seemed to harden and distort his features. It was like Mom all over again. He said he didn't want me or anyone else from the family around. Then he said something that really scared me. He said, 'But maybe it's a good thing you're here, Annalee. It will make it easier on Janet when I kill myself.'"

She felt woozy with fear—terrified that she had done the wrong thing by coming. Back at the house, Janet told her not to take it personally. These days, suicide was nearly all Mike talked about.

They hid the car keys, for fear he'd drive himself over a cliff. They hid the medicine for Janet's sheep.

They kept a twenty-four-hour vigil. If Mike arose at night, either Annalee or Janet would get up, too. The blackness of his moods would ebb and flow, but despair colored all.

On mountain hikes, Annalee positioned herself between Mike and ledges—"I knew no matter how self-destructive Mike might be, he would never do anything to hurt me." Annalee stayed three weeks, and then Barbara flew out from Vermont for a three-week shift.

It was dreadful. The Prozac was having no effect. Mike was skeletal. He was like a very old man. Each day was something to be endured.

Janet became convinced she was going to lose him. Mike had built a prison of his own dark logic. One morning, as he and Barbara walked down the long gravel drive to the mailbox, he sought his sister's permission.

"Mom did it, Barbara. It's okay," he said.

"No, Mike. Mom did it, but it's *not* okay," said Barbara. "I loved her dearly, and I was so sorry to see her go. I know the pain she went through. But it's not okay. What Mom did is not okay."

"When would it be okay?" he asked. "Suppose I had an accident and lost my finger. Would it be okay for me to kill myself?"

"No, of course not."

"Okay. Now suppose I lost my arms and legs. I was just a torso; would it be okay then?"

"No, Mike," argued Barbara, explaining that there were many tragically maimed people who had adjusted and found happiness in their lives.

"Okay, I'll buy that. Now suppose I was just a head, and they had me hooked up to all these machines. Would you let me go now?"

"No!"

"You aren't getting the point," Mike said.

"I am getting the point! You are trying to box me in! You are trying to box me into saying it's okay to kill yourself. I guess next you're going to ask me if it's okay if you're nothing but an eyeball on a tray! Nothing you can say would make me say that it's okay. Nothing!"

"What if there's no way to bring me back?" he asked, pitifully.

"Mike, you came out of it the last time."

When Prozac failed, Janet checked Mike into the hospital at the University of Seattle to try electroshock. He went glumly, but willingly. The doctors there, who see a lot of depressed patients, said Mike was the worst case they had ever encountered.

Then, miraculously, the day after his first shock treatment, he was okay. Completely well.

"I came to see him in his room and he was sitting on the bed smiling," recalls Janet. "He said, 'I'm back!'

"The results were immediate. He had not only bounced back, it was like he had bounced too far back. He was just exhilarated. All traces of the depression were wiped out, so much so that he didn't even remember much of it. He kept asking me the same things over and over again. He didn't remember Annalee coming, or Barbara. He kept asking me, 'What was I saying?' and 'What did I do?' I'd tell him, and two hours later he'd ask me the same question again. He apologized profusely. I think he was really horrified when we explained to him what he had been like. He went out and bought me an Audi. He said it was for putting up with him."

Early in 1993, Mike got a job at the Yakima Farm Workers' Clinic, so he could satisfy his NHSC commitment without moving away. The clinic served the area's growing Mexican population, most of them poor. The job paid next to nothing, but then, Janet's business was thriving. It seemed perfect—and something happened that made it more so, as far as Mike was concerned.

A pregnant young woman came into the clinic, early in her term, who didn't want to keep her baby. She had checked "abortion or adoption" on her chart. Mike and Janet had been through all kinds of hell trying to have a baby.

Mike was determined to handle the matter discreetly, and ethically, but he wanted that baby. He didn't mention his interest to the mother during her clinic visit. But once the young woman was sold on adoption, she eventually selected Mike and Janet to be her baby's parents.

The clinic put up a fight, claiming Mike had steered the baby his way. But he wouldn't budge. He wrote off the job (even though that meant resuming the long-running battle with NHSC) and hired a lawyer to push on with the adoption. He had lost a baby once; he was going to save this one.

"On November fifteenth I got a phone call, real scratchy," says Annalee. "It was Mike on the car phone. He and Janet were on their way to pick up the baby. He was so excited. All through that period, he was just so thrilled. I flew down for Christmas. It was the first time in years Mike had even wanted to celebrate Christmas. Dad flew out. We hiked up into the mountains and cut down a tree and brought it home. We decorated it together. I was just entranced watching Mike with the baby. He was just wonderful with her."

They named her Daniela. Happily unemployed, Mike became Dr. Dad. All through that winter he was triumphant. He toted the baby everywhere. When he stopped in the emergency room to show his friends, he held Daniela in both arms over his head, beaming, so joyful it moved some of his friends to tears.

In May, abruptly, that joy began to fade. Mike said he felt bad living off Janet. He missed being a doctor. The NHSC battle was roiling again, with the cost of relocation even greater now that Janet's business had taken root. With Mike, rational worry tilted readily into irrational darkness. And the cloud rolled back in.

Mike's doctors already knew he did not respond to conventional drug treatments. Janet didn't know if she could face another ordeal like the one two years earlier. Their hope was down to electroshock. It had worked before.

This time it didn't. In all, Mike went for seven electroshock sessions in Seattle in May. He would rally after some of them for a few days, then

slip right back into despair. It was the same story. Losing weight. Unable
to rouse himself from bed. No pleasure in anything. Eventually, Mike resisted going to the hospital. "What's the point?" he would ask. Each time a
treatment failed he was plunged deeper into depression. He obsessed over
past mistakes, missteps that had hurt others.

Mike's ghosts were real. Like most people who live more than four
decades, he had accumulated lasting sorrows and regrets. Healthy people
keep such memories in perspective; they build a context that enables them
to acknowledge error, learn, and go on. Mike could not. Locked in depression, he became convinced he was a terrible human being.

Janet worked out a system with Mike's doctor, Ray Silves, to have
him involuntarily committed if things got too bad, and at the end of May
she made the call.

The Yakima County Sheriff's Office dispatched a squad car, and
Mike was carted off in handcuffs, crying, shouting angrily, begging Janet
not to let them take him in.

"It was the hardest thing I've had to do in my life," she said later.

Annalee flew down from Anchorage two days after Mike was committed. As she walked into the hospital lobby, Mike was waiting, arms
folded, skeletal again, scowling severely.

"I heard a rumor you were in town," he said, shouting so that everyone in the lobby could hear. "I am being held here against my will. I don't
belong here. They have no right to keep me here."

For nearly an hour, Mike ranted about the injustice. He said he would
never have another thing to do in his life with the medical profession. It
was an outrage! He was a doctor! When an orderly came out to tell him
dinner was being served, Mike shouted, "I'm on a hunger strike. You can
put that in my chart!"

"I will," the orderly said.

"See how it works?" Mike asked Annalee. "They lock me in here
unjustly, saying I'm sick, and if I get angry about it, that's used as evidence
to prove how sick I am. Will you help me get out of here?"

Annalee felt confused. Mike did, in fact, seem sane. If she hadn't
known anything about what had led up to his commitment, or Mike's history, she would have sided with him in a minute. But she did know.

"I had to leave when visiting time was over, and I just left him there
ranting," she says. "It was scary. It was enormously hurtful to see him there,

so utterly humiliated. They had strip-searched him when the sheriff brought him in."

He got out. Mike had a lot of friends in the medical community. Some came to his aid, challenging Dr. Silves's diagnosis. Janet had desperately wanted to keep Mike in the hospital for the full two weeks allowed by law—"Frankly, even if they couldn't help Mike, I needed the break," she says—but she was reluctant to side openly against her husband.

He came home cheered by his victory, and within fifteen minutes was talking again about killing himself. He sat in the big wicker chair in the corner of the living room before his bookshelf, facing out over the valley, locked inside the pain.

"You could see it in his face; you could always see it in Mike's face," says Annalee. "His mind was just churning, churning, churning."

"I just don't know how I can do this anymore," he said, and broke down sobbing.

Mike tried to smile when Annalee flew home the next day, but it was more of a grimace. Then he went back to the hospital for more electroshock. It didn't help.

On Friday, June 10, Dr. Silves gave him a new drug, a thyroid medicine called thyroxan. The doctor said it would take three to four days to know if it would help. They would know by Tuesday. If it failed, they'd try another round of electroshock.

Mike left the office, drove to the hardware store, and bought plastic tubing, duct tape, and clamps.

When Janet came home from work that night, Mike told her, "I want to have a good weekend. Just the three of us here together."

They passed a quiet night with the baby. On Saturday, Janet got a call from a client, and Mike sat and listened quietly to her half of the conversation. When she was done, he started to cry.

"It just seems like I'm from another planet," he said. "I listen to you sounding so professional on the phone. There's no way I could have a normal conversation with someone like that. I listen to you, and I can't even imagine anymore what it's like."

It had been a frightening fall. Just eight years ago he had been the most promising resident in his medical class in Philadelphia; now he wasn't even working. It was a struggle for him to make it through the day.

"For you, I've become this drogue," he said, referring to the small anchor used to slow a boat at sea.

He told Janet that she had saved his life more than once, and shouldn't have bothered. Janet pointed out all the wonderful things he had brought to her life. A loving relationship, the dream house in Yakima, all their wonderful adventures, her thriving business, their baby girl.

"You've helped me make my dreams come true," she said.

The conversation wound on all day. That night it grew fierce.

Janet told him she couldn't take it anymore. Mike acted hurt. "I feel like you've just given up," he complained.

"Mike, I haven't given up," she said. "I'm tired of just putting out and putting out all the time and not getting anything back. If you don't love me, you don't love Daniela, and you don't even love yourself, there's just nothing I can do about it!"

Mike apologized, and cried, and tried to console her. Sunday he was morose. He talked for a long time on the phone with Annalee. He was crying. They were both crying. He said he felt it was hopeless.

"It scared the shit out of him that the electroshock treatments weren't working," Annalee recalls. "He thought that would be what would save him. He said he was feeling worse than he had ever felt before. He felt terrible about what he was doing to Janet and the baby. He was convinced nothing was going to get better for him, that it would be just like it had been with Mom. He didn't think he could go on."

"Why don't you go somewhere else," Annalee suggested. "Look for some cutting-edge treatment. Anything."

"I don't have the strength," he said.

More to the point, he didn't have the hope. Mike read and understood the medical journals. He knew that a small percentage of bipolar patients could not be helped, were doomed to deepening spirals of despair.

Annalee didn't know what to tell him. Truth was, she was haunted herself by her mother's last ten years. Annalee had found Jeanne once in 1974, half dead from a deliberate overdose. She had phoned the ambulance, and, in effect, saved her mother's life.

"But for what?" she asks. "When I looked back at her last ten years, it was sheer hell! What did I save her for?"

Annalee believed she was talking to her brother for the last time. What could she do? Finally, sobbing, she tried to say and yet not say what he most wanted to hear.

"Mike, if you can't keep doing this, I love you, I admire you, you've been such a wonderful influence in my life." She knew he wanted her to say it was okay if killing himself was the only way out, but she couldn't say it. Instead she said, "I want you to stay. But no matter what happens, I'll understand. I could never hate you. No matter what."

Mike called her back a while later and told her not to worry.

"I'm going to make it," he promised.

Annalee hung up the phone and shuddered. She wanted to feel relief but didn't dare.

On Monday, Janet went to work, and Mike took Daniela to the hardware store, to buy plastic guards for the electrical sockets. She had begun to crawl; it was time to baby-proof the house.

He spent part of the afternoon with his daughter by the pond out back, and caught a trout, which he fixed for dinner. He and Janet had a long, slow meal with a bottle of wine, then watched a videotape of *Remains of the Day*. At the end, as the old butler allows his last chance for happiness to slip away, Mike burst into tears.

Still, it had been a good day. Mike went to bed hopeful. Maybe the thyroid pills were taking effect.

He woke up Tuesday feeling awful.

"I can't even put together two good days in a row anymore!" he complained bitterly, wailing that he would have to keep going through his nightmare "again and again and again!"

Janet stayed home all morning. She figured he'd be okay in the afternoon—he was supposed to go riding.

His brother-in-law Peter Miller called, just to check in.

"I'm having a tough time right now," Mike said, and started crying.

"Look, this thing passes, you know it does," said Peter. "All you have to do is ride it out, man."

Mike told Peter that he didn't think he could. "It's so painful. It's worse than having your legs broken or having your toenails pulled out one by one."

Eventually, Peter got angry at Mike, as he often did. "You kill yourself, goddammit, and I'll come out there and dig you up and fucking piss

on you," he said. "First of all, for what it would do to your family and to
me. I'm your friend. And think of the message that sends to the kids."

"But it's just so painful," Mike said, in tears. "You don't understand."

Still, Peter felt no special urgency about this conversation. He had
talked to Mike about suicide so many times that the subject no longer
alarmed him. He assumed Janet would have Mike in the hospital if that's
where he needed to be. He told Mike he'd call back that night.

Janet left for work at two-thirty. Mike tried to say good-bye at the
car, but Janet had learned to avoid good-byes.

"I won't get any rashes," Mike said. "See you later."

When she was gone, Mike called his neighbor and begged off the
riding lesson. He fetched the tubing, loaded up the Nissan, and drove up
to the ridge.

Janet knew as soon as she turned south on Forty-second Avenue early
that evening and saw their magnificent house straight ahead in the distance, alone high on the ridge. It just looked peaceful, and suddenly . . .
empty. When she drove up the winding driveway she saw that the horses
hadn't been fed. Then she saw the car was gone.

Stuck to the front door was a tiny yellow leaf of memo paper, on
which Mike had scratched in tiny script:

> *On a small road*
> *On Ahtanum Ridge*
> *That turns north from where*
> *We gather rocks for terracing*
>   *Love Always,*
>   *Mike*

Mike McConnell's decision to kill himself drove a second stake through
his family's heart, already scarred by his mother's suicide. Mike's choice
dramatically divided them.

Annalee and Janet were one faction. For Janet, who had worn herself to exhaustion trying to keep Mike alive, grief was tinctured with relief. She understood. More, she *respected* Mike's choice, even romanticized
it as a final, loving gesture. So did Annalee, who had grown so close to Mike
during the struggle and had promised not to hate him if he succumbed.

But this loving acceptance rubbed the rest of the family the wrong
way. To them, Mike's suicide was a betrayal. Their grief was colored with

anger, frustration, and fear that bipolar disorder might someday claim yet another member of their family. Somehow, they felt, to honor Mike's terrible decision was to make that more likely.

Barbara, the middle child, felt pulled in both directions—"as usual," she says. "I guess it's my role."

Janet, at the memorial service five weeks after Mike's suicide: "It was a beautiful death. . . . Anyone who knew him knows that if anyone could have beaten this thing, it was Mike. He tried so hard. He desperately wanted to live. We all wanted him to stay. But the reasons we had were for ourselves. He was in so much pain. He had this terrible disease. As health professionals, we had both seen the futility of keeping people alive long past the point where it makes sense for them or society. . . . As hard as it is for us to face, I know what he did was right for him. [Quoting from the Gospel of John:] 'Greater love hath no man than this, that a man lay down his life for his friends.'"

Marilyn, outdoors, just after the service: "This was not a 'beautiful death.' I resent any suggestion that suicide is an acceptable outcome for this illness, that it's okay under these circumstances. What Mike did, what my mother did, is not okay. Most people who have this problem work their way through it without treatment. I have children. My children are at greater risk of committing suicide because of what Mike did, and what my mother did, just because they're growing up in a family where suicide is part of their experience. And I'm angry about it."

Ed, standing next to her: "We all went together to see this shrink after Mike did it. It's probably something we should have done as a family years ago, I don't know. But I told the shrink, 'If any of my other kids so much as hint that they plan to do this, let me know. I'll shoot 'em first.' It would be better than living through this again."

Peter, back home with Marilyn in Vermont: "It's easy to second-guess from this far away. This was the only way out Mike could see for himself. Maybe something else could have been done. Maybe not. But don't give me this 'beautiful death' bullshit. It's a fucking tragedy."

Annalee, at her home in Alaska, sobbing: "I really believe if he had taken as much as he could take . . . it wasn't fair to ask him to keep on taking it. . . . No matter how hard on us it would be to lose him, he didn't deserve that much pain. I couldn't ask him to keep on enduring it . . . I never could actually bring myself to say . . . 'It's okay to kill yourself' . . . but I wanted him to know . . . I wanted to leave him with this feeling . . . I wouldn't resent him for it . . . hate him for it."

Barbara, home in Vermont: "I've been struggling really hard with this, with trying to feel that what Mike and Mom did was okay, but that suicide is not okay for anyone else. It isn't easy. . . . There's no closure with suicide. You can't come to terms with it. You can't. That's the terrible thing about it. So I don't think there was anything beautiful about what my brother did, much as I love him. 'Beautiful' is living life to the fullest. Suicide is not beautiful."

FIGHT WITH FAME (NORMAN MAILER)

DECEMBER 1984

Norman Mailer was one of the writers whose work initially inspired me—particularly Armies of the Night, Of a Fire on the Moon, *and* The Executioner's Song—*and I undertook this story just to get a chance to meet him in person. After the story appeared, I was surprised to receive a complimentary letter from Mailer. He wrote, "Research is research, and we all can do it, but insight is rare. My God, have I become that transparent?" His words of encouragement meant a lot to me, and still do.*

Norman Mailer has done it again.

He has this new book called *Tough Guys Don't Dance.* It's a murder story. Now, it's no literary alp, not even in the pyramid range, really. It's more the size of a sand castle, modest but nicely crafted, and with what will likely be a similar lifespan. But even Norman Mailer is entitled to aim low now and then, and, face it, tough guys and murders are Mailer's meat. So Random House was happy enough just before publication to throw a dinner party in Washington, D.C., to tout the book and show off its new hotshot writer. And after dinner, reporters were invited to ask questions. That was when he did it.

"This book is like an illegitimate baby," he said. "It was written in two months, therefore born out of wedlock, and I'm struck by the fact that the event took place"—*imagine here the publicists from Random House, starting suddenly like deer downwind of a hungry lion, gulping their last swallows of champagne and wheeling around in their chairs*—"When I read it, I don't wince, which is all I ever ask for a book I write"—*no, not true, not true! Not of you, Norman, an author who typically aims for nothing less than immortality with each new effort, and even if it were true, it's damn faint praise*—"I could have tarnished myself, but I didn't"—*there's still time . . . only a few tables are in the way, we could maybe gag him and wrestle him out that side door before he can say another*—"I'd come to a point in my life where I really felt up against it. If I didn't write a book in two months"—*oh, no!*—"I owed my former publisher a large sum of money"—*Oh, NO! . . . only two tables, have to dodge Norman's fabled right uppercut*—"I couldn't write a word for months and had been drawing an advance. . . . If I didn't write it"—*no! Norman, no!*—"with all I owed the IRS and my old publisher, I'd have to begin cheating Random House immediately."

Too late. A publicist's nightmare. It would be hard to script a paler pitch for what really is, *really,* quite a readable little book. But Mailer's remarks were out, and the line on *Tough Guys* took on a life of its own. *New York Times, Washington Post, Time, Newsweek,* the wires—straight from the author's big mouth. He wrote it in two months to pay his bills. Why didn't he just do an American Express commercial, for God's sake?

So we find ourselves, three months later, at a small news conference on the seventh floor of the slick, modern Random House building in New York. Assembled in a long working conference room are five reporters, including the estimable John Barkham, of John Barkham Reviews. They have been invited by the publisher to talk with Norman Mailer about his new book. *Tough Guys* was published several weeks before, and despite the line on the book and a couple of prominent, nasty reviews—some critics clearly resented handling tainted goods—it has been holding steady in the middle of most best-seller lists.

Mailer enters on time, escorted by a crisp Random House executive named Carol Schneider, who stays roughly twelve inches off the author's left shoulder at all times. At sixty-one, Mailer looks less pugnacious than pudgy. He is like a boyish grandfather, respectable but full of mischief. He looks flushed—this could be the result of having been recently in the sun, or it could be the afterglow of a long press agent's lunch, perhaps both.

Whatever, his manner radiates vigor. His blue eyes, under a spray of white eyebrows, are quick and playful. He stands on the balls of his feet and seems always intently aware of where his hands are—in his pockets, gesturing, pointing, striking out at some elusive invisible enemy dodging just in front of him. Mailer's clipped white curls are a happy mess. He has exceptionally large ears, the kind of ears kids probably teased him about when he was little. They protrude like supersensitive listening devices, making his face seem wider than it is long. He wears a navy blazer and a white shirt with fine stripes of pink, yellow, and blue. His gray slacks are belted tightly, rounding his belly out desperately over and under it. His collar is open, and his silk tie is yanked askew. In sum, he appears on this day like a man ready to make an effort but willing to go only so far. And, typically, there is that cheerful, reckless look in his eye.

Mailer wastes no time seizing the wheel at this small event.

"I have a story we can start with, 'cause I learned something over the weekend," he says, his voice a staccato huff. He explains that he has just returned from a film festival in Colorado. He describes the festival briefly and says he showed a film, *Maidstone,* a controversial 1963 effort about which few people have shared or even understood Mailer's abundant enthusiasm. "Before the movie began, I talked about it, and I had everybody laughing and laughing. And I talked about it, how bad it was, everything that was wrong with it. And I thought—I really like the movie, you see— I thought they'd see that I was kidding them. And instead, what happened is—there were two hundred and fifty people in the theater at the start of the movie, and by the time the movie was over, there were eighty left. One hundred and seventy people walked out. I counted them.

"So I was thinking of that because when I was in Washington, then we were talking about *Tough Guys*—that was before the book came out— I started joking about it. I said I wrote this thing in two months, and I hope it's good and so forth, blah, blah, blah. And, of course, a lot of people took it very seriously."

Ah ha! Mailer had come around to the point. Ears perk up around the table. Tape recorders edge closer.

"You see, I *did* write the thing in two months—I want to get into that—but if I had thought it was not a good book, I never would have talked that way. I would have said, 'I worked on this thing for five years, I went back to it many times, and I suffered over it terribly. It came to birth through great pain, and I hope you like it.'"

This comment is delivered like a punch line, and it leaves Mailer's small audience laughing. In person, much more of the comedy in Mailer's view of himself comes across than it does in his prose. One of the reporters, ignorant of the earlier remarks, asks, "What did you say about the book on that occasion, that you have come to regret?"

"Well, I don't regret it, I just think it was chancy what I did, and silly." Having won the audience over with wit, Mailer now turns serious.

"What I did was, I started talking about how I had written the book in two months—which is absolutely true—and that, ah . . . I don't remember what I said."

Mailer looks over at Schneider.

"Do you remember what I said?" he asks.

Touchy here. Clearly, elaborating on the earlier statements is not a good idea. Mailer is looking for some coaching. For those present who weren't quite sure what is going on, the scene has come into focus. It is an act of contrition, of sorts. Mailer isn't exactly eating his words, just taking them back in his mouth, chewing them over again, and assembling the remasticated material with greater care.

"You discussed financial things," says Schneider, discreetly.

"I talked about how much I was in debt, and about how I was writing this book to get out of debt. Sometimes you write a bad book that way, and sometimes you write a good book. And that I actually thought that I had written a good book."

"You made the analogy of being a gambler," says Schneider. "You said you had made 'a pretty good bet tonight,' which was a *positive* thing."

"Oh, you mean that thing, that I took a big chance?" Mailer asks.

"Yes."

"Well, the chance I took was just that when I started writing it, I had built up in my mind that I had to write the thing in two months. Looking back on it now, a year later, that two months was not necessary. . . . But I had set it in my mind that I had to do it in two months. And I think, looking back on it, what it was, was that I needed that. Because if you write a book, if you say to yourself ahead of time, I've got to write this novel or this work in three months, two months, six weeks, eighteen weeks, or whatever, if you give yourself a severe deadline, then it's equivalent to having to drive a hundred miles to a hospital with a pregnant woman in the rear seat, and you have to get there, say in one hundred minutes. Now, if you're driving that hundred miles in one hundred minutes on a mountain road, you're going to do the best driving you've ever done in your life.

"As it was, it brought this *intense* concentration to the very center of my head. I've never lived with a book as closely as I did with this one for about sixty-one days. In comparison to my normal rate, if I had written this book the way I'd normally write, I would have spent eight months on it, ten months, just in the writing. And the other element of it that was odd was that, as far as in relation to my own work, this was as finished a first draft as I've ever written. I then had about eight or ten months to work on the book, and I did, but none of the work was structural.

"If you've got a poem"—Mailer, charmingly, pronounces this word "pome"—"or a book of poems you feel is in fairly good shape, one of the pleasures of being a poet, I've always thought, is that you can sit there for eight or ten months and work on these poems, and after reading one several times, you may change a word, you may not. You may then change and put the original word back. That's what I did with this work after I'd finished it."

Absolutely amazing. He has gone from a rush job done under financial pressure to a work as polished, as fastidiously turned and tenderly fitted as a volume of the finest verse.

Norman Mailer has done it again.

Tough Guys is an okay little book. Remarkable, really, for how quickly it was written and for what reason. Whatever difficulty it faces in literary circles owes more to Mailer's mouth than to his prose.

Which is nothing new. It will take at least one generation of critics to sort out Mailer's writing from the things Mailer has said about his writing. This confusion goes beyond his work. Because the subject matter of so much that Mailer writes is Mailer, it will take biographers a lot longer to sort out the actual Norman Mailer from the things Norman Mailer wrote about Norman Mailer from the things Norman Mailer said about Norman Mailer.

This is a writer who has stalked the intellectual wilds of America for the last forty years like a great wounded bear, too belligerent to tame, too big to kill. He achieved worldwide literary acclaim at age twenty-five with the publication of his novel *The Naked and the Dead*. In the years that followed, he wrote two more novels that were critical disasters before turning to essays and nonfiction in *Advertisements for Myself*. While he continued to produce novels, none measured up to the mounting success of his nonfictional writing, primarily *Armies of the Night, Of a Fire on the Moon,* and *The Executioner's Song*. Now, in his seventh decade, Mailer has returned again to fiction with his long-awaited Egyptian novel *Ancient Evenings* and the less ambitious *Tough Guys Don't Dance*.

Through this long career, his reputation has been through more radical swings than that of any other contemporary author. After blowing Mailer's literary dimensions to such outsize proportions when he was only twenty-five, many of the critics and academics responsible have come to regret it in the decades since. Their abundant early praise had helped create, perhaps prematurely, a literary giant, and he has been stomping unpredictably across the landscape of American letters ever since. He is a man who has accumulated more ex-wives than most men have suits and who once stabbed one of them in a drunken rage. A man who once tried to pick a fight at a news conference with the world heavyweight boxing champion; a man who once noted, in his celebrated essay "The White Negro," that it took a kind of courage for two teenage hoodlums to beat an aging candy store owner to death; a man who labored to free from prison an author/murderer who then promptly killed again (about whom Mailer would subsequently, pleading for a lenient sentence, utter a remark that might well serve as his own epitaph: "Culture is worth a little risk").

More than one big-time book critic has had second thoughts about this post–World War II wonderboy. But Mailer's reputation was too big to quash after the reception given to *The Naked and the Dead* in 1948. It gave him The Writer's privilege of having an important opinion of his own—even, or perhaps *especially,* about himself. No one has had the last word on Norman Mailer ever since.

"Mailer had the most developed sense of image; if not, he would have been a figure of deficiency, for people had been regarding him by his public image since he was twenty-five years old," Mailer wrote in *Armies of the Night.* "He had in fact learned to live in the sarcophagus of his image—at night, in his sleep, he might dart out, and paint improvements on the sarcophagus. During the day, while he was helpless, newspapermen would carve ugly pictures on the living tomb of his legend. Of necessity, part of Mailer's remaining funds of sensitivity went right into the war of supporting his image and working for it. Sometimes he thought his relation to this image was not unlike some poor fellow who strains his very testicles to bring in emoluments for his wife and yet is never favored with carnal knowledge of her."

Mailer went off to World War II like the rest of his generation, took careful notes, and returned home to produce the kind of novel everyone was waiting for. *The Naked and the Dead* is still often called the best novel written about World War II. It is also the most conventional work Norman Mailer has ever written. He was playing by the rules.

The book "was written out of what I could learn from James T. Farrell and John Dos Passos with good doses of Thomas Wolfe and Tolstoy, plus homeopathic tinctures from Hemingway, Fitzgerald, Faulkner, Melville, and Dostoevski," Mailer explained in 1976. "With all such help, it was a book that wrote itself. It had a style-proof style. That is to say, it had a best-seller style: no style. Very few people failed to read that book with some interest."

And, *voila!* It made Norman Mailer famous. Mailer was one of the first of his generation of writers to feel the full force of literary fame in the modern world. What made the change so difficult was how damnably hard it made it to write.

"It changed my life," Mailer said in an interview with biographer Hilary Mills. "After *The Naked and the Dead,* for seven or eight years, I kept walking around saying nobody treats me as if I'm real, nobody wants me for myself, for my five feet eight inches, everybody wants me for my celebrity. Therefore my experience wasn't real. All the habits I'd formed up to that point of being an observer on the sidelines were shattered. Suddenly, if I went into a room, I was the center of the room, and so regardless of how I carried myself, everything I did was taken seriously and critically. I complained bitterly to myself about the unfairness of it, until the day I realized that it was fair, that was my experience. It's the simplest remark to make to yourself, but it took me ten years to get to that point.

"Then I began to realize that the kind of writing I was going to do would be altogether different from the kind of writing I thought I would do. After *The Naked and the Dead* I wanted to write huge collective novels about American life, but I knew I had to go out and get experience, and my celebrity made it impossible. I then began to realize that there was something else that I was going to get which would hopefully be equally valuable, and that was that I was having a form of twentieth-century experience which would become more and more prevalent: I was utterly separated from my roots. I was successful, and I was alienated, and that was a twentieth-century condition."

Mailer was one of the first American writers to realize that American media had created a kind of instant, disposable, pasteurized, and homogenized culture that was layered like sweet frosting over the real matter

of life. This was the candy Olympus he now inhabited. His fame assured
invitations to appear on TV talk shows and to be interviewed by popular,
glossy magazines. He was his own best subject matter. If people were so
interested in Norman Mailer, then he wasn't going to leave the subject to
amateurs.

Beginning with *Advertisements for Myself* in 1958, the book that Mailer
says was the turning point in his career, the one in which he finally discovered his personal style and method, he has struggled to live up to, or
to become, whatever it is that The Writer needs to be in this age. At a time
when it seems no single intelligent mind can have a coherent grasp of life,
Mailer has been one defiantly opinionated intellect. Asked to write about
a major public event—a political convention, a demonstration, or even a
trip to the moon—Mailer did more than just accumulate a mountain of
information, interview the experts, and relay the sum of it in an entertaining way. He set himself, Norman Mailer, smack in the middle of whatever
it was, let it happen to him, and then wrote about how it looked and felt
and smelled and sounded and tasted, and about what it made him think—
as if he mattered! And he did matter! It redeemed the role of the individual,
unexpert, but intelligent man, the honest citizen—The Writer—as an essential part of the world.

More than the lives of any of his contemporaries, Mailer's life became a public life, his writing became the story, ultimately, of himself—
or himself as The Writer—even when he wasn't at the center of the story.
The Writer's job was to experience, observe, and make sense of the world,
and that's what Mailer has done. In the process, he has accumulated more
than any other contemporary writer a permanent record—in fiction and
nonfiction—of the *interior* life of his age, of its intellect and emotions, of
its beliefs and superstitions, of its hopes and fears, its genius and its folly.
Whether anyone agrees with Mailer is utterly beside the point. As Mailer
himself has said, defending his admiration for Argentine author Jorge Luis
Borges despite Borges's reactionary opinions, "I detest having to think
of a writer by his politics first. It's like thinking of people by way of their
anus."

Those who dismiss Mailer angrily because they don't agree with him
miss the point. The point is, ideally, that we *all* should live and think and
talk as courageously and defiantly as Jorge Luis Borges, or as Norman
Mailer. We are not supposed to all agree with him. Norman Mailer's spe-

cial hell would be a place where everyone always agreed with him. He would have no one to fight.

After helping to define novel-length journalism and immediate autobiography as legitimate literary forms during the 1960s and 1970s, Mailer has turned once more to fiction.

Throughout his career, he has insisted that he is primarily a novelist. At the height of his success with nonfiction, this was interpreted as his insistence on being taken as seriously as a novelist, no matter what form his writing took. But Mailer never really bought that. To him, the biggest challenges were always looming off ahead. The Novels.

His big step in that direction, a transitional work, was *The Executioner's Song,* which many regard as his masterpiece. It was a book with a masterful grasp of America, as attuned to the odd complexities of Gary Gilmore's rural life as to the cynical priorities of the urban hustlers who marketed Gilmore's macabre execution. It was a book that stretched every facet of reporting and writing to ultimately deserve Mailer's paradoxical subtitle *A True Life Novel,* which was impressively sanctioned when it won the Pulitzer Prize for fiction in 1979. He had used novelistic techniques in the past but always in reporting an event through his own eyes. This was the first long piece of nonfictional storytelling that Mailer ever wrote without placing himself in the story. He adopted a pose much more like that of a novelist, an omniscient narrator with full powers to manipulate characters, viewpoint, and scene, to tell a true story. He even set out to imitate the voice of the writer Mailer has always most admired, Hemingway.

"I spent a lot of time in Utah before I started writing *The Executioner's Song,* and I came away fascinated with the speech of people out west, and how they said so much in that flat, laid-back way," he says. "So I thought I'd see how simple a style I could work with. And one of the things that did was it brought back my respect for Hemingway. Because what I saw was a style that wasn't bad, but it wasn't one quarter as good as Hemingway's style. So that gave me new respect for him. I'd always secretly thought it was a little easier to write like Hemingway than, in fact, it is."

It was as though Mailer had come full circle. He had begun his career trying to be a novelist in the Hemingway mold. His own fame and the pressures it brought to bear on him forced him off in an altogether different literary direction, into journalism, essays, and extended nonfictional writing. Now he had found his way to a perfect marriage of the two forms, a nonfictional novel written in imitation of Hemingway, but—especially in the second half of the book, "Eastern Voices"—Mailer through and through.

Then, last year, the return voyage was complete. Mailer finished his long-awaited "Egyptian novel," *Ancient Evenings.* It was a richly imaginative and powerful book, the work of a great novelist attempting to speak in a heightened, invented language of magic and metaphor. The book is narrated by a man newly dead and, through him, by his great-grandfather, a man who has lived four lives. The story undulates from one state to another, from the eerie confusion of a consciousness caught between life and death, from the battlefields of an ancient civilization to the subtle shifts of palace intrigue. *Ancient Evenings* is an attempt to break through the normal cultural constraints of fiction. It speaks to a kind of universal consciousness, free of place and even time. It deals with man's loss of God, or the gods, and with the essential mystery of death. Critics will be debating the value of *Ancient Evenings* long after Mailer is gone, but few would argue that it is not an audacious effort.

After a book like that, it was no wonder that the literary world was somewhat skeptical of a modest effort like *Tough Guys Don't Dance.* And such a precedent helped to explain why Mailer's initial comments on the book fueled this skepticism about it, and why Random House might have felt the need for this damage-control news conference, which, after about an hour, is coming to a close.

Before it does, John Barkham addresses the issue directly.

"Norman, was this book by way of relaxation after the Egyptian novel?" he asks.

"It's never relaxation to write," says the author, showing only faint umbrage. "I was trying to do a mile a minute over mountain roads. When I was working on it, I felt like I might bust a blood vessel. I thought, I'm working *so hard* on this one. When it was over, I probably, uh, looking back on it now the answer to your question is, from the outside and maybe even from the inside, yes. After *Ancient Evenings,* it was relaxing because I could hold it all in my head at once. In *Ancient Evenings,* I always felt a little bit

like a furniture mover. You know, I was always taking a piano up four flights
of stairs."

Writing a murder mystery would be perfect relaxation for the man
who carried copies of Dashiell Hammett and Raymond Chandler all
through the Pacific in his duffel bag during World War II.

"I'd been thinking of doing one for many years," he says. "And I've
always loved Hammett and Chandler. Whenever I get tired of writing, I
go and read them, and reread them. I read them five times, eight times.
Every one of their books. This is over many years, over forty years.
They're a tonic. So, I've always wanted to write a murder mystery, and
I've always been very curious about how it would turn out. And I also
knew I could never write a book the way they do. Because they had a
different psychology than I do. You know, I think to write a quick, brisk
detective novel, where the emphasis is entirely on reaction, you have to
have a notion of people that's *executive.* That is, you have to be able to
dismiss them completely in a sentence and not worry about whether that
character has more stuff going in him or her than you've given them. I've
never been able to do that. I always linger over my characters, finger
them, paw them."

Mailer's conscious approach to his early nonfiction, the books about
himself, was to write fast, to present his thinking raw. In his return to fiction, Mailer is again the careful young writer who compiled biographical
details about each of his characters in *The Naked and the Dead* on three-by-
five cards. He is writing again with extreme deliberation and with careful
control. He is trying to improve on his performance, trying to write his
best books.

"My age is on my mind," he says. "I'm sixty-one, and I feel that it's a
likelihood that I've got ten or twelve, I don't know how many more years
of good writing, but obviously I will outlive that period at which I can write
well. So I want to make the books count now. Which is not to say I wouldn't
do journalism. If something were big enough in a way or, to me, exciting
enough in a way, I could well wind up doing journalism, because I like it,
I enjoy it. I enjoy the writing of it much more in certain ways than fiction,
because there isn't that terrible worry there, it's more of a relaxed performance. But I would have to believe it counted for something.

"When you write a novel—if you're the kind of writer I am—you
don't know where you're going when you start," he says. "You don't know

how you'll finish it. Every time I've known how a book was going to finish, I'd write a chapter, and I'd never get past the first chapter. This has happened three or four times over the years. And those are the books I never finish, the ones where I plot out the thing completely in advance. And I realized after a while that, for me, knowing what the plot of my book was going to be in detail would be like being married to someone whose every habit you knew. And there was just no life left in the relationship. And there's something stifling about a book whose end appears to me immediately. I prefer to discover the end of a book. That gave me great pause, because in writing a novel—the big difference between writing a novel and writing nonfiction is that, if you're writing nonfiction as I have about an event most of the time, in fact all the nonfiction I've done has been about an event, the story is given to you. And one of my favorite notions is that God is a better novelist than the novelist. In *The Executioner's Song,* for example, I kept being amazed at how good a novelist God was. How much better God was than I was as a novelist, because in places where if I had had the material up to there I would have gone in a certain direction, and the real direction was more interesting.

"But, nonetheless, even if you're not as good a novelist as God, you do have to make these godlike choices when you're writing a novel. And you have to decide where the characters go. When you're writing about an event, the story has been handed to you. Whether it's a good story or a bad story, it's there. And all you have to worry about is your style. And the amount of energy you can put into the writing. And the amount of inventiveness you can bring legitimately to these facts. But your problems are essentially simplified. It really is a classic discipline, the end is given you, and then you have to fulfill the details artfully."

Mailer says he has been trying to make up his mind which of two potential novels he will write next. He says he has just about made up his mind, but stops short this day of saying what the book will be about.

"In announcing it, I think you take away the possibility of it," he says. "I don't know why."

On some days, he is less reticent. Anyone who talks as much as Norman Mailer has left clues elsewhere. Like in a 1980 interview reprinted in his book *Pieces and Pontifications:*

"After I finish the Egyptian novel, I've then got a second book I want to do about a spaceship in the future, maybe two or three centuries from now, and I'm appalled by the difficulties of the task."

And there is a hint in the last page of *Ancient Evenings*, as the narrator describes his journey after death in terms of shifting time, of sailing past comets and through magnetic fields.

So it does seem *Tough Guys Don't Dance* was a quick, money-making stop off the great highway of Norman Mailer's progress. No matter. The true measure of literary worth is not the sweat on the author's brow but the satisfaction in the belly of his reader. And one thing Mailer's readers ought to be accustomed to by now is an unpredictable menu. He takes devilish delight in it. It is, after all, the perfect revenge for someone trapped in the panoptic eye, as if to say, You may see me, but you can't *know* me. It is the same motivation that prompted *Advertisements for Myself* and everything that came after it. The last word on Norman Mailer is Norman Mailer—this from an interview in *Pieces and Pontifications:*

"I've always felt as if the way people react to me is not to me but to the latest photograph they've seen of me. So I can change the photograph and have the fun of observing the reactions. The devil in me loves the idea of being just that much of a changeling. You can never understand a writer until you find his private little vanity, and mine has always been that I will frustrate expectations. People think they've found a way of dismissing me, but, like the mad butler, I'll be back serving the meal."

THE FIGHT
ROCKY LOST

SEPTEMBER 1984

Only a movie star would have an ego big enough to commission a statue of himself, and then donate it to one of the premier art museums in the world. Only Sylvester Stallone would have the colossal cojones to suggest that it be placed at the center position of the museum's front entrance. The gesture provoked a one-of-a-kind battle in Philadelphia over the nature of art. Today, the infamous Rocky statue stands in front of the Spectrum, one of the sports venues in South Philly. To me, this is an outrage. The statue of Julius (Dr. J.) Erving, an actual living-breathing local sports legend, is shunted off to one side, and nowhere is there a statue of, say, Joe Frazier, a flesh-and-blood local pugilist who became champion of the world . . . in real life! Instead we have this schlocky monument to Stallone playing a fictional Philadelphia boxer. Go figure.

O nce upon a time, in a far-off land of palm trees, sand dunes, and major expressways, there lived a dashing and possibly brilliant young movie star known throughout the land because he had written, directed, and starred in two very similar, but very successful, films about a lovable palooka from South Philly who becomes, on a diet of sheer willpower, raw eggs, and milk, champion of the boxing world.

One day this bright young star, who was named Sylvester Stallone, hit upon an especially good and supremely generous idea. His third film about Rocky Balboa, the lovable palooka, called for a bronze statue of the champ to be ceremoniously unveiled on the very spot where he had paused in earlier films to lift his arms and leap in silent tribute to himself. So, the star wondered, why not commission a *real* statue? Not just a prop, but a genuine *work of art*. And then, as a way of thanking all Philadelphians for their help in making the films, why not let the gracious city keep the statue *right there*. Right there at the top of the same steps he had made so famous!

The handsome and supremely well-built actor/writer/director decided to take a break from hefting heavy bars of iron and steel and honing his heavyweight script to telephone some of his friends. He told them of the idea, and they rejoiced in it and saw that it was good. Now, even though the actor had only the nicest intentions, it occurred to some of his friends, men with smaller hearts, but with minds more subtly attuned to the benefits of publicity, that the actor had a very good idea indeed. And they thought, in their small-hearted but keen-minded way, It is no wonder that his friends call him *Sly.*

But it so happened that at the other end of the land, in the city of Philadelphia, there lurked near the top of those famous steps something even grander, something famous throughout the world. They called it the Philadelphia Museum of Art, an imposing and serious institution run by imposing and serious people. In fact, the steps where the actor had decided to place his statue actually *belonged* to the art museum! And the famous art museum decided that it did not want the famous actor's statue on its front steps, so . . .

"Now, you got people who just want to deal with this in a negative frame of mind," says Art Gorman, the Philadelphia truck driver who fought very hard to save the Rocky statue. "You got people who want to make out how Sly's on this giant ego trip, you know, that all's he wanted was to get a statue of himself set up on top of the art museum steps. I tell you, Sly ain't like that. He's good people, good people. The man was tryin' to *give* something and, hey, what he was givin' wasn't bad, you know what I mean? Hey! It wasn't bad."

Gorman cares. A lot. This thickset man of thirty-three with carefully styled brown hair and heavy hands wears his Kensington heritage like a uniform, a man as up-from-the-streets as they come, a man uncommonly proud of being common. He plucks a Marlboro from his pack, lights it, and tucks it deep between the first and second fingers of his right hand, which is closed to a half fist. The Rocky movies were important to Art. Hey, Rocky speaks his language, you know? Everything about the films, which he has on videodiscs at home, vindicates who Art Gorman is and where he is. They depict his world: hard-core Philadelphia. His man Sly got it just right. And the statue? Why, Art turns positively artistic when he talks about the statue.

"Heeey, that's a great statue. You seen it? You can look at it and know at a glance what it is. But mostly it's good for the inspirational value. I like what it exposes to the younger set—you know, about the hungriness you need to survive, about how determination is the only ingredient that measures up to winningness. I admire Stallone for providing us with a character like Rocky, but the character is the guy I think of most. Still, if you've met Sly, I mean, the guy *is* Rocky, if you know what I mean. There's no way he can say he isn't. He's pretty good with his dukes—in real life, he ain't bad. You gotta like the guy. I mean, there's a whole lot of Sylvester Stallone in Rocky Balboa. Rocky *is* Sly. Most people don't know that. He is."

Public art is often controversial. That can be good, because if you go to the trouble of erecting a large statue in a busy place, you want people to notice. If no one does, you have failed. But just because a work of art is controversial, that doesn't mean it is good.

People notice the Rocky statue, partly because of the controversy, but also because there's something appealing about a piece of movie fantasy slipping through a peculiar warp into reality. It's as if Dorothy woke up back at the farm in Kansas to discover she still had the ruby slippers from Oz. Only trouble was, the peculiar warp this particular nine-foot 1,500-pound statue had to slip through was the Philadelphia Art Commission.

After all, Philadelphia doesn't put just anything on public display. This is a city that has a world-famous, fifty-foot-tall clothespin standing on a pedestal in its Centre Square. Things like that don't happen accidentally. Like any civilized community, Philadelphia has arbiters of good taste.

When Stallone decided to donate the statue of, well, let's face it, *himself,* to the front steps of the world-famous Philadelphia Museum of Art, he did not approach the city's art commission. Instead, he went to people who better appreciate public relations. He instructed his retainers to contact Philadelphia's Commerce Department, the men and women who had been helping his movie crews use the city as a backdrop for the Rocky films for half a decade. When the commerce people heard the star's idea, they rejoiced, for they, too, saw that it was good.

"United Artists today phoned to advise that they have granted a commission for a sculpture of Sylvester Stallone as Rocky as a gift to the City of Philadelphia!" That's what commerce worker Betty Croll wrote in a memo to her boss, Dick Doran. She told the movie people that the official acceptance "should best be done by the mayor. . . . Obviously it is an outdoor piece planned for the museum . . ."

Doran liked the idea. He penned on the memo: "Good. The mayor should definitely do this."

Then Doran decided to write a letter to a wealthy and powerful man named F. Eugene Dixon Jr., the president of the Philadelphia Art Commission, which has the final word on placement of art on public property. Doran wrote about plans for *Rocky III* and concluded with this: "A part of the planning includes a statue of himself as 'Rocky' by a recognized sculptor to be placed in the courtyard of the Philadelphia Museum of Art. I hope we can count on the approval and support of the Art Commission for this proposed venture." Then he signed the letter, "Cordially, Dick."

It took several days for the missive to reach F. Eugene Dixon Jr., what with the inconvenience of routing his mail from the art commission headquarters in Center City to the esteemed president's farm in Montgomery County. "Fitz," as he is known to those who love him, began his letter to Dick by apologizing for the delay. As for the rich and famous Hollywood star's planning to make a third in his series of very similar, but very successful, films, Fitz was delighted. But on the matter of the statue, er, well, ". . . if the planning for this film includes a statue of Sylvester Stallone to be erected somewhere in the courtyard of the Philadelphia Museum of Art on a temporary basis, that is one thing. If, however, this statue is to be placed somewhere in the courtyard on a permanent basis—I hope you are jesting!"

Fitz was the sort of gentleman who used the word "jesting." He signed the letter, "With best regards, as always," then "Sincerely yours, Fitz."

Oh sad, oh unhappy day!

The bare boughs of Fairmount Park stirred stiffly in a cold, cold wind. It was December 10, 1980. One by one, the Guardians of Good Taste gathered in the columned chamber of Memorial Hall to pass judgment on the Hollywood star's generous gift of himself—or himself as the lovable palooka he had cast, then recast, and now threatened to cast again, both on-screen and in bronze. Who were the lofty eminences in plenum there? There were the knighted fourteen of the Fairmount Park Commission; the excellently tasteful art museum president, Robert Montgomery

Scott, and his exquisitely discerning director, Jean S. Boggs; the exalted mayor's trusted aide in all matters related to commerce, Dick Doran, and his retinue of paper carriers and assistants; and, enthroned above all others, the nine esteemed countenances of the Guardians of Good Taste, the Philadelphia Art Commission, F. Eugene Dixon Jr., in from the farm, presiding.

Far too modest to attend on his own behalf, the rich and famous movie star sent a telegram of apology and a delegation. Attending were two of his movie company assistants, men of shrewd mind and pleasant manner, one of whom wore a hot pink shirt. And, to present, nay, *unveil* a scale model of the gift itself, the star sent the very artist he himself had commissioned to execute the genuine Work of Art, sculptor A. Thomas Schomberg, who was accompanied by his wife.

Schomberg is a tall, bearded man who primarily sculpts figures of athletes in action. His personal philosophy was conveniently spelled out, sans capitalizations, in a handsome brochure accompanying the model of his statue:

"i believe that time, heredity, and environment combine to produce that individual human behavior which is inherent in us all. through my personal development i have tried to thoroughly understand the techniques utilized in the past (in particular hellenistic greek and 19th century french sculpture) and apply those techniques to a 20th century theme. i feel we have created the greatest athletes in the history of man and this social development, only one of an infinite number, happens to be the subject i most relate to. had i traveled west in the 19th century, i might have developed as a remington or a russel, but, living in 1980, one has to be influenced by the competitive athlete."

Or at least, one supposes, by a rich and famous Hollywood star portraying a famous athlete.

Stallone had long admired this modern-day Frederic Remington's work. The actor had purchased two of his boxing sculptures from a gallery in the MGM Grand Hotel in Los Angeles. So when the wonderful and supremely generous idea occurred, the star called Schomberg and offered him a $53,000 commission. Stallone himself put in about a week's worth of time posing for the sculptor, and permitted his idolized, wilting, chiseled, pouting features to be caked in plaster for the formation of a mask. Working from that and more than eight hundred photographs, Schomberg fashioned the twenty-eight-inch sculpture that stood that sad day on a polished conference table in Memorial Hall.

The sculptor humbly explained that this miniature muscular man with outstretched arms was *not* just a statue of Sylvester Stallone, but was, rather, a fighter striking a pose that makes a "classical statement of perfection" that harks back to such Greek works as *Apollo of Belvedere* and that the victory it represents—Rocky's technical KO of fictional champ Apollo Creed (just a coincidence there with the name)—recalls the attitude of ancient Greeks during the Peloponnesian War.

Schomberg further explained that he had planned the work to stand atop the front steps, but that he would not protest if the assembled commissions, in all their wisdom, opted to display it immediately inside the front doors of the museum. He concluded, tastefully, with a tribute to art commissioner Joe Brown, an aging sculptor and former boxer, whom Schomberg confessed he had admired since "I was this high," indicating with one hand the height of a child. He implored Commissioner Brown to help him with this ambitious project. And with that, he sat down.

Silence fell over the chamber. Commissioner Brown pondered his response. He knew of Schomberg, too.

("The man has been writing me letters for years telling me how great he is. You know, I think he's the only young person to write me who I have failed to answer. I didn't know who the hell he was, and I didn't want to know. Back in my studio I have what I call my 'nut' file. He's in it.")

But the commissioner couldn't exactly speak his mind after hearing Schomberg's sincere words of praise. So even before Brown spoke, he decided not to comment on the worth of the statue that stood on the table before him ("I thought it was a bad statue") and instead spoke about the Hollywood star's generous idea.

"It's in bad taste," this Guardian of Good Taste said.

Didn't Schomberg realize that what he and the others were proposing was an imposition on the art museum and the city of Philadelphia? "You're trying to promote a movie—no, not even a movie, but a sequel to a sequel of a movie! And to do it you want to exploit a fine art museum. It's in bad taste."

Stung, the sculptor rose to speak. He had not meant to *impose*. Why, his work was designed to "enhance the architectural environment" of the famous museum's courtyard. Schomberg was hurt and disappointed. ("It was as if he had criticized one of my children.")

Then rose art commissioner Meyer (Pat) Potamkin, mortgage broker and tireless regulator of Philadelphia's public aesthetics. Why, *this,* he said, this work conceived and executed as a genuine Work of Art, was mere *illustration!*

Sensing Emotion in the great hall and, close behind, its constant companion Confusion, the sage art commission president F. Eugene Dixon Jr. quickly requested a recess. Gathering about them their satin cloaks of true expertise, their gilded gowns of high motive, and delicate trains of political connection, the Guardians of Good Taste repaired to an antechamber with commerce director Doran to talk turkey.

Speaking on behalf of the city's commercial interests, Doran made a final plea. Hey, guys, this thing may be a promo, but it's a *great* promo. This would be good for the city. Good for the art museum. He cleverly recalled that attendance at the hallowed art museum had doubled after the first Rocky movie. Commissioner Brown allowed as how, if the city put go-go dancers on the front steps, they might be able to do better than that.

Because truly great men rarely argue long in a time of decision, even in matters of profound importance, a compromise was soon reached. The Good Taste Guardians would allow the statue of the Hollywood star to stand on top of the museum steps for only as long as it took him to film the sequel to the sequel of his very successful film, thank you just the same. Afterward, the Guardians would decide whether the statue would be placed anywhere on permanent display. Commissioners Brown and Potamkin objected, but were overruled. They preferred to reject the statue outright.

Art Gorman heard on the evening news that night that his city had rejected the Rocky statue. The precise politics didn't matter much to him.

"We both sat down, me and my girl, and we were *astonished,* you know? They flashed a picture of the statue on the TV screen, and I said, 'Hey, not bad!' I was angry and very disappointed. You figure, there's so many things that art commission has on display around here that the common people can't even understand. So who are they to take this picky-pick attitude toward the statue and its quality and all that? You know, 'Art is in the eyes of the beholder'! At least when you look at the Rocky statue, you know what you're beholding! And to think that Mr. Stallone had prepared this statue—which has a lot of inspirational value all by itself—and this city was honored enough to be chosen to house it . . . and our own art commission wouldn't accept it!"

Gorman was up most of the night. This really bugged him. He was then a truck driver for *The Philadelphia Journal,* so he knew how to muster publicity. And determination? He had gotten a heavy dose from Rocky himself. If the Philadelphia Art Commission wouldn't accept the statue, then Art Gorman was going to get the people of Philadelphia to accept it.

And, lo! A petition drive was born.

The next morning, he lobbied his friends on the *Journal* staff for coverage, and he got it. He had petitions and leaflets printed. A handout read:

ROCKY STATUE SHOULD BE BACK IN PHILLY. REMEMBER ROCKY I. WHEN YOU AND THE KIDS WENT TO THE MOVIE, WHAT DID THEY AND YOURSELF FEEL SEEING PHILLY ON THE SCREEN INSTEAD OF NEW YORK OR SAN FRANCISCO? "PRETTY GOOD HA!" WE EVEN HAD A ROCKY II DIDN'T WE? NOW WE ARE PROMISED A ROCKY III BUT WE ALSO HAD A STATUE OF ROCKY. BUT THAT'S NOT TRUE ANYMORE. THE REASONS HAVE ALREADY BEEN HEARD. WHY WE DON'T KNOW. WHY DON'T YOU VOICE YOUR OPINION IF YOU FEEL THAT THE STATUE SHOULD BE BACK IN PHILLY AS DID "SLY." DROP ME A LINE AND I WILL SEE THAT YOUR LETTER REACHES MR. SLY "ROCKY" STALLONE.

Gorman took to the streets and back alleys. He withdrew $5,000 from his own bank account to finance the project. "You didn't see it? We had this forty-foot Rocky banner. Beee-yoo-ti-ful! What we was doing is something that is never going to happen in a thousand years again. I did it because I had my heart in it." He took to South Philly and Roxborough and Kensington, where the real people live. And, lastly, he took to City Hall.

His campaign stretched through winter to spring, when on-location shooting began for the third very similar, but very successful, film about the lovable palooka from South Philly. The statue was erected, right on top of the art museum steps. It was exciting. Gorman actually met his hero on location for one of the scenes.

"I told him that I just wanted him to know that not everybody in Philadelphia feels the same way as the art commission." Gorman's wide face lights up with the memory. "Stallone reacted. He said he couldn't make heads nor tails as to why they were so taken off, so not willing to accept it. I think he respects the character enough to want to see the character rest where he most relates, and the best place for that statue—I don't care what anyone else says—is *still* the art museum steps."

Seeing the uplifted arms of that bronzed champion really fired Gorman up, but the feeling was short-lived. The art commission was willing to keep the statue—or store it or who knows what—after the filming was over, but Stallone's movie crew quietly disassembled the statue at 5 a.m. one day and took it home. It had been standing only three days.

By the summer of 1981, the campaign was dragging. No one seemed to know the exact whereabouts of the genuine Work of Art. Gorman had signatures, signatures, signatures. They were easy enough to get. But progress—well, progress was harder to come by.

He took to haunting the offices of the art commission. Maybe a common man could talk some sense into these people.

"He nearly drove me crazy in here," recalls Kathleen H. McKenna, art commission director. "I kinda like the guy. He's a colorful character, an interesting individual. He had a point well taken. He would say," and McKenna attempts an impersonation of Gorman's gruffer voice, "'Look, lady, let me put it to you this way. What we've got here is a statue that the public can relate to.' That's basically what he had to say."

But McKenna was hardly in a position to influence the Guardians of Good Taste. She listened sympathetically to Gorman and tried to tell him gently that what he hoped to accomplish was just plain impossible.

Indeed, things were looking bad. It was like the scene from *Rocky,* the original *Rocky,* the big fight scene, where the hero has been knocked down. His eyes are swollen almost shut and bleeding. His head reels. He reaches desperately for the ropes. Gorman's forty viewings of the film had prepared him well for McKenna's disparaging words.

"When she told me the statue would *never* stand on top of the steps, that did it. That took any doubt away. I wasn't going to be beat so easily. I figured, This is it. Now I go for broke. I took a job, and I was going to finish it. I was in the arena, right? I was the one who was going to do this thing, right? People were counting on me. I had all those signatures. *Kids* would stop me on the street."

First District city councilman Jimmy Tayoun is known in the dark, wide corridors of City Hall as a man who knows how to get things done. "Yeah, well, I saw the kid walking around like a nut handing out his leaflets and asking for signatures, and, like everybody else, I didn't pay any attention to him at first," recalls Tayoun. "But I looked at the leaflets, and I noticed that the kid was living in my district. So, I said, 'Yo, kid. Com'ere. Talk to me. What's your problem?' Like that."

Tayoun can smell a populist issue a mile off. A man of the people. He'll put his arm around perfect strangers, standing about a foot closer than most folks, establishing instant intimacy. It didn't take 2,000 signatures to tell Jimmy Tayoun that this was your basic common-folks-versus-cultural-elitists fight. Or which side he was on.

"So I told the kid there was tremendous merit to what he was doing." The more Tayoun thought about it, the more he liked it. "Yeah, I figure, you put the statue up on top of the steps and who knows how many people are going to come and see it? It'd be a real attraction. So maybe some people would go on then and step inside the art museum and see the [Alexander Calder] mobiles and other stuff in there, you know? Kids, too. I figure, maybe some kids'll get titillated, I mean, *titillated,* by real art. You never know. It might be the best thing they ever did over there."

Not that Tayoun has strong feelings about art, or even about the statue. Not at all. He doesn't even *like* the statue.

"You know, the Rocky statue is not a good statue," he says, leaning forward and tapping his listener's chest with his forefinger as if to confide inside information. "If it looked more like Rocky I would like it better, but it doesn't look that much like him. I went over to see it. I'm a realist. I look at things, and I like 'em to look like what they're supposed to look like. But this one? It don't look nothin' like Sylvester Stallone."

No, it was not aesthetics that motivated Tayoun. It was politics. The councilman shared Gorman's outrage that the Guardians of Good Taste, some so-called experts of art, could reject a popular work on behalf of people who probably would *like* to have it—yes, right there on top of the art museum steps. So, in September, as a kind of warning shot, Tayoun introduced a resolution, the legislative equivalent of a nice suggestion, "asking the art commission to reconsider its arbitrary and capricious decision regarding the 'Rocky' statue, and to permit the statue to be placed at the art museum in Philadelphia."

Two months later, after the nice suggestion was ignored, Tayoun had the council's legal authors draw up a document that, if approved, would have been much more than a suggestion. It would have been the law.

"The legal draftsmen told me the bill was unconstitutional, that it contradicted the charter, which gives the art commission authority over deciding where to display things publicly in the city, but I didn't care," Tayoun recalls. "I thought it would make an interesting legal test in court. It was an egalitarian kind of thing. I mean, I don't think these people should have the right to dictate to everyone else what is art."

Tayoun's proposed ordinance succeeded where his resolution had failed; the art commission took him seriously. At the public hearing on the bill, those who came to argue against it outnumbered Tayoun, Gorman, and the handful of supporters rounded up by the Kensington truck driver. Gorman knew he had come as far as he could go. The enemy was arrayed before him with a staff of killer attorneys on leash.

"They made it pretty clear that in order to do what we wanted, we would have to change the charter," Gorman remembers. As any self-respecting up-from-the-streets Philadelphian knows, charter changes are nothing to be trifled with. Not even the Bambino, beloved former mayor Frank Rizzo, could get the charter changed. Gorman knew it was time to stop fighting and start talking.

"They had worked out the compromise before the meeting even started," he says, with newfound insight into the legislative process. The Hollywood star's generous gift of himself would stand atop the art museum steps again, briefly, to mark the world premiere of the sequel to the sequel. Then, on July 11, it would be shipped to a large square of cement in front of South Philly's indoor sports arena, the Spectrum.

"They figured, We'll put it down by the Spectrum; I mean, you and me go to see hockey, so we don't know art from a hockey puck, right?" explained one of the officials who helped chisel the compromise. "Actually, this sort of thing happens fairly often. Museums are always getting gifts of artwork they don't want. During World War II, there was a handy solution. There was this crucial shortage of bronze, you see . . ."

Oh sad, oh unhappy day! Workers finally wrapped the giant statue of the Hollywood star in soiled, graying mattresses and hoisted and blasted it off its perch atop the Art Museum steps. It was a hot August day. The July 11 deadline had not been met because the eminent parties involved fell to arguing about who was going to pay to remove the genuine Work of Art. At the height of this dispute, one member of commerce director Doran's staff offered an explanation:

"The city is in no position to pay for removal of the statue. Clearly, the statue has overstayed its welcome on the front steps of the art museum. The art museum just wants the thing *off* their front porch. I can tell you that the city of Philadelphia is not going to spend a cent to ship some statue of Sylvester Stallone all over town. We figure, the statue was a promotion for the film, which has made, by current estimates, more than a hundred fifty million already this summer. Then, since it is going to the Spectrum, there was some talk of trying to get them to pay for it. . . ."

The Guardians, by now, had grown impatient. At a meeting held shortly before the statue was finally removed, it was seriously suggested that the lot of them march out and just push the statue off its pedestal, as a sort of, you know, protest, but this was rejected as undignified.

As the wait wore on, hundreds of tourists from across the land posed for snapshots, fists held high, before the sculpted version of the man who had beaten the odds, beaten Apollo Creed, and seemingly beaten, at least for a time, Philadelphia's high and mighty Guardians of Good Taste.

Then one day a kindly construction contractor appeared with the right equipment and a soft heart for Rocky Balboa. When he and his men were done, only a chipped pedestal remained on the art museum's steps. The Guardians rejoiced at the sight, and knew that it was good. And in good taste.

Today, in the famous City of Brotherly Love, the Hollywood star's generous gift stands, muscular and proud, outside the Spectrum, the same sports arena where he captured and defended and defended his crown. Common people come from all over the land to admire the work of A. Thomas Schomberg, the famous sculptor, and ponder its true meaning. The sculptor is gratified that his work will be permanently exhibited in Philadelphia, "which has one of the finest collections of public art on display anywhere in the world." The Guardians of the world-famous art museum breathe easy, confident that the artistic sensibilities of the Spectrum's patrons are not easily bruised. And Gorman, though somewhat disappointed, feels vindicated and proud. (There remains, however, in some quarters, the lingering suspicion that those Hollywood slickers put one over on the old hometown.)

And out in the far-off land of palm trees, sand dunes, and major expressways, the dashing and possibly brilliant young actor/writer/director has modestly avoided further comment on the matter. Alone under the red-orange smear of Southern California's setting sun, he most assuredly ponders other things (*Rocky IV*?), and in the rare moments of silence can hear, all across the land, the ring of cash drawers and the crank of turnstiles, happily ever after.

MAYBERRY VICE

FEBRUARY 1986

When The Inquirer *went on strike in 1985, I called a friend at* Rolling Stone *and begged for an assignment. This story was her idea. When it came out, it demonstrated for me one lucrative side benefit of having a story in a national magazine. I had been writing magazine articles for years, but this one prompted dozens of calls from movie producers. I sold the rights to Warner Brothers, and split the earnings with my editor and with Mike White and Rudy Legenza, the heroes of the story. The movie never got made, but it gave me some valuable experience with Hollywood, a nice payday, and lifelong friendships with Rudy and with Mike, who died suddenly of a heart attack just a few years ago. Mike and Rudy suggested that I contact some FBI agents in Philadelphia, a tip which led to my first book,* Doctor Dealer. *So all in all, the time I spent on strike was the most lucrative period of my career up until that time.*

Cocky as ever, the skinny Puerto Rican kid knew he was on to something. Now he would call these cops' bluff. Maybe then this Blanco and his lieutenant would leave him and his friends alone.

Only his cigarette cast light behind the corner bar where he waited. There were boards on the windows. It was the summer of 1983, and the kid wore a black net T-shirt. His jeans, also black, descended to a pair of puffy white ankle-high basketball shoes the size of ski boots, made larger still by laces left loose and untied. Tires cracked on gravel; the kid flicked the cigarette and clomped across the lot.

At the wheel of the black Chevy, Lieutenant Rudy Legenza turned off the headlights. Beside him sat Blanco, Detective Mike White, whose mind flashed Mickey Mouse when the thin black figure in great white boots stepped out in the open. Mickey scurried into the backseat and closed the door. He could hardly wait with his news.

"Listen. On my way over here tonight, this guy stops me, this Colombian guy, and he offers me a gram of coke. I promised to meet him five minutes from now. So I need a hundred bucks."

Mike groaned. "Why did you do that?"

"You should *never* set anything up without telling us about it first," said Rudy. Rudy was in charge; you could hear it in his voice.

This was not the reception Mickey expected. What was with these cops? Blanco and the lieutenant had busted him a few days ago. Nothing serious, but they had enough to lean, to make him work on their stupid little cases. At this meeting here, he was supposed to collect all of ten bucks to buy a few lousy joints and a hit of acid from the fat American over on Dexter Street who was dealing right out on the sidewalk. How chickenshit can you get? "What are you fuckin' with high school kids for?" he'd asked. "I hear there's a Colombian living over on Washington Street who gets twenty kilos of coke from Miami every month! And you're busting *me?*" And now he was offering them a Colombian who was ready to deliver a gram right off the bat and they were coming down on him like he had done something wrong!

"Hey, look," he said. "I told the guy I'd buy it, man. I have to go back. He's probably waiting right now."

No answer. Mike and Rudy stared at each other. In the dim light, Mike's sandy-red beard looked gray, there were lines under his eyes. Rudy is a shorter, wider man, with bright streaks of gray in his black hair and beard. They felt foolish, embarrassed. They knew how penny-ante these street busts were. Now Mickey Mouse here in the back seat had put them on the spot. Who was going to tell him their drug investigation was authorized to spend, count 'em, twelve more bucks?

They'd started three days ago with $200. It was all they could wheedle out of the chief. But even Mike and Rudy hadn't figured things would move this fast. Were they going to tell this kid that the Central Falls, Rhode Island, police were ready to bust *him,* were after the stupid American kid on Dexter Street for dealing a dime of dope, but weren't interested in a Colombian with a gram of coke because they couldn't afford the buy? For a hundred dollars?

Both detectives pulled out wallets. Mike's got three kids, so he didn't even have twenty. Rudy, the bachelor, was frowning down at that week's spending money. He turned on the overhead light and reluctantly began copying the serial numbers of his own bills.

The chief would understand. Surely.

*   *   *

Police headquarters, on Illinois Street, is a low, two-story brick bunker with white trim, basic municipal modern. It sits dead center of Central Falls, which means that no point in the jurisdiction is more than a half mile away. Even with 20,000 people jammed inside those boundaries, the smallest city in the smallest state is still what you might call a manageable district.

In the lobby there's a Coke machine and a row of four hard plastic chairs. On one wall there's a framed photo display of all thirty-seven members of the force. Mike and Rudy are pictured as they looked before they made detective: beardless, in uniform. The centerpiece of the display is a larger picture, that of a man whose meaty Irish countenance fills all available space. This is the man who scowled at spending $200 to chase drug dealers in the dark, when that's the kind of work that should be left to the state; this is the man who held the experienced opinion that Central Falls (*his* Central Falls) had no more of a drug problem than any other American city (that is, unstoppable), and whom Rudy had decided not to awaken and consult last night when he counted out a hundred dollars of his own money to the Puerto Rican kid with the giant shoes. This is Chief James F. Galligan.

The detectives' office is upstairs, in a long room with light-blue cinder-block walls. Old Glory flaps at eye level out the front window. Mike and Rudy sit in opposite corners. The small bulletin board over Mike's left shoulder displays a yellowing newspaper ad of his older brother, Jack, in a trench coat with an upturned collar. Jack is a TV reporter in Providence. In the corner of the board there's a blue-and-white bumper sticker: I SURVIVED CATHOLIC SCHOOL. Rudy's corner is uncluttered. A few pictures from hunting magazines are tacked to his own bulletin board. His desk is just inside the door. Any shit that flies through lands in his lap.

Mike hardly glanced from his paperwork that morning when Rudy stood up and announced, "I'm going down to see the chief about my hundred dollars."

Mike figured this was no big deal. Forking over that money was the kind of decision you have to make for yourself on the street. Still, he sensed they were out on a limb on this one. The undercover drug work was something Mike had pushed. At thirty-two, he was five years younger than Rudy, and had been on the force half of Rudy's fourteen years. He was entitled to be more gung-ho. Mike had even taken courses with the Drug Enforcement Administration in Providence on his own time. They taught things like how to tail people without being noticed. He and Rudy were too well-known in Central Falls to make undercover buys themselves, so Mike recruited his cousin Frank Dougherty, a uniformed cop in Lincoln, the next town over, to help out—without pay, of course. Rudy was the one who had to sell the idea to the higher-ups, and Rudy was the one who'd be second-guessed.

The meeting with the chief lasted less than ten minutes. James F. Galligan was a man of few words. Rudy came out laughing, but you could tell he was angry.

"I almost didn't get it back," he said. His ears were red.

"Rudy? Rudy Legenza?"

"That's me. Who's this?"

"This is Ralph. You know, Ralph Mott." Rudy didn't know, but he'd learned not to discourage people.

"Hey, Ralph," he said warmly. "Nice to hear from you. What can I help you with?"

"You did me a favor a few years ago, Rudy. I think I might be able to return it. Can you meet me, say, up at the Store 24 tomorrow morning?"

This happened often to Rudy. He'd grown up in Central Falls and seemed to know everyone—except Colombians, that is. Rudy's parents had worked in the wire mills. Back in the fifties, their neighborhood had been the Italian corner of Central Falls. If a cop caught Rudy anywhere else, he'd get a boot on the rump and a stern suggestion to get back where he belonged. Nowadays, you did that and you'd be up on charges. It hurt Rudy to drive down the old block and see it in such disrepair. Theirs had been the typical Central Falls tenement, a three-story wood-frame with shingles. The city had block after block of them. Rudy's old place, like many, had been reno-vated with low-income-housing grants, its bleached wood shingles replaced with shiny striations of aluminum siding. It gave the neighborhood an insti-tutional look.

After hanging up the phone, Rudy remembered who Ralph Mott was: a drunk, pleasant when sober. Rudy had picked him up five years before, after Mrs. Mott came in black-and-blue. Eventually, she wanted to drop the charge. But Rudy told Ralph they were going to prosecute anyway. At the metal desk in the interview room, an airless closet with yellow walls, Rudy made him sweat for a half hour. Ralph was pleading when Rudy finally made a show of giving in. He tore up the summons and said, "You owe me one. Don't let this happen again." As far as he knew, it hadn't.

Rudy was waiting in the parking lot outside the store when Ralph walked up. He looked the same, bedraggled and strung out. Rudy bought him coffee, and they leaned against the black Chevy in the morning sunlight.

"What have you got for me?" Rudy asked.

"Some people next door to me, Colombians. They were making such a racket that I couldn't sleep, so I watched them out the window. At first I thought they were breaking into this car across the street, but when I looked closer I could see they were taking the door panels off. I saw them taking out packages of this white stuff from inside the car door."

"What do you mean, 'white stuff'?"

"I don't know. It was in packs that looked like plastic, about six inches wide and a foot long. I seen on the TV where they had it hidden in door panels like that. If I didn't know better, I'd say it was cocaine."

At the metal desk in the interview room, the kid from Dexter Street was more indignant than scared. Just a fat nineteen-year-old with acne and blond hair jutting out in all directions. He was trying to act tough.

Mike read him his rights. "Want to say anything?"

"Yeah. What are you bothering me for? What are you bothering my friends for? We're small-timers. We don't hurt anybody. Why don't you go after the Colombians? The big guys are making a fuckin' mint, and you're busting me for pot."

"So, tell me about the big guys. I'd be happy to go after them."

"Right. I bet you would. What about the Colombian on Foundry Street—Gomez? He's got shipments coming straight up from South America through Miami. He must be dealing fifty kilos a month to the East Side of New York!"

Mike was getting tired of hearing this. "Yeah, yeah. Now tell me where Jimmy Hoffa is buried."

"Holy cocaine, Batman! I think we're getting snowed under here!"

Mike was always kidding around. Yet this talk of coke and Colombians was starting to trouble him. Rudy felt it, too. They mulled over the mounting evidence as they cruised their familiar maze of streets.

A few months before, they had begun noticing strange cars, expensive cars, with out-of-state tags. There were no fancy restaurants here, no hotels or motels, no tourist attractions. So they had plugged the tags into the computer and found that some of the people who owned these cars had been busted—cocaine.

"I got a call from a friend who works at the bank, a guy I went to high school with," Rudy said. "He called and he said, 'People are coming in here changing small bills for large bills.' So I said, 'Well, what do you mean?' So he said, 'They're bringing in small bills and they're taking all our fifties and hundreds.'"

"Jesus."

"He says they're also making out a lot of money orders, and they're making them for just under the ten-thousand-dollar maximum, so it doesn't have to be reported. They're making a lot of money, in other words, and it's all going, my friend says, to three people who have the same account number down in Miami."

"Laundering in small amounts," Mike said.

"Yep."

"Colombians?"

"Colombians."

The first of the Colombians had been recruited in Central Falls in the early seventies. They were textile workers. Most of the mills around Central Falls were textile mills. The Colombians were willing to work for a lot less than Americans. And once the migration started, Central Falls became a cultural beachhead for Colombians. The flow north turned to flood. They came even after there were no more jobs. The urge to come north transcended immigration laws, language barriers, unemployment. As the tide mounted, longtime residents started moving out, driving down housing costs and accelerating immigration. Today the city is officially one-third Colombian; unofficially, maybe half. Next to New York and Miami, Central Falls has the largest community of Colombians in North America. Now Rudy and Mike were thinking it had plenty of coke, too.

"How are we supposed to get at somebody dealing in amounts like this?" asked Mike. "We'd need a couple of thousand just to set up a buy for an ounce! And we already spent our two hundred dollars."

"You mean three hundred," Rudy corrected.

"We need help," Rudy said.

"DEA?"

"Yeah, but we need more. We've got to have something definite—or they'll think we're nuts."

When the brawl inside spilled out the front door, it was no longer something Mr. Blanco could ignore. Mike was doing his standard Saturday-night detail at the Sportsman Cafe, one of the few occasions when he still wore a uniform. The Sportsman is a barn-sized bar and dance hall, the center of Colombian night life—on Saturday nights, that is. There'd been a stabbing some years back that closed the place down, and when the city liquor authority allowed it to reopen, it was for one night a week. The chief liked to keep two men in uniform on the scene, just in case.

Mike and Skip Jameson, the officer sharing the detail, leaped into the fight, pulled two men apart, and cuffed them. Mike radioed for a cruiser, and within minutes the men were gone. All in a night's work. The crowd had already drifted back to the music inside when Mike was approached by a man he recognized but didn't know by name.

"Mr. Blanco, I want to talk to you." The man was small, middle-aged, with a broad, flat nose. He gestured toward the darkness around the side of the Sportsman. Mike left Skip under the portico and walked back to the tall fence that kept cars from spilling onto the parking lot of McDonald's next door.

"One of those guys you just busted is a big dealer," the man said.

"Coke?"

"Yeah."

"What do you mean by 'big'?"

"I don't know. Kilos. He gets weekly shipments from Miami."

"How?"

"By car."

The story was familiar, but this was no punk kid or drunk telling it. Mike got excited. This might be the break they needed. He tried to keep the man talking.

"No. No. Not here. People will see. But I will come in." He walked across the lot to a car, got in, and drove off.

Mike phoned Rudy in triumph. Rudy had his hometown confidants, but Mike's years outside the Sportsman Cafe earned him access to the insular Colombians. He knew names, families, where they lived, who they went out with. Maybe now it would pay off.

He hung around the office the next few days, but the man never called or came in, never approached Mike again.

But his tip was good. One of the Colombians busted the night of the fight had been carrying a gram. He got himself a pricey lawyer, and he wouldn't talk. But the lab tests on the coke . . . Well, normal purity on the street is between 10 and 20 percent. This stuff came back, certified, 98 percent pure.

"Mike, I'm having a problem with my daughter. Could I bring her in— you talk to her?"

Mike told the woman on the phone, "Sure. Bring her down."

They were waiting in the lobby, mother and daughter, less than an hour later. Mike was surprised at how young the girl was. He guessed ten. She turned out to be twelve. She had this crazy spiked crop of brown hair and lots of makeup. She looked bored and annoyed. Mom looked weathered, about forty.

In the interview room, Mom stood, the girl sat behind the desk. Mike took one of the metal chairs, turned it, and straddled the back.

"Okay. What kind of problem?" Mike suspected she had been shoplifting Top Forty cassettes.

"Well," began Mom unsteadily, drawing breath, "she has been staying out all night; she hasn't been coming home; she was gone for two days, and I looked everywhere and couldn't find her. I finally found her in front of this house on Dexter, and she was sittin' out on the front steps, and she had this white shit all over her nose. You wanna hear what she was doing?"

With her eyes averted and a pained smirk on her face, the daughter looked like she was trying to will herself onto a different planet.

"Yeah. What was she doing?"

"She was giving these Colombian men blow jobs to get a little of the coke they have."

Coke whores: the latest clue, *Andy of Mayberry* meets *Miami Vice*. Rudy said, "They picked up this one girl over on Lonsdale Avenue the other night. She used to babysit for my friends' kids." It disgusted him.

He and Mike were weaving through orange cones set out on Broad Street for repaving crews. It was shortly after dawn. The crews weren't out yet, but Mike and Rudy had been up all night on another fruitless stakeout. They had watched people coming and going from the place on Dexter Street. That was all they could do, watch.

They were on their way to Kentucky Fried Chicken for an early sandwich and coffee before heading in for another day's work. It was a cold and sunny November morning. They were still talking about coke whores when Walter Alvarez drove by, going the opposite way in his white Corvette.

"There goes the Nitwit," noted Rudy.

It was hard not to notice Walter. They had learned about most of the suspected coke dealers the hard way. Whispered information, corroboration. There were a few big names that kept coming up: Carlos Arroyave, the cheerful ladies' man in Lincoln with the pretty, pregnant young wife; Roberto Tabares, the tall, beer-bellied businessman in Pawtucket; the flamboyant Gomez brothers, who had an apartment just three blocks east of headquarters. But nobody had to tell them about Walter. Mike had known him for years. He had watched Walter get more and more outrageous. Mike and Rudy could tell that Colombian dealers felt they had nothing to fear from the police in Central Falls. But Walter took things a step further. In recent months he had started calling himself the Snowman. He drove the white Corvette and wore white suits, white shirts, white shoes. He was the Prince of the Sportsman on Saturday nights.

Just as Mike and Rudy sat down at Kentucky Fried, Walter walked in and ordered coffee. Mike said, "That son of a bitch turned around and came back just to let us know he doesn't care that we're watching him."

Sure enough, Walter strutted by their table on his way out. "Greetings," he said. Walter's white shirt was unbuttoned to the waist, and a white towel was wrapped around his neck. And there was something new. Walter had bleached his bushy moustache white!

"Weird," was all Rudy could say as Walter's great bushy head disappeared out the door. "That guy," Mike said, "is just begging us to bust him."

Roll-call room, on the second floor of headquarters, looks like a classroom. Writing surfaces are attached to chairs, and behind the sergeant's podium is a long blackboard. The room smells of stale coffee and tobacco, leather and chalk.

Mike strode in as the morning shift was getting ready to leave. There were friendly hoots as he asked to say a few words. He stood to one side of the podium, addressing a roomful of blue winter uniforms.

"Rudy and I just wanted to take a minute here to tell you that we have reason to believe there are some major cocaine deals going down here in Central Falls. I know that's maybe hard for you to believe"—Mike could see the looks on their faces—"but Rudy and I have been gathering a lot of information that I can't be too specific about right now. We just wanted to ask that you keep your eyes and ears open and be careful of any out-of-state vehicles you might stop. We're talking about people moving hundreds of thousands of dollars of coke and probably armed."

There was silence. Mike stuffed his hands into his pockets and turned to leave. But as he reached the door, he heard someone from the ranks mutter, "You boys have been watching too much TV." And the room erupted in laughter.

After asking for Mike White, the Hispanic woman on the phone sounded reluctant. She wouldn't say her name.

"I just want to meet with you and talk," she said.

"Okay, when?"

"Now."

"Where?"

"Someplace away from Central Falls. No one must see us together. No one must know I called you."

"My partner and I can meet you in Providence."

"Partner?"

"Yeah, Lieutenant Rudy Legenza. If you trust me, you'll have to trust him. We work together."

They agreed to meet in the parking lot of a downtown hotel in Providence, about a fifteen-minute drive. The woman said she'd be in a new green LTD. Mike and Rudy grabbed their coats.

When the woman's car drove into the hotel lot, they automatically noted the license plate. The woman looked Colombian. Mike stood up outside for a moment and waved to her. She was in her twenties; she was finely dressed in pressed blue wool slacks and a white sequined sweater.

When she climbed in the backseat, Rudy drove toward I-95. They cruised into Massachusetts as they talked.

"... If they discover that I came to you, I will be killed." She spoke with quiet resolve, describing a man she knew well. She said she had personal reasons for wanting him arrested. He controlled "a lot" of cocaine, she said, which came up from Colombia through Miami, then to Central Falls in regular deliveries by car. The man supplied major dealers in New York, Boston, and Providence and throughout New England.

"How much is 'a lot'?" asked Mike.

"One customer in Boston gets twenty kilos a month, and he has many customers like this."

Mike and Rudy looked at each other. "That's a lot."

She laid out the operation: names, dates, addresses, amounts. She had more answers than they had questions. Mike scribbled notes as fast as he could. She stopped several times to stress her danger.

"You must understand. They will kill me. I will just disappear. Not only me, but also my family—in America and Colombia. They keep lists of the relatives, even the children. They know where to find them. It is a simple thing for a Colombian to disappear from Central Falls. It is said that they went home to Colombia. Who is to know if it is true?"

Mike and Rudy stayed calm and professional, reassuring her. But after they dropped her off down the street from the hotel, Mike whooped for joy. *It was true!* If this information checked out—and they were sure it would—then cocaine traffic in Central Falls was bigger than their wildest suspicions.

Then it sunk in. Jesus, they were in over their heads.

Mike stood next to Rudy's desk. Rudy sat behind it. They were nervous. Sitting in front, sipping coffee, was Dan McCarthy, head of the DEA in Providence. McCarthy is a tall, slow-talking, very Irish fellow with a shock of white hair. He has puffy eyes and the look of a man who stays out late. On either side of McCarthy sat two police detectives from Pawtucket.

Mike and Rudy didn't know what to expect. There was a good chance McCarthy wouldn't believe them. A cocaine ring in Central Falls? Or maybe he knew all about it, and they would seem foolish, two local cops stumbling where they didn't belong. All they really wanted was in on the case. No one knew the city like they did. No one had their contacts. Maybe they could help. They could almost taste it.

They had planned it the night before: once things got started, Mike would do the talking. For a while he'd been the community-relations officer, so he was used to speeches. Mike had rehearsed what he was going to say. That morning, he began, "We've got a street drug problem here just like every city in America, you know? And when we started working on that more and more, we started gettin' more and more information of a drug nature, you know? And the information we got was outrageous. That, you know, this guy's dealin' twenty kilos a month, this guy is dealin' fifty kilos a month, just wild stuff."

"Stuff that we didn't believe," said Rudy.

"Yeah," Mike said. "But as we found out more and more, we heard this stuff more and more, and then the out-of-state cars, you know, it all started to fit."

Mike told of Rudy's talk with Ralph Mott, the stories from the kids he busted, the skittish man at the Sportsman and the lab results. He told about Rudy's banker friend and the girl with coke on her nose. He told them about the Snowman and about Carlos Arroyave and Roberto Tabares and the Gomez brothers. He saved the meeting with the woman for last.

"So we asked you to come here . . . We don't know what you can do to help us, but we'd like to get some help, because Rudy and I would sure like to do something about this."

McCarthy's face betrayed little. Mike finished, feeling lame, as if it all added up to very little.

Then McCarthy spoke: "Not only is what you have told me true, but there's more."

Exhaust clouds on a winter night are enough to give you away. So Mike and Rudy had to freeze in the car outside the Newport Creamery in Pawtucket. Another night of backup.

The DEA agent had pulled into the lot some time before, waiting to meet a dealer and set up another buy. Mike and Rudy were parked about a hundred yards off, away from the tall spotlights on the street side. Their job was the same unglamorous task they had performed nearly every night for the previous two months: wait, watch, stay inconspicuous, be there in case the agent needs help.

It was now January 1984. At that first meeting with McCarthy, Mike and Rudy had learned that the DEA had two agents in Central Falls. The feds had been feeling their way in. As McCarthy listened that morning, he could see months of dangerous undercover work spared—Mike and Rudy could guide his people. If he had a face, they had a name, an address, a contact, a relative. Working together, they had made progress in two months. One of McCarthy's agents, Pegg Cafolla, had already made buys from Arroyave and Tabares, two of the biggest people they were after. In a few months, if all went well, they'd be ready for a sweeping bust.

This meeting at the Creamery was late. When the toes and fingers were numb, Mike and Rudy decided to dash inside just to get warm, pick up coffee. It would only take a minute. But once inside—"Charlene!"

"Mike!"

"Paula!"

"Michael!"

Cousins. Rudy was used to it. How many first cousins can one man have? There were times it seemed like Central Falls was two-thirds Colombian and one-third Whites and Doughertys. These were Whites.

"This is my partner and my friend, Rudy Legenza," Mike said.

Rudy shook hands with the two women. "We got to be getting right back out, Mike."

"Okay, just a second. I haven't seen Paula and Charlene in years!" The Whites started catching up on family history. "... And then Danny, he's three now," Mike was saying.

"Three!" the woman exclaimed.

"Danny plays Star Wars with Michael, who's six—"

"Uh, Mike," Rudy said. He edged toward the door and looked out. The agent's car was gone! Rudy pushed through the doors and ran around the corner of the building. Gone!

"Mike!" Rudy called. "No car! Let's go!"

They sprinted back out to the lot. All sorts of drastic scenarios were going through Rudy's head. But before they got to the car, they spotted the agent again. He had moved to a spot under a light. Mike and Rudy climbed sheepishly back in their car.

"From now on," Rudy said, "I'll get coffee myself."

Mike had to push his way through the dancers, noise, and smoke of the Sportsman to get back to the john. He was in uniform, in the heavy blue coat and gloves that preserved him in the cold outside. These days he had more reasons than usual to mind his own business outside, but once or twice a night he'd push his way back through the crowd when he had to take a leak. Onstage was a dance band playing rock, rumba & roll.

In the men's room, Mike spied six feet under one of the stall doors. Due to his extensive police training, as he would later say, "I knew something was amiss."

The stall door was unlocked. It pulled right open and brought Mike face-to-face with Walter Alvarez, the Snowman himself, white suit, white shirt, white shoes, white moustache and all. Two men in the stall with Walter pushed out on either side of Mike, who, in his bulky overcoat, nearly filled the doorway. They stopped before fleeing, though, and turned to see what would happen. The Snowman faced Mr. Blanco with a flat-out look of amazement. Cupped in the palm of his right hand was a tiny bit of white powder.

A lot flashed through Mike's mind. Walter was someone he, Rudy, and the DEA wanted. They were already setting him up to see if they could score something big. He didn't want to arrest Walter. Not for the half gram in his hand. So he hesitated, figuring Walter would ditch the coke in the toilet. Then he could throw him against the wall and yell, "If I ever catch you with that again, I'll throw you in jail so fast . . ."

But the Snowman froze. He stood there with the stuff in his hand and gaped. With the others watching, Mike had no choice but to arrest him. As Mike led him through the crowd to the front door, the Snowman's admirers pressed close, dismayed. "Oh, Blanco! What are jou doeen? What are jou doeen with Walter?" Mike shared their chagrin.

After Walter was taken off, Mike sprinted to Kentucky Fried to phone Rudy. The call got him out of bed.

"Rudy, I blew it."

"Blew what?"

"Walter. I arrested Walter Alvarez."

"For what?"

"A half a gram."

Rudy was washing his car in the garage under police headquarters the night the Gomez brothers, Jaime and Jorge, blew themselves up.

"Rudy, you better get over here," the fire captain said on the phone. "You're gonna want to see this."

It was a crisp February night. Rudy's black Chevy Malibu was still wet, shining in the streetlamps, as he drove down blocks of dark tenements to Foundry Street. He saw the hoses when he turned the corner.

In the upstairs apartment, Rudy had to keep moving or the floor would burn through his tennis shoes. Smoke stung his eyes. He held a handkerchief over his mouth and nose. The walls and ceiling were scorched black. The air was choked with smoke and steam. It seemed like the whole place was sweating. And there was this foul odor.

The captain took Rudy back to a bedroom. There was an overturned mattress and bedspring to one side of the room, a dripping bureau on the other. On the bureau was the biggest bag of coke Rudy had ever seen. It must have been a pound. He had never seen much more than a gram. This must have been worth a hundred grand on the street.

In the kitchen, globs of white paste stuck to the floor and walls, and the odor was particularly strong. As they pieced it together later, the Gomez brothers had been working one of the tricks of their trade. Cocaine sold as powder is more readily suspected of having been cut, or diluted, than cocaine in rock form. A quick test can easily measure the purity of either powder or rock, but most small buyers don't carry testing equipment and tend to be in a hurry. So even though the powder in the bedroom tested almost 100 percent pure, the Gomez brothers had been turning it into rocks.

They were mixing powdered coke with acetone (which accounted for the odor) to make a white paste, then warming the paste under heat lamps to evaporate the acetone and harden the paste into snowball-sized rocks. Acetone, however, is highly flammable, and the brothers' lab technique was flawed.

Jaime and Jorge turned themselves in the next morning. Rudy thought, Some people just can't wait to get busted.

* * *

Special agent Pegg Cafolla was a looker. Before joining the DEA, she had worked as a radio reporter in Providence, where she had known Mike's brother. She had thick brown hair and big brown eyes and a street-smart way of talking. She didn't mind a little excitement. This Central Falls assignment was her first.

On the day before the big bust—it was April 16, 1984—Pegg's job was to get back in touch with the two Colombians she'd been buying from for nearly six months, and arrange the big buy for the next day.

Pegg drove to Lincoln that afternoon. She would see Arroyave first. Carlos was a small, scraggly man with deep lines in his face. You could kid around with Carlos, make him laugh. Pegg felt more relaxed with him than with Tabares, who made her nervous. Tabares was a big, broad man, all business. He got pissed if she showed up five minutes late for a meeting. Tabares had these small eyes that were so brown they seemed black. Pegg always felt like he could see right through her, could see DEA stenciled in pink right there on the inside of her skull.

She slowed in front of Arroyave's big brick apartment building, turned down the driveway, and followed it back to the parking lot in the rear. Carlos's apartment was on the first floor. Pegg could feel her heart pounding. Carlos answered the door holding his newborn baby. He smiled, every inch the house-husband, a diaper slung over one shoulder of his blue button-down shirt. He showed Pegg into the living room. All the furniture looked new.

Pegg leaned forward on the sofa, making it clear she did not intend to stay long. Carlos sat down with the baby in the lounge chair.

"I'd like to pick up a key or two tomorrow,' she said, "because, you know, I can move it. I'm going to a party tonight, and I should be able to make arrangements there."

"Well, I won't have two keys until Thursday, when I get another shipment in, but right now I can give you one." His accent was heavy. Since the whole idea was to grab Arroyave with the cocaine, Pegg didn't want to buy now.

"I can't right now, Carlos. I've only got half the money with me."

"I'll tell you what. Why don't you take it anyway, and if you can move it, just pay me tomorrow."

"What time should I come by?"

"How about noon?"

Pegg wanted to avoid making the bust there because of the baby. "Why don't we have lunch," she suggested. "I'll meet you at the Dragon Villa."

"Okay, great."

Arroyave got up, still holding the baby, and walked down a hallway to the bathroom. Pegg walked out to the kitchen. He returned moments later with a blue plastic box. There was a kilo of cocaine packed in a plastic bag inside. Pegg took it out just to turn it over in her hand admiringly. It would be worth as much as several hundred thousand dollars cut and broken down. Pegg promised him $30,000.

Arroyave fetched her a grocery bag, and she walked out without paying a cent. She was still in a mild state of shock when she drove up alongside her partner's car in a shopping-center lot a few miles away. Both agents rolled down their windows.

"Did you order up?" asked Rick Scovel, the other agent.

"Yeah, I ordered up."

"Where do we pick it up?"

"He gave it to me."

"He what?"

Pegg just reached over with the brown bag and dropped it in his lap.

It was still dark the next morning when Rudy picked up Mike. They drove to Providence for the six a.m. meeting.

At DEA headquarters, just across the street from the big gray U.S. courthouse, there was an alphabet of feds—DEA, FBI, U.S. Marshals, and INS agents—and cops from several nearby towns. They sat down in a large conference room. McCarthy explained that they had twelve targets, with Arroyave and Tabares at the top of the list.

A "Class One dealer," in DEA terminology, is someone who handles at least four kilos of coke a month and has at least four people working for him. In the Boston metro area of more than three million people, the DEA could identify ten Class One dealers. In the Central Falls area, population maybe 50,000, they could now identify twenty-five Class One dealers. Ten of the twelve people targeted this day were Class One, McCarthy said. All were likely to be armed and dangerous. The agents were divided into pairs.

Rudy and Mike split up. They would be bit players this day, but they were unquestionably the happiest cops in the room.

Rudy was backup for the Tabares bust. He and his DEA partner waited in a car at one corner of the Almac supermarket lot in Pawtucket and watched as Tabares drove up, right on time at ten a.m., rolling his big white Oldsmobile up alongside Cafolla's car.

"Got it?" Pegg asked.

"Yeah," Tabares answered.

"Do you have another one, Roberto? I really need two."

This had been prearranged. Pegg had ordered a pound from Tabares the day before, but the agents were unsure where he kept his stash. The DEA hoped Tabares would go off and fetch another pound. There were agents around the neighhorhood, to see where he'd go. Mike was in a car outside of Tabares's house.

Tabares took the bait and drove off. When he returned a few minutes later, he was in a different car and was not alone. This time a woman was with him.

Pegg was startled when they pulled up. Tabares stopped his car a few spaces away. The woman in the front seat looked Colombian. Her small features seemed set in stone.

Pegg stepped out of her car and walked around to speak with Tabares. He was nervous. He gestured to the space between him and the woman, to a box wrapped up like a birthday present, with colorful paper, a bow, and balloons. Next to the box was a plain brown paper bag; Pegg assumed this was the second pound.

"Just a sec," she said, and walked back to her car to get the money. She leaned inside to unlock the trunk. Lifting the trunk lid was the signal for backup to start moving in.

Pegg strode directly to Tabares and handed him the money bag, but at just that moment he spotted the cars. He pushed the money bag back into Pegg's hands. His leg went for the accelerator. Seconds went like long minutes for Pegg. She had her gun under her sweater, stuck in the waistband at the small of her back, but she was sweating so much that the cold gun was starting to slide down her pants. Pegg dropped the money bag and drew her gun.

"Get your hands up! *Los policías!*" she shouted. Tabares spoke English, but Pegg had to make this stone-faced woman understand. Tabares's hands shot up. The woman hesitated; one of her hands crept behind her back.

"Get your fuckin' hands up or you're history," Pegg said, hoping her tone would penetrate the language barrier.

Slowly, the woman raised her hands. When Rudy and the others ran up, they found a pistol on the seat behind her.

That was the worst moment of Mike and Rudy's day. The rest was clock-work: ten targets, ten collars. Arroyave surrendered in his car with Pegg's second kilo of cocaine and a hurt look on his face. More searches that day turned up twelve pounds of coke and $105,000 in cash.

It was the money that got to Mike and Rudy, amazed them, even months afterward, even now, a year and a half later, with more than a hundred fifty cocaine arrests on the books in Central Falls, with forty of those major dealers, twenty-four of them convicted (one acquitted), five on the lam out of the country, and more than a hundred cases pending.

Their $200 investigation blew apart the biggest coke center in the Northeast, one of the biggest in the country. It hauled in over a hundred kilos of pure Colombian cocaine. But still, it was the money: it turned out their little town was moving a cool $100 million a year.

And money is what Mike remembers from the day of the big bust. He was in Tabares's bedroom and spotted a thick package, wrapped in duct tape and aluminum foil, under the dealer's dresser. Got to be a kilo, he thought. But when he tore at the edge of the package to peek, he found instead cash, more than he'd ever seen. It counted up to $47,000.

He remembers that number, forty-seven. Later that day, after they'd wrapped it up, he and Rudy invited the feds to a saloon down the street. Flush with Irish goodwill, Mike stepped to the bar and called for beers. He dug in a pocket and pulled out his money—then scanned the poor scatter of coin on the bar. He was exactly forty-seven cents short.

So he had to bum it from Rudy.

Carlos Arroyave was fined $30,000 and is serving a ten-year sentence in federal prison.

Roberto Tabares is serving a nine-year sentence in federal prison.

Walter (the Snowman) Alvarez was convicted of cocaine possession and given a one-year sentence. While in custody, he was convicted of a prior rape charge and sentenced to twenty years in prison.

Jaime Gomez is serving a seven-year sentence in federal prison.

Jorge Gomez is serving a five-year sentence in federal prison.

Mickey Mouse and the American kid on Dexter Street were not prosecuted.

The Colombian who sold the gram to Mickey Mouse was convicted and given a one-year suspended sentence.

Ralph Mott is holding down a steady job. His name was changed in this story to protect his identity.

Special agent Pegg Cafolla is working in Detroit.

Mike White and Rudy Legenza are still patrolling the one square mile of Central Falls, Rhode Island—now with avid cooperation from the DEA, the FBI, the Royal Canadian Mounted Police, and Interpol.

COPS ON
THE TAKE

JULY 1984

This piece was my first extended work of narrative nonfiction, and tells the story of how a major police corruption scandal unfolded in Philadelphia. It ran in four issues of the Inquirer Sunday Magazine. *When the first part appeared, it was illustrated with a cover photograph of a Philadelphia police badge altered to show a row of dollar signs at the bottom instead of a badge number. Large numbers of Philadelphia police marched down Broad Street in front of* The Inquirer *building to protest this defacing of their departmental symbol. It was by far a larger display of outrage than any prompted by the revelations of corrupt police behavior.*

Waiting for the fat man with the moustache on the corner of Thirteenth and Vine, Donald Hersing pulled on a Marlboro and dug his chin deeper into the upturned collar of his tan leather jacket. It was a cold March afternoon, 1981. Out on Vine Street rumbled ten loud lanes of traffic. Steam rising from sewers and manhole lids diffused to a sunny silver sheen and disappeared. From where he stood, shifting his weight from foot to foot on the icy sidewalk, Hersing could look up over three cluttered blocks of rooftops to City Hall, straight to the stone gaze of old William Penn.

The fat man with the moustache had stopped by the new whorehouse on this corner a few afternoons ago. He had spoken to Cinnamon, the manager. He said he was a police detective. He knew what was going on here. If she wanted to do business in Philadelphia, she would have to see the right people, do the right thing. Cinnamon understood. This statuesque, busty redhead had worked in the city a long time. She knew how the game was played. That was why Hersing had hired her.

I don't own the place, she had told the detective, I just run it. You want to talk to Don. She promised to pass the message along.

Hersing was to meet the detective in front of Frank's Tavern, which was next door. Hersing flicked one cigarette to the pavement and lit another. Cinnamon had explained what to expect. He had $300 in his right pants pocket. He hoped that would be enough to keep the heat off his whorehouse, but just in case, he had $200 more in the other pocket. He was cold. Fists of gritty air from passing trucks bumped him off balance and steeped him in the stale odor of spent fuel.

This whole thing annoyed him. Even before it had opened, several weeks earlier, Hersing had lost interest in the whorehouse (or "nude modeling studio," as he preferred to call it). He felt he had been roped into it. During the first weeks he had hardly set foot in the place. There were several reasons for his unease, but the biggest was pride. Pimping didn't fit his self-image. He had no moral qualms. And the idea of easy money was appealing. But Hersing felt irksomely *amateurish,* out of his element. Even if he had liked the idea of being a pimp, he knew, as he put it, "I wouldn't make a pimple on a pimp's ass."

So he had limited his involvement with 1245 Vine Street to stopping in late at night to pick up cash. Cinnamon complained that she might just as well hang the money out on the end of a long stick and let Hersing drive by and grab it, he seemed so loath to enter the place. For practically the whole first year of operation, profits from the whorehouse would primarily go to repay the $20,000 his partner had put up to rent the place and renovate it. Hersing himself was making next to nothing at that point, which contributed mightily to his resentment about even having to drive in each night and pick up the money.

And now this! Was he going to have to deal with the Philadelphia police, too?

These things turned in his mind as he waited for the fat man with the moustache. He longed for his old life in the Caribbean. But Hersing's fond memory of the tropics slipped away as swiftly as his breath, a mingled vapor of smoke and steam, vanished before this gray winter vista of Center City.

His contact pulled up in a blue Chevy Nova. Stepping into the car, Hersing introduced himself to a small round man with a round face and a gruff, up-from-the-streets Philly manner. The detective shook his hand and smiled. He said his name was George Woods. He was a vice officer assigned to the central police division. Woods did most of the talking. He kept telling Hersing to relax. Once things were taken care of, there would be nothing to worry about. Just to make conversation, Hersing asked him about the car, and Woods told him that it was a standard city police under-cover vehicle.

Woods drove to a diner at Fifth and Spring Garden Streets. The diner was a classic affair, a chrome car with horizontal red stripes set on a brick base. Inside, business was easing toward the slow middle of afternoon. The air was still heavy with the odor of a hundred quick lunches. The two men slid into a booth of slick turquoise Naugahyde. There were mini-jukes beside each green Formica table, but the rock music that filled this joint jangled from a small radio a waitress had perched up on the wall of steel kitchenry behind the counter. Hersing ordered a cup of coffee.

He sipped it as the vice officer explained how things would go. The scam was as old as police work. There would have to be busts. But if Hersing paid up each month, Woods would make it easy on him. It sounded like a good deal. It would be wrong to say that Hersing had expected this, but none of what Woods said surprised him. He didn't know the ropes in Philadelphia well, but Woods evidently did. Hersing listened with interest as the detective explained that the district attorney's office did not bother prosecuting prostitutes. It was a waste of time and tax dol-lars. Whoring never earned trials or convictions, but arrests alone were serious harassment. The threat of arrest was enough to discourage ama-teurs. A full-scale brothel bust would close down business for at least a day, and might send half of the shop in for booking. Whores might wait for hours in a jail cell before their pimp showed up to bail them out. It meant costly delays and attorneys' fees, and it tended to frighten off the clientele.

There was pressure from above for arrests, Woods explained, but if Hersing cooperated, Woods could satisfy his inspector with a minimal disruption of business. When it was time for a bust, he would simply tip off 1245 Vine Street, and Hersing and Cinnamon could pick a prostitute to take the pinch. Woods would arrest the woman and see to it that she was booked and released as quickly as possible. That would cost a few dollars more. Later, the case would be dismissed. They always were. Hersing dubbed the system "Dial-a-Bust."

Woods took out a pen and scribbled something on a napkin. He pushed it across the table.

"This is how much," he said.

It said $500. Hersing passed Woods $300 under the table. Outside in the Nova, on the way back to Vine, he reached into the other pocket and gave him the rest. Then Woods dropped him off in front of the studio.

Such was Donald Hersing's introduction to the City of Brotherly Love.

It offended him. Didn't they know who Donald Hersing was? Didn't they know he wasn't their average sucker pimp? Didn't they know he was a man who took law enforcement seriously? That he was *not* the sort of man they ought to be pushing around?

Even his best friends saw Donald Hersing as a peculiar, boastful character with shadowy connections. He had a new get-rich-quick scheme every week. The schemes usually involved other people's money.

Hersing was forty-six years old. At times, to look at him, he seemed much older than that, and at other times he seemed younger. It depended on his mood, or maybe on how many beers he had the night before. He was only of medium height, but he managed to look gangly. His arms and legs were long and thin, but his belly was wide. He walked balanced back on his heels, gut first, his long arms beating a wide cadence by his sides. Hersing favored casual knit pullover shirts and double-knit trousers with flared cuffs that he tended to wear too short, so that when he sat down his calves in black hose jutted up, as thin as table legs, from boots that reached just over his ankles. His head was small in proportion to the rest of his body. Hersing's light brown hair was cut short and parted on the left side. His face angled in two deep furrows down his cheeks, ending in a narrow, receding chin. His skin was pink. It was lightly pocked from some childhood skin disease. Hersing still had exquisitely sensitive skin. Overnight an infection could blow up his hands or his feet with little bumps or deep red blotches. He was a chain smoker and an erratic eater. Most days, he looked unhealthy.

Hersing grew up during World War II, which was not a happy time to be German-American in Trenton, New Jersey. The fourth of five children, he was born in 1934. His father, who kept his fluent German to himself, ran a restaurant. His mother worked as a dietitian at the state hospital in Skillman. Hersing attended Immaculate Conception grammar school and Trenton Catholic High, where he is remembered by classmates as a "cocky kid" who played football and basketball and seemed fascinated by gadgets and police work. He was addicted to "Dick Tracy," and even sent away for a correspondence course on fingerprint identification. He would point to the space-age gizmos featured in the comic strip—the two-way wrist radios and so forth—and tell his friends that someday these things would exist.

But what Hersing remembers most is not fitting in. Hardy homefront heroes in the township passed an ordinance restricting the liberties of German-Americans. They were not allowed, for instance, to own short-wave radios—nobody was going to beam to Berlin any delicate wartime secrets from the basements of Trenton, New Jersey. Hersing's father didn't own a shortwave radio anyway, but the ordinance worked its effect. Children at his school taunted him and his brothers and sisters, calling them "Nazis"—"You know, my father used to talk to Hitler every night, that kind of mentality." He fought with the children who called him names.

It was, perhaps, partly out of a desire to prove himself that Hersing forged his mother's signature on documents to enter the Marine Corps when he was only sixteen. He stayed in for three years and liked it, he says, but was discharged when he began suffering migraine headaches. After leaving the Marines he married and went to work for a friend's father who owned a car dealership in New Jersey. At the time, American dealers were making good money selling cars to GIs stationed in Germany. When he was offered a chance to go over as a salesman, Hersing jumped. The idea of foreign travel excited him. And he had extended family in that country, in Frankfurt and Wiesbaden. His employer sent him to a Berlitz language school, where he picked up German quickly—partly, he figures, because his father had spoken the language around the house when Hersing was a small child. He stayed in Germany with his wife and young son for six years.

Although he lacked college credentials, Hersing had accumulated his own odd international education by the time he returned to the Trenton area in the early 1960s. He prided himself on being smarter than most people suspected, which enabled him, he thought, to see through people, people who were cheating him or sneaking behind his back. He moved his family across the river to Levittown when he took a job in a dairy, and a few years later went to work for a tile factory. But these more conventional jobs bored him. His real fascination was still police work. He wanted to be a detective, a man who finds people and figures things out. But to be a detective, first he would have to wear a uniform and work his way through the ranks of a local police department. That held little appeal. And he wouldn't make as much in uniform as he did in the tile factory.

So he found his own way into police work. At the time, the Bucks County jail would issue "body receipts" for prisoners who had escaped or defendants who had skipped bail. If you could find those fugitives, the body receipts could be cashed in with local bonding companies, which were out a lot of money for every bail-jumper on their books. Hersing was good at it. He paid his own expenses, sometimes traveling to different states in search of his man. He says he found it easy to find people. "They don't realize it, but people leave tracks," he says. "Once you know where to look, it's pretty easy to find them." The hardest part was capturing a man once Hersing found him. He couldn't enlist the help of local police. Usually the charges were too small and too distant for them to intervene; besides, Hersing would lose his commission. So he devised his own methods. He would send a telegram, and then wait for his target to show up at the Western Union office to pick it up. Hersing usually carried a gun. He didn't mind describing himself to people as a bounty hunter. It sounded dangerous. And the work was occasionally lucrative. He cashed in some body receipts for as much as $6,000. Just for a few days' work.

Bounty hunting led to full-time private detective work. Hersing worked on accident investigations, divorce cases, and internal investigations for companies in the Levittown area. He even tracked down AWOL soldiers to collect commissions from the FBI. Hersing inhabited two worlds, one foot on either side of the law. He had a sweet tooth for the night life, for the bars and whores and pornography stores. He even opened a bar and lounge, which closed after he was arrested and subsequently convicted on bad check charges. But he also had friends on the other side of the law, in the courthouse and in the local Bucks County police departments. He kept odd personal hours, usually sleeping during the day, and seemed to work very little. He was not a person to be relied on for punctuality or for keeping small promises. He loved to tell stories about himself, and had a way of telling them that accented his own importance, or bravery, or intelligence, as if he were always trying to *convince* people. Those who knew him well recognized enough truth in the stories Hersing told not to dismiss them altogether. Seated in the corner of a seedy bar with his standard sixteen-ounce can of Pabst, Hersing might look like a drunk. At times he cultivated that image. But there was more to him than that. He could be savvy and articulate and when he talked one always sensed that he was sitting there beside himself watching himself, and quietly sizing up whomever he was talking to. The local police detectives and FBI agents considered Hersing a valuable contact, somebody who moved comfortably in places they could not easily go, who could find things out that no one else knew.

So Donald Hersing became the sort of man with whom everyone worked, but whom no one wanted, officially, to know. He saw himself as a freelance law enforcement expert. He took college courses in criminal investigation techniques and learned how to use sophisticated electronic surveillance equipment. Like most men given to self-aggrandizing talk, Hersing was full of self-aggrandizing notions. He read *Soldier of Fortune,* a magazine full of stories about mercenaries and spies, and—seeing himself as a sort of international figure—longed for international adventure.

Hersing sought adventures of his own. In the early 1970s, through contacts at a company in Conshohocken, Pennsylvania, named Criminal Research Products, Hersing was introduced to a whole network of American companies that manufacture sophisticated police equipment, things like fingerprinting kits, lie detectors, fluoroscopic investigating kits, and electronic eavesdropping equipment, all the stuff he had fantasized about as a kid. These firms published catalogues of the stuff, which read like *Fascisti* wish lists. Though it wasn't always legal to export these things, arrangements could be made. With help from contacts he made in Philadelphia and New York through the Conshohocken company, Hersing began pursuing sales leads in the Caribbean and in Central and South America. His first trip was to San Juan in 1976, when the Puerto Rican government inquired about electronic beeping devices that attach to car bumpers, making a car easier to follow. Hersing flew down to demonstrate the equipment and teach them how to use it.

His contacts spread rapidly. While he was in San Juan on one of his early trips, he was contacted by representatives of the rightist government of Dr. Joaquin Balaguer in the Dominican Republic, which was also interested in the bugging equipment he had brought down. His relationship with the Balaguer regime blossomed. For two years, Hersing maintained a home in Santo Domingo. He learned to speak Spanish, and enjoyed the advantages of living well in a poor country—he was able to rent a fine home and employ, for a pittance, a staff of servants. He taught the Dominican police how to use the equipment he sold. Through the late 1970s, Hersing felt that he had become the soldier of fortune he wanted to be. He traveled extensively, carrying his catalogues and trunks of equipment so prized by governments with strong enemies among their own people—to Colombia, Peru, Bolivia, and Ecuador. As he was ushered hurriedly past customs officials in seedy alien airports, in his hushed meetings with *generalissimos,* Hersing was living a life he had only dreamed about back in Bucks County.

Sometimes his wife and son lived with him in Santo Domingo, but they kept their home in Levittown. Hersing was often away for months at a time. When he was in Levittown, Hersing enjoyed the new aura of international mystery that surrounded him. A lot of people just assumed that he was working for the CIA, and Hersing, in so many words, encouraged the notion. He might have been. He was certainly in a position that the CIA would have found interesting. But, again, Hersing had one foot in each world. He had the contacts of an international spy, but he was working primarily for himself.

When Balaguer lost power in 1978, Hersing's exciting new life began to unravel. Investments he had arranged for financial backers at home soured. The more socialist government in the Dominican Republic refused to honor contracts made by the Balaguer regime. He made fewer and fewer tropical excursions. Soon he was back in Levittown permanently. Then his marriage fell apart. By 1979, Hersing was living alone, unemployed, bored, and in debt.

But he stayed busy, in his own way. The subject of whorehouses first came up in the fall of 1980. During his Caribbean period, Hersing had met William Robertshaw, a construction contractor in Princeton, New Jersey.

Robertshaw flew down to visit Hersing in Santo Domingo, and had invested in some of his friend's projects there. When the deals fell through in 1978, Robertshaw lost a bundle—he estimates about $30,000. It was this loss that the two men were feeling when they decided to open the whorehouse in Philadelphia.

The idea came, at least indirectly, from Cinnamon. Hersing had met Cinnamon, whose real name was Mary Angeli, in a Bristol Township pornographic bookstore, where she was managing a small prostitution business in the back room. Through her, he had become acquainted with Philadelphia's flourishing underworld of strippers, pornographers, pimps, prostitutes, and swingers. One day that fall Hersing remembers showing Robertshaw an ad in *The Philadelphia Journal* for a "nude modeling studio," a place where he says his friend Cinnamon had once worked. The ad featured a saucily smiling woman in a bikini and spiked heels. Both men were impressed by how openly the studio was advertising. And there were quite a few other ads like it in *The Journal.*

It was Robertshaw who suggested getting into the whorehouse business, as Hersing recalls. "He said it must be very lucrative. Bill Robertshaw had a good brain when it comes to money. He said, 'Look at the size of those ads! Can you imagine what they cost? They must cost about five hundred dollars each! They must make big money to do that. Why don't you open one of them up.'"

At first Hersing didn't act on the suggestion. He had no experience running any kind of business, much less a nude modeling studio. But then, about a month later, Hersing says, Robertshaw asked him about it again. The man was serious. So—what the hell? Hersing was unemployed anyway. He and Cinnamon went down to Philadelphia and found a building. It was a three-story corner townhouse on the north side of Vine Street, within walking distance of the city's commercial center but far enough away so that men could come and go inconspicuously.

He and Robertshaw signed a lease and went to work. Robertshaw sent down a crew of carpenters to spruce up the place. They divided the first floor into seven rooms. There was a reception area in front, complete with Polaroid cameras—Cinnamon said there were always a few weirdos who really did want to take pictures. Behind that were six "session" rooms. Each room had a mattress on an elevated platform, a chair, a lamp, and a table.

Upstairs were showers for the girls and a phone. They boarded up windows and painted the exterior of the house with an odd flesh tone Cinnamon had picked out. Gold carpeting went down. Fake wood paneling went up.

Despite his reservations about managing whores, Hersing was impressed. The place was, he thought, no dump. It would cater to an above-average clientele, and should do a good business. But right away the negatives began to outweigh everything else. It was clear to him that Cinnamon was really in charge. She was, after all, better qualified. As soon as he had introduced her to Robertshaw, Cinnamon more or less took over. She talked Robertshaw into paying for fine details of furnishing that Hersing considered extravagant. Just days before the studio was to open, it occurred to Hersing that he didn't even know where to find whores. Cinnamon told him not to worry, she would take care of that, too. Hersing felt unnecessary.

Besides, he still had his law enforcement work. He was still a private detective. That was the kind of work that really excited him. One of his clients was Cinnamon. She had hired him in the summer of 1979 to help her deal with a local patrolman named Joseph Minnichbach who she felt was harassing her.

Hersing placed a tape recorder under Cinnamon's bed in a local hotel. As he tells it, Cinnamon then arranged for Patrolman Minnichbach to have a liaison there with a prostitute. The recorded evidence led Hersing's friend, Bristol Township police chief John Tegzes, to fire the officer. The episode caused a scandal in the township that was still raging. Hersing had gotten a degree of satisfaction out of the case that was hard to explain.

It was not the first time he had felt that way. He had been gratified in the same way eight years before, when he had helped the FBI and Tegzes, then a detective, with an internal probe that led, in 1976, to the indictment of three township detectives for illegal wiretapping—one man pleaded guilty, another pleaded no contest, and charges were eventually dropped against the third. Hersing liked catching bad cops. There was something especially pleasurable about it.

Over the years, especially as his own unorthodox "law enforcement" experience grew, Donald Hersing had developed a peculiar love-hate relationship with police. Official law enforcement agencies, like the cliques of youths who had called him "Nazi" as a child, would never consider him one of their rank. It bothered him. He wanted to be recognized by them as at least an equal, if not for the expert he believed himself to be. Here was a man who spoke three languages fluently, who taught classes in other nations on how to use police equipment, whom the local police and the FBI had been coming to for years in his hometown when they needed help. Few things disturbed Hersing more than to be treated like an ignorant criminal, or to be taken for a sucker.

So it had especially disturbed Hersing when he was notified, at about the time he returned from the Dominican Republic, that he was being investigated on smuggling charges. U.S. Customs officials were looking into some shipments of wiretap and polygraph equipment, semiautomatic rifles, and tear gas that Hersing had arranged while he was in Santo Domingo. To try to help himself, Hersing volunteered to assist with a federal investigation of the mob in Bucks County. That was dangerous work. Some of the people under investigation had been known to kill. Compared to this, the Bristol Township sting was a prank. Hersing hoped that if he helped the FBI enough, the Bureau would get the potential smuggling charges against him dropped.

He tried hard. But in January 1981, a group of U.S. Customs agents knocked on his door in the dead of night and arrested him. He had been indicted by the U.S. attorney's office and a federal grand jury in Philadelphia. Hersing was furious, but, more significantly, he was insulted. Didn't they know who Donald Hersing was?

"Those customs agents were asses, complete asses," Hersing says. "They were totally incompetent—and I'm not saying that out of bitterness. I mean, they couldn't use a camera, they didn't know how to take fingerprints. The tape recorder wasn't running for thirty-five minutes when they were interviewing me. And, then, the ability to separate people, see. If you're an investigator, you know when you're talking to a 'strapper'—we call 'em a 'strapper,' an asshole—and when you're talking to a guy who has technical knowledge, who really is experienced in the field of police work. You talk to him different than you talk to the average guy.

"And you don't insult him, because you know when he gets back up, he can hurt you."

* * *

Everybody called George Woods "Georgie" or "Woodsie." He was round. He had grown fat serving the people of Philadelphia, but, at thirty-nine, Georgie was still dapper and had a sometimes comic flair. His face, like his body, seemed as wide as it was long. His round cheeks and double chin framed small features: a nose fitted close to his face, small eyes, small mouth. Georgie had a rakish dimple in the middle of his chin, and a trim moustache on either side of the wide dip at the middle of his upper lip. He combed his thick brown hair back into what would have been a ducktail if it were long enough in the back.

Georgie knew the streets of Philadelphia. He had grown up on them, and had spent most of his fourteen years in the police department patrolling them in uniform. He had faced scrapes. In 1971, patrolling up in the Northeast, he had stopped to shoo two boys who were loitering in a shopping center at Red Lion Road. In the argument that ensued, one of the boys tore a radio antenna from a car and beat Woods severely with it until the patrolman managed to draw his revolver and shoot him in the thigh. Five years later, in the Woodhaven Apartments in the Northeast, Woods and his partner coolly confronted and then shot to death a man with a shotgun who had taken a hostage aboard an old bus. Woods was a tough cop, but a likable guy who could see humor in even a bad situation. He had been transferred to the central police division as a vice detective exactly one year before 1245 Vine Street opened for business, so he knew his way around the neighborhood. He saw himself as a kind of pavement philosopher, a cop who was nevertheless one of the street people his job required him to police. He would say things like "What was said to me, was said to *me*," with a wink intended to convey exactly what that meant, though others weren't always sure.

It is not surprising for a kind of conspiratorial camaraderie to develop between vice detectives and the pimps, prostitutes, numbers runners, and two-bit bar owner/gambling impresarios they are supposed to harass. Often a guy like Georgie Woods has more in common with the common folks than with the stern office faces at headquarters demanding a certain number of busts—enough to match last year's totals, but, for God's sake, not too many, *we don't want to be settin' precedents here, Woodsie.* Prudes and heavies don't get assigned to vice; they couldn't stomach it. To know what's going on in the whorehouses and bars means *mingling* in the whorehouses and bars, and, face it, not all of these people are altogether bad. There are cops in Philadelphia who remember the neighborhood numbers man as maybe the one person on the block who would lend their family money for groceries when things got tight. And cops are human, too. Prostitutes make it their business to be alluring, and pornography does have its appeal. You get friendly with a bar owner, and . . . What? You gonna bust him for paying off a handful of quarters when somebody wins a hand on the video poker machine?

Georgie Woods inhabited a dark and often tempting world. People were making big money peddling flesh and porn. The district attorney wasn't prosecuting it. That, from where Georgie stood, looked like a tacit endorsement, or at least an admission that there was no getting rid of it anyway. So the only control the city exercised over vice was the threat of arrest. This made Georgie Woods a kind of power in the Center City sleaze districts. He could pick whom to bust and when. If you were on his good side, maybe most weeks he would look the other way.

And Georgie was modestly ambitious. He had a wife and kids at home, and his youth was plumping quickly to middle age. Slipping Georgie a regular portion of the ill-gotten gains was one surefire way of staying on his good side. And Georgie, who could hurt you, could also be real pleasant.

In March of '81, Philadelphia was thawing out of an exceptionally cold, white winter. More than the weather had been bleak. Ronald Reagan was slashing federal funds for social service and employment programs vital to big Northeastern cities. Philadelphia's transit workers were preparing to walk off the job. Even the anticipated return of the world champion Phillies was clouded by an imminent ballplayers' strike. At JFK International Airport in New York, police apprehended an unemployed South Philadelphia longshoreman named Joey Coyle. Coyle had a one-way ticket to Acapulco and $165,000 stuffed in his new cowboy boots. Police had been searching for him for weeks, ever since two million-dollar money bags had dropped out of the back of an armored car and into Coyle's lap. For a few weeks, fugitive Coyle's stupendous luck and daring flight had captured the collective imagination of a struggling town.

The whorehouse at 1245 Vine was in its first months of operation, and business was good. Cinnamon ran the place strictly. Each prostitute paid for a weekly medical checkup to ensure against venereal disease. She kept six women working eight-hour shifts. Each whore paid $25 per shift. Customers paid the house $25 for a photo session. Whatever else was exchanged in the back rooms was between them. On a good night, Hersing would pick up $700. Even on slow nights, the total was rarely less than $400. Out of that came upkeep, rent, a $150 weekly salary for Cinnamon, and money to repay Robertshaw's initial investment.

What was left over was enough to prompt Hersing and Robertshaw and a few other partners to invest even more heavily in vice. They opened a smaller whorehouse "modeling studio" at 2209 Walnut Street, and started a private club called the Morning Glory on Vine Street, two blocks west of the place Cinnamon ran. With three operations to oversee, Hersing spent a lot of time in Philadelphia. He often took a room overnight in the Holiday Inn at Fourth and Arch Streets.

His Walnut Street studio was like a discount version of 1245 Vine Street. Up a quick flight of stairs from the sidewalk, it had a cramped waiting room with two chairs and a magazine rack stuffed with well-thumbed back issues of *Hustler* and *Sports Illustrated*. Doors to the session rooms were just two arm-lengths from the chairs. The manager sat behind a small desk in a closet-sized room to the right, directing traffic like the receptionist in a dentist's office.

The Morning Glory was in a two-story rowhouse of orange brick that was boarded up in front with plain brown panels, notable to the eye only because it bore along its western edge a long hand-lettered vertical sign, an anachronism, advertising "Rizzo for Mayor." It was sandwiched between a delicatessen named The Bonanza on the corner and a bar named Doc Watson's. The club got around having to acquire a liquor license by admitting only members, who consisted mostly of *Inquirer* and *Daily News* printers and truckers whose odd shifts brought them in and out from late afternoon until the blue hours of morning.

The club caught on quickly. It was quite a bacchanal. Patients in beds at Hahnemann Hospital, which towered over the south side of Vine on that block, could look down from their windows and see a steady parade of men in work clothes going in and out of the building with the plain brown door and the big "Rizzo for Mayor" sign on top. Although the activities in the building had nothing to do with the former mayor, there was enough traffic in and out to spark rumors that Rizzo was plotting a comeback. Inside, the club's video poker machine offered more than a free game for a winning hand. On a small stage, some of the girls from Cinnamon's stable performed hugely successful acts of indecent entertainment. One of the *Inquirer* truckers, a stocky fellow with curly hair and a great bull belly, had even become a regular part of the show. Each night, naked, he would take turns whipping and being whipped by the female performers. He would soothe his welts in the whirlpool bath at the Philadelphia Athletic Club a block away, where he had become infamous as "the porno king," and then bounce back for more every night. The Morning Glory had a special arrangement with uniformed central division police, Hersing says. It was paying $75 per week to be allowed to keep serving after the 3 a.m. curfew for selling alcoholic beverages.

And there was still Georgie. By the time Hersing met Woods in April for the second payoff, he had to discuss buying protection for two whorehouses. They met on the littered sidewalk in front of the old Broadwood Hotel building on Broad Street. Hersing paid Woods $500 as they walked around the block. They would give the Walnut Street brothel a month or two to get on its feet.

During April they had a Dial-a-Bust. It worked like a charm, but it was more costly than Woods had explained. Woods said he needed $75 "grease" money to speed the prostitute through booking—$25 for the sergeant and $50 for a judge's assistant. Then there were $300 in attorneys' fees to get the charges dismissed. Hersing even had to pay a $100 bonus to get a whore to volunteer for the fall! Then, in May, Woods set $300 a month as the price for protecting 2209 Walnut Street. The first payment for that whorehouse would come due in June.

Hersing didn't like it. He was supposed to be running this business, but it felt as if the business—the whores and now the cops—were running him. As the weeks went by, he went from feeling put upon to feeling pinched. Woods was bruising his pride at the same time he was picking his pocket. It wasn't enough that the detective kept upping the ante; he was also making life difficult with his Dial-a-Busts. It was insulting. Deep inside, Donald Hersing, international law enforcement expert, was seething.

"I just couldn't believe that they were so open about it!" says Hersing. "The way they squeezed ya! It pissed me off twice as much. We were paying right and left, and they were still harassing us with busts. Cinnamon didn't like it. At one point when they called up demanding a girl for a sacrifice, because Woodsie needed a bust that night, Cinnamon just closed the place up and ran away! All the girls beat it out the back door. Who likes getting arrested, man? You got to sit around down at the station house all night. You lose money. Aletia, the Spanish girl they arrested one night, they wanted to take her out drinking first. She said, 'Hey, man, I got to make some money! Take me to the jail and get me out! I gotta get back to work!'"

So after making only the first two payoffs, Hersing called an old FBI contact in Bucks County, Chick Sabinson, and told him what was going on. Sabinson referred him to the Philadelphia FBI office, where Hersing was identified as "a longtime Bucks County informant." He was assigned to two young agents who happened to be available, Mike Thompson and Andy Lash.

Thompson is a friendly, loquacious former Air Force pilot who has preserved intact his honey-sweet, down-home North Carolina accent. He is solidly built with a tawny complexion and dark hair. The brown eyes under his thick eyebrows betray a lively sense of fun. Lash, who joined the FBI right out of college, is the more soft-spoken of the two. Where Thompson is puckish, Lash is pensive. Where Thompson is dark and solid, Lash is pale and slight. They are friends, and their personalities balance nicely. Lash is from Seattle. When they met Donald Hersing, Thompson was thirty-four years old. Lash was only twenty-eight. Neither man had been assigned to Philadelphia for two full years.

They met Hersing for the first time on May 4, 1981. Their first impression of him was lousy; he was definitely not the sort of man they would invite home to dinner. But when they came to know him better, they were surprised by certain things. They were surprised by the extent of his past work and associations—he didn't seem all that sophisticated, but he knew a lot. And despite his lifestyle and associations, they were surprised to find that Hersing was also a loving family man. Hersing had settled down with a warm and friendly woman who would soon become his second wife. She had two small children from an earlier marriage whom Hersing treated as his own. They maintained, at least on the surface, a normal suburban existence: two cars in the garage and a small boat docked at the Jersey Shore. When the agents met Hersing's son from his first marriage, now college-age, they were impressed: "Obviously a boy who cared for his father, and who was well brought up," Thompson says.

During the two years they worked with Hersing, Thompson and Lash found out a lot of contradictory things about their informant. He could be maddeningly unreliable, untrustworthy, boastful, and stubborn, but he had a real talent for playing his undercover role and an extraordinarily precise memory. What's more, they *liked* him. And he was damned effective.

At their first meeting, however, this chain-smoking operator struck them as odd and unsavory. The story he told sounded typical. Their office already had information that Philadelphia police were extorting money from gay bars in the city. And there was a much more promising investigation soon to begin concerning information that certain police were taking money to allow petty gambling with video poker machines in city bars. Hersing's case sounded to Thompson and Lash like an isolated instance, a maverick vice officer lining his pockets in a not-particularly-novel sort of way. And they were curious about Hersing's motives. It didn't make sense. The man seemed to be profiting from the arrangement he had with this Georgie Woods. Why was he offering to trap him?

Hersing wasted no time in explaining his law enforcement credentials to Thompson and Lash. "Right from the start, he was sure he knew how to conduct this investigation better than we did," Thompson says, chuckling at a memory that is comical only in retrospect. Hersing seemed eager to get started, which was unusual. The agents were more used to leaning on a source, coercing cooperation. "We had nothing to force him to help us," says Thompson. "He came to us on his own. It was obvious that Don *liked* doing these sorts of things. He *liked* tape-recording people. He *liked* being part of an investigation. We took him at his word. He said he hated dirty cops. Whatever his reasoning was, as far as we were concerned he was a private citizen who was willing to help. And that was good enough for us."

So the agents got permission from their headquarters and from the U.S. attorney's office to employ Hersing as an informant and to place a tape recorder on his telephone.

It was the beginning of what would become one of the biggest police corruption scandals in any city's history. Two years later, twenty-three Philadelphia police officers, including the second-highest-ranking member of the force, would be under indictment. Some of the toughest and most popular officers in the department would be in jail. The FBI would be opening doors that led down dark, greedy corridors of police power. They would uncover corruption so deeply rooted that it could only have evolved over decades, perhaps even generations. They would discover that many city police officers considered it their due to receive payoffs from petty criminals, that they regarded such money as the rightful spoils of the arrest powers they wielded on city streets.

It was a system ripe for scandal. And it was about to be cut down because of one proud, unsavory man, a seedy bar and brothel owner, who—for his own reasons—got fed up.

Don Hersing contacted someone else on or around May 4. After what he felt was the double-cross he got from the FBI on his smuggling charge (he had pleaded no contest in January and, in April, had been sentenced to three years' probation) Hersing was taking no chances.

When he had worked with Bristol Township police chief John Tegzes, Hersing got to know a reporter for the *Trenton Times* named Stryker Meyer. Meyer was in his early thirties, a blue-eyed man with a boyish mop of brown hair who went by the nickname "Tilt." A Vietnam veteran, Tilt Meyer had been around a bit more than most reporters his age. He was the kind of reporter cops liked, not the effete college-boy type who usually wrote them up. Meyer had a hardbitten, cynical quality. He considered information wrong until proven otherwise. Hersing liked him. Meyer seemed like just the sort of guy whom Hersing might want to have write down some of his exploits someday.

On a cold evening that month, Hersing was sitting in a car with Meyer outside Bristol Township police headquarters. Meyer was pumping Hersing for details about Cinnamon and the township cop she had tape-recorded. Suddenly Hersing said, "You want to hear a *real* story?"

Meyer said yes, and Hersing started telling him about the work he had begun in Philadelphia.

"I work for the *Trenton Times*," Meyer told Hersing. "I couldn't care less about a police corruption investigation in Philadelphia."

But the more Meyer insisted that he didn't care to know, the more Hersing seemed intent on telling him the story.

"He was worried the FBI wasn't going to pay him, or that they would just drop the investigation and leave him hanging," Meyer says. "He was worried he was going to be caught and killed. I told him if he was really afraid for his life, then he ought to have someone completely outside the government who knew what was going on. The original idea was that I would write a story about the Philadelphia thing only if something went wrong. At least that way he wouldn't just vanish one day without anyone suspecting what happened. I even promised I would go to Washington with the guy and stand by him, if it came to that."

FBI Tape #1:

"This is Special Agent Michael W. Thompson. The date is June 1, 1981. The time is 11:47 a.m. I have placed a recording device on telephone number 923-8660, extension 7527, located in room 527, Holiday Inn, Fourth and Arch Streets, Philadelphia, Pennsylvania, for the purpose of monitoring calls between PH 721-OC [an FBI code number identifying Hersing] and Detective George Woods of the Philadelphia Police Department."

The phone rings.

"Central police division, Officer Pezzano."

"Is George Woods there?" Hersing asks.

"George Woods? Yes. He's here. Hold on."

"Thank you."

Woods's voice comes on. "Hello. Can I help you?"

"Georgie!"

"Yeah."

"Roger." Hersing gives Woods the code name they used.

"How are you?"

"How are you, Georgie?"

"Fine. Fine."

"How was your weekend?"

"Okay."

"Okay? I haven't seen you in a while."

"Yeah, I know."

"When you wanna meet?"

"Four. Three-thirty."

"I can't make it today. Can you make it tomorrow, Georgie?"

"Sure. When?"

"Anytime in the afternoon. You know I'm not morning people."

"Eh, two-thirty?"

"Two-thirty. Where at?"

"At the, ah, restaurant."

"Okay."

"See ya."

"See you, George. Bye."

June 1, 1981, was the day John DeBenedetto took over command of the central police division.

It covered everything between the Delaware River and the Schuylkill River, from Poplar Street down to South Street, all of William Penn's original city. The central division is the plum front-line police job in Philadelphia. Cut into two districts right down the middle by Broad Street, Central includes decaying black and Hispanic neighborhoods to the north and the meticulously preserved historic redbrick districts of Society Hill to the south. At its core are the vital avenues of commerce, legitimate and illegitimate, that crowd into a few square miles around City Hall. In the eastern Sixth District are Independence Hall, the Liberty Bell, and the revitalized riverfront plazas of Penn's Landing. In the western Ninth District are many of the city's most prestigious financial institutions and law offices. Around the tan brick Ninth District building at 20th Street and Pennsylvania Avenue, which serves as division headquarters, are the wide, landscaped ovals and parks that sweep west toward Fairmount, the spot from which the Philadelphia Museum of Art surveys Center City. Central division encompasses nearly all of what most people traditionally mean when they say Philadelphia, past and present, rich and poor, beautiful and ugly, good and bad.

There were more than four hundred uniformed officers assigned to police this area. Each district was supervised by a captain, who was assigned four lieutenants and four sergeants. In addition to the regular organization, there were a number of special squads. Enforcement of vice laws got special attention in central division, because it was where prostitution, porn, and gambling were most heavily concentrated. There was a separate lieutenant in charge of vice operations, and a four-officer vice squad (one of them George Woods) whose job it was to root out vice on the streets.

Commanding it all was the inspector. Center City was John DeBenedetto's fief. The top post at Central was a perfect place for an ambitious cop to prove himself and get ahead. It was also the best place for a crooked cop to get rich.

Inside Central headquarters, in one of his first days on the job, the new division commander assembled all of his nonuniformed men, including George Woods, and explained a few things. If there was any protection money being collected, the new man said, he wanted to know about it. Pronto.

DeBenedetto had a tough reputation, with the manner and frame to match. Woods and the other men knew that he recently served as a staff inspector in the department's internal affairs division. DeBenedetto didn't care to be popular. He wasn't above boasting about the number of badges he had collected in that job, nailing policemen who didn't play by the rules. So the new boss had everyone's ear when he explained the way the game was gonna be played. *All* protection money was to be passed up to him. He would spread it around accordingly. From where Georgie Woods sat, DeBenedetto's system meant the end of a good thing. What with Central's eight lieutenants and eight or nine sergeants above him, and the other vice squad guys, whatever payoffs made it down to his pocket would be just a fraction of what he was collecting on his own. Woods kept his mouth shut.

The Georgie Woods empire was not going to volunteer its own throat.

The Chuckwagon Restaurant was on the first floor of the old Broadwood Hotel, three blocks north of City Hall on Broad Street. It was a sixteen-story maroon brick building, its rooms empty, the hotel having shut down years ago. It was set directly across the street from the sad, broken-down shell of the old Philadelphia Record building and the gothic spires of Roman Catholic High School. For some reason having to do with poor street cleaning habits and airflow at street level in that part of town, paper trash, dirt, and debris seemed to accumulate under the brown marquee in front of the hotel. Pedestrians walking in front of it had to dodge small whirlwinds of trash, and squint to keep the blowing dirt out of their eyes. Just down the block was a badly graffitied Broad Street subway entrance. From the shadows below wafted up the potent odor of urine. In the basement of the old brick building were the swimming pool, handball courts, gymnasium, and saunas of the Philadelphia Athletic Club. The club's name was spelled out in an elaborate mosaic tile on the lobby floor, encircling a portrait of Atlas struggling with the weight of the world. Just off this lobby, to the immediate right of Atlas, was the Chuckwagon. It was a good spot for a quick cafeteria-style lunch, and it had cold beer and wine in its coolers.

Earlier in the afternoon, before keeping his appointment with Woods, Hersing had met Thompson and Lash at the Holiday Inn on Fourth Street. They had wanted to strap a small Nagra tape recorder under his shirt, but Hersing didn't want to wear it. He was worried that Woods would search him. The agents managed to talk him into putting it on, but when Hersing drove past the hotel on Broad Street he saw that Woods was waiting for him with another man. Woods had never brought along anyone else before.

This spooked Hersing. There were agents positioned at tables inside the Chuckwagon, and Thompson and Lash were staked out nearby. But Hersing didn't like the way things looked. He drove on up a few blocks and turned the corner. Then he stopped at the first telephone booth and called the FBI office. He spoke to John Anderson, Thompson and Lash's supervisor, and explained the situation. He asked if he could take the recorder off. Anderson told him to go ahead. So Hersing took off the recorder and left it in his car.

The man with Woods turned out to be Ray Emery, his partner. Emery was younger than Woods. He looked to be in his early thirties. He was about the same height as his partner, but was in better shape. He had a dark complexion and beard. Hersing thought he looked Italian. Emery didn't say much. They picked up coffee and went to a table.

Woods seemed troubled. The detective complained about his new boss. This inspector was, he told Hersing, "a hungry son of a bitch," and "all the boys at the top are hungry."

Woods told Hersing that he would like to have the July payoff early. Hersing took advantage of the requested favor to ask for one in return. There were some "hippies," he told Woods and Emery, who were running a whorehouse next door to his Walnut Street operation. They were cutting into his business. Hersing wanted Woods to make trouble for them, and he remembers that Woods promised to look into it.

Then, as he had done in the diner two months before, Hersing passed money to Woods—an envelope with $500 inside. It was the monthly payoff for 1245 Vine Street. Hersing had written the word "Insurance" on the envelope. The bills, in denominations of $20 and $100, had been counted out and their serial numbers carefully recorded by the FBI. Hersing agreed to meet with Woods again toward the end of the month to make a $1,100 payment, the $500 owed for 1245 Vine's July protection, and the first two $300 payoffs for 2209 Walnut.

Seven days later, early in the afternoon on a Wednesday, Woods stopped in at the 1245 Vine Street studio and told the manager that he had to make a bust that day over at the Walnut Street whorehouse. Later, Thompson wrote up an account of what happened.

A confidential source provided the following: Sources advised that George Woods, detective, Philadelphia Police Department (PHPD), Vice Squad went to 1245 Vine Street on June 8, 1981 and told the assistant manager, Evon, that he needed to make a vice arrest at 2209 Walnut Street. Both these places are owned by the same person. Evon called the owner of 1245 Vine Street and 2209 Walnut Street and Woods talked to him. Woods stated he needed to make a bust at 2209 Walnut. Woods told the owner that he would only arrest one girl and she would be out by the afternoon. Woods also said the charges would be dismissed later. The above call took place at 12:45 p.m., June 8, 1981. The owner of 1245 Vine Street called 2209 Walnut and told a girl named Lola that he wanted her to take a "hit." Woods went to 2209 Walnut and made the arrest at approximately 1:25 p.m., June 8, 1981. Woods went into 2209 Walnut, set up a session with Lola and then arrested her for solicitation. This was all set up prior by Woods and the owner of 2209. When a set up "bust" takes place the owner gives the girl arrested an extra $100 for her trouble.

The next afternoon the busy detective again stopped by 1245 Vine to phone Hersing. He explained, cryptically, that the new inspector was pressuring him to make arrests. He had had to move fast the day before. Now he wanted to make sure that Hersing wasn't upset. He wanted to reassure the whorehouse owner that their deal was still on.

"What was said to me, was said to me," Woods explained. "So before anything gets screwed up, I said I'll take care of that. Right?"

"Yeah. That's cool," Hersing said. "That's cool."

"So, eh, everything worked out fine."

"Good."

"Right?" Woods asked.

"Right."

"Did you hear? . . . She was only there four and a half hours."

"No. That was good, George. I appreciate that."

"I greased the way a little bit."

"Good. Good. I appreciate that."

But as Philadelphia's spring warmed to summer, the new inspector was making things hotter and hotter for Georgie Woods. The plump vice detective was feeling the heat. As July approached, he planned to take a vacation, a long drive south with the wife and kids. That was why he wanted to be paid off early.

Friday, June 26, was an unusually cool, sunny summer day. The baseball strike was three weeks old. Frustrated city children were finally being freed from their classrooms. The bitter winter had forced school closings earlier in the year and delayed summer vacation.

Hersing drove into the city from Levittown that morning. He was supposed to meet Woods in his room at the Holiday Inn that afternoon, but he had to see a doctor about his feet. Hersing had slipped and hurt his feet while working on his boat. They had swollen and developed a horrible rash. It was scary. His feet were bright red. He could hardly walk. Hersing was worried that there was something wrong with his circulation. He had called Woods to postpone the meeting, and Woods, who was leaving on vacation the next Tuesday, had agreed to come by that night at about 10:30.

Hersing was in a third-floor room. He was soaking one foot in a tub of ice water. The other was propped up on a pillow. Thompson and Lash had hidden a tape recorder behind the dresser across the room. They waited downstairs, and watched as Woods breezed in. The detective walked over to the house phone and called Hersing to tell him he was on his way up. Hersing asked Woods to bring up some beer, so the detective detoured into the hotel bar before crossing the lobby, carrying one bottle in each hand, to a waiting elevator. After Woods hung up the house phone, Hersing switched on the tape recorder.

Woods found Hersing with his feet pitifully soaking and propped. He clucked sympathetically as he entered the room.

"You should see underneath the ice," Hersing said.

"What's he say? What's the doctor say?"

"I'm taking water pills, doing a lot of blood tests, shit like that. Blood sugar and all. That all turned out good. He told me my fucking liver was enlarged."

"An enlarged liver," Woods said. "My, that's always good for you." And the two men chuckled. Their conversation had an easy familiarity to it now, in contrast to the awkwardness that first day when they drove together to the diner. They had gotten to know each other. They talked like partners. As their meetings became more relaxed and friendly, the detective dug himself deeper and deeper into the trap.

Hersing showed Woods a gold bracelet. Woods collected gold. The detective eyed the bracelet appreciatively under a lamp.

Hersing complained that the women running his whorehouses were driving him crazy, fighting with each other. Woods listened sympathetically and offered advice: "Separate 'em," he said. "Send Yvonne over to Walnut Street. Send her to Bucks County." Hersing complained about how bad business was getting. He suspected that some of the women with their own pimps were ripping him off.

"My advice to you is," Woods said, very deliberately, offering up a piece of homespun wisdom off the beat, the way he liked to do, "you know what you got . . ."

"Uh-huh," Hersing said, listening.

"You might not know what you're gettin'."

Hersing nodded. It took a moment for some of the things Georgie said to sink in. Hersing complained that business was off anyway. Woods again sympathized. He said business would be bad this summer: "You know, a lot of people are saving their bucks up, too."

"Yeah, for vacations," Hersing said. He asked Woods when he was leaving on his vacation.

"Wednesday morning."

"Guess you're looking forward to that, huh?"

"Yes and—*yes* eighty percent, *no* twenty percent."

"What's the twenty percent?"

"Well, I don't know. I guess you might call me a workaholic."

"I don't know how you work all them fucking hours you work. I really don't."

"Well, I put it like this," Georgie explained. "If you don't stay on top of it, you're not going to *be* on top of it."

"Yeah, that's for sure."

"Now, I got three places yet to go tonight."

"What fucking time you quit?"

"When the job's done."

"Yeah, but when is the job done?"

"The job's never done," Georgie said. "The job's never done."

"Did you ever get a chance to talk to your boss?" Hersing asked. He was pushing Woods to let him deal with the top man. Woods's tone changed. He spoke quietly, putting the request off.

"No. It will happen. Later on, you'll see." Then Woods complained about how ugly things were getting, how the old system was being reorganized. "This guy, this new boss? He's got a hangup on machines."

"Yeah, somebody was in about our machine," Hersing said, referring to the video poker machine at the Morning Glory.

"Yeah. The lieutenant."

"Your lieutenant?"

"Yeah," Woods said, then added hurriedly, as if something had just occurred to him, "Don't say nothin' to him." Woods was on slippery ground here. Hersing had been pushing him to strike a deal with the higher-ups, and he had, after all, been telling him how "hungry" his new bosses were. But if the inspector discovered his private enterprises, the Georgie Woods empire, he was cooked. Woods fumbled for an explanation. He said, "Because he don't, eh, eh, eh, he doesn't like, eh, girls."

Hersing misunderstood. "I thought he liked Terry," Hersing said. He had heard that the lieutenant had an eye for the woman who managed the Morning Glory.

"No, that's not what I'm saying," Woods said sharply, recovering. "That's not what I'm saying. I'm saying two different things."

"Yeah," Hersing said. He was confused. Woods tried to explain.

"He likes, see, he, he sees through Terry, like, he just, all he wants to do is get his—he wants to fuckTerry." He fumbled on trying to explain his way free of this mess. The lieutenant liked girls, but he didn't like taking money to protect prostitution.

"Why is that?" Hersing asked.

"I don't know. I, eh," said Woods—now just why wouldn't a cop want whorehouse money?—"I'll put it like this. I really, eh, think it has something to do with the Knapp Commission."

"What the fuck is the Knapp Commission, if I don't sound too dumb?"

The Knapp Commission was a major police corruption probe in New York in the 1960s. A lot of New York cops were indicted for taking money to protect vice operations. It had started with this Happy Hooker, Xaviera Hollander, Woods said. "Because of her, they started this Knapp Commission in New York, which indicted a lot of fucking people. And it was a big fucking exposé in New York . . . I've heard him mention it once. I don't pursue the matter with him, right?"

Woods and Hersing chatted then for a while, comparing notes about mutual acquaintances, bar owners, bookies, crooks, warning each other about whom to trust and whom not to trust. Rapping was a survival technique in the world they inhabited. Word got out about people and places to be avoided. Georgie, the gold collector, collected these tidbits, too. He prided himself on it. When Hersing mentioned that he had gone down to a bar called the Waiting Room with this loan shark, Woods cut in.

"You gotta be crazy."

"Why?"

"Stay the fuck away from . . ."

Hersing thought he was referring to the loan shark.

"Not him!" Woods said.

"The Waiting Room?"

"Yeeeeaah," growled Woods knowingly.

"Why is that?"

"Feds got that so fucking wired it ain't funny."

"Really?"

"Oh, oh yeah," Woods said, chuckling now, as if to say, *How could you be so ignorant . . . ?* "Stay the fuck away. They've had that fucking place fucking wired for almost a year now, a year and a half."

Hersing's mind flew for that second behind the dresser to the FBI machine turning silently, listening, recording. There was something delicious about moments like these, he thought, about collecting them silently, deferring revenge, about being the only one in the room who really knows what's going on, especially when the other guy thinks it's him.

The two men wrapped up their business. Hersing handed over $795. They agreed that would cover the July payments. The bracelet, which was worth $375, would take care of the $300 Hersing owed for the protection of

Walnut Street during June. The extra $75 of value would reimburse Woods for what he gave a sergeant and a court official during the June Dial-a-Bust. Woods actually owed Hersing a few bucks back, but Hersing waived it. "You can have it," he said. "I know you're going on vacation. You can use it."

"All right."

Before he left, Hersing told Woods that he was going to be taking over an apartment down on South Street. Maybe they could meet there next. And Hersing asked if Woods would consider accepting less money during July and August. After all, as Woods had agreed, business fell off badly in the summer. Hersing said they might have to lower the price of a session to $20. Woods promised to talk it over with Ray Emery, his partner, and get back to him. He sounded sympathetic.

"Okay, George. I appreciate you bringing up the beer."

"You take care of yourself," Woods said, and then called Hersing "Roger." He laughed, and said, "Why am I calling you Roger?" Roger was the old code name, back before things had grown more informal between them.

"We'll get together for a drink when you get back," Hersing said.

"Sounds good," said Woods as he walked down the hallway toward the elevator. "Hope your legs work out all right."

"Thanks, George."

Downstairs, the FBI agents saw Woods leave an elevator, cross the lobby, and exit into the night. They waited a few minutes just to make sure he was gone. Alone upstairs, Hersing sat a few minutes and then, groaning, he pulled his feet from the cold tub and walked across the room to turn off the recorder.

The meeting had lasted about forty-five minutes. They had at last gotten a payoff on tape. This meeting would prove to be the meat of their case against George Woods, but it had fallen short of their hopes. Woods hadn't taken the bait when Hersing pressed him about meetings with higher-ups. Maybe they were on to just an isolated instance of corruption. But what was all this talk of the new inspector being so "hungry"?

As Thompson and Lash returned this new scrap of electromagnetic evidence to their office safe that night, it was clear that Woods was not going to open any doors for them. Hersing would have to explore a new route, one that had opened up unexpectedly just a few weeks before.

*   *   *

George Woods offered at best a paltry police protection service. Every time the plump little officer with the moustache called to arrange a "Dial-a-Bust" at one of Donald Hersing's whorehouses, Hersing was out about $500 in legal fees, courthouse payoffs, and compensation to the prostitute who agreed to take the pinch. That was on top of the monthly payoffs of $500 for the 1245 Vine Street studio and $300 for the one at 2209 Walnut Street. The women hated it. It was a hassle.

And Hersing could see that things weren't getting better. Ever since the central police division got its new commanding officer, Woods seemed under even more pressure to make arrests. It was either because this new inspector, John DeBenedetto, was eager to make life difficult for the sleaze merchants in his division, or because Donald Hersing (and the FBI) were paying off at the wrong level.

What would turn out to be Hersing's last payoff to Woods took place early in August at Kelly's Irish Pub, at Broad and Race Streets. An FBI agent with a tape recorder was positioned near the two men as they met and exchanged $500, but there had been so much noise in the bar that the tape was worthless. At that point both Hersing and the agents were through with Georgie Woods anyway. Hersing, in his role as a whorehouse owner, was getting fed up with Woods's costly, almost comical Dial-a-Busts, and was eager to start doing business with someone who could offer him serious protection.

Hersing's ticket to the upper ranks was a police detective whom he had met through his accountant, Gene Botel. Botel had brought the detective along one March afternoon to meet Hersing for lunch at Fireman Jr.'s, a luncheonette directly across 13th Street from the Vine Street whorehouse. The detective's name was Abe Schwartz.

Botel and Schwartz were friends. Abe was everybody's friend. He had served for forty-one years in the Philadelphia Police Department—one of the longest careers of anyone on the force. Technically, Schwartz was a detective in the east division, assigned to investigate applications for gun permits. But he counted among his good friends the highest-ranking members of the department. They told jokes about Schwartz's popularity in the department, like the one about the pope: "Who's that guy in white in this picture of Abe Schwartz at the Vatican?" East detectives had thrown a lavish banquet the year before to mark Schwartz's fortieth anniversary on the force. About four hundred people crowded into Pinocchio Ristorante on

Cottman Avenue, among them Commissioner Morton Solomon, former deputy commissioner Harry Fox, and Inspector James J. Martin, who was then Schwartz's boss. It had been a big departmental social event, with the atmosphere of a retirement party. But Abe had no intention of retiring. He would have missed the work too much. For Abe, his work and his social life were closely intermingled.

At sixty-one, Abe was bald as a rock on top, but his squat frame showed none of the encroaching softness or frailty of advancing age. He was built wider in the middle than at the ends, which made him look at first glance like someone with a paunch, but on closer inspection it was clear that Abe was in great physical condition. He still played tennis like a man thirty years younger, and his handshake was one your grip remembered. Over dark round eyes, his brows seemed fixed in a perpetually quizzical arch, curving up to a vertical crease where his forehead closed on the wide bridge of his nose. He was a vigorous, fun-loving man, a *character*. Abe called everybody "brother," whether it was in the steam baths of the Philadelphia Athletic Club or the boardrooms of the Police Administration Building. It was just Abe's jovial way of relating to the world. During World War II, Schwartz had served in North Africa, Italy, and France, assigned, of all things, to the Naval Combat Blimp Squadron; that was just the sort of odd detail that had added to his reputation as a delightful character. He had started with the police department as a clerk after the war, and worked his gregarious way quickly through the uniformed ranks. By the mid-fifties, he was already a dapper, respected detective, given to expensive suits and a dazzling variety of colorful hats. During the leisure-suit period, Abe's wardrobe blossomed in bright pastels, checked shirts with huge white collars, and colorful ties as wide as a man's hand. Abe didn't mind drawing attention to himself; he reveled in it. Attention seemed at times to be for Abe almost an end in itself. Over the years, as his circle of friends grew to legendary proportions, Schwartz became a sort of unofficial supply sergeant for the department, and for anyone else he met. If you wanted to buy something, anything, Abe could find you a deal—if he didn't just happen to have what you were looking for already in the trunk of his car, which was a veritable treasure chest of goodies, everything from discount clothes to cartons of fresh cookies. He was like a one-man "old boy" network, Abe was, always ready with a smile, a joke, a crunching handshake, and the right connection. Abe trafficked in connections. He saved photos of himself with Grace Kelly, with Golda Meir, with David Ben-Gurion. He had been assigned to help escort a few presidents of the United States through Philadelphia over the years. Abe's job was bigger than its official description, just as his lifestyle was considerably grander than the average police detective's. His salary was modest, about $25,000 a year, and his wife, a nurse, worked full-time in the city school system, but they and their three sons lived better than most two-public-servant families. They had a home and a boat on Long Beach Island, and in addition to their permanent residence in Northeast Philadelphia, they owned a condominium in Florida and valuable stocks and bonds. An official estimate of the Schwartzes' worth, made the previous year, was $300,000. This was the memorable man with the year-round deep summer tan, with the round jowls and wide hooked nose, with the playful eyes and wiseacre smile, whom Donald Hersing met over lunch in April of 1981.

At first, Hersing hadn't mentioned his new friend to Mike Thompson or Andy Lash, the FBI agents working with him. Abe didn't know Georgie Woods, and he didn't seem to have anything to do with the central police division. But, gradually, Hersing and the FBI agents recognized this amiable detective for the unofficial mover and shaker he was.

Right away there were deals. Knowing Abe Schwartz meant being in the process of delivering something to him or waiting for him to deliver something to you—though it wasn't always clear what the precise terms of the trade-offs were. Sometimes Schwartz just enjoyed doing people favors, asking nothing in return but good feelings. In Hersing's case, the whorehouse owner/informant understood right from the start that there would be advantages to making friends with the detective. Nothing explicit was offered in return, but Hersing had promised to find Schwartz a videocassette recorder. He also gave Cinnamon, the woman who managed his Vine Street whorehouse, the nod to arrange private parties with prostitutes for Schwartz and his friends at her apartment on South Street.

This was the apartment that Hersing, in June, was preparing to take over. It was in a row of angular brick townhouses in a modern rowhouse development named Washington Square West. Located on the leading western edge of the thriving bohemian South Street retail district, the development was the vanguard of the affluent residential neighborhoods expanding south from the Center City enclave of Society Hill. Across the street, on the corner, was a men's clothing outlet called Big-Hearted Jim's.

Down the rest of the block were the battered shells of empty old rowhouses, their boarded-up fronts laminated with posters. Cinnamon had fallen behind in the rent, which was about $525 a month. The FBI was eager for Hersing to establish a permanent base in Philadelphia, so they could wire it for both pictures and sound. Abscam had proved—just a few blocks west at the Barclay Hotel—that there is no better way to present evidence of payoffs than for the jury to actually see the money and goods change hands.

But, so far, outside of Schwartz's fraternal affection, it was not clear what Hersing could expect in return for the sexual liaisons. Thompson and Lash were eager to find out. Although no quid pro quo had been spelled out, there was something more than affability in Schwartz's manner. It was obvious that the old detective *expected* favors from Hersing.

In the weeks before the meeting with Woods at the Holiday Inn, Hersing had phoned Schwartz a number of times to make sure arrangements with whores had come off as planned, and to find out why the police seemed to be paying special attention to his studios. There had been a few days early in June when patrol cars were parked out in front of 1245 Vine Street for hours at a time. It had kept business away. Hersing had asked his friend why, and Schwartz had promised to look into it. When Hersing called him on June 17, Schwartz was annoyed that he had gone to a lot of trouble to find the information, and Hersing hadn't bothered to return his calls. There was no *how ya doin', brother* on the other end of the phone this time.

"Where the hell you been?" Schwartz said. "Boy, you're the most unreliable son of a bitch!"

"Man, I called a couple of times for you."

Schwartz then came directly to the point. Hersing had promised to find a videocassette recorder several months ago. Schwartz was impatient. He asked peevishly, "Where's that thing you told me you had for me previously?"

"I have it for you," Hersing lied.

"Uh-huh," Schwartz answered skeptically.

"I have it for you," Hersing insisted. Then Schwartz became quieter, more helpful. He told Hersing that the patrolmen had been watching a suspicious cargo container in the neighborhood; this was the reason for so many police cars near Hersing's whorehouse.

"Now, you asked me and then you never called me back," Schwartz said. "That's bullshit, ya know? I went to a lot of trouble to get that for you and that's what the hell happened there."

Before hanging up, Hersing asked if Schwartz had wanted an automatic timer for the recorder.

"No."

"Okay."

"No. I just need a fucking machine like you promised me. I should have had it three weeks ago, Don."

"All right. Abe, next phone call I make to you I'll be calling you to come and get it."

That conversation had piqued Thompson's and Lash's interest in Schwartz. Who was this guy? Neither of the young FBI agents knew Philadelphia well enough to have heard of Abe Schwartz before. They knew him only as this gun-permits investigator with an interest in prostitutes. Hersing kept telling them that Schwartz was well connected, but they had no way of finding out more about him without tipping off the police department to their investigation. Thompson and Lash had learned just enough about Abe Schwartz to be intrigued by him. He seemed to know exactly what Hersing was up to, yet was unfazed by it. And he seemed to want that videocassette recorder badly. The agents figured that they ought to take Schwartz for what he seemed to be: a good person to know. So they decided that it was time to buy Abe Schwartz a Betamax. Before they did, however, they wanted to wire the apartment at 707-A South Street. If something as large as a videocassette recorder was going to change hands, they wanted the transaction on tape.

So in July, the FBI began renting the apartment. It was a sterile duplex, walls painted white. On the first floor was a living room, dining room, and kitchen. Upstairs was a bathroom and two bedrooms. Underneath the stairs was a closet with noisy air-conditioning equipment inside. This would serve as a surveillance hideaway for Thompson and Lash. FBI workers installed a door without a handle on the closet entrance. It could be opened only with a key. If anyone asked, Hersing was to tell them that behind the door was air-conditioning equipment and he did not have a key to open it. Inside was a small TV monitor, headphones, and a metal box containing audio recording equipment. They wired the front room upstairs for sound and picture. Small, sensitive microphones were set right into the walls. The television camera was hidden inside one of the stereo speakers.

It peered out through the fine mesh of the speaker's cloth front. The stereo faced an L-shaped couch ensemble with a coffee table set in the angle formed between its two parts. The stage was set.

With the apartment wired and ready, the FBI bought Abe Schwartz a $900 present. Mike Thompson and Andy Lash shopped around a little to get a good buy, and settled on a Sony Betamax in the Radio 437 store in the 900 block of Chestnut Street.

They wanted the sales receipt to be made out in Hersing's name, just in case Schwartz bothered to check. Picking which agent to pose as Hersing was easy. Once, when the agents and their informant had been buying furniture for 707-A South Street, a salesman had asked slender, fair-haired Lash if he was Hersing's son. Thompson and some of the other agents in the FBI office had had a good laugh over that, and never let Lash live it down. Another time, over lunch, someone told Lash he looked a little like the actor Don Knotts, and Hersing had quickly said, "No way, Andy's more handsome than that!"

So it was Lash who introduced himself as Don Hersing and asked for the Betamax. When the sales clerk brought the box out, he called across the store, "Don! Don!" But Lash, who was chatting with his partner, failed to respond until the man crossed the store and tapped him on the shoulder. It would be one of the small lapses the two agents would laugh about later.

Soon afterward, Hersing phoned his friend Abe.

"Abe?"

"Yeah."

"How you doing, brother?"

"All right, brother. Who is this?"

"Don."

"Who?"

"Don."

"Holy Christ, a voice out of the fucking past. You son of a bitch."

"Hey, guess what?"

"No, no. Don't tell me."

"I got it."

"Naaah, I don't believe it!"

"I got it!"

"You son of a gun."

"I got it, Abe."

"Yeah? Where's it at?"

"It's in my apartment. I took over Cinnamon's apartment on South Street."

The two men made arrangements to meet the next day.

Wednesday, August 19, was the day Navy fighters shot down two Libyan jets over the Mediterranean Sea. Thompson, who had flown Air Force jets for six years before joining the FBI, would read the next day's stories with interest. *The Philadelphia Journal*'s enthusiastic headline read: "U.S. Guns Down Madman's Warjets." Nine games into the second half of the strike-broken baseball season, the Phillies had toppled to last place in their division, having lost their third game in a row to Cincinnati at the Vet the night before. The day was sunny and the humidity, which typically turns the air to broth in Philadelphia at that time of year, was taking a day off.

When Abe Schwartz stopped by the South Street address shortly after 11 a.m. that morning, temperatures were in the middle seventies. FBI cameras would preserve him that day dandy as ever: straw hat with a dark band, lightweight suit over a cotton shirt with an open collar, dark handkerchief folded into the right breast pocket of his breezy suit coat.

Hersing met him at the door and escorted him directly upstairs. Abe knew the apartment. He had stopped in with his friend, Inspector Jimmy Carlini, for a party that Cinnamon had arranged. He hardly glanced at the big open Sony box next to the coffee table. He stepped around the table, hat in hand, and flopped back on the portion of the L-shaped sofa that was against the wall, draping his left leg over his knee.

"How ya feel?" he asked Hersing, who looked rumpled and pale. Hersing, as usual, had been up all night. He was tired. His sport shirt, a short-sleeve pullover with one thick stripe down the right side, dangled loosely out over the waist of his bell-bottom trousers. He knew the most important things about the meeting with Abe were, first, to give him the Betamax, and, second, to see whether Abe could fix him up with somebody more influential in the department than George Woods.

"Pretty good," Hersing said. "I had this problem with my legs." Hersing sat on the other part of the sofa, at a right angle to Schwartz, and hiked up one trouser leg to show off the remnants of his rash.

"Holy God!" Schwartz said, examining the leg. "Howdja do that?"

Schwartz had a way of talking right over top of Hersing, not letting him finish what he was saying, so that the two men were frequently talking at the same time. Their conversation was less a give-and-take than an organic, aimless flow that somehow arrived at mutual understanding. Schwartz was suddenly warm and friendly toward Hersing. Brothers. All they had they had in common. The gift of the Betamax had won his favor.

"You look good. You look good," Schwartz said, lying.

"Do I?"

"How's business?"

The old detective seemed genuinely interested in poor Don Hersing's legs, even bending over to hike up one of his own pants legs to show off where he had gotten sunburned on his boat. After Hersing wound out a long story about how he had originally injured his legs falling on his boat, Schwartz said, "I'm always falling on the boat. I'm always falling on the boat."

Schwartz was full of advice that day, but he was wary. Downstairs in the closet, watching on the TV monitor and doing their best to follow Schwartz's convoluted syntax, Thompson and Lash were surprised at how cagey the detective seemed. Every time Hersing would try to talk turkey, Schwartz's voice dropped so low that they worried their microphones might not pick it up.

"I was tellin' ya about getting hit," Hersing said.

Schwartz mumbled something back so softly that the microphones couldn't pick it up. Even Hersing had a hard time making out what Schwartz was saying.

"Nobody here?" Schwartz asked.

"Huh?"

"Nobody here?"

"No, just me."

"The guy had told me, just—see, you got a new man here—and . . . ah, my other friend said, 'Why don't you get him in and get him to help you there.' But then I didn't hear from ya, and, I say, he was kinda leery of you, too. Jimmy."

"Why?"

"I don't know. Somebody got all excited about you."

This was what Hersing feared most. Surely, Hersing thought, word about this undercover work would eventually get back to these city cops.

After all, Bucks County was just a twenty-minute drive north of Philadelphia. But as Schwartz talked, it became clear that Inspector Carlini had grown leery of Hersing for an entirely different reason. It stemmed from a botched sex party Cinnamon had arranged for Carlini and Schwartz.

"Well, another thing that pissed off Jimmy," Schwartz said. "The time you set something up and you sent Cinnamon and set something up here?"

"Yeah?"

"We came here and this fucking girl comes down high as a fucking kite and she went on and on. . . . And Jimmy said, 'Let's get the fuck out of here.' And he was pissed off."

Hersing understood what Schwartz was saying. The inspector couldn't risk being involved in a scene like that. Schwartz was annoyed that Hersing had not handled the matter himself. Carlini could be a valuable friend, Schwartz whispered. "Here's the man you want to entertain, you want his friendship." (At the stern instructions of Thompson and Lash, Hersing had not directly set up Schwartz and the others with prostitutes. The FBI wanted to avoid embarrassing revelations later on.)

As the men talked, the Rolling Stones performed their plaintive hit "Angie" from the speaker where the camera silently ran. Hersing crushed out a cigarette. Then he leaned over and plucked from the Sony box a plastic bag full of pamphlets with information about the videocassette recorder. He handed the packet to Schwartz.

"A new one," Schwartz said, referring to the machine. "I didn't know that." He pulled out glasses from an inside coat pocket and put them on to peruse the instructions.

"It's a beautiful job," Hersing said, meaning the machine. "A beautiful job. And look, you know, in the beginning I just, eh, just couldn't handle it. The thing that was strapping me was paying my partner off. . . . That has everything. You can set it to record a certain day, a certain time . . ."

"Yeah, all right! 'Record one TV program while viewing another,'" Schwartz read appreciatively. "I'd given up on you, you know that? I didn't hear from ya."

"What'd I tell ya? I said, Abe, next time you hear from me I'll have it."

"Yeah, but for crying out loud."

"Like I say, I was strapped then and a lot of things come up, you know, with that case I had and all that."

"Yeah, I know." Affable Abe did not sound sympathetic. He clearly had expected to get the machine long before this. But then he warmed up again. He thanked Hersing for the machine. "I hope I see more of you now," he said. They talked about their boats. Schwartz grew animated describing his flat-deck twenty-footer. He sat up on the edge of the couch and, using his hands to block out the shape on the coffee table, described its dimensions in detail. "We just float along the bay," he said. "I love it. I *love* it."

It was such a chummy scene, and Schwartz seemed so resolutely circumspect, that at this point Thompson and Lash, downstairs in the closet, began to despair of collecting any useful leads from the detective. But, finally, Schwartz got around to business again. His voice dropped abruptly.

"Listen, this friend of mine in the DA's office? He was on TV a couple of weeks back. They had this whole thing about this pornography."

"Yeah?"

"He's, eh, good people. He likes, ah, I think whatever he likes, he'll be able to get it, right?"

"Of course."

"You know what I mean?"

"Absolutely."

"He's good people."

Having promised to set up Schwartz's friend with whatever kind of sex he was looking for, Hersing also promised to get Schwartz some X-rated tapes for his new machine. Then Schwartz said something that made Thompson's and Lash's ears perk up in the closet downstairs. He indirectly promised to help set up a meeting between Hersing and the new man in the central division, George Woods's boss, Inspector DeBenedetto.

"I'll work on that other thing for you," he said.

"Do that. That's important."

"That is. You should know him."

"Because this fucking Woodsie . . . he's a real fucking prostitute. You know what I think's happening?"

"Who's he working for?" Schwartz asked. Hersing named the lieutenant directly over Woods. Schwartz was shocked. Here Hersing knew *him*! Abe Schwartz! He knew Inspector Jimmy Carlini! And he was dealing with a vice officer and his lieutenant? Schwartz was dismayed by Hersing's innocence.

"Christ! The big boss is Jimmy's best friend!"

"You know, I heard that."

"Very best friend! What are you paying?"

"Five, eh, five a month."

"Why don't you see the head guy?"

"But, you see, the thing I think, Abe, is happening—Woods is not telling his lieutenant he's getting the five a month."

"Then he's not even telling the inspector."

Schwartz now had the undivided attention of the FBI agents watching and listening downstairs.

"That's what I figured," Hersing said. "You know, 'cause he come to me the other day and he said, 'You gotta take a bust.' I said, 'Hey George, what the fuck is this? I pay. Why do I have to take a fucking bust?'" Hersing said that Woods told him, "I got to make it look good to the lieutenant."

Schwartz decided to straighten his brother out. He never mentioned DeBenedetto's name, but Hersing understood that the detective was referring to the new central division inspector.

"You want to talk to him?"

"Yeah."

"And you're gonna take care of him, will ya?"

"Oh, yeah."

"He's good people. I'm gonna talk to Jimmy."

"Eh, I would rather deal with the inspector than with him," Hersing said, referring to Woods.

"Always talk with the top man. I'm surprised at you, Don."

Hersing said that he was wary of DeBenedetto because the inspector had once been a staff inspector in Internal Affairs, the police division charged with rooting out corrupt officers.

"Right," Schwartz said. "Well, so was Jimmy. That don't mean nothing . . . Take care of the head man. I'll . . . try to set it up for you."

"I appreciate that."

"All I want is . . ."—and Schwartz gestured to the videotape recorder on the floor and spoke rapidly, whispering, "You took care of me now—I'm gonna get fucked . . . ten times. That's all I want."

"Hey," Hersing said, indicating, *no problem*.

"And I, I don't like to go over there," he said, referring to the Vine Street whorehouse. "I want to come here." Schwartz asked if Hersing had anything *good* for him.

"Oh yeah," Hersing said. The detective said he would like for something to be arranged for the next day. He stood up and put his hat back on. Stepping around the coffee table, he stooped and lifted the box with the Betamax without bending his knees.

"You strong enough to carry that, Abe?"

"It's for me, ain't it?" the detective said, walking out of the room, the weight of the machine bending him slightly backward.

"That's the best they got, too," Hersing said.

Now the hunt was on. Schwartz had taken the bait and disappeared into woods neither Thompson nor Lash had ever explored. They were delighted. Listening to Schwartz, one of the most veteran members of the Philadelphia Police Department, the two young FBI agents felt like they were getting an education in big-city police work. It was disillusioning, to say the least. When Schwartz had casually tossed off the fact that it *didn't matter* that DeBenedetto and Carlini had worked as staff inspectors for the department's internal affairs division, it said a lot about the corruption Hersing was finding. It suggested that Georgie Woods was, in fact, an anomaly. Not because he was taking money, but because he wasn't collecting it for someone else!

The fast-talking police detective in the straw hat was not only confirming their worst suspicions, he was *expanding* their worst suspicions. Prior to the meeting, the only indication they had that Schwartz was corrupt was his enjoyment of Cinnamon's whores. But for all they knew, Schwartz and Carlini just used their position to con men like Don Hersing into throwing them wild parties. There were certainly questionable ethics involved, but hardly indictable activity (Carlini, in fact, would never be indicted). But Abe Schwartz, with his quickly lowered voice and his *brother-now-that-you've-taken-care-of-me-I'll-take-care-of-you* talk, had turned this minor FBI probe into a major investigation.

Abe Schwartz was as good as his word. Six days later, Hersing got a message on his answering machine to call Inspector John DeBenedetto. He called back immediately, and DeBenedetto told Hersing that he wanted to see him that afternoon. So at 2 p.m. Hersing took a cab over to the tan stone central division headquarters at Twentieth Street and Pennsylvania Avenue.

He was directed inside to DeBenedetto's office on the second floor. But, after climbing the stairs and stepping out into the second floor, Hersing walked straight into George Woods. The detective was sitting behind a typewriter at his desk outside the inspector's office.

Woods was clearly shocked to see Hersing walk in. He jumped up and crossed the room, shooing Hersing out the door and back down the stairs. "Get outta here!" he said. If the inspector ever found out that Woods was collecting money from Hersing on his own, he was in trouble. Woods rushed Hersing back outside. Annoyed, Hersing strode back to the cab. As he was climbing in the back door, Woods came hurrying out the front door and got in next to him. He told the driver to cruise around the block. They stopped a few blocks away at an auto repair shop.

What was Hersing doing at headquarters? Woods wanted to know. Hersing said that DeBenedetto had asked him to come in. He could see that this put the detective in a bind; Hersing was nervous, too. He didn't know what Woods would do. Finally, the detective just told Hersing to leave.

Woods told him, "If he calls you back, come back, but if you do come back make sure you don't mention my name to him."

Hersing wasn't sure what to do next. He didn't want to cross Woods just yet. For all he knew, DeBenedetto might really be straight. If he told the inspector that he had been paying Woods, it might blow everything. He had to feel his way. So he went back down to the apartment and phoned the inspector. He told DeBenedetto that he had gotten delayed at a doctor's office. The inspector agreed to meet him the following day at the Parkway Room restaurant.

Hersing was wary of Inspector DeBenedetto. The man had George Woods positively spooked. And, even if Schwartz said it didn't mean anything, DeBenedetto *had* been in Internal Affairs. Hersing had heard that the new inspector was a tough man. He wasn't eager to start dealing with him.

Truth was, Hersing's sore feet had begun to turn mildly cold when it came to this investigation. It had been almost four months since he had first gone to the FBI. Then, he was primarily interested in getting George Woods off his back. They had quickly collected enough evidence to nail him. But as the case expanded, as Thompson and Lash grew more excited about it, Hersing's interest waned. It was taking a lot of his time. He had finished paying off the money his partner, William Robertshaw, had lent him to start up the whorehouses and the club, and was now starting to make money. With DeBenedetto looming as a new target, the undercover work was looking less exciting than dangerous. It was starting to place demands on his time and on his wallet. It was a constant hassle. The FBI seemed to have trouble coming up with cash in time to meet expenses. When he started working as a source, Hersing had spent mostly his own money. This had been fine initially, while he was excited about the case, but now it had become a drain. He wanted to know how much money the FBI would pay him when it was all over. All Thompson and Lash would tell him was that, while it was customary for the FBI to bestow a cash award on sources after a case was complete, the amount depended on the outcome of the case and the level of contribution made. They weren't making any promises. Hersing was also worried because he was still on probation for the previous smuggling conviction. One of the rules of his probation was that he could not work for the government. He couldn't come right out and tell his parole officer what he was doing, but the man kept asking questions.

Thompson and Lash were exposed to Hersing's growing reluctance in a multitude of ways. There would be whole weeks when they couldn't find him. Their phone calls routinely went unanswered. Hersing frequently failed to show up for meetings they had scheduled. They had begun to sympathize with the annoyed voices of the Philadelphia policemen in their growing stack of tape-recorded conversations.

On August 27, the agents were eager for Hersing to wear a tape recorder for his first meeting with DeBenedetto. If the inspector was going to cut his deal with Hersing, it would be at this meeting. But Hersing balked. He was afraid of DeBenedetto. He thought the inspector would search him. The agents, reluctantly, had to agree that it was possible. So Hersing went to the first meeting without a body recorder.

It was a cloudy day, more humid than hot. Moisture and pollution hung like a bright fog over the view from Spring Garden Street toward the dense green foliage along the Benjamin Franklin Parkway. The Parkway House was a tall apartment building of pale orange brick that was the last major structure before Spring Garden Street opened out into the sculpted green spaces and busy traffic ovals laid out before the Philadelphia Museum of Art. DeBenedetto lunched regularly in the bar and restaurant on the first floor of the Parkway House. It was just a two-block walk out the front door of central division headquarters. The inspector always sat at a round table to the right, just past the bar, in a little space between the kitchen entrance and a wide green pillar. On the wall behind him was a collection of framed prints: a big color photograph of Philadelphia, an aerial view from behind the art museum looking east to Center City; a soft purplish shot of Boathouse Row in the fog and two Norman Rockwell prints; one of John F. Kennedy at the 1960 Democratic convention, and another of an old woman praying over her meal at a luncheonette. From where he sat, DeBenedetto faced across the restaurant a wall of curved greenhouse windows shaded by plants suspended from a high ceiling.

DeBenedetto looked like the heavy he was reputed to be. He was a wide-shouldered man with a broad face that was both fleshy and square. Even his double chin seemed regimented, falling from under a strong chin to a hard second line of defense just over the Adam's apple above his collar. His eyes were set wide apart, and were more horizontal than round. Hard black pupils stared out of long fleshy slits that echoed the squareness of his brow and chin and jaw. DeBenedetto had a wide straight nose and a small, tight mouth. There were deep, old creases angling down the middle of both cheeks, but these were more the remnants of a young man's angular face than the deepening lines of age. DeBenedetto's hair was regulation trim, a touch of gray cropped short at the temples. He didn't smile. It was the kind of face that didn't smile easily. DeBenedetto's very lack of expressiveness added to the appearance he gave of being strong, set, determined. He looked just as Hersing thought he should look.

Two FBI agents seated at another table observed Hersing come in around noon and greet DeBenedetto. He was introduced to the inspector by Gene Console, the restaurant manager. DeBenedetto was wearing a white uniform shirt with police insignia on the collar and silver buttons on the pockets. Hersing sat down and ordered a cup of coffee. He never had much of an appetite at these sessions. Besides, Hersing was usually asleep at this hour. There was no search. DeBenedetto was brusque. He was willing to do business with Hersing, but, unlike Hersing's relationships with Woods and Schwartz, there would be nothing buddy-buddy about it.

He asked Hersing right out if he had been paying off one of his men. Hersing wasn't sure how to answer. He wasn't ready yet to trust DeBenedetto, or to throw Woods to the wolves. What if the inspector was laying his own trap? Hersing hedged. DeBenedetto reassured him.

According to Hersing, the inspector told him that he had been recommended by two people DeBenedetto respected very much. Then he made it easier for Hersing to answer. He asked, "Is it the little fat guy with the moustache?" Hersing said yes. DeBenedetto wanted to know how much he had been paying. Hersing told him five hundred a month. Hersing recalls that the inspector's face grew flushed. He said that he hadn't known anything about the payoffs and that he wasn't getting a dime out of it.

Hersing remembers that DeBenedetto then told him how he had gathered all of his people together the previous June for a "soul-searching" session.

"He said he gave them time for soul-searching and they could confess all their sins and tell him anything they had to tell him, and that they had their opportunity and they didn't," Hersing recalled later. DeBenedetto explained that all the money was supposed to be passed up to him. He passed about $50 of each payoff back to each member of the vice squad—it was easy to see why Georgie hadn't been eager to play along.

So Hersing and the inspector struck a new deal. He would still pay the $500 per month. At first Hersing did not mention his Walnut Street studio or the Morning Glory, the private after-hours club he owned on Vine Street, for which he had been paying extra. DeBenedetto said he would call him back later with the details of the arrangement. He wasn't sure whom he wanted to have picking up the money. Hersing told DeBenedetto how Woods's system had worked. He explained the Dial-a-Busts. He recalls that the inspector scoffed—*when you pay*, he said, *you don't take hits. That's why you pay!* He told Hersing that if he knew of anyone else who was paying off people in his department, it would be like throwing money to the wind. Then DeBenedetto also made arrangements to begin collecting for the Walnut Street whorehouse and for a video poker machine at the club.

As for the fat officer with the moustache, well, DeBenedetto said, he would take care of him. His officer had been disloyal. It was curtains for the freelance empire of Georgie Woods.

More than most large urban institutions, a police department is deeply rooted in the community it serves. While a 7,000-member force like Philadelphia's has its share of college-educated officers, some even from other places, most city cops are educated on city streets. As in most occupations, real experience counts for more than academic degrees. They don't give doctorates in street smarts.

If they did, John DeBenedetto would be among the first in line. His formal education had ended with a high school diploma from a correspondence course he took years after joining the force. One of eleven children, he had grown up in the tight-knit old neighborhoods of South Philadelphia. The characters who ran the bars and the numbers and the whores grew up with John DeBenedetto, played with him in the alleys, went to grade school with him, just as the people who ran the police force and the fire department and City Hall did. Some of the better-educated, smoother officers in the department's upper echelons regarded DeBenedetto as a crude man. But to those who came to police work up from the street, DeBenedetto was recognized as a force to be reckoned with. He was not a fancy talker, and there was nary a philosophical bone in his body, but DeBenedetto was a shrewd, tough man. One high-ranking city policeman who came up through the ranks with DeBenedetto described him as "one of the finest policemen this city ever had." He was known, primarily, as a detective. And he had quite a reputation. "If John was looking for you, you were caught," says one of his men. He was *talented*. Some detectives work best the way Abe Schwartz worked, by cultivating people, earning their confidence and picking their brains. That was not DeBenedetto's style. He had that special intuition, that serendipitous sixth sense it takes to assemble and interpret the miscellany of objects and information that constitute evidence in a criminal investigation—a recovered bullet, a piece of cloth, a scrap of conversation, a number hastily scrawled on a sheet of paper. DeBenedetto had a patient, methodical, analytical approach to detective work that set him apart.

His most famous case was the Judy Lopinson murder, back in 1964. She was a pretty young artist married to a bar owner with mob ties. One day in June she was found murdered, executed, shot through the head at close range in the basement room of her husband's Chestnut Street place, Dante's Inferno. Dead with her, killed in the same manner, was her husband's partner. Her husband, Jack, had been shot through the thigh. Lopinson told police a dramatic story of gunmen who had first executed his wife and his partner, then wounded him in a wild gun battle before fleeing. Months later, it was John DeBenedetto who fished a missing revolver from deep Delaware River waters with a powerful electromagnet, and who was instrumental in piecing together the case that convicted Jack Lopinson and sent him away for life. In the news photographs DeBenedetto is a slender young fellow in street clothes with curly hair and hard eyes and a tight, cynical grin, one big pinky-ringed hand holding up the recovered pistol for the cameras, with a look that says, *Hey, this guy didn't fool me.*

There were lots of less glamorous cases, too, the kind of day-in, day-out work that earned DeBenedetto a reputation inside the police department to match the more ephemeral praise outside. As a captain in Southwest Philadelphia during the early seventies, DeBenedetto supervised fifty-man police escorts for schoolchildren through racially charged neighborhoods, and managed to contain potential violence. He had been honored in 1977 by the city's Commission on Human Relations for this work. Later, as a staff inspector in the internal affairs division, his reputation for dogged pursuit, combined with his stiff, silent personality, had made him unpopular to many on the force. Many interpreted his gruff style as arrogance, so they resented him all the more when he dragged some cop in for a petty scam and took away his badge.

They would have resented DeBenedetto even more if they had known that even while DeBenedetto was busting cops for breaking departmental rules, he himself was collecting money on the side. In 1978, in addition to his salary, which was approaching $40,000 a year, DeBenedetto had made about $10,500 just by collecting payoffs from two charity bingo operations. In 1979, he made $15,900. In 1980, it was $22,050. And in 1981, the year DeBenedetto took over the central police division and began expanding his network of graft, he earned $27,775 from the bingo games alone. Evidence would later show that he was collecting $100 per month for vending machines owned by Penn Regal Vending all over the city, and

$50 per month for the machines owned by D & G Amusements. During that year and also in 1982, men working for DeBenedetto were also collecting monthly payoffs of $50 for machines owned by a vending machine company named Mr. Music, and $75 per month for machines owned by Appel Vending. This, along with the whorehouses and bars and gay clubs that paid anywhere from $100 to $500 monthly, added up to more than $120,000 of graft over his first year and a half as commander of central division.

According to those who knew him during these years, it is unlikely that such payments greatly troubled his conscience. Better than most people, cops recognize that there is a wide gulf between the ideal world—spelled out in laws and oaths of office and departmental guidelines—and what really goes on *out there*. Perhaps it was easier for someone who came to law enforcement with a fancy education and a head full of ideals to march through his career on the straight and narrow higher road, in step with the departmental motto, "Honor, Service, Integrity." But for someone who grew up on the streets, there were certain realities that spoke a lot louder than even the most eloquent rhetoric. Power has an unspoken vocabulary.

Something Inspector John DeBenedetto understood, for instance, was that Philadelphia's beleaguered prosecutors have more work than they can handle trying to convict those charged with violent crimes or theft. As a matter of policy, petty gambling, prostitution, and blue law offenses (such as serving alcohol after the state-mandated closing time) are simply not prosecuted. For gambling, the district attorney had an arbitrary standard of 1,000 bets per year. Anyone arrested and charged with fewer gambling offenses than that was set free. As for prostitution, it had been a long-standing informal policy that as long as it went on behind closed doors and there was no community outcry, the city left it alone. The same criterion went for blue law violations. Cracking down on these things makes more enemies in the community than friends. So, in the big city, gambling and prostitution and after-hours clubs flourished. Most brothels in Philadelphia maintained only the most thinly veiled pretense of being a "massage parlor" or "photo studio." In magazines like *Philadelphia Scene*, their actual services were openly and lewdly advertised.

These policies put police officers like DeBenedetto in the middle. They had the power, even the obligation, to arrest prostitutes and gamblers.

But if those who were arrested were simply set free, then what was the point? The arrests amounted to little more than harassment. For the bar owner or pimp, getting busted was bad for business. To a bar owner who wanted to pay customers who won on his electronic poker machine, or wanted to stay open two hours after the law said he must close, or to a massage parlor manager who wanted to avoid being shut down for a day or two because of a police raid—to these people, paying off the police was simply a business expense. People like Donald Hersing *sought out* John DeBenedetto.

And even the straightest of cops could be tempted by the kind of money being offered. People offered John DeBenedetto money not to do something he may not have particularly *wanted* to do anyway. Why the hell not? The payoffs even injected a little logic into an otherwise illogical enterprise. You harass the people who don't pay. You leave the people who do pay alone. After all, society loves its vice. Most of these places are owned by legitimate businessmen. The public likes it, patronizes it. *Nobody* complains. Even if you do bust them, nothing happens. After a while, the money offered so eagerly had the look of *found* cash. You might as well be picking it up off the sidewalk. It even gave those in command positions like DeBenedetto a certain discretion over the bars and whorehouses. One could almost see it as quality control. If a place was too sleazy, or if it bothered a community, John DeBenedetto would be the first one to close it down.

Playing the game this way was lucrative. The money on the side was *tax-free-the-drinks-are-on-me-boys!* money. And DeBenedetto's expenses had gone up. He had separated from his wife and was embroiled in divorce proceedings. He was living in a nice apartment on Twenty-third Street in the Fairmount section, within walking distance of his office. His kids were approaching college age. And DeBenedetto had a daughter with cerebral palsy, which entailed expenses for doctors, therapists, special schools, and equipment. The extra money went a long way toward meeting the heavy demands on John DeBenedetto.

He had long ago faced a choice that, at some point, almost every police officer faces. From the police academy right on up, the department spells out its policy and responsibility on such matters explicitly. No one blunders into graft blindly. As one high-ranking officer explained:

"It's not organized. It's not institutionalized. Corruption is an individual choice. When a cop decides to take money, that's an *individual* decision that he makes. He doesn't discuss it with his commanding officer. He doesn't even discuss it *with his wife.*"

Inside the police department, estimates of those who take money range from as many as two thirds of the force to as few as 1 percent. Even if only 1 percent had made the same decision as John DeBenedetto, it would have meant that there were seventy armed men in the community extorting money from petty criminals. Seventy men in blue, feeding off their city's sleaze. Seventy cops who were, on the one hand, taking paychecks from society to harass bookies and pimps and petty gambling impresarios and, on the other hand, taking payoffs to leave them alone.

This was the hypocritical subworld Mike Thompson and Andy Lash of the FBI had been guided into by their eccentric, chain-smoking, brothel-keeping, and otherwise strange and maddening source: Donald Hersing, private eye. In George Woods and his partner, Ray Emery, they had snared a couple of small-time operators. In Abe Schwartz, they had reached for someone almost too slippery to grasp. But in John DeBenedetto, the new man, the boss, the inspector, they had happened on a great old tree with roots spread deeply through the city of Philadelphia. When and if they brought down DeBenedetto, the crash was going to rustle a few leaves in the forest.

Catching the inspector was not going to be easy. Because he was afraid of being searched, Donald Hersing had not worn a hidden tape recorder for his first meeting with DeBenedetto at the Parkway Room. FBI agents positioned at tables nearby could see the two men in conversation, but they could not hear them. DeBenedetto had taken no money from the whorehouse owner that day. He was obviously too cagey for that. He had cut his deal with Hersing, explained his terms, and said he would send one of his lieutenants to pick up the money. Mike Thompson and Andy Lash knew that it would take more than just the word of their disreputable informant to convince a judge or jury of DeBenedetto's guilt.

On August 30, three days after the meeting, Hersing called the inspector. DeBenedetto was friendly but abrupt. He said he would send a vice squad lieutenant, John Smith, over to Hersing's apartment on South Street to pick up the first monthly payoff.

Hersing drove in from his home in Bucks County that afternoon at three, but Smith didn't show. Thompson and Lash had geared up the video and audio recording equipment. It was uncomfortable in the apartment. The air conditioner hadn't been working right all summer, and the place had not been built to encourage airflow. As the afternoon passed, it grew stifling. The three men were impatient. After about two hours Hersing dialed the inspector again. A receptionist answered the phone and asked for Hersing's name. Then Hersing was put on hold for a moment.

"Don?" DeBenedetto said.

"Yeah."

"Yeah, howya doin'!" DeBenedetto spoke heavy nasal Philadelphia-ese.

"All right, John. What happened? He didn't show up yet."

"Did he call ya?"

"No."

"I told him to. . . . He said he would call ya. I just spoke to him a little while ago. He said he'd call you from his house. You gonna be there for a while?"

"Yeah, I was, but I was getting ready to leave because I was—"

"Ah, well, wait a while. I'll tell him. Let me call him at home, tell him that you're waitin' for his call. Okay?"

"Okay."

"What I think he wanted to do was kinda meet you on the outside, you know? Everybody is afraid of everybody. Ya know what I mean?"

"All right. Well, tell him I don't care, you know."

DeBenedetto said he should wait a few minutes because Smith was probably on his way home from work. Hersing said he would meet with the lieutenant anywhere he wanted to meet.

"It'll make him feel more comfortable," the inspector said.

"It's all right with me, John."

"All right. Okay. I told him, I said, 'Look,' I said that, you know, I mentioned a couple of friends"—Hersing understood DeBenedetto to mean Detective Abe Schwartz and Inspector Jimmy Carlini—"I said, 'If they'll go in his house, I'm sure you can go in.' You know what I mean?"

Hersing asked whether Detective George Woods was going to be with the lieutenant. He wasn't eager to see Woods again, after having snitched on him during his first meeting with the inspector.

"No. Georgie is now a uniformed policeman"—and he emphasized the word "po-lice-man"—"in the Twenty-fifth District." The 25th was a

North Philly beat. If Woods was back in uniform, it meant that he had been demoted. He had been demoted and assigned to patrol city streets. "He's no longer with us," DeBenedetto said. "We decided he should go back because he did something very disloyal." Hersing gathered from the inspector's tone that he had relished busting Woods. DeBenedetto had also demoted and transferred Woods's partner, Ray Emery. Hersing thought, *Boy, no wonder everybody is afraid of this guy.*

"He ain't gonna give me any repercussions, is he?" Hersing asked, referring to Woods.

"Fuck no. No. He went away. You know what he told the lieutenant? 'I got caught.' That's all, you know what I mean? . . . I don't see any problems with him. Let me get you Smitty."

Smith never did call that day. The vice squad lieutenant had been Woods's supervisor, and it was Hersing's impression that Smith had been in on the payoffs all along. But he wasn't certain. If Hersing was right, then this new arrangement placed Smith in an awkward spot. If Woods and Emery had kept silent to protect the lieutenant, Hersing was the one remaining threat. Under those circumstances, dealing with this odd, talkative whorehouse owner would make Smith mighty uneasy. Hersing and the FBI suspected that this was why Smith kept putting off the meetings DeBenedetto arranged. One meeting after another was postponed. Three more weeks would pass before the lieutenant came by.

Finally, on September 17, Smith rang the doorbell at the South Street apartment. As usual, Thompson and Lash were hidden in the closet with the air-conditioning equipment on the first floor, under the stairway. They had turned on their camera and microphones to record the anticipated payoff. But, to the agents' chagrin, Smith asked Hersing to step outside. Hersing ran back in and got a jacket. The mild summer was quickly turning to fall.

The lieutenant was rotund. He had a great, thick hawk nose that protruded down to the tip of his upper lip. Smith's graying hair was in crisp regulation trim at all times, as it had been during his years of uniformed service, but the lieutenant had acquired a trendy flair since joining the detective squad. He had let his sideburns grow down almost to his earlobes, and wore a pair of wide, steel-framed aviator-style glasses. He was fifty-three years old. Eight years earlier, an admiring reporter had written that

Smith looked like George C. Scott, but he lacked the actor's voluptuous facial features. Smith's eyes and mouth were small. His neck plunged straight from chin tip to tie knot, making his head seem, from the correct angle, almost perfectly round. This gruff man had spent twenty years of night work in uniform, policing the poverty-blighted, crime-ridden neighborhoods of West Philadelphia, and returning at daybreak to his wife and three kids in a quiet Catholic neighborhood in the Northeast. His wife had worried about him desperately during those years. A phone call in the night when he was gone was enough to turn her blood cold. She knew that her husband was proud of his reputation for physical courage, and no matter how much she begged him to be careful, she knew that he never hesitated, when the situation called for it, to mix it up with the "bugs," as he called the hoodlums he chased in those days. In a long newspaper interview eleven years ago, Smith had called his West Philadelphia beat a "jungle district." And like many police officers who spent violent years patrolling hostile communities, even then Smith was cynical about the system he fought to uphold. He had glimpsed its shortcomings firsthand while at the same time getting kicked around and insulted by those who despised him for working to uphold it. Compared to that life, his job on the vice squad was a breeze. *If* you knew how to handle it. And lucrative. *If* you were careful.

And Smith was careful. For his first meeting with Hersing, Smith had brought along a young vice investigator named Larry Molloy, a big plainclothes officer. As Smith motioned Hersing into the back seat of a tan station wagon, Molloy strolled out to the corner of Seventh and South Streets to keep an eye on things.

In the car, Smith was surly. He accepted the $500 payoff, and explained that this money was just for the whorehouse at 1245 Vine Street. There would be more due for Hersing's other businesses, the Morning Glory after-hours club on Vine Street and the "modeling studio" at 2209 Walnut Street. As soon as he had taken the money, Smith laid into the whorehouse owner. According to Hersing, Smith said he had heard that Hersing was spreading around a story that Woods had been sharing his payoffs with "an Irish lieutenant." Hersing was a notorious talker, a man who loved to tell stories about himself. Smith wanted the talk to stop. After learning of Woodsie's fate, Hersing understood why. He was flustered. He swore that he hadn't told a soul, and, moments later, promised not to do it again.

The lieutenant spelled out arrangements for future payoffs. If he was unable to stop by and pick up cash, he said, Hersing could give the money to Molloy. Thompson and Lash remember that Hersing came back from the meeting shaken. He didn't like Smith.

But through the rest of September and October, Hersing's businesses ran smoothly. Gone was the almost comic "Dial-a-Bust" system. Paying off higher-ups promised to end these busts altogether. But even though, for the time being, Hersing's police hassles seemed to be over, Smith's bullying bothered him.

The FBI, of course, shared Hersing's eagerness to stop dealing through Smith. They were far more interested in getting the inspector himself on tape. They knew that DeBenedetto was manipulating the payoff system, but if the inspector kept dealing through Smith, the charge would be harder to prove.

In his efforts to get Smith out of the way, Hersing turned to his buddy Abe Schwartz. If anybody could get this surly lieutenant off his back, Schwartz could. But when Hersing approached him, Schwartz turned out to be no help at all. He just wanted to borrow some X-rated tapes for his new Betamax. He told Hersing he would have to work out his problems with the top man.

By now, Hersing was perturbed by the whole investigation. Thompson and Lash were exasperated. They knew they were into a big case. DeBenedetto had mentioned something to Hersing about paying off for video poker machines. This touched upon a separate—perhaps even bigger—investigation under way in the FBI office, one that would eventually implicate police officers citywide. But just as Thompson and Lash's supervisors and the U.S. attorney's office were getting hot for this Hersing case, their eccentric source seemed to be backing off. Hersing kept canceling meetings. He didn't return phone calls. He kept no regular hours anywhere. When they could find him, they would arrange for Hersing to set up another meeting with DeBenedetto. He would agree to wear a body recorder and get some of the inspector's machinations on tape. Hersing would phone DeBenedetto and set up the meeting. Then, on the appointed day, he would decide, on his own, to call the inspector and cancel it.

Hersing was feeling put upon. He was still worried about how much the FBI would eventually pay him for all this work. Working with easygoing Georgie Woods had been one thing. Working with men as menacing as DeBenedetto and Smith was something else. Thompson and Lash kept trying to talk Hersing into wearing a body recorder for meetings, especially because Smith kept refusing to come inside the wired apartment, but Hersing was afraid. Before almost every meeting he suspected that he would be searched. Smith was usually abusive and threatening. Furthermore, he had recently gotten into an argument with Hersing's brother at the Morning Glory.

On top of these investigative hassles, Hersing's prostitution business was giving him trouble. His prime competitor, a swank whorehouse called Chic, was pressuring him. Chic's owners were making noises about buying 1245 Vine Street, right out from under him. Hersing and his partner, Robertshaw, were just renting the place, and Robertshaw didn't want to buy it.

Hersing felt himself edging farther and farther out on a limb. He wasn't at all convinced, after all this time, that the FBI wouldn't just suddenly decide to drop their investigation and leave him hanging. And if they did follow through on it, indict these Philadelphia police officers, convict them and lock them away, what was going to happen to Donald Hersing? He couldn't very well expect to stay in Philadelphia. What would he do? There were going to be a lot of powerful people mad at him. When he first went to the FBI, Hersing had hoped he would be able to limit his involvement in the case to just making some undercover tape recordings—as he had done for smaller FBI operations in the past, up in Bucks County. But it soon became clear that this case was different. Hersing was the linchpin in an ever-expanding FBI probe. The agents had explained the federal witness protection program to Don and his new wife, Donna, but the idea of changing their names and going off to live someplace where no one knew them was hardly appealing. They would have to leave friends and family behind. One of the requirements of the witness protection plan was that you could leave no forwarding address, and you were not allowed to contact people from your past life. It was not a happy prospect. Hersing's businesses would fold. What would he do for a living? There were weeks when Hersing just wanted to pretend that none of this had ever happened.

But extricating himself from the situation was harder than going along with it.

Smith and Molloy stopped by the apartment again on October 21 to collect that month's payoff. Thompson and Lash waited in the closet with their monitors, but again the wary lieutenant refused to come inside. Instead, Molloy came to the door and said Smith wanted to talk to him in the car. Hersing climbed into the front seat of a white Thunderbird, and Smith chewed him out again. As they talked in the car, Molloy again spent the half hour standing on the corner, looking around.

Thompson and Lash were feeling discouraged. The investigation seemed stuck. Then, in November, things got worse. Hersing's Vine Street studio was raided. Some of the women were arrested, and he had to close the place down for a day. When he called DeBenedetto to complain, the inspector didn't want to talk about it. At first DeBenedetto said that the morals squad had made the bust, and that he had no control over them. "They usually only go around one time this winter," he told Hersing. Later, after checking into it, the inspector told Hersing that the raid had occurred because of a complaint from Roman Catholic High School up the street, at the corner of Vine and Broad. It seemed that one of the students had wandered into the studio, bought a session with one of Hersing's prostitutes, and contracted the clap. His mother had complained to the school, the school had complained to the district attorney, and the district attorney had leaned on the force. Hersing said he didn't believe it. He suspected that the complaint was a hoax, cooked up by his competitors.

Despite DeBenedetto's reassurances, there were more raids. By the time Smith was due to stop by 707-A South Street again for the November payoff, there had been two raids at Vine Street and one at Walnut.

For this meeting, Thompson and Lash had talked Hersing into wearing a body recorder. He wore it strapped in an elastic holster in the small of his back. As the agents wired him up, Hersing eyed the equipment with disdain. Citing his experience as a private detective and his work selling electronic surveillance equipment to governments in the Caribbean, Hersing told the agents about equipment he had worked with that was much smaller and more powerful. The agents had never heard of the super-

snooping devices their informant described. They figured that they would
have, if such things existed. As Hersing had become more and more difficult to work with, their patience with his self-importance and his supposed
expertise in law enforcement was wearing thin. While Hersing lectured,
the young agents would look at each other and roll their eyes.

This time Smith didn't insist that Hersing step outside the apartment.
After three months of dealing with him, Smith was more relaxed with Hersing.
He stepped into the dining room to take the payoff, and the two men launched
into a long, rambling conversation about whores and whorehouses. Hersing
was surprised by how knowledgeable Smith was. The lieutenant described
with glowing appreciation an Asian whore he had encountered working at a
different studio. He offered to give Hersing her name and address. Hersing
allowed as how a "well-built Jap" would do wonders for his business. Then
he complained to the lieutenant about the three raids. Smith would only say
that it was the work of the morals squad, not the vice squad, and that he didn't
have anything to do with the other group.

As this conversation wound on, Thompson and Lash listened from
just a few feet away inside the closet under the stairway. With the air-
conditioning unit running, it made quite a racket in their enclosure, so they
couldn't hear much of what was being said outside. Since one of their func-
tions was to protect Hersing, Thompson felt obliged to try to keep track
of what was going on. The solid, dark-haired agent crawled down to the
floor and peered through the crack at the bottom of the door. All he could
see were feet. Then, abruptly, the air conditioner kicked off. Alarmed by
the sudden silence, just an arm's length or two from Smith and Hersing
through the thin door, the two agents were afraid to breathe. They could
suddenly hear Smith's and Hersing's voices clearly on the other side of
the door. Thompson was still contorted on the floor, trying to look out of
the crack. They felt trapped and ridiculous. They would laugh about it
often, later. Thompson would joke that their FBI training had enabled them
to hold their breaths for the entire time. But, at the time, it was a long, har-
rowing ten minutes before the air-conditioning equipment kicked on again.

Smith collected the money and left.

The next week, Vine Street was raided again. The morals squad arrested
a prostitute who had been the toast of the whorehouse all that week after

her pinup appeared in the "Winner's Circle," a daily feature in *The Phila-delphia Journal* that displayed a seductively posed young woman in a bikini. The raid occurred on a Saturday night. On Monday morning Hersing phoned DeBenedetto to complain.

The inspector asked if it was the same group that had made the earlier pinches.

"Yeah, same guys," Hersing said.

"Oh, boy. I don't know. I'll have to see. I'll have to find out who they were and you'll have to get together with them."

"Yeah, you can make that so I can get together with them so it won't happen again."

"Yeah, well, I'm gonna set something up."

"'Cause I tell you what, John, my girls are ready to walk out on me."

A few days later, Hersing called DeBenedetto again.

The inspector said, "I talked to that fellow and he is gonna talk it over with his, ya know, friends, and he is going to get back to me. And I'll set up a meet, for you to meet him."

And again, a few days later, DeBenedetto told Hersing on the phone that Hersing's original suspicion about what had sparked the morals squad raids may have been correct. The inspector had heard a rumor that Tracy Summers, the manager of Chic, had paid the morals squad to make trouble for Hersing. DeBenedetto said his boys would be paying Summers a visit in return. He had already spoken to Chic's lawyer.

"I put it on him," the inspector said. "I put it right on him about that. And I says, 'I want this stopped. I don't want no wars starting.' I says, 'If you're going to start, we're going to start.' He swears, no. He swears, no. But, ah, we're paying her a visit today anyhow."

"Tracy?"

"Yup."

"Good."

Thompson and Lash couldn't get over how much the inspector of the city's central police division sounded like a mob boss. They were more determined than ever to complete their case on him. After the November meeting with Smith, the agents had had a long talk with Hersing. They had decided that Hersing should stop making payoffs.

"We felt that was the only way that we could get to DeBenedetto, because it looked like he was going to continue dealing through Smith," says Thompson, who nevertheless felt, at the time, that the tape-recorded phone calls and Hersing's testimony alone might have been enough to convict the inspector. "We wanted him to be more active in the taking of the money. We knew he was corrupt, we knew he was taking the money— he was getting it through Lieutenant Smith—but we wanted him to come after the money or say something stronger than what he had said already. So we felt stopping the money would maybe generate something."

There was another reason. It was increasingly difficult to set up these meetings with Hersing. The agents recognized that their informant's interest in the case had fallen off. He was impatient. To the agents, his every move—every call he made on the bugged telephone, every payoff he made—added to their growing store of evidence, but, to Hersing, the agents were just intruding on his life. He was less and less willing to do things that seemed uncomfortable or unnatural to him just because the FBI thought it would be a good idea. And besides, Hersing was beginning to know his way around Philadelphia, and the business wasn't bad. He had gotten rid of Woods—DeBenedetto had taken care of that for him—and he genuinely liked Abe Schwartz. And then the inspector had sort of taken up for him in the battle with Chic. Knowing that when Hersing's role in the investigation became public his satisfying lifestyle would end, Thompson and Lash couldn't help wondering if, down deep, Don Hersing was no longer as determined as they were to send these men to jail.

So the decision to take a break would be mutually advantageous. Hersing would make no payoffs during December, January, or February. The investigators would wait to see what happened.

During December, the first month that Hersing made no payments to the police, he traveled to Florida for his son's college graduation. On his return, in the first month of 1982, his competitor, Chic, bought the building on the corner of Vine and Thirteenth Streets, the location Hersing had so carefully selected more than a year before. His competition put a small red awning over the doorway with the name "Chic II."

In response, Hersing and his partner Robertshaw simply moved over two doors, to 1241 Vine, and signed a five-year lease for the first floor of the townhouse on the other side of Frank's Place. The bar was now sandwiched between warring brothels.

Into the second month of the payoff moratorium, Hersing noticed a change in the attitude of his contacts in the police department. He continued to complain to Abe Schwartz about the three busts at Vine Street., but Schwartz had turned suddenly cool. Where the ebullient detective had once carried on long, rambling conversations with the brothel owner, now Hersing could hardly shake a word out of him. It was like Schwartz was trying, without actually coming out and saying anything, to give Hersing a message. The detective would answer the phone:

"Hello, can I help you?"

And Hersing would say warmly, "Yeah, Abraham!"

The detective would answer again, flatly, as if he hadn't recognized the voice, "Abe Schwartz."

"How you doing, Abe?" Hersing would persist with the friendly tone.

"All right," Schwartz would answer.

"You don't recognize my voice again," Hersing would complain.

"Yes I do, brother," Schwartz would say.

Whenever he phoned DeBenedetto, the inspector seemed to be out. If he got Lieutenant Smith on the phone, Smith would complain that he was too busy to talk. He would tell Hersing to call back later, and when Hersing did, the lieutenant would be out. He told Hersing that he kept "erratic" hours.

On January 29, Hersing paid Schwartz a visit at the detective's office on the second floor of east division headquarters at Front and Westmoreland Streets. He had two X-rated tapes to deliver, *Debbie Does Dallas* and *Blondie*. Schwartz had a friend who was going to make copies for him. Thompson and Lash again wanted Hersing to wear a body recorder for the meeting, but Hersing wasn't about to walk into a police station wired.

Schwartz didn't have much time for his "brother" Don. They discussed the lack of payments during the previous two months. Schwartz told Hersing that the inspector had been going easy on him because of the three morals squad hits and because Hersing had had to clear out of 1245. When Hersing complained about the detective's abrupt change in manner toward him on the telephone, Schwartz said that they suspected their phones were being tapped. He told Hersing that two FBI agents had been spotted across town. No one knew what they were doing, but people had become more careful about talking on the phone.

Another month went by. On February 26, Hersing phoned DeBenedetto.

"How you doing, John?"

"Okay. What, what did you do, go to Europe or something?" The inspector sounded distinctly unfriendly.

"No, I didn't go to Europe. We moved. We had to move out of that building."

"Yeah."

Hersing started to explain, but DeBenedetto abruptly cut him off. "What's on your mind?"

"Can we arrange a meeting with them people you mentioned?" Hersing was referring to the morals squad.

DeBenedetto said he was still trying.

"They're knocking me nuts," Hersing complained.

"Well, we ain't been bothering you."

"No, no, no. I know that. But I'm saying them other guys."

"Well, I'm trying to work something with them."

"You know what's happening, John. Tracy's going to move into that— Chic is moving into our old building."

"Well, I don't know," the inspector said. "If they are, they're gonna get their balls knocked off."

"Well, they're, I think they're the ones behind motivating it."

"Nah, you're wrong. You're wrong. When, if you ever come around here and I see ya, I'll explain it to you."

They arranged to meet on the following Tuesday, March 2, but at the last moment Hersing again called to cancel. They set up the meeting instead for Thursday at lunchtime in the Parkway Room.

Thursday, March 4, 1982, dawned cloudy and cold. Thompson and Lash met Hersing at his apartment. The agents succeeded this time in persuading their undercover source to wear the tape recorder. They set the small Nagra into the elastic holder and again strapped it to the small of Hersing's back. They gave him $500 in marked bills. It was time to start paying off again.

By noon, the clouds had cleared. Lash drove across town to the Parkway Room ahead of the others. He would be observing the meeting from another table. Thompson followed Hersing's Thunderbird, a new car, white with a red top. The agent parked on Spring Garden Street to keep watch outside in case DeBenedetto decided to leave the restaurant with Hersing. The FBI had even placed a tape recorder in Hersing's car, in the event that one of his payoff sessions wound up there.

When Lash arrived he was escorted to a table by Gene Console, a short, friendly man with thick hair and a soft, handsome face. A big color photo portrait of Console, framed, hung prominently up over a mirror on the east wall of the restaurant. It pictured the restaurant manager in a tasseled leather jacket staring off wistfully, and looked a bit like the kind of picture one sees on the album covers of popular country singers. There were ceiling fans overhead, slowly turning. Temperatures were still in the thirties, but the noontime sun streaming through the restaurant's high greenhouse windows on the south wall bathed the dining room in warmth. Lash knew that DeBenedetto liked to sit at the round table in the front corner of the place, behind the thick pea-green pillar. So he was pleased when Console gave him a table nearby.

Hersing came in a few minutes later, wearing his short tan leather jacket and double-knit trousers. Console met him at the entrance to the dining room. Lash could overhear Hersing explain that he was there to meet the inspector, so Console sat him down at the round corner table. Hersing ordered a cup of coffee and lit a cigarette. Console walked over to the bar and rang DeBenedetto at central division headquarters down the street.

A few moments later the inspector and his lieutenant strode in. DeBenedetto looked crisp and official in his white uniform shirt and tie. The portly Smith was dressed casually. Lash could see right away that there was nothing at all friendly in the way they greeted Don Hersing today.

"Howya doin', John?" Hersing said, smiling.

"Oh, somebody told me you left town," said Smith, pulling out a chair. "I haven't seen you for so long." Then the lieutenant let the inspector handle things.

"Where have you been for four months?" asked DeBenedetto.

"Where have I been? All over." Hersing looked across at the two men with a hurt, quizzical expression.

"Yeah, but you ain't seen us for four months."

"Yeah, I know."

"Well, we got, we got a little message for you. I want you to get something straight." DeBenedetto accused Hersing of mentioning his name in three city bars.

Hersing was confused. "Where, John?"

And the inspector listed two places.

Hersing denied it in a hurt, pleading way. He spoke in a whining, nasal voice. "I didn't even know you then, John."

"Let me tell you something," DeBenedetto said. He wasn't even listening to Hersing. "I don't want to do business with you no more. This money don't mean anything to me. Understand what I mean? So you operate the way you want to operate, but I don't want to do business with you anymore. Okay? Because if you think you're gonna walk around this fucking city, come around every four months and we have to chase you all the fuck around . . ."

"John, things has been bad, man." Now Hersing's tone was obsequious.

"Well, call us up and tell us 'things has been bad,'" the inspector said, mocking Hersing's tone. "But not you, you want to play a cute game, you wiseass. Now, I try to put you in touch with a certain guy, Delvecchio"— John Delvecchio headed the morals squad—"and you've dumped him two times."

Hersing was truly confused. Delvecchio had never arranged a meeting with him. (Delvecchio, in fact, never did meet with Hersing, and although a federal grand jury would later name him as an unindicted coconspirator, he was never charged with a crime.)

Hersing whined, he pleaded, he swore to DeBenedetto that he had never stood up Delvecchio. "I swear to God. Honest to God I didn't, John."

"Let me tell you what we're going to do with you. We're not going to do any more business with you. See that club, that club is going on our list as regular clubs. We're going to start hitting you in the afternoon, we're gonna start breaking your fucking balls, because you broke my balls for four months."

"John, I'll make it up."

"You ain't gonna make nothing up," DeBenedetto snapped. He leaned toward Hersing across the table, and spoke in a low, threatening tone. "We're done with you. You're done. You want to get on our after-hours club list, it's okay with me. But that's as far as we're gonna go. We ain't gonna do no business with you otherwise because I ain't gonna chase you all over the fucking United States. . . . You know why you're around to see me now? Because you need me. You need me, don't you? You want me to help you out, don't you? Well, I ain't gonna help you out—you're going, you're going down the tubes. I'm gonna tell you another thing. You moved out of that one place, right?"

"Yeah."

"Now where are you?"

"Twelve forty-one."

"Just had a complaint," Smith chimed in. "You don't know about the complaint from Roman High School, huh?"

"No."

"You don't know about the kid getting the clap in there and going home and telling his mother? You don't know about that?"

"No, I don't."

"Well, I'm tellin' ya," DeBenedetto said. "If you would be in contact with us, we would know what's going on."

Despite his overbearing manner, DeBenedetto seemed, suddenly, to be backtracking from his initial outburst. Now he was convincing Hersing how valuable they were to him. He evidently cared about the money more than he said, thought Hersing. The inspector went on. He explained that they had tried to let Hersing know what was going on, but couldn't find him. He said they weren't about to leave recorded messages on his answering machine. "Now, if you think we're *about* to talk into a machine, you're wrong," DeBenedetto sneered. Hersing's mind rested suddenly on the gentle hum at the small of his back—*Hmmm.*

"And I'll tell you. We don't know whether we—frankly, we don't want to do business with you and Delvecchio doesn't want to do business with you. 'Cause you've got a big mouth. You just get drunk and talk."

Hersing protested. He said he never drank anything harder than beer. He swore that he had never mentioned their names.

"Listen," DeBenedetto said. "Let me tell you something. Nobody we do business with mentions our names. . . . Frankly, Don, I'll tell you. You came recommended to me by a guy that I like. Otherwise you would have never gotten near me. See? Now this guy vouches for you and Carlini vouches for you. And they never dealt business with you, see? Now I told them about you, and they don't even like you. 'Cause, I don't know. That talk shit."

Again, Hersing protested that he had never mentioned DeBenedetto's name. Smith explained that it wasn't necessary to say his name; if he identified the inspector by rank, people knew who he was talking about. Hersing said that he had only been in one of the bars DeBenedetto had mentioned, and that had been before DeBenedetto took command of the central division.

"What the fuck?" the inspector said. "They don't put dates on these things! But you're tellin' people you *got* us. And you don't *got* us. Because we ain't seen you for four months. And you didn't call us up. You didn't say, 'Hey, fellas, things are rough. I'm getting a lot of pinches.' We know that. We know you were taking pinches. We know that."

Again DeBenedetto accused Hersing of setting and breaking appointments with Delvecchio. Hersing swore he hadn't. "John, I swear on my *mother*," Hersing said, God apparently not having been sufficient.

"Now he knows that man for over twenty years," Smith interjected. "Now who's he supposed to believe?"

"I know the fucking guy from my *neighborhood*," DeBenedetto said.

But Hersing insisted that he had never heard from the morals squad. He hadn't. He was genuinely puzzled by the inspector's accusations. DeBenedetto continued abusing Hersing. They went back over the story about the high school kid that supposedly contracted venereal disease in Hersing's place. They said the district attorney wanted Hersing "off the face of the earth."

"And you were never aware of the complaint, right?" Smith said. "How the fuck can you operate a business like that?"

"Yeah, but if somebody don't tell me, how do I know?"

"Well, how will they tell you if you stay away?" Smith answered.

This went on and on. Lash couldn't overhear the conversation, but he could tell Hersing was taking his lumps. He overheard Hersing pleading, "I swear to God . . ." The officers were hunched over the table, leaning toward Hersing. Lash could tell that their undercover man was doing his best to hang on.

DeBenedetto told Hersing they were "putting him on the back burner." Finally, they let up a bit. They started to talk business again. Despite the bluster, they clearly weren't serious about refusing money from Hersing. They encouraged Hersing to stay in touch with them. Then they could tip him off about things. They wanted to know if Hersing was making money now, after all the hits and the move.

"Are youse operational now at 1241?" DeBenedetto asked.

"Yeah. We're coming back up on our feet now. I mean, if you give me a little bit I'll make it up, John. I got something with me."

"What have you got with you?"

"Five."

"Five hundred?" the inspector said, sarcastic. He looked over at Smith comically, and the two officers laughed.

"John, if you, if you give me—"

"What kind of—are you *Jewish?*"

"No, no, John."

"You think I'm a fucking Jew. You think he's a fucking Jew."

"John, John, no. John, give me a couple of weeks and I guarantee I'll make every bit of it up."

"Oh, guess what? Hold that five hundred and add it to whatever you've got in a couple of weeks. Okay? Then come around when you want to talk business."

"Okay. Okay."

"And in the meantime, we have no alliance."

"How much, how much in arrears do you know you are?" Smith asked. "This is one, right?"

"This'll be three payments."

"What?" Smith asked.

Hersing could see that wouldn't do.

"Four. This'll be the fourth."

Then DeBenedetto said, "You hold that five hundred and add, and add something *substantial* to it."

"How about if I add fifteen [hundred] to it and make it two [thousand]?"

"I'm gonna talk to Delvecchio," the inspector said. "If I went there, even assuming you could get Delvecchio, how much do you think you're gonna have to pay him?"

"I have no ideas, John, whatever you say. . . . If I can get him off my back, then I can operate. But we're running on low key. They're sending three and four times a day somebody into the fucking place."

DeBenedetto said there was no use in doing business with Hersing if the morals squad was going to keep locking his girls up.

"I'm gonna talk to Delvecchio tomorrow. Let me put you on the back burner for a while. You hold that five hundred, we'll tell you how much it is."

He told Hersing to call him the next day at 11 a.m., after he met with the head of the morals squad. Then the two officers stood up without further ceremony and began to walk off.

"Thanks, John Smitty, have a good day," Hersing called after them.

"I will," said Smith.

But DeBenedetto and Smith didn't leave. Instead they walked over to the bar. Hersing sat for a few moments alone. On the restaurant's sound system, Jimmy Buffett sang his hungover lament, "Margaritaville." Hersing called for his check and finished his coffee, which he hadn't touched, and crushed out his cigarette. When the waitress brought his check, Lash watched as Hersing stood up and put on his jacket, took a bill out of his wallet, placed it on the table, and left. Hersing nodded and said goodbye again to DeBenedetto and Smith as he passed them at the bar on his way out.

Lash stayed at his table for a while longer. In a few minutes, a well-dressed man with dark hair came in and greeted DeBenedetto and Smith. They returned to the table. The man in the fine suit sat in the same chair that Hersing had been in, and the inspector and the lieutenant sat back in their chairs. It seemed to Lash as if the same scene was being enacted again with a different person. Then Lash left. He would see the man with dark hair again.

When Hersing left the restaurant he walked back up the street to his Thunderbird. He got in and took a couple of deep breaths, turned on the ignition, and put on his seat belt. The weatherman on the radio announced that the temperature was thirty-two degrees, and predicted a warmer day tomorrow. Soft music began to play.

Just before he reached back to the machine in the elastic holder and turned off the tape, Hersing muttered to himself with disgust.

He said, "Filthy cops."

It had gone better than Thompson and Lash had dared expect. Halting payoffs for a few months had, so to speak, drawn the beast from his lair. Now they had DeBenedetto on tape spelling things out clearly. The inspector of the central police division bullied Hersing like a mob enforcer, exhibiting what a prosecutor would later term "amazing venality." Thompson and Lash knew that this revealing glimpse of DeBenedetto would enable any jury to see past his rank and reputation.

They also noticed that after the March 4 meeting, the one they came to call the "browbeating session," their informant's interest in the case revived; DeBenedetto and Smith had insulted Hersing. He felt pushed around and squeezed, the way he had felt the year before when George Woods had upped the ante on him. Hersing mostly blamed Smith. The inspector's accusations about missing meetings with John Delvecchio especially bugged him. He figured the lieutenant was feeding DeBenedetto false stories about him, hoping to poison Hersing's dealings with the boss because he feared the inspector would find out he had been in on Georgie Woods's Dial-a-Bust system. Hersing had felt stupid and powerless sitting there just taking it that day. *Didn't these guys know who Donald Hersing was?*

For the next three weeks, Hersing kept calling DeBenedetto to see if he had arranged a meeting with the morals squad, but the inspector kept putting him off. He called his friend Schwartz, but affable Abe seemed to have grown completely cool.

Finally, Hersing got a message. He was to meet with Smith back at the Parkway Room on Wednesday, March 24. Thompson and Lash again wanted their informant to wear the body recorder, but, again, Hersing was afraid. He was sure he would be searched. A few weeks before, in one of his calls to DeBenedetto, the inspector had said something about having Hersing "checked out" before they could start doing business again. And then, when he talked with Lieutenant Smith on the phone to set up the meeting, he had asked how much money he should bring with him. Smith had told him to bring nothing, just himself.

So now, at this first meeting since the browbeating session, Hersing was jumpy. The agents were especially reluctant to let him go without the recorder. They felt that they were at a crucial point in the case. Today Hersing would find out exactly how much it would take to get back into the inspector's favor. They suspected that Smith was going to spell out the amount at this meeting. But they weren't going to force their informant to wear a tape. They argued with him. Agents would be inside and outside the restaurant observing, they said. Nobody had searched him yet. But Hersing was adamant. He went to the meeting without the body wire.

He arrived at the Parkway Room first, and Console showed him to the usual table. After a few minutes, Smith walked in with Larry Molloy. But instead of coming to the table, Smith ignored Hersing and walked to the bar. Molloy came up to the table and asked Hersing to accompany him to the men's room. As agents at a nearby table watched, Hersing followed Molloy into the men's room.

According to Hersing, once inside the lavatory Molloy told him to drop his pants. Hersing asked why, and Molloy, who was apologetic, said he had to search him. Hersing took off his trousers and his underpants. Molloy frisked him, even reaching up in his armpits. Then they came back out to see Smith. On their way out, Hersing recalls, Molloy offered him some advice. "He said, 'Look, if you are behind four payments, why don't you give the boss an extra payment, which would make it five payments, and get back in his good graces?'"

At the table, Hersing said, Smith told him he was behind four months of payments. That would mean that he owed $2,000. But again, Hersing said, Smith explained that it would be pointless to make any payments until an arrangement was worked out with the morals squad.

So Smith met Hersing at the Parkway Room again on April 1. It was at that meeting that Hersing was told a deal had been made with the morals squad. He would have to pay the $2,000 in arrears, and the new arrangement would be $500 monthly for the vice squad, another $500 monthly for the morals squad, and $300 monthly, on top of all that, for Hersing's after-hours club, the Morning Glory. The payoffs would fall due the 15th of each month.

The lieutenant was in a friendly mood—friendlier, in fact, than he had ever been. The agents watching the two men in the Parkway Room stayed for several hours. Hersing was ordering drinks for himself and Smith, and they were obviously loosening up. They seemed to be having a good time. So, finally, the agents left.

According to Hersing, he and the lieutenant eventually left the Parkway Room and went to the Morning Glory, where they stayed until early the next morning. Just before dawn, Hersing drove Smith back to his car at division headquarters. Then Hersing drove home to Levittown.

A few days later, Hersing got his instructions for making the arrears payoff. He was told to leave the money under a napkin at the Parkway Room on April 6. So he drove over that afternoon, ordered a cup of coffee, and slipped an envelope with $2,000 in it under a napkin. Then he left. After he had gone, Gene Console picked up the napkin with the envelope in it. He put it on the kitchen counter. When DeBenedetto and Smith came in, he retrieved it and put it on their table. Donald Hersing was back in business with the Philadelphia police.

After the night they went out drinking together, Smith became more friendly with Hersing. The informant secretly despised Smith, but he played along. Even when he was on the lieutenant's good side, Smith could be insulting and abusive. It was a bizarre relationship, wary on one side, entirely bogus on the other.

But with whatever easing of tension this newfound camaraderie brought, Smith finally felt relaxed enough to come upstairs in the apartment at 707-A South St. Two weeks after Hersing had dropped off the $2,000 at the Parkway Room, the lieutenant stopped by to pick up the regular $1,300 monthly payment for April. Thompson and Lash watched the TV monitor downstairs with delight as Hersing handed over the money and the lieutenant counted it out. This, coupled with the Parkway Room recording of DeBenedetto, was what prosecutors liked to call "incontrovertible evidence." Hersing and the lieutenant chatted on for about twenty minutes. Then Smith announced that he had to get going. It was late in the afternoon.

"So you're not allowed to go out with me anymore?" Hersing asked.

"Afraid so," Smith said. The inspector wasn't happy about his lieutenant's night on the town. He had told Smith that he shouldn't be seen out drinking with Hersing.

So Smith left. Thompson and Lash rewound the videotape and returned it to the safe at FBI headquarters in the courthouse on Market Street. Several days later, after prosecutors had seen the agents' official written account of the meeting, the U.S. attorney's office asked to see the recording. Thompson and Lash got out the tape, walked across the building to the prosecutors' office, set it into a videotape recorder, and sat back to watch.

In a moment the picture came on, *but there was no sound!* For some reason, the videotape had no sound for the first nineteen minutes, during the most crucial portion of the meeting. The agents had had a backup tape recorder in the closet, but they had never turned it on. Hearing the conversation through their earphones, they had assumed that the audio equipment was picking it up, too. It was a great disappointment.

So they set up anxiously again a week later, when Smith came back to the apartment to pick up $1,300, this for the month of June. Again he came upstairs. Hersing gave him a beer, and the lieutenant tipped him that state liquor board agents were investigating the Morning Glory. Then, when Hersing handed over the envelope with "Insurance" written on it, Smith did something that flabbergasted the agents in the closet downstairs, something that even made up for the foul-up during the previous meeting. The man who had been so coy for months about even entering the apartment suddenly offered to spell things out for the informant (and, eventually, a jury) explicitly.

"You know how this is broke down?" Smith asked Hersing.

"No."

"That's three for the club."

"Right."

"Which is what everybody pays."

"Oh yeah, you told me, go ahead."

"Okay? A nickel for us and a nickel for the other squad."

The lieutenant went on to explain that the vice squad had an advantage over the morals squad because the latter normally was busy following up on complaints. The vice squad had more latitude with its power.

"We can go out and pinch anybody, anytime we want," Smith said. "We don't need no fucking paper. Just because I want to, right?"

This brief explanation confirmed not only that Smith knew what he was doing, and what the money was for, but that Hersing's payoffs were part of a larger pattern. The FBI couldn't have gotten more if they had injected Smith with sodium pentathol.

This time the agents didn't wait a day before replaying the videotape to make sure that it worked. It was all there this time, sound and video. Right there in black and white.

*   *   *

After that meeting, the FBI was through with Smith and DeBenedetto and their helpers. Hersing's contacts had spread, opening up new, wider avenues to probe. Agents were following these new leads into a widespread system of police payoffs involving video poker machine gambling in city bars. An investigation into police extortion at gay bars had led another team of FBI agents to John DeBenedetto.

So it came as no disappointment, though it was a surprise, when the central police division decided on its own to stop doing business with Donald Hersing.

On July 27, Hersing called Smith to arrange a meeting. Smith came to the phone and said he would stop by 707-A South Street that afternoon.

He stopped by about 8 p.m. This time, as in the past, he had Molloy with him and he refused to step inside. Hersing walked outside with him.

"Look, we don't do no more business with you," he said, according to Hersing. "This is it. No hard feelings. Forget it."

And that was it. For whatever reason, the police officers had shut the door on Hersing for good. Thompson and Lash figured that they probably just got tired of dealing with someone they considered unreliable. Either that or word had gotten back to DeBenedetto and Smith about some of the undercover work Hersing had done in the past. He had, after all, worked with the FBI in Bucks County investigating police corruption. There was also the fact that, during the May 26 meeting, Hersing had told Smith about an electronic device that could be used to tell whether a phone was tapped. He had gone on and on, revealing a familiarity with electronic snooping devices that may have alarmed the lieutenant, who tended to be an extremely cautious man anyway. Whatever.

"We don't know," Thompson says, "and Smith and DeBenedetto aren't talking."

It didn't matter. The inspector had closed the door too late.

It was time to tell the commissioner. By September 1982, the FBI was thirteen months along in its probe of corruption in the Philadelphia Police Department. At least seven of Police Commissioner Morton Solomon's men, including the commander of the city's central police division, were certain to be indicted. John Hogan, the special agent in charge of the Philadelphia FBI office, felt it was time that his friend Solomon got the bad news.

It was a task rued by the tall, gray FBI man. But despite concerns for secrecy expressed by William B. Lytton, the assistant U.S. attorney who was preparing the cases for prosecution, Hogan wanted to let Solomon know. His office depended heavily on the city police. The two law enforcement organizations worked together every day. Hogan and Solomon were professional and social friends. News that Hogan's agents had uncovered a major scandal on the city force would disturb and embarrass his friend.

Hogan himself found it disturbing. He didn't like investigating cops. He had been a cop all his life, and knew what a hard and sometimes thankless job it could be. But for the same reason that the news he bore saddened him, it also sickened him. Corruption like the large-scale graft that his men had discovered in the Philadelphia Police Department tainted everyone in law enforcement. He wasn't about to shy away from what had to be done.

So on September 30 Hogan phoned the commissioner's office and set up a meeting for that afternoon. Such sessions were not uncommon. Hogan and his associates often walked the few blocks north from their offices to the Police Administration Building, better known as the Roundhouse, a modern, curved concrete structure at Eighth and Race Streets. Hogan preferred discussing sensitive matters face-to-face, and in his line of work, most matters were sensitive. At about 1 p.m. Hogan and John Anderson, a younger man with broad shoulders and dark hair who had been supervising the agents conducting the probe, strode across the Roundhouse's front plaza, past the giant statue of a cop holding a small boy, and checked in with the receptionist. They were given visitors' badges. Then they took an elevator up three floors to Solomon's office.

The commissioner, a portly man with thin white hair, was seated behind his big desk just inside a set of wide double doors. He waved the FBI men in. Solomon had a spacious, green-carpeted chamber of an office. The windows just behind him looked out over Race Street. On the sill was a replica, almost four feet tall, of the statue outside. On the left was an arrangement of chairs and a table for more informal talks, and beyond that was a door that opened onto a conference room. Hogan and Anderson took two chairs, swung them over to the front of Solomon's desk, and sat.

Hogan came right to the point. Their whole conversation lasted only about a half hour. He and Anderson told the commissioner that the FBI had been investigating corruption in his police department, and explained that they were not going to be able to give him many details. Solomon listened gravely. He said he understood. They outlined the general nature of the evidence that their agents had assembled.

"The commissioner showed no real outward emotion as we talked," Hogan says. "I think he may have been surprised that our office had been investigating his department.... Commissioner Solomon had been a member of that department for many years. He was a reform-minded commissioner appointed by a reform mayor [William J. Green]. We got the impression that it was a problem he had long been concerned about, just as there are things that worry the commander of any large organization. I can't emphasize enough how completely cooperative Commissioner Solomon was. He said he would help us in any way he could. What were his exact words? He said something like 'If you can root out only one of the corrupt officers on this force, we would be grateful.' That was how strongly he put it."

Hogan explained that there was a lot of work yet to be done. Solomon said he understood the need for secrecy. He told the FBI men again, as they were leaving, that he would cooperate in any way he could.

What the FBI did not know was that someone else was privy to the secret details of its case.

In 1981, when Hersing had first approached the Bureau, he had also begun telling the same story to his friend Tilt Meyer, the *Trenton Times* reporter. The arrangement was that Meyer would not write the story unless something happened to Hersing, or until the undercover operation was completed.

But by the fall of 1982, Meyer and his editors were not just interested in the Philadelphia corruption story, they were impatient to print it. The reporter had been hearing about this big-time police corruption probe in Philadelphia for more than a year. Through all those months, Hersing had talked with him often. Sometimes they met. Mostly, Meyer would get phone calls at all hours of the day and night. Hersing was usually eager to fill him in on the latest. Sometimes he was full of bluster and brag. Sometimes he was angry. Sometimes Hersing went on and on complaining about the FBI; about how the Bureau couldn't be trusted and how it was nickeling-and-diming him and his wife. Sometimes Meyer could see that Hersing was genuinely shaken and fearful. He would listen, ask a few questions, take notes. It was a shame this probe wasn't under way in Trenton, his home turf. Then Meyer would have a scoop people would remember for a long time.

As it was, the reporter was content to bide his time. At least the central figure, Hersing, was a Trenton native. That would give him a slight local angle. And there would be something delicious about scooping all the Philadelphia press with a major story right under their noses. Still, a police corruption probe in Philadelphia was of only marginal interest in this central New Jersey city. Meyer had little difficulty at first keeping his promise not to write until Hersing gave the go-ahead.

But as the months went by, Meyer says, his editors grew more and more eager. News organizations can only sit on a story for so long before it hatches, and Meyer's editors were afraid that this story would soon hatch, with or without them. At first, Meyer says, he resisted; he had promised Hersing. But then he found out that Hersing had also been talking to another reporter, a competitor from the *Bucks County Courier Times* named Karl Stark.

Fearing he was about to be scooped, Meyer stopped by the FBI office in Philadelphia during the last week of October and talked to John Anderson. The FBI supervisor listened with mounting chagrin as the reporter explained all that he knew. Hersing had obviously been talking to Meyer all along. Although he was officially able to neither confirm nor deny Meyer's story, Anderson says, he could see that Meyer wanted to do the right thing.

Anderson says he told Meyer: "We aren't using Hersing as much as we did in the beginning, but there are still things we want to do with him. We aren't ready for this thing to break yet."

Meyer wanted something more concrete. He says he told Anderson that if going ahead with the story would jeopardize the investigation, he would wait until there were indictments—but he wanted to know early enough to be first with it. Anderson conferred with prosecutor Bill Lytton. Then he called Meyer back and said that he couldn't offer any deals, but that he would prefer it if the newspaper would wait.

For Meyer, with the imminent threat of the story breaking elsewhere, this was not enough.

Over that weekend, Meyer phoned his source. Hersing was angry. The reporter said he knew Hersing had also been talking to Stark. Hersing denied it. Meyer said he had given the FBI a chance to call him off, but they wouldn't. He and his editors feared the story would break anyway. He said he felt that he might lose his job if he didn't write the story. His wife was about to have a baby. Hersing was not unsympathetic. But he also knew that the size of whatever reward he got at the end of the case would depend on how well the FBI felt that he had cooperated with them. Leaking the story to a reporter would hardly improve the Bureau's estimation of his work. He reminded Meyer of the promise.

Meyer said he was sorry, but the story was going to run. Later, he got a call from Hersing's wife, Donna, who was crying. Didn't he know that he could be jeopardizing her husband's life? Meyer felt bad about the whole thing.

Anderson got another call from Meyer on Sunday. The reporter could hold off no longer. He told Anderson that his editors were really pushing him. There was nothing he could do. The FBI supervisor could only repeat the standard line: he would neither confirm nor deny the story.

The story ran under a big black headline the following morning, Monday, November 1, 1982: "FBI Probes Philly Cops; Sting Operation Big as Abscam."

Meyer did not mention Hersing by name in the story, referring to him only as "a Trenton native," but the information had Hersing's grandiose stamp. The story reported that two hundred FBI agents were being assembled to begin handing out subpoenas to the vast number of suspects in the probe.

Karl Stark's story ran the following day.

First Assistant U.S. Attorney Bill Lytton found out that the story was going to break the night before. He was at home in Chester County with his wife and two small children. He remembers that it was Halloween.

Lytton is a bookish man who looks every inch the prosperous young liberal Republican lawyer—pin-striped, cotton-shirted, silk-tied, and straight-laced. Reared in St. Louis, Lytton went to Georgetown University and then to American University's law school. He had worked for

Senator Charles F. Percy (R., Ill.), monitoring legal issues before the Senate Judiciary Committee, prior to landing a job in the federal prosecutor's office in Philadelphia in 1978.

He looked younger than his thirty-three years, with a few stray strands of brown hair falling over a broad forehead, a soft, friendly gaze, and a slightly reticent smile. Lytton was an idealist, a man with an academic appetite and appreciation of the law and law enforcement. He would describe the FBI probe in a way that might make the FBI agents he worked with squint quizzically at each other—"It was essentially a proactive investigation," Lytton says, "where you proceed by looking at objective facts, taking whatever other input you can get, and trying to develop some sort of hypothesis. It's very scientific in a way; you set up a hypothesis and see whether you can prove it or not."

Agents Mike Thompson and Andy Lash worked closely on the case with Lytton and another assistant U.S. attorney named Bob Hickok. Lytton estimates that he talked to either Thompson or Lash daily for almost two and a half years. Although the U.S. attorney's office and the FBI have different responsibilities—the Bureau collects information; the Justice Department, working with a federal grand jury, decides what to do with it—Lytton and Hickok and the agents followed the more typical current practice of working closely together through every step of the case. "We gave them some advice they took during the investigation," Lytton says, "and they gave us some advice during the prosecution which we took."

Lytton and Hersing might as well have come from different planets. They had met over lunch with Lash and Anderson at the Moshulu, a floating restaurant at Penn's Landing, and the whorehouse owner says he took an immediate dislike to Lytton because of the way the prosecutor talked to the waitresses. He regarded Lytton as a snob. As for Lytton, the most he will say about Hersing is: "He was a source, an informant, and as such he inhabited the world we were investigating. You get used to working with people like that when you're a prosecutor. It's part of the job."

As evidence accumulated against the Philadelphia policemen, Lytton felt a mounting sense of outrage—a righteous, intellectual revulsion. He would find just the right expression for it in an old dissenting opinion by U.S. Supreme Court Justice Louis D. Brandeis: "Our government is the potent, the omnipresent teacher. For good or ill, it teaches the whole people by its example. Crime is contagious. If the government becomes a law-breaker, it breeds contempt for law; it invites every man to become a law unto himself; it invites anarchy."

As a law enforcement official, Lytton felt that the kind of corruption he was seeing in the Philadelphia Police Department undermined his own integrity, and that made him mad. "It is very difficult, I think, to deal with citizens and make them have faith in what you're doing, when they know that other people doing exactly the same thing, perhaps for a different governmental level or structure, are corrupt. It's an insidious, cancerous problem. Once the people out there start to think that people in law enforcement are corrupt, they tend, I think, to have a feeling that, well, maybe everybody is corrupt." That was not the sort of world in which Bill Lytton wanted his son and daughter to grow up.

He also found the threat inherent in such corruption so chilling that he feared retribution from the police department. He made sure that his wife carried phone numbers of FBI agents with her at all times. He even went to his son's school and spoke to his teacher. He wanted to make absolutely sure that the school would under no circumstances release his son to anyone without hearing from him first—especially if the person in question identified himself as a law enforcement officer.

Lytton had known for about a week that the *Trenton Times* was on to the story. After Meyer first phoned Anderson, the FBI supervisor had met Lytton for lunch outdoors in Independence Mall to discuss how to handle the reporter. They decided not to cooperate, but began preparing to move fast if the story broke prematurely.

When he got the word, on that Halloween evening, that the story was about to appear, Lytton was angry. At that point, with their hidden video camera and tape recorders, he believed that they had already gathered enough evidence to convict Inspector John DeBenedetto, Lieutenant John Smith, Detective Abe Schwartz, and four other officers. "They were dead in the water," he says. But there was more they wanted to do with Hersing. Lytton knew that after the story had been published, their informant's cover would be blown. Everyone involved was angry at Hersing, too. They knew it was his big mouth that had caused this.

But there was no time for recriminations. Lytton knew that he had to move fast. He went to work very early that Monday morning.

"It was sort of like being in the Situation Room," Lytton recalls. "We were hoping to beat the newspaper, and I was curious to see what evidence we would be able to gather. It was a hectic time."

Lytton had prepared subpoenas in advance in case of an emergency like this. There were certain pieces of evidence that he wanted to secure before the targets of the probe knew what was happening. One of the subpoenas demanded reports from the police department's internal affairs division. Lytton didn't want DeBenedetto and Smith to be able to claim that, in extorting bribes from Hersing, they had just been playing along with him because they were investigating him. If there were no Internal Affairs reports on such a case, then the inspector would have a hard time proving such a claim. He also wanted all the papers in John DeBenedetto's desk. There were references on the tapes to the inspector's "lists." And Lytton wanted all the papers he could collect from the desks and lockers of Lieutenant Smith and Detective Schwartz.

He did not have any direct knowledge that they would find information inside the desks and lockers, so he didn't call a judge to ask for a search warrant—which would have entitled the FBI just to seize the material outright. Instead, Lytton drafted forthwith subpoenas, which would order the suspects to deliver the contents of the desks and lockers immediately to the grand jury. Normally a suspect would have the right to challenge such a subpoena, and there would have to be a hearing to determine whether or not the suspect would have to comply. But in a conversation with the city solicitor's office, Lytton had learned that the police department's rules and regulations permitted the department to search individual lockers and desks. This meant they could proceed without waiting for search warrants if the department cooperated.

On the morning before the story broke, Lytton started making phone calls to recruit the assistance that Commissioner Solomon had promised.

Thompson and Lash's first concern that morning was for their informant's safety. They drove out to Hersing's home in Levittown and rang the doorbell and banged on the door. There was no answer. Thompson recalls that both he and Lash were worried that Hersing might be lying dead inside the house, but, on the other hand, with the hours he kept they knew that he might just be dead asleep. They walked around to the back of the house and banged on Hersing's bedroom windows. Finally, the bleary-eyed informant came to the window. They warned Hersing of what was happening, and urged him to be careful. He wasn't unduly worried, so they left and returned to Philadelphia.

When they got back, Lytton handed subpoenas to the agents and sent them out to do their work. It was an exciting day for Thompson and Lash. A year and a half of work was riding on these cases. This was their last chance to collect evidence before their suspects were tipped off.

Lytton had alerted the city solicitor's office. Lawyers there called the police department's internal affairs division, so it would be ready to help. That afternoon, after returning from Hersing's house, Thompson, Lash, and FBI agent John O'Doherty met Chief Inspector Robert Armstrong at the internal affairs division office at Third and Race Streets. Thompson and O'Doherty, along with an assistant city solicitor and a police inspector on Armstrong's staff, drove across town to central division headquarters at Twentieth Street and Pennsylvania Avenue. They carried subpoenas for the contents of John DeBenedetto's desk and John Smith's locker. Armstrong and another staff inspector from his division drove over in a separate car. In order to comply with departmental regulations, these police officers would actually conduct the searches as Thompson and O'Doherty stood by. Lash, accompanied by another lawyer from the city solicitor's office and another Internal Affairs officer, drove east to Abe Schwartz's office in east division headquarters, at Front and Westmoreland Streets.

Armstrong's car arrived at Central first. According to Thompson, the city inspectors went upstairs in the building and told DeBenedetto that two FBI agents were on their way with subpoenas. Just as Thompson arrived at the door of DeBenedetto's office, he remembers seeing "a five-by-seven, dark brown or black notebook" lying on top of the inspector's desk. DeBenedetto was in the office. Thompson says he turned momentarily to say something to someone in the hall, and, as he did, DeBenedetto abruptly left through a side door to the same office. When Thompson entered, the notebook was gone.

DeBenedetto came back a few moments later as the Internal Affairs inspector was pulling things out of his desk. Thompson asked DeBenedetto about the notebook, which one of the other staff inspectors had also seen, but DeBenedetto said he didn't know what they were talking about.

Thompson says, "He was a little shocked that we were there. His basic thing was, you know, talking to the other city police inspector saying, 'What is all this about? What can I do?' And he kept saying, 'Sure, go ahead, go through my desk. I don't have anything to hide. I don't understand all of this.' I explained to him that he was under investigation and that if he would like to talk to the U.S. attorneys he could, that he should call, he could call me or anybody else and that we would be available to listen to him."

Thompson says DeBenedetto had the desk of a pack rat. They filled two large boxes with the contents of his desk drawers. They found messages and notes from one and two years ago, old yellowing calendars, telephone numbers, business cards, and lists—lists that included names of people who Thompson knew were making payoffs. Beside the names were written numbers—"250, 300"—that corresponded to the amounts of protection money that the FBI agents suspected were being paid. At first glance, it looked like a good haul.

On this day, Thompson thought the inspector seemed supremely confident that there was nothing in the desk to incriminate him. DeBenedetto did not yet realize how much the FBI already knew. It was logical for him to assume that the bits and pieces of administrative detritus in his desk couldn't add up to anything substantial. Besides, Thompson thought, with all the stuff packed in that desk, it was extremely doubtful that DeBenedetto had a clear idea of exactly what was in there.

Smith did not have a desk, so O'Doherty and one of the city inspectors collected things from the lieutenant's locker, including a list of bars and modeling studios with figures written alongside each name.

As he returned to the federal courthouse with these cartons of new evidence, Thompson remembers pondering just how confident DeBenedetto had seemed that morning. For the first time it struck him just how much of a shock the Philadelphia police had coming. So far as he knew, there had never been a serious investigation of graft like this in the police department. Perhaps it was no wonder that DeBenedetto was so confident that he would not be caught, or that he could bluff his way through.

Thompson had no idea exactly how confident the inspector really was.

Because early that evening, DeBenedetto took Thompson up on his offer. In a move that would later make his defense attorneys groan, the inspector phoned Bill Lytton.

*　*　*

The prosecutor almost dropped the telephone with surprise when DeBenedetto identified himself. Lytton had been talking with Thompson about the notebook the agent thought DeBenedetto had removed from his desk. They were both disappointed that the inspector had been able to spirit it away. Then the phone rang.

"It was after five o'clock, which was why I answered the phone rather than my secretary," Lytton recalls. "The voice said, 'Mr. Lytton?' I said, 'Yes?' 'This is John DeBenedetto,' and it was, in fact, the voice I recognized, having heard it so many times on the tapes. I said, 'Yes, sir?' And he said, 'I'd like to come in and talk with you.' And I said, 'Fine. When?' And he said he was going to go home and change, and he would be in around six-thirty. And I said, fine, I'd be there and I'd be glad to talk with him. He said he wanted to get this whole thing straightened out, implying that there had been some terrible mistake."

Lytton hung up the phone and turned with the news to Thompson, Lash, and Bob Hickok, the other prosecutor assigned to the case. The four men were dumbfounded. They spent the next hour or so discussing how to handle the meeting.

"We decided not to tell him what we had," Lytton says. "We would just ask him questions and see how much he hung himself."

The four men were hungry. They had been running around so much all day that none of them had eaten. But they were afraid to leave. They didn't want to miss DeBenedetto. Finally they decided that they had enough time to run out for a quick bite. But in the hallway, on their way out of the courthouse building, they ran into the inspector. He had come early.

DeBenedetto looked impressive and commanding in a gray business suit and a white shirt. From the inspector's photograph, and from tape recordings of his voice, Lytton had pictured a much bigger man. In person, the inspector was decidedly shorter—under six feet—than the prosecutor, and weighed less than he did. He was hardly the threatening presence Lytton had expected. It seemed odd to be suddenly looking down on this brown-haired man with the wide, square face.

The inspector appeared calm and friendly.

"I'm here to clear all this up," he said.

The four men turned around and walked back with DeBenedetto to the U.S. attorney's conference room. DeBenedetto sat on one side of a long, narrow table and Lytton, Hickok, Thompson, and Lash sat on the other.

Thompson then advised the inspector of his rights. He was not under arrest, so there was no legal necessity for it, but the prosecutors and the agents had decided beforehand to do so, just to be careful. They told DeBenedetto that they were investigating police corruption. DeBenedetto said he understood. The agents asked if he would sign a standard waiver form, which is a formal acknowledgment that he has been informed of his rights to stay silent and to have a lawyer present. For the first time the inspector seemed leery. He refused to sign, but he repeated that he understood his rights.

Thompson and Lash brought into the room the boxes of material taken from his desk earlier that afternoon. The boxes had not been opened. Lytton asked DeBenedetto if they could open them and look through his things, and the inspector told them to go ahead.

"He said we could look at anything we wanted," Lytton recalls. "He was very, very cooperative at that point, when he still thought he could probably talk his way out of it." (Later, at a pretrial hearing, DeBenedetto testified that he had not given his permission for the boxes to be opened. Lytton calls the testimony "an absolute, outright, boldfaced lie, and DeBenedetto was not a very good liar, either.")

So they opened up the boxes and went through the contents with him. He explained what a lot of the material was—much of it was legal papers pertaining to his ongoing divorce proceedings. Then Lytton began questioning DeBenedetto. He asked about his career, his assignment to the central division. DeBenedetto obligingly listed all the people working for him. He even said he would be willing to take a lie detector test.

Then Lytton began asking the inspector more specific questions— questions to which he already knew the answers. Inside a black binder on the chair next to him were transcripts of tape recordings and FBI reports going back to the origins of the investigation: to Donald Hersing's 1981 meetings with George Woods and Ray Emery, the vice squad officers who first extorted protection money from him; to his phone calls and meetings with Detective Abe Schwartz, who had fixed Hersing up with the inspector; to the meeting where an angry DeBenedetto had first learned from Hersing that Woods was collecting money without passing it up to him, and the subsequent phone call in which the police inspector explained, with relish, how he had demoted Woods and Emery because they had been "disloyal"; to Hersing's ugly encounter with the inspector and Lieutenant Smith at the Parkway Room after he had withheld payoffs from them for four months—the notorious "browbeating session" where DeBenedetto demanded more money than the $500 Hersing had brought along. . . . It was all there, in the black binder.

The prosecutor's questions started with Woods and Emery. He asked why the inspector had transferred the officers soon after taking command. DeBenedetto explained that it was not unusual for an incoming inspector to replace members of his own squad with his own people. There was no problem with either Woods or Emery, he said. There had been no special reason for their transfer.

Lytton asked what DeBenedetto would mean if he called one of his men "disloyal." The inspector seemed puzzled. He said "disloyal" meant disloyal. If somebody lied to him, he would consider that person disloyal. Lytton asked what he would do if he found out any of his men were taking payoffs. DeBenedetto said he would "put a man back if he were dirty."

This went on for nearly two hours. At one point, as he grew more uncomfortable, DeBenedetto took a rubber band from his pocket and began twisting it in his hands. Lytton led DeBenedetto through a litany of questions drawn from the material in the binder. DeBenedetto said he had never been offered any money. If anybody had ever offered him money, he would have thrown him out, DeBenedetto said—it would have been the last time that person ever spoke to him. He presented himself as the image of an honest cop, even pointing out that, while he was a staff inspector with Internal Affairs, he had personally busted thirty-four cops for corruption. When Lytton asked about Donald Hersing, DeBenedetto acknowledged that he vaguely knew Hersing, referring to him as a "punk," saying he was "crazy." He said he had agreed to meet with this fellow—"Maybe his name was Hersing"—at a restaurant because he was a friend of Abe Schwartz's. But as soon as this guy mentioned money, DeBenedetto said, he stopped him. He also said he had never had Lieutenant Smith meet with this man for any reason.

"At that point he probably figured we only had Hersing's word against his, which wouldn't have placed the inspector in too much trouble," Lytton says. DeBenedetto told Lytton confidently that he would gladly return at any time to answer any further questions.

Finally, Lytton said, "Inspector, I've got some bad news for you. We've been tape-recording your conversations for eighteen months." He put the binder on the table. "Here are the transcripts of those conversations, and you've been lying to us for two hours."

DeBenedetto reacted angrily. He said, "You don't have me on videotape."

"We've got you on tape, Inspector," Lytton said.

"Well, you can't say that I've been lying. You haven't asked me any specific questions."

"We've asked you very specific questions," Lytton said. "And you've lied to us about them."

Agent Lash remembers that the inspector seemed to undergo a stark transformation when confronted with the evidence against him. Suddenly, the cool, commanding figure seemed nervous, shaken. DeBenedetto got up and began to pace, working the rubber band in his hands, as Lytton read to him from the transcripts. Lytton read the portion of the tape where DeBenedetto describes Woods as "disloyal," and then he read the portion of the Parkway Room tape where the inspector tells Hersing, "You take that five hundred dollars and add something *substantial* to it."

Lytton asked if DeBenedetto was still willing to take the lie detector test. At that point, according to Lytton, the inspector said:

"I came down here to help myself, but I can see I can't help myself here. I'm leaving."

According to the FBI report of the meeting, DeBenedetto also said, "I thought this was an investigation, but if I'm a target, there is nothing that I can provide that would help me." He said he would tell his bosses that he had attended the meeting, that "there is a ton of evidence, and that the FBI has me on tape." Then he got up to go.

Lytton said, "We'll be in touch."

And Inspector DeBenedetto was gone.

The next day John DeBenedetto retired from the force. So did John Smith and Abe Schwartz. A week later, George Woods retired.

After that hectic first day of November, it was time for Bill Lytton to begin presenting the case to a federal grand jury. The U.S. attorney cannot indict anyone without grand jury approval, so Lytton approached the jury with two things in mind: winning the indictments, and using the jury's subpoena and contempt powers to gather more evidence.

To Lytton's surprise, the *Trenton Times* story, and the subsequent storm of publicity in Philadelphia, actually helped his case. Over the next few weeks Lytton, Thompson, and Lash began getting anonymous tips— a lot of them—that pointed to people all over town. There were evidently quite a few citizens who were fed up, as Hersing had been, with police officers who played both sides of the law.

Hersing's conversations with DeBenedetto and Smith had already led the FBI to other bar and whorehouse owners who were buying police protection. The inspector had even mentioned the name of a vending machine company operator who was in league with him. These leads, along with the tips that now came flowing in unsolicited, spun the prosecutor and FBI agents on a four-month tour of Philadelphia's underground. By this time, too, a team of other FBI agents was busy following up new leads, tracing what seemed to be a labyrinthine web of police corruption extending throughout the city.

To bolster their cases against the first seven men they were preparing to indict, Lytton, Thompson, and Lash assembled a cast of characters rich enough for a nineteenth-century novel—pimps, bookies, well-heeled lawyers, homosexuals, bar owners, prostitutes, and madams. Unlike Hersing, most of these people were at first unwilling to cooperate. No one wanted to testify against a criminal conspiracy in which all the participants were turning a profit. That had been the problem with cracking this kind of graft all along. The bar and vending machine and brothel owners were making a lot more money by buying police protection, and the police weren't about to blow the whistle on themselves. That's why Hersing had been so remarkable.

To obtain the cooperation of new witnesses, the agents would often pretend to know a lot more than they did, and they knew enough to be convincing. One advantage the agents had was that the people making money in vice were easy to lean on. The FBI needed only to subpoena them to testify before the grand jury. If they wouldn't talk, Lytton could threaten them with a contempt citation, which meant they could be held in jail for many months—or possibly up to three years—until they agreed to talk. If they lied, as two vending machine company officials later did, they could be charged with perjury. With jail looming as a likely prospect, it usually didn't take long to persuade a potential witness to take the stand.

One of the first to be persuaded was Tracy Summers. Summers ran Chic II, Hersing's aggressive competitor, a lavishly appointed brothel at the corner of Thirteenth and Vine Streets. The place was decorated with red chintz carpeting and wallpaper and gilded picture frames with mirrors and pop art prints. It had a heart-shaped whirlpool bath on the first floor and session rooms upstairs—each room equipped with a TV monitor showing explicit pornographic films. There was even an elaborate torture chamber upstairs, complete with a rack, chains, whips, and assorted other sadomasochistic treats.

Summers's name had come up often enough in the tape recordings for Thompson and Lash to know that she was also making payoffs. She was a plump woman with enormous breasts who often dressed in a baggy blue sweatshirt and bell-bottom blue jeans. Her skin color was smoky brown, and she often wore an extravagant, curly black wig. Her smile and manner were warm and soft, but the long scar down her left cheek spoke of a harder side.

To Summers, prostitution was strictly business—lucrative business. Basically, Summers believed that men are animals. Sex is not a drive, but a *need*. She was proud to provide the service. All society could ask is that the girls be clean, and that they not peddle drugs or shake down customers. Her business belonged underneath a rock, where she would just as soon people left it. She was mortified when the FBI agents came by and suggested she testify against the police. *Whatever for?* The last thing Tracy Summers wanted was to draw attention to herself. As for paying off the cops, hey, that was life! She didn't mind. How are you going to change that?

Thompson and Lash found Summers to be cool and articulate when they served her with a subpoena.

"The FBI agents said that I had two choices," she recalls. "Either to testify, because they already knew what was happening—that is to say, they knew about the payoffs—or I would go to jail. I called my attorneys when they first approached me, and I did what my attorneys told me to do."

Testifying under immunity at the trial, Summers would acknowledge that she had been arrested many times for prostitution, that she lived in an $80,000 penthouse condominium in Center City, that she drove a

Corvette, that she employed seven or eight girls, and that, yes, she still turned tricks herself from time to time. Summers testified that she had been making payoffs to the police for several years, and pointed to the officers in the courtroom who had received them.

Another witness was smooth and friendly Gene Console, from the Parkway Room restaurant. He was mortified to be incriminating his good friend John DeBenedetto, but he really had little choice. Console would testify that he had picked up an envelope Hersing dropped off at his restaurant and delivered it to DeBenedetto. He would say, reluctantly, that, yes, he often did that sort of thing for his friend the inspector.

There was also Bert Spennato, a 300-pound full-time pimp who wore a long black leather overcoat. Spennato swore that he was getting out of the business for good after testifying about the payoffs he had made, first to Officer Woods, then to DeBenedetto's men. He would tell how DeBenedetto had hurled an ashtray across the room in anger when he found out that the pimp had been paying off Woods without his knowledge.

When Thompson and Lash went looking for Spennato at his whorehouse, the Gallery, at 2132 Market Street, they were accosted in an extremely friendly way by two nearly naked women. The agents asked to speak to the manager, and pulled out their FBI identification.

"And immediately, wraps start coming on," Thompson says. "We're talking to these girls, you know, they won't give you their names. You say, 'What's your name?' and they say, 'Monica.' And you say, 'Monica what?' And they answer, 'No, just Monica.' So while we're standing there talking, this guy, a customer, comes up the stairs, and walks up right behind us. He just stands there. I guess he figures he's just going to wait in line. He's after us. He's just looking around quietly, and then he obviously overhears something about the FBI or a subpoena, and he just sorta slowly— he doesn't run or anything—he just sorta slowly turns around and starts heading back down the stairs. Well, the girls see him leaving, and they realize that's a *customer* leaving, and they chase him! The two girls run out from behind the desk yelling, 'No, come back! They'll be gone in a minute!' and all. But once that guy got to the bottom of the steps he must have broken into a run. He was outta there. He must have thought we were raiding the place or something."

And then there was Joseph Weiss, a Center City lawyer. Lytton had gotten a phone call about Weiss. The tipster had said that Weiss would be a good person to talk to about payoffs to police. He mentioned a "massage parlor" called Ozzie-Oz at Nineteenth and Market Streets. Lytton just put the name on a stack of other leads and forgot about it until, by chance, he happened to spot Weiss's name one day while flipping through his legal directory.

"So I thought, I'll just call this guy," he says. "You know, 'Hello, Mr. Weiss, this is Bill Lytton with the U.S. attorney's office. I wonder if you could come down and see me.' And he said, 'What's this about?' and I said 'I'd prefer to talk to you in person, but I'd like to talk to you about the current investigation into police corruption.' And he said, 'Do I need to bring a lawyer?' And I said, 'If you want. It's up to you.' I said, 'You're not a suspect or anything, I just want to talk to you.' He said, 'I'll be there tomorrow.' And he stopped by the next day."

Andy Lash wasn't there that day to recognize the dark-haired man in the fine suit. But Weiss turned out to be the man Lash had seen on a previous occasion, meeting DeBenedetto and Smith at the Parkway Room immediately after those two officers had met with Hersing and browbeaten him about falling behind on his payoffs.

Anderson and Thompson were with Lytton on the day Weiss came in for questioning. Lytton asked Weiss about Ozzie-Oz, and the lawyer said, yes, he had represented that place. He had met DeBenedetto once, he said, but had never paid him off. Lytton asked him if he would mind sitting outside his office for a moment. When the lawyer stepped out, Lytton conferred with Thompson and Anderson. They didn't believe Weiss. So they decided to try to bluff. They called him back in.

"I said, 'Mr. Weiss, this investigation has been going on for a year and a half. We have used almost every type of investigative technique available, including videotapes, audiotapes, surveillance photographs, informants. We've issued subpoenas and, as a result of all that, we believe you've not been fully candid with us.' All of that was true. It was just the juxtaposition of everything that led him to believe that he had been taped. And he said, 'Well, you're right, I haven't been fully candid with you.' Apparently sitting outside my office for that five minutes had really shaken him up."

When Weiss started telling them the truth, Lytton was flabbergasted. "I couldn't believe it worked!" he says.

Weiss would later tell the jury that he had paid off DeBenedetto several times, that he had met with the inspector in the central division office and DeBenedetto had outlined to him how, for $500 a month, Ozzie-Oz would have no police problems. Weiss was the first witness they found who would testify that he had actually put money in John DeBenedetto's hand.

Meanwhile, many of the seemingly unconnected leads chased by different FBI investigations were ending in the same place. An informant led the FBI to a numbers runner named Alfredo Morales. They began watching Morales, and observed two of DeBenedetto's men, Vincent McBride and Larry Molloy, stopping by Morales's house on a regular basis. Morales would reluctantly testify, through an interpreter, that he had been making payoffs. A city schoolteacher named Diane Lusk would testify that she ran a club called Rainbows on Walnut Street that had a substantial gay clientele, and that DeBenedetto and Molloy had bullied their way in one evening to demand regular payoffs.

By February 1983, Lytton and the FBI had assembled enough information to indict John DeBenedetto, John Smith, Abe Schwartz, George Woods, and three officers who had played relatively minor roles, McBride, Molloy, and Ray Emery. They were all accused of extorting and conspiring to extort money from businesses. The government also named former inspector James Carlini and John Delvecchio, a plainclothesman, as unindicted coconspirators, which meant that the FBI had evidence of their involvement, but not enough to accuse them of a crime.

Seven men in blue went on trial. Each had spent years putting criminals behind bars; now each faced that prospect himself. Thompson and Lash saw them as the kind of cops who wouldn't hesitate to risk their lives in a more traditional law enforcement role, to jump in to stop a fight, to save someone being attacked or apprehend an armed man. But they were men who, upon entering the alluring netherworld of vice, had lost their moral bearings; they no longer had as clear an idea what their role was, whether the crimes they were assigned to prevent were really crimes, or whether the criminals they were assigned to apprehend were really criminals.

"Any of these guys, taken out of the vice area and put in a regular police line of work, they'd do an excellent job," says Lash.

*   *   *

Of all the men indicted, Thompson and Lash felt the least sympathy for John DeBenedetto, the man who had headed the central police division. After their encounter with the inspector at Lytton's office, after hearing his repeated denials of things they knew to be true, after hearing him boast about the thirty-four "badges" he had taken as a staff inspector in the internal affairs division, it was hard for the agents to summon any pity or respect for the man. He was by far their most important catch. They had pieced together a frightening portrait of the man known to some on the police department as a "supercop," the man who had been such a cocky, effective young detective twenty years before. The new picture was of an ambitious, hypocritical street Caesar, using his considerable powers of arrest not to enforce the law but for personal profit. The prosecutors' estimated total of payoffs to DeBenedetto during a year-and-a-half period was $120,000—and that was only what they had been able to document. Evidence indicated that the actual total was a lot higher. A small part of what DeBenedetto collected—about 20 percent—was distributed down through the ranks, but the great bulk of it had stayed in the inspector's hands. And he had just gotten started! DeBenedetto had only taken over the vice-rich central division in June 1981. The agents felt good about having cut short his career. To them, there was nothing sad about it.

But for some of the others, there were mixed emotions. Before any of them were officially indicted, Thompson and Lash drove out to their houses to deliver "target letters," letters informing the men that they were targets of the investigation and offering them an opportunity to cooperate with the probe.

When they drove out to Larry Molloy's house in the northeast on December 14, 1982, they were greeted at the door by a little girl, one of Molloy's three small daughters. She ran inside yelling, "Daddy! Daddy!" Molloy's wife, Janet, peeked out the door at the agents. Then her husband came to the door. The agents gave him the letter and talked to him out in the yard. Molloy acted dumbfounded. "He says, 'I don't know what you're talking about!'" Lash recalls. "'I'm a driver for Smith at times, but, me? Nah, you got the wrong guy.'" A week later, Molloy called the U.S. attorney's office and came in to hear firsthand what evidence they had on him. He listened in silence as Bill Lytton explained the case. Then he got up and said, "Thank you." As he walked out the door, Molloy turned back to

Lytton and said, facetiously, "And you and your family have a nice Christmas, too, prosecutor."

"I knew then what it felt like to be hated," Lytton recalls, "and, believe me, it was not a pleasant feeling."

Thompson and Lash said they took pains to offer the men a chance to avoid discussing the case in front of their families. On the visit to Smith's home on February 1, 1983, the lieutenant's son, a pleasant young man, opened the door. He invited the agents inside. Thompson and Lash asked Smith if he preferred to talk with them alone, but the lieutenant said no. As the agents explained what they had against Smith, his wife and son sat alongside him. It was a polite, but difficult, encounter.

When they stopped by Vincent McBride's house two days later, they were again greeted at the door by children. One of the little ones was wearing cute new pajamas, the kind with feet on them.

Lash turned to his partner and complained, "Why do these guys have to have kids?"

The jury trial of John DeBenedetto, John Smith, Abe Schwartz, Larry Molloy, and Vincent McBride took place in early May of 1983. It lasted nine days. George Woods and Ray Emery were tried separately the following month. During the first trial alone, Bill Lytton lost twenty pounds to work and worry.

Donald Hersing monopolized testimony at both trials. His account of the long investigation was punctuated by the playing of tape recordings, audio and video. As Lytton had hoped, the tapes spoke mostly for themselves.

Hersing held up well under cross-examination. He bristled when the defense attorneys called him a "pimp." The first question from Robert Madden, counsel for DeBenedetto, was: "Mr. Hersing, when did you first begin selling flesh?" But Hersing knew that the tapes formed an unshakable buttress to his credibility, and he rarely slipped. He adopted a punctilious formality for the courtroom—for his long-awaited moment of revenge—often addressing the defense attorneys as "counselor."

Still, the informant had one surprise in store. Hersing had taken a liking to Abe Schwartz, the man with so many friends, over the last year and a half. Under cross-examination by Schwartz's attorney, Jeffrey Miller (the same lawyer who had once defended Hersing against smuggling charges), he testified that Schwartz had had nothing to do with the conspiracy. Thompson and Lash did their best to listen impassively to the testimony. They were familiar with Hersing's feelings about Schwartz, so it didn't surprise them too much when he took up for the veteran detective on the stand. They were confident that the tape recordings would make Schwartz's role obvious to the jury, regardless of Hersing's testimony.

On the third day of Hersing's testimony during the first trial, Miller asked: "The indictment alleges here police officers were paid some one hundred twenty-five to one hundred thirty thousand dollars. Isn't it a fact that if monies were paid, not a nickel to your knowledge was paid to Abe Schwartz?"

"Yes, it would be safe to say that," Hersing said.

"Did you ever pay, Mr. Hersing, any money in the form of a bribe or a kickback or a premium or a gratuity to Abe Schwartz?"

"No, sir."

"Now, Mr. Schwartz is charged with conspiring, plotting—whatever—to extort money from you. Did he ever extort any money from you?"

"No."

Of course, Miller had not asked about the sessions with prostitutes, which Hersing had arranged for Schwartz at the detective's request. But he did ask about the $900 Betamax videocassette recorder Schwartz had asked for, and received, from Hersing.

"When you met with him about the Betamax, that had nothing to do with any illegal conspiracy, did it?" Miller asked.

"No," Hersing said.

Thompson and Lash could only look at each other and wonder.

Following Hersing to the stand was the parade of characters the FBI had rounded up in the months after the story broke. About all the defense attorneys could do was try to discredit these witnesses by emphasizing how unsavory many of them were, how untrustworthy and crooked. None of the defendants at either trial took the stand in their own defense. Instead, they presented their own parade of witnesses—fine, upstanding people, family members and friends—each of whom convincingly showed the jury that there was another, human, honorable side to the men they had heard and watched on the tapes.

The most stirring defense came when A. Charles Peruto Sr., the pugnacious trial lawyer representing John Smith, addressed the jurors on the seventh day, just as they were about to retire to deliberate. Peruto and the others knew that they had not accomplished much with their stinging cross-examinations or their character witnesses. Instead of trying to argue away what the jury had seen and heard, Peruto, at least, was going out in a blaze of oratory. He acknowledged that his client and the others had taken money. It was the character of the crime he wanted the jury to weigh against the character of the men charged. Wasn't losing their careers and reputations enough punishment for such a commonplace crime? How can these cops be guilty of extorting money from people who were delighted to pay them off? "Who made the phone calls?" the defense attorney asked. "Who wanted the meetings? Who was it that was dying to get connected? . . . Poor little Mr. Hersing, poor little Mr. Hersing, the cockroach . . .

"Let me tell you something. They are a special breed of men. Philadelphia isn't the safest of the ten major cities in the United States (it would come out, years later, that the department faked its crime statistics) because these fellows were sleeping on the rest of their jobs. Sure, it's irrelevant. It's irrelevant that they had outstanding performance ratings. It's irrelevant that John Smith was commended over and over. It's irrelevant that they put their lives on the line."

Peruto denounced the FBI for hiring a "pimp" to bring down these men. He invoked the Boston Tea Party, urging the jury, as ultimate judge of the law, to acquit the men in a protest against the federal government's tactics in the case.

"One juror, one juror that says *Enough! I am not going to go along with this garbage!* is all that stands between an injustice and justice. Don't concern yourselves. No way is John Smith ever going to patrol our streets again or command policemen. No way can he or Mrs. Smith or his sons and daughters hold their heads up. You can't give that back to them, but you can sure stop this nonsense. . . . One of you stand up and say . . . *We are not going to stand for this anymore! We are people!* If that is flag-waving, I'll wrap myself in it.

"We forget all about John Smith, don't we? Don't we, because it was almost forty years ago that he was on the battle lines for our country. If this very trial were taking place in 1946 and I put up his service record, you would walk him out. Are we so callous that we forget? Do we forget those guys who fought on Bunker Hill? Do we forget those people who put down their lives constantly to give us those principles instead of headlines?"

Each day during the trial, outside the courtroom, the agents had small interactions with the men whom they had stalked for so long. Inspector DeBenedetto had, in their estimation, changed utterly. He looked as if he had lost weight, and seemed pale. His lawyers described him as a shattered man. The once-commanding figure sat meekly through the trial with his hands folded in his lap.

Lieutenant Smith, they said, treated them with great politeness. His wife came over and spoke to them several times. The Smiths both wanted to let the FBI men know that there were no hard feelings. "It was like they wanted us to know that they understood we had just been doing our jobs, and that they thought we had acted professionally," Thompson says. "Whatever was happening, they didn't hold it against us personally." Once, Mrs. Smith actually hugged them.

Abe Schwartz was, true to form, dapper, cheerful, and pleasant. It was hard not to like the guy. Of all the men on trial, Schwartz seemed the most confident. Despite the embarrassing conversations on the videotapes, the thread linking Schwartz to DeBenedetto and the others was tentative at best. Schwartz had been extremely circumspect most times. Lytton was hoping the jury would be able to see Abe Schwartz as part of the larger context. But Hersing's surprisingly friendly testimony had to have given the detective a boost. Right up to the end, the detective thought that there was at least a very good chance that he, of all those on trial, would be acquitted.

Mostly, the agents took a liking to Georgie Woods. The chubby, moustachioed officer had simply resigned himself to his situation. His attitude, according to Thompson and Lash, was the same as the one DeBenedetto had described on the tape after he had found out that Woods was collecting payoffs on his own. His attitude was, simply, "I got caught."

Woods even retained his irrepressible sense of humor. One day during the trial, the agents happened to get on the same elevator with the former vice squad officer. The doors closed on the three men.

They were riding upstairs in awkward silence, avoiding each other's eyes, when Woods suddenly turned to Thompson and Lash and said:

"Hey, guys, how 'bout we just forget all of this?"

* * *

They were all found guilty, Schwartz and Emery of conspiracy, the others of extortion and conspiracy. John Smith, who had collected so many bribes for his boss, DeBenedetto, was sentenced by Judge John B. Fullam to serve six years in Eglin Federal Prison Camp, a minimum-security facility at Eglin Air Force Base in Florida. Vincent McBride was sentenced to three years at Montgomery Federal Prison Camp at Maxwell Air Force Base in Montgomery, Alabama. Larry Molloy was sentenced to three years at Eglin; after nine months he was put in a program that enabled him to work at a catering business in Philadelphia and return to a local jail facility each night.

George Woods was sentenced by Judge Louis L. Pollak to four years at Eglin. Ray Emery, Woods's former partner, was sentenced to three years at Montgomery. Lytton had recommended that partners be separated. That way, he thought it more likely that one of the men might relent and agree to cooperate with the continuing investigation.

Abe Schwartz was stunned by the verdict against him, according to his lawyer, Jeffrey Miller. All along, Lytton had been confident that the tape-recorded evidence made Schwartz's role in the conspiracy too obvious to deny.

Prior to sentencing on August 1, Miller urged Judge Fullam to treat his client leniently. He pointed out that the prosecutors had not shown that Schwartz had taken any money, and that his client, of everyone, had been the least culpable. He cited the testimony to Schwartz's fine character, and reviewed briefly the detective's forty-year career in the force.

"We have submitted photographs to Your Honor showing Mr. Schwartz with Grace Kelly, Golda Meir, Yitzhak Rabin, and David Ben-Gurion," Miller said, "and Mr. Schwartz was involved and secured numerous presidential visits."

"Not to be cynical," Judge Fullam interrupted, "but it could also be interpreted that Mr. Schwartz had good connections and was able to line up soft and cushy jobs as opposed to hard beat work."

"I think that is true," Miller said, "but I think those who have worked those kind of jobs know they are not cushy. They are generally around-the-clock things, sitting outside hotel rooms."

"There is a feature of this pro-sentence report which I think requires some comment," Fullam said. "That is the remarkable accumulation of assets which Mr. Schwartz has succeeded in achieving."

Miller explained that Schwartz's $42,000 home in the northeast was originally purchased twenty-eight years ago for $13,000, that the $80,000 Long Beach Island home was purchased years before for only $7,800, and that Schwartz had put down only $22,000 to buy the $57,000 Florida condominium. Miller backed away from the subject matter quickly. He spoke at some length about Schwartz's military record and charitable work. Then the defense attorney returned to what had been proved against his client.

"Basically, what the evidence showed about Mr. Schwartz . . . was that he told Mr. Hersing if he wanted to pay somebody he should go see Mr. DeBenedetto, and Schwartz would try to connect him with Mr. DeBenedetto."

"No, it went a little further than that," Fullam said. "The plain implication was: Mr. Schwartz viewed it as a matter of course that police would be paid off, and that any businessman who needed a favor and didn't pay off the police was an idiot."

When Miller had finished, Lytton added a few points about Schwartz's considerable assets. Living off a detective's annual salary of about $25,000, Schwartz owned, in addition to his three homes, $60,000 in stocks and bonds, and had about $15,000 cash on hand.

"Plus the ability to have educated all his children," the judge said. Then, addressing Schwartz, "Those of us who have done it find it remarkable that you have any money left over." Pointing out that an officer of Schwartz's stature had more responsibility to set an example to younger men, Fullam then sentenced Schwartz to four years at Eglin, and fined him $10,000.

On the same day that Schwartz was sentenced, John DeBenedetto appeared in court again. In addition to the charges for which he had already been convicted, the inspector had also been charged with filing false income tax statements for the previous two years. He had originally pleaded not guilty to these charges, but had since decided not to contest them.

To Lytton, on this day, the proud, commanding figure seemed thoroughly beaten. Robert Madden, DeBenedetto's attorney, told the court that his client had written out a letter expressing his feelings and his position. "We have discussed it at length and he felt he would be unable to address the court at the time of sentencing," Madden said. "He feels emotionally drained."

Madden reviewed the other side of DeBenedetto's twenty-nine-year service record, the "supercop" side.

"He was a good cop," Madden said. "He cared about the citizens of Philadelphia. He cared about cleaning up crime. . . . I met Mr. DeBenedetto prior to initiation of this investigation and he talked proudly about what he was doing in Center City to prevent muggers. . . . He was proud then. Today he is no longer proud." Madden asked the judge to put himself in the inspector's place. "Think about the fact that you are a judge. You have served your community for years. If you were disgraced in front of all your friends and family in the manner Mr. DeBenedetto was, what could be more devastating to you as an individual? He is humiliated. He is crushed. He is broken. . . . He can't go out in public. He can't hold his head up in front of his family. He is just beaten."

But DeBenedetto was not beaten completely. He had refused to co-operate with the continuing federal probe into the widespread departmental corruption his case had revealed.

"This case, as presented, was enough to cause many of us to become ill," Judge Fullam told DeBenedetto. "It exhibited police officers as parasites. Unfortunately, the evidence leaves little doubt that what we have seen here is the tip of the iceberg. And the real tragedy, again, is that so many other officers who are totally honest, who are doing their job, who are risking their lives, are placed under a shadow. I note that none of the defendants have been forthcoming with the government with respect to their obviously extensive knowledge of other instances of corruption in the department. That is their choice. But it is a choice they must accept the consequences of."

Fullam sentenced DeBenedetto to serve eight years at the Montgomery Federal Prison Camp.

The day after he sentenced DeBenedetto, Judge Fullam was criticized publicly by the Fraternal Order of Police. Robert S. Hurst, president of FOP Lodge 5, demanded that the judge apologize for his "slanderous remarks." There were also those in the department who, while deploring the crimes for which DeBenedetto and the others were convicted, were nevertheless alarmed at the severity of Fullam's sentences. These sentences struck them as inappropriately harsh, compared with what perpetrators of major crimes of violence sometimes receive. Federal prosecutors, on the other hand, credit the stern sentences with helping them get further cooperation from police sources as they continued to look for corruption in the department.

During the following year, sixteen more police officers would be indicted, and would plead not guilty to charges of racketeering and extortion in connection with the alleged systematic shakedown of vice operators. Those indicted would include men in places of high authority. Five were lieutenants. One was a captain. One, Joseph DePeri, was a chief inspector. And one, Deputy Commissioner James J. Martin, was, at the time of his April 10 resignation, the second-highest-ranking officer of the force.

This later set of federal indictments would portray corruption so endemic that the department itself had been turned into a "criminal enterprise." According to the indictments, beat cops were collecting money citywide from bar owners and bookies, and were being rewarded with small portions of the take after passing the money up the ranks.

With the $25,000 he was paid by the FBI for his undercover work, Donald Hersing moved to Florida, where he leased a lovely suburban home with a swimming pool in back. Hersing opened an after-hours club catering to the same kind of randy, late-night, no-holds-barred customers as those who had patronized the Morning Glory, his after-hours club in Philadelphia.

Within months after his arrival in Florida, he was having problems with the local government, feuding over the club's hours of operation, over whether customers were really bringing their own booze or the club was selling it, and over the whores who plied their trade among the club's early-morning clientele. Hersing again felt harried and out of sync with his true self. He insisted that the club was just a temporary thing. What he really wanted was something closer to law enforcement, something like supervising hotel security. He wondered if maybe he could get a reference from the FBI.

The Bureau had offered to include Hersing in its federal witness protection program, but that would have meant changing his name and not being able to stay in touch with his family or friends. He didn't want any part of it. Besides, this had been Hersing's biggest caper. He had gotten his revenge. Who could give up the chance to gloat a little bit? To pull out the newspaper clippings and tell the story of Georgie Woods and Abe

Schwartz and John DeBenedetto, and the whorehouses he had owned in Philadelphia, and how the local police had tried to lean on him?

Him! Donald Hersing! A veteran private investigator. A man so expert in electronic surveillance equipment and techniques that he had traveled the Third World as a salesman and teacher. A man who spoke three languages fluently. A man who had been nabbing crooked cops for years.

Him! Did they think he was just some pimp they could push around? *Didn't they know who Donald Hersing was?*

ACKNOWLEDGMENTS

I owe thanks to a platoon of editors for helping me make these stories presentable enough for publication. The ones who come readily to mind are Toby Lester, Yvonne Rolzhausen, Robert Vare, Bill Eddins, Carolyn White, Charles Layton, and David Boldt. I'm grateful.

Thanks also to Terrence Henry, whose research was a big help in the articles that originally appeared in *The Atlantic Monthly*.